1988

P9-ASN-776

EARLY CHILDHOOD PROGRAMS
Human Relationships and Learning

EARLY CHILDHOOD PROGRAMS
Human Relationships and Learning

EIGHTH EDITION

KATHERINE READ

PROFESSOR EMERITUS
SCHOOL OF HOME ECONOMICS
OREGON STATE UNIVERSITY

PAT GARDNER

CHILD DEVELOPMENT PROGRAM
SANTA MONICA COLLEGE

BARBARA CHILD MAHLER

CHILD DEVELOPMENT PROGRAM
CALIFORNIA STATE UNIVERSITY, CHICO

HOLT, RINEHART AND WINSTON

New York   Chicago   San Francisco   Philadelphia
Montreal   Toronto   London   Sydney
Tokyo   Mexico City   Rio de Janeiro   Madrid

TO DOCIA ZAVITKOVSKY
who has worked unceasingly over the years
for quality programs to meet
the needs of children.

Library of Congress Cataloging-in-Publication Data

Read, Katherine.
  Early childhood programs.

  Rev ed. of: the nursery school and kindergarten/
Katherine Read, June Patterson. 7th ed. c1980.
  Includes bibliographies and index.
  1. Education, Preschool—United States. 2. Day
care centers—United States. 3. Nursery school
teachers—Training of—United States. 4. Socialization.
I. Gardner, Pat, 1930-   . II. Mahler, Barbara Child.
III. Read, Katherine. Nursery school and kinder-
garten. IV. Title.
LB1140.2.B24   1987   372'.21   86-25770

ISBN 0-03-007172-0

CBS COLLEGE PUBLISHING
Holt, Rinehart and Winston
The Dryden Press
Saunders College Publishing

PREF~

The eighth edition of *The Nursery School and Kindergarten* brings with it a new title. As the title, *Early Childhood Programs* suggests, this edition includes the increasing varieties of centers that care for young children today. There are all-day centers to meet the needs of parents who work outside the home, while other centers offer educational experiences in half-day programs, mainly for three- and four-year-olds. Some centers care for infants, and some have special programs for toddlers and parents. There are home-care programs. After-school care has become part of some programs. This text is appropriate reading for teachers in each of these programs.

We have added two new chapters in this edition, one on "Computers and Television" and another on "Becoming a Professional Person." In "Computers and Television" we discuss some of the many questions being raised today about the use and value of computers and television in programs for young children, and we present recent experiences with using a computer in a center. In "Becoming a Professional Person" we discuss practical questions related to teacher training, experience, and professionalism. The rapid increase in numbers of centers has brought an acute need for more trained professional teachers.

There are changes in organization in this edition with six main parts: Part One, The Setting; Part Two, Basic Teaching Skills; Part Three, Guidance in Experiences Common to Everyone; Part Four, Understanding Behavior; Part Five, The Program Evolves Through Experiences; Part Six, Concerns of Parents and Teachers. Each part contains new material which will serve as an introduction to the various topics introduced. We have tried only to suggest possibilities and to stimulate thinking. Every teacher will select what is best for his or her needs in particular groups. Teaching and learning are part of a creative process, a process of exploring and constant discovery.

We have tried to present the material in as simple and direct a way as possible so that it may be easily understood by anyone interested in young children. We start with essential points, things most necessary to know in dealing with young children. We then return to these points, amplifying them in later sections, adding more information which can lead to more advanced or profound thoughts. We have tried to spiral our way up to more complete understanding in a process that never ends. Although the material is based on research findings, we have not stressed the academic approach. An annotated bibliography at the end of each chapter and references in the bibliography at the end of the book provide material for further study.

The emphasis in this edition remains as in previous editions on understanding human behavior, the child's behavior and our own, as well as on the process of learning. Everyone working with young children needs to gain more understanding of the significance of behavior and the needs of individuals if she or he is to guide a child wisely and help him learn.

We have faced the dilemma caused by the lack of a pronoun to cover both the male and female genders. We have decided to resolve it by using *she* for the teacher and *he* for the child on the basis that more teachers of young children are likely to be female and the child is about equally likely to be a boy or a girl. We realize that this may not satisfy every one.

We express our thanks to Millie Almy for her suggestion of the title and its definition. We continue to be indebted to Betty Lark-Horovitz for her gift of children's drawings to be used as headings in the chapters of the book. We are also indebted to the professional organization, The National Association for the Education of Young Children, for many quotations from their recent publications and for their emphasis on quality education for young children. We are also grateful to the many colleagues who have helped us in writing this book, as well as those whose thoughtful reading and comments have helped to shape it: Martha Abbott-Shim, Georgia State University; Nancy Andreasen, Cabrillo College; Thomas W. Draper, Brigham Young University; May Kanfer, Sarah Lawrence College; Grace Mills Koopmans, Fort Steilacoom Community College; Susan W. Nall, Southern Illinois University at Edwardsville; Catherine M. Prudhoe, University of Delaware; Mary Carolyn Pugmire-Stoy, Ricks College; Helen Warren Ross, San Diego State University; and Billie Warford, Montana State University.

We appreciate the valuable contribution Jean Berlfein has made by the photographs she has provided for this edition. Our thanks are also extended to Laurie Schneider for her skill in capturing children in action at John Adams Children's Center and Hill 'n Dale Family Learning Center. Other excellent photographs were contributed by Deborah Hansen and Denise Maldonada, teachers at First Step School in Santa Monica. Louise Dean and Marc Pettigrew were generous in providing fine pictures of the outdoor setting and children at Los Angeles Valley College Campus Child Development Center. Barbara Mahler provided pictures from Chico State Child Development Program. Carol Sharpe sent pictures from her nursery school class at Bakersfield College, taken by Jim Fisher and Pat Schroeder. Dorothy Hewes contributed pictures taken by a student, Jim Hollander, in the Child Development Laboratory at San Diego State University. Carol Chamberlin supplied pictures from the Santa Monica Child Development Center and Laboratory Preschool. We owe a debt of gratitude to the photography department at Santa Monica College for their assistance with the photography.

We acknowledge the contribution our husbands have made by their support and patience, and we give special credit to Charles Gardner, who took on the task of preparing the index.

We also express our thanks to Nedah Abbott and Herman Makler, our editors, and to the staff members of Holt, Rinehart and Winston who worked with us on this edition.

The three of us, as authors, have pooled our knowledge and our different experiences in the production of this edition. Communicating from a distance has often been difficult but we have found the process stimulating. We have enjoyed our contacts. We hope that we have produced a more useful book than any one of us might have achieved alone.

K.R.
P.G.
B.C.M.

CONTENTS

12 ◆ The Role of Play in Social Relationships   196

13 ◆ Feelings of Security and Confidence   223

14 ◆ Feelings of Hostility and Aggression   245

Part Six: CONCERNS OF PARENTS AND TEACHERS

PART ONE

◆

THE SETTING

Mommy and Maya
(girl 4 years 1 month)

1 ♦ Introducing the People in the Center

Education shall be directed to the full development of the human personality and to strengthening of respect for human rights and fundamental freedoms. (DECLARATION OF HUMAN RIGHTS, UNITED NATIONS)

INTRODUCTION

"The single most important thing in human cultural behavior is literally and specifically the way we bring up our children."[1] This statement by an anthropologist points to the significance of the task of those responsible

[1] W. LaBarre. (1949). The age period of cultural fixation. *Mental Hygiene, 33,* 200, 221.

3

for bringing up children, whether they are parents, or teachers, or members of any other group relating to young children.

For many years people have been concerned about meeting the needs of children. Today their concern is based on more knowledge. However, with more knowledge comes increased responsibility for providing each child with what he or she needs for sound growth. Research findings have emphasized the importance of the first year of life and the necessity of meeting adequately the physical, emotional, social, and intellectual needs of the young child.

The educational programs we shall consider support, complement, and supplement parental care and enhance the child's development. They are programs in which children learn as they play and share their day-to-day life experiences with other children, guided by adults who have an understanding of child growth and development and of the learning process. These are also programs in which adults learn more about human behavior and relationships as they observe and participate.

The material presented here is addressed specifically to those who are beginning to teach in centers, but it can serve those who care for young children anywhere. Anyone with young children, even the most experienced person, needs to learn as well as to teach. The two processes are inseparable.

For convenience and to avoid tedious sentence structures, we will use the pronoun *she* for the adult and the pronoun *he* for the child. As Donaldson states it, "While the word 'child' does not convey any information as to sex, there is no similarly neutral personal pronoun in English. We have followed here, though not without some heart-searching, the tradition of using the masculine 'he' when a neutral sense is intended. It is particularly desirable when one is speaking of education not to suggest that boys are somehow more important. The ideas in this book apply equally to boys and to girls."[2] As Smith added, "We wish to acknowledge the known fact that teachers and students are both male and female. Their excellence in either of these positions is not determined by their sex."[3]

What promotes optimum overall development in young children? What do teachers need to know about development and learning? What skills do they need in guiding young children? We shall be looking for answers to these and other questions—even though the answers may often be incomplete.

There is a tendency today to try to hasten a child's intellectual development by teaching, for example, what may be more appropriate for first grade children to much younger children. Pushing children in their development may shortchange a child, depriving him of firsthand ex-

[2]M. Donaldson. (1978). *Children's Minds.* New York: W. W. Norton.
[3]A. Smith. (1985). From a personal paper, "Mistakes, a tool for learning."

periences on which later learning depends. The best preparation for all children lies in their completing each stage, having as full and as rich a variety of experiences as possible, consistent with each child's own style and pace of learning. Each child should feel more self-confidence because of successful learning.

Young children's needs are the same, whether at home or in a center. Young children are in a crucial period of development, physically, socially, emotionally, and intellectually. Each child is an individual, different from any other. Each child needs understanding guidance that respects his own rate and style of growing and learning. Each child needs a rich variety of experiences in exploring and discovering as he tries to make sense out of the world.

The emphases in this book are on human relationships and learning and on teaching as a creative process. The order of presentation of the

Young children's needs are the same whether at home or in a center.

Valley College, Campus Child Development Center

material does not indicate the degree of its importance. We must begin somewhere and spiral our way upward, going over subjects at new levels. Some matters of immediate importance will be presented simply and later developed in more depth. Although we may wish we could start out with a complete background of knowledge, we must be content to learn each step of the way. The more knowledge we have, the more we perceive there is to know. The going demands our best efforts. It is never dull. It remains challenging. It is always rewarding.

THE CHILDREN

A center for young children is a place where people are important. We will start by introducing the people one finds there, beginning with the children.

The children are the most important people whom we will meet in the center. They are the people from whom we will learn the most, not just because they are the most active and the noisiest but also because they show us more clearly how they feel. Their responses are relatively simple and direct, and they act as they feel. When a child is angry, he may cry or kick or throw something, or he may yell at his mother or his teacher, "Go away. I don't like you." He has neither the capacity nor the inclination of the adult to modify his responses. His patterns of behavior are less likely than an adult's to be influenced by a fear of consequences.

We learn from children for another reason. Their behavior changes rapidly. In different environments or under different circumstances they blossom forth with quite different behavior. We can see the effects of our handling when we watch a child's response.

By watching children, we see too that they are surprisingly different. Each one has his own way of meeting situations. Let us introduce some children, so that we may feel acquainted and thus be better able to understand what may lie behind the behavior of other children with other names. In this way we can see the special uniqueness and the many similarities between children whom we will meet in the centers where we may be working.

CHARLES, WHO IS FIGHTING TO FIND HIS PLACE.   Charles, three-and-a-half years old, a rosy-cheeked, brown-eyed boy, comes running into the school in the morning, greeting the teachers and the children with enthusiasm and plunging into activity. Everything captures his attention: a new book on the table, a bird's nest brought in by one of the children, the pin on the teacher's dress, the garage of blocks that the children are building. Observed over one fifty-minute period, he engaged in more than thirty activities with apparent wholehearted interest.

The children are the most important people whom we will meet in the center.

John Adams Children's Center, Santa Monica

He is eager to join other children in whatever they are doing and makes many attempts to get others to join him. He directs any play that he is engaged in with a flow of excellent language and a vigor and enthusiasm that overwhelms the opposition. But the other children drift away from him or reject his advances, perhaps because he cannot brook opposition. He hits or bites when blocked or even when there is no apparent provocation. He is impulsive and quick, and thus it is difficult for the teachers to keep him from attacking others. He is constantly taking things from other children. If he sees someone using a tricycle, he immediately wants it. If he sees someone swinging, he wants to use the swing himself.

He has picked up many adult verbalizations which he only partially understands. He knows that words are often used to justify acts. "I want to swing," he cries, when he sees Jill on the swing. "Why?" asks Jill reflectively. "Because I have to learn how," he answers her. He quickly gets on the tricycle that Bruce has left for a minute. When Bruce cries, "I want it," his answer is, "When people get off trikes, I have to get on and ride around." Usually he does not wait until people get off. When he is absent with one of his rare colds, Mary's comment is, "I'm glad. Now he won't bite me today."

His behavior often surprises the teachers as well as the children. One morning as he started to pour a drink, he said to the teacher cheerfully, "Do you know what I'm going to do?" To her negative reply, he answered, "I'm going to pour this water on the floor." He did just that before her startled eyes. And then, he immediately mopped it up willingly and became absorbed in watching the way it ran down the corridor, exclaiming, "The water doesn't wait for me."

His observations and his approach to problems reveal an attention to detail. He enjoys stories and listens with sustained attention as an adult reads. He looks thoughtful when adults give explanations and seems to understand the reasons for requests or suggestions. One gets the impression that he can see the value of constructive ways of interacting with people but that his own feelings get in his way and are often more than he can manage. He is eager for social contacts but gets carried away by his impulses, and he appears genuinely sorry when he hurts another child.

Typical of Charles's behavior is the following incident. As he came on to the playground one morning he saw Bill on a tricycle. He ran to him, grasping the handlebars firmly and saying in a persuasive voice, "Give me your trike, Bill. I want to pull you." Bill made no move to give up the tricycle and Charles repeated the request several times in the same persuasive tone. Then still talking, he pushed Bill off and rode away, calling back, "I'll be right back, Bill. I'm only going to take a little ride." Bill ran after him and grabbed for the tricycle. Charles hit him, and the teacher had to intervene and help Bill recover his tricycle. Deprived of the tricycle, Charles threw himself on the ground, crying loudly. Suddenly he jumped up and ran to the shed where the toys were kept, calling to Bill to wait for him. He came out with another tricycle and rode after Bill, trying in vain to get Bill to play with him.

The demands for adjustment have been heavy for Charles in his home. The family has moved many times. Charles's parents think he is a difficult child to manage. They seem to expect adultlike behavior from this little boy. He has been spanked, threatened, made to sit on a chair, and reasoned with. They appear to have little understanding about what a load their expectations have been for him or how often he has been confused about what is expected. A new baby at home has complicated the situation further. Again, his parents have not recognized what the addition of the baby to the family has meant to Charles. They have succeeded in making him hide his feelings to such an extent that they report that "he adores his baby sister and is very sweet to her." His biting at school is probably related to this situation at home.

Three astronauts on their way to outer space.

Santa Monica College

Anxious to conform to adult standards, eager for friendships with children, and having strong drives and confused feelings, Charles is very much in need of guidance and quite able to profit from it. He needs to be with people who will reduce the difficulties he has to face, who will give him suggestions for solving his problems acceptably, and who will interpret the needs of others to him. Because of his intellectual capacity, his strong drives, and his physical vigor, he can be either a damaging influence or an inspiring one, depending on the guidance he is given. With the leadership qualities he possesses, he may go in either of these directions.

JEAN, WHO HAS LIVED UNDER FAVORABLE CONDITIONS.   Jean, who has just turned three, is a small, sturdy looking child. She is one of the youngest children in the group, but she is independent and resourceful and plays with all the children. She entered the group several months after school had begun, but she was soon acquainted with everyone and everything. Being the youngest in a family of four children may have helped her to adapt easily.

Jean appears to like people and to trust them. She approaches other children easily and is not defensive in her responses to their approaches. If they reject her, she turns to something else. She is seldom rejected, however, for when she joins a group it is with a purpose in mind. She brings an idea or some new material. She is primarily interested in activity and joins groups of active children who are carrying on projects.

Jean has many interests. She loves music and, although a vigorous, active child, will occasionally spend as much as half an hour listening to music. She paints, uses clay, builds with big blocks, and is often busy in the housekeeping corner. She stands up for herself and will hit another child who tries to take something from her. Her social skills are excellent and seem to reflect a realistic appraisal of what other children are like. She solves her problems well, both with materials and people. She is matter-of-fact and impartial in playing with other children. Her sympathy is apparent and intelligently given. One day, for example, she took a child with a scratch to the first-aid cabinet to get a bandage.

An example of how she copes with experience occurred on the second day she stayed at the center for lunch. She followed the teacher's directions carefully and seemed to enjoy the experience very much, taking additional servings of everything, including dessert. The dessert consisted of fruit and cookies that the children had helped make earlier in the morning. When Jean asked for another cookie, the teacher told her to go to the kitchen and ask the cook for one, since there were no more on the table. This teacher was not aware that plans had been made to let each child take a cookie home after lunch. Jean trotted off in the direction of the kitchen. When the teacher glanced up two or three minutes later, she saw Jean again going in the direction of the kitchen, but this time she had her coat on. For a moment the teacher was puzzled, and then she realized what must have happened. The cook, when asked for a cookie, had told Jean, "You may have one when you have your coat on ready to go home." So Jean trotted to the coatroom, put on her coat, and was returning. She must have felt that adults make strange requests! She was given her cookie. With it in her hand she went back to the coatroom, removed her coat, returned to her place at the table, and happily ate her cookie.

Jean had kept her purpose in mind and carried out the confusing directions. She accepts things as they are!

Jean's confidence spills over to others. She takes care of herself, faces problems, and feels comfortable. Others are more comfortable and confident and purposeful because of her presence. Without actively leading, Jean is a strong force in the group.

JUAN, WHO WATCHES OTHERS.   Juan is a beautiful Hispanic four-year-old who gravely watches what goes on around him in the center. His mother was very glad when Juan was able to enter the center. From the time he was an infant, she had been taking him with her when she did housework in various homes. He had been a good baby and cried very little, but it had not been easy for her to manage. She was a single parent and supported herself and the child. As Juan grew older, he played quietly or watched her as she worked. He understood that he was not to touch the things around him or to disturb other people. By the time he had reached the age of four, his mother felt that he needed to be with other children and to start learning more than she could teach him. She spoke only Spanish with Juan, and she wanted the child to learn English before entering public school. She had already tried to teach him his letters, without much success. She was relieved when she found that the center would accept Juan.

When Juan entered the center he was able to let his mother leave after the first day. He made no protest. But now after several weeks in the center he is still a "watcher." He seems interested in what the other children do; but when they approach him or make an effort to draw him into play, he smiles shyly and withdraws. He seems bewildered and prefers to play alone. Teachers have not heard Juan speak in Spanish or English.

Juan is skillful in manipulative play with puzzles or in stringing beads. He does not often use the large blocks or engage in any vigorous play. He follows the teacher's directions, given in English or the minimal Spanish spoken by one of the staff. He fits into the routines of the school. He sits quietly at the table at lunchtime and rests when told to do so. He remains passive, doing what is suggested but initiating little.

What is Juan really like? The teachers feel that they do not know. Is he responding to his early experiences in which he needed to be "good"? Do the teachers need to learn more about his cultural patterns in order to draw him out? Or is he a child who simply needs more time to move into all new situations? How can he be helped to do more exploring, discovering, and creating on his own? How can he be helped to communicate in Spanish or English?

The teachers are slowly finding ways to win his trust. They hope to help him change his passivity into a confident zest for experience. They hope to help him find friends. They hope to help him discover his own patterns of learning as he grows in the center.

ELLEN, WHO FINDS IT HARD TO TRUST THE WORLD AND THE PEOPLE IN IT.   Ellen, nearly five, was born with a physical deformity requiring corrective surgery. She was in the hospital several times as an infant and very young child. When Ellen was in the hospital, her mother was not able to stay with her and could only see her during visiting hours.

Ellen is physically normal now, but she bears both the scars of her

This girl expresses her thoughts and feelings in painting.

Valley College, Campus Child Development Center

operations and the psychological scars left by her hospital experiences. Her hospitalizations and surgery came at a critical time in her development, when she should have been learning to trust herself in the world. Instead, she learned to be suspicious and unsure of herself. She is very jealous of a younger brother who was born shortly after her last hospital stay.

Ellen's parents were eager for her to enter the center. The bonds of affection between Ellen and her parents are close, but they felt that she would gain a great deal from being with others. They were delighted when she was enrolled.

When Ellen entered, she moved rather clumsily and often pouted. She was a heavyset, stolid-looking girl with thick dark hair. Her motor coordination was poor for a child of her age, and she avoided active play. She did not join the children in playing on the jungle gym or the ladderbars. She seemed aware of her lack of skill and was defensive about it.

Ellen needed her mother when she first entered. She did not remain near her mother, but she would protest vigorously if her mother indicated that she was going to leave. She seemed to want to be sure that she could control the matter of her mother's leaving. Both the staff and the mother believed that it was important for Ellen to feel that she could keep her mother there. They knew that she would feel sure of herself in time. Meanwhile, the teacher tried to build a good relationship with Ellen. Ellen had accepted help from her teacher from the beginning but seemed to keep her interaction on an impersonal level. She was suspicious of people.

Over a period of many weeks, her teacher continued trying to maintain a warm, friendly relationship with the child, giving her extra encouragement when she tried something new or was successful in any motor skill. She also let Ellen decide as many things as possible. When she had to refuse to comply with one of Ellen's requests, she did so firmly and

Doll washing is serious business.

Santa Monica College

matter-of-factly, explaining the reason and adding, "I would like to let you do it, but I can't because. . . ."

In addition, her teacher made a point of including many items for dramatic play of the doctor–nurse–hospital variety. She read stories about children and hospital experiences. It took a long time before Ellen became interested in these books after she had enjoyed a lot of messy play—getting her hands into sticky clay and playing with water. By this time, she viewed her teacher as her special friend, which seemed to make her feel more secure, and she began using the dramatic play materials.

The change in Ellen by the end of the year was rewarding to everyone. She was enjoying active play, using her body freely, and keeping up with the other children in climbing, riding a tricycle, and engaging in other large muscle activities. She sometimes talked with her teacher about what had happened to her in the hospital as though what she experienced there was really a thing of the past for her. She was steadily making progress in learning about the world and the people in it and in finding it rewarding to achieve, to build skills, and to cope with stress. The center had been successful in providing Ellen with some of the support she needed.

THE PARENTS

Parents Are Important People

Next we will look at some of the parents we may meet. Parents are important people; they are the child's first teachers. They give the child his first experiences with loving relationships: they serve as his first models; and they direct his first learning opportunities.

They are also important because they are people with feelings and needs. They must cope with difficulties and seek personal satisfactions. Their relationships with the child are loaded with some of the deepest human feelings. We need to know something about parents and to respect the part they play in bringing up the children we meet.

Parents are all different. What are they like? What does the center offer them?

Charles's parents are glad to have him attend the center. They are both very busy people. While they are proud of this handsome little boy and love him very much, they often find him difficult and trying. He does not fit easily into the dream they have of a well-behaved child who does them credit. They look forward to the time when it will be easier for him to understand what they want. They are glad to shift the burden of caring for Charles to the center for a time. Charles's father has never come to the center, and his mother seldom has time to visit. She has to get back to the baby or on to some engagement.

Jean's parents lead a full life. At the moment it is full because of their four active children. They enjoy them all, but Jean has a special place because she is the baby. Jean is well able to hold her own with the others. The mother really wanted to keep her at home, but she knows that Jean wants to play with children and is eager to go to school. The mother often drops in for a visit and has stepped in quietly to help on occasions. She thinks that teaching in a center would be a delightful experience and wonders if it might be possible for her to do this later when her children are older.

Juan's mother is relieved that the center has a place for Juan. Having her son in the center makes it much easier for her to manage her work. She feels glad that Juan is with other children, learning English, and learning what he needs to be ready for school. The mother is hesitant to talk to teachers, but she did shyly say that she hopes the center will observe some Hispanic customs with holidays and foods. She feels that education is important and that she herself was denied many opportunities. As they leave each day, she asks Juan in Spanish, "What did you learn from your

A teacher sings with the group.

Valley College, Campus Child Development Center

teacher today?'' She is not sure just what the center does to teach the children, but she is happy that Juan enjoys going there.

Ellen's parents are very grateful to have Ellen in the center. They feel that she is thriving in this situation, so different from her separation experiences when she was hospitalized.

Ellen's mother was glad to stay with Ellen as long as the teacher felt it helped her. Ellen's father willingly carried the extra work at home. The mother observed with interest what the teachers did at the center and how they guided the children. She feels that she learned many things that have helped her understand better what Ellen needs and how she and her husband can encourage Ellen's development at home. Both parents feel that the teachers care about Ellen and are watching her development with pleasure. The burden of concern they had known earlier has been lifted. They welcome conferences with the teacher and are glad of the help they have received.

As we can see, all of these parents have different needs. They look at the center and the teachers in different ways. For all of them the school and the teachers play an important role in their lives.

Charles, Jean, Juan, and Ellen are like some of the children whom we will meet in the center. Their parents are like some of the parents there. What are the other adults in the center like?

THE ADULTS IN THE CENTER

Adults Are People with Feelings That Need to Be Understood

Adults are people with the same kinds of feelings as children, but they are likely to express their feelings less directly and openly. Their responses have been modified by many experiences that have taught them to control and often to conceal their feelings even from themselves. An adult who is angry seldom hits or throws, but she may demonstrate her anger by performing a task poorly or criticizing for no apparent reason. Many times the adult's responses are as inappropriate or unacceptable as the child's, but they are harder for us to relate to the cause. The responses of an adult do not change as quickly as a child's, perhaps because these responses are patterns of behaving that have been in use for a long time.

But there is an important difference between the child and the adult that gives the adult an advantage. The adult has a greater capacity to be objective, that is, to look at her own feelings and behavior. Because of this capacity the adult can modify responses and make them more appropriate, as she comes to understand them. Understanding ourselves, what we feel and why we respond as we do, is very important to all of us. We need to understand ourselves, for our feelings will influence the relationships we build and maintain with other people.

Self-understanding is especially important for teachers, because children are influenced by the feelings of teachers. It is important for us as teachers to learn to understand our feelings, so we can be honest and realistic and respond in appropriate and constructive ways to people and to situations. We are in a better position to help children understand themselves when we understand ourselves.

We Are Likely to Feel Inadequate in a New Situation

We will start by looking at how beginning teachers or student teachers will probably feel as they start working in a center. We will try to understand these feelings, because it may help us understand the feelings of the children as they, too, enter a center.

Most people who begin working with children in centers are entering a situation that is new to them. They may not be sure of what to do. They do not know the children or the teachers, and they are unfamiliar with school procedures. They may not know simple things like where the paints or the mops are kept. Even though they have been given directions and have been shown through the school, they are sure to find that they have forgotten or were not told many of the things they need to know. Unexpected things keep happening, things for which they are not prepared.

In these situations a student may try something that does not work out the way she expects. She may greet a child cheerfully only to have the child reply, "I don't like you." She may follow the example of the teacher in approaching a group with the words, "It's time to put things away now," but she may get a different response from the children such as, "We're not going to."

She has many questions. Should she interfere when one child hits another? Should she just watch? Should she ask an experienced teacher for help? What should she do?

It is not comfortable to feel unsure and inadequate. It is easy to blame someone or something as a defense against this feeling. A student may become critical, disapproving of the teachers and the program and what the children are allowed to do. Or she may turn away from the unfamiliar or difficult situations. She may busy herself with familiar things or spend time with the passive, "easy" children. She may do a great deal of needless talking or giving directions as a way of reassuring herself. She may even blame herself for not knowing what to do. Any of these responses may make it harder to become more adequate.

We Need to Feel Comfortable about Being Inadequate in the Beginning

All these responses are natural. In a new situation everyone has feelings of inadequacy, and these feelings are not easy to face. The important thing is to realize the feelings and to understand something about why they are there.

First of all, students can expect to feel inadequate when they begin participating in the center and probably for some time after that. They cannot possibly be prepared for all that may happen. No one can give instructions that will cover everything, certainly not in the time there may have been for preparation. Of course, students will not feel sure of what is expected of them or of what they are supposed to do. The teacher who is guiding them may not be sure of these things herself, as she does not know them yet or know what is possible for them.

What students can do about the feeling of inadequacy at this point is to feel comfortable about having it. It is all right to be inadequate when one begins a learning experience. No one should expect to know in the beginning what will be learned in time, and no one should expect that of herself. There is a lot to learn at first. Students might as well try to live as comfortably as they can with this feeling and enjoy their successes as they begin to have them.

We Have Other Feelings, Too

The feelings we must face and deal with first are usually feelings of inadequacy. But there are other feelings that encourage us. We have some successful experiences, too. A child's face lights up when he sees us come into the room, and we know that our relationship with him is a source of strength. He is seeing us as someone who cares, who can be depended on, and who has something significant to give to him. It makes us feel good inside to be this kind of person for a child. It gives us confidence.

Or a child may bring us a drawing he has made, saying softly, "It's for you." It is the kind of gift that warms the heart. We are rewarded, also, when we watch a child struggle and then succeed in actually cutting through the piece of wood with the saw or spooning pancake batter into a pan, all on his own. The glow of satisfaction on his face or expressed through his body makes all our planning and teaching efforts seem worthwhile. We share in his accomplishment. We can truly feel that we are engaged in "the most important thing in human cultural behavior," as we succeed in helping a child to act and to learn with confidence.

WHAT DO WE NEED TO UNDERSTAND ABOUT OURSELVES?

We Were All Children Once

It is important for us to understand ourselves, if we are to understand others. We are all alike in many respects, and we all have some common experiences that may influence our responses. In the first place, all of us were children once. We can never escape that fact. What happened to us then still influences what we are like now. Some of us may wish that our childhood experiences had been different. Others may feel grateful on the whole for the events of their childhoods. But whatever the case may be, we can understand ourselves better by trying to understand what children are like and by observing how things affect them.

The way our needs were met during the period of dependency, when we were tiny and helpless and dependent on the adults around us, still affects what we do. If we lived with people who met our needs with warmth and love, if we were fed when we felt hungry and played with and cuddled when we wanted attention, then we were *satisfied* during this period. If the adults around us were themselves satisfied people who did not try to prolong needlessly our dependence, then we were free to become independent when we were ready. If we grew up under conditions like these, we are now neither fighting against being dependent nor seeking reassurance by constantly demanding more protection than we need.

Others of us may have lived with people who did not provide pleasant experiences during our period of dependency. We were not fed when we felt hungry. We were left to "cry it out" when we felt helpless and alone. There may have been many reasons for such handling by our parents, such as lack of knowledge of the real needs of infants, poor health, too many

The center is a laboratory for human relationships.

Valley College, Campus Child Development Center

responsibilities, or the influence of our parents' own childhood experiences. Under these circumstances, we may have fought against being dependent, finding it hard later to accept the necessity of being dependent in any situation. Or we may have continued seeking to have our "dependency needs" met by trying to be more dependent than we need to be, as though to make up for what we did not have earlier.

We Were All Members of Families

Another factor influencing our behavior is the position each one of us held in our families. Some of us were only children; others were oldest, youngest, or any number of middle positions. The position means different things in different families. Families are likely to be competitive. Children want attention and compete for their parents' or each others' attention. Some are more successful than others in getting it.

In the center, for example, a teacher who happens to be the youngest in her family may identify with the youngest child in the center and resent seeing him teased. She may want to see the aggressor punished, just as she wanted to see punishment given to those who teased her when she was a child. Under the guise of wanting to be "fair" she may try to impose a "justice" that really belongs to a situation from her own past, from which she has not yet succeeded in untangling herself. When we recognize that patterns of past feelings still exist, we have a better chance of handling situations in the present with understanding.

We All Met Frustrations in the Growing-Up Process

Let us take one more example of the way our childhood patterns enter into how we feel and behave in the center and elsewhere. As a result of the frustrations that are an inevitable part of the growing-up process, we all have feelings of resentment and hostility, and we handle them better if we can recognize them. It is needless, and may be damaging, to try to deny these feelings. We have them because as babies we were subjected to many limitations. The baby can't reach the toy he dropped. He trips and falls when he tries to walk. He isn't allowed to touch interesting objects. Frustration rouses resentful and sometimes hostile feelings.

How much hostility a child feels depends somewhat on whether the adults in his world help to minimize the inevitable frustrations, or whether they aggravate and increase frustration by a mistaken idea of "teaching" the child. If the necessary limitations are imposed firmly but with gentleness by a comfortable, confident, loving person, they will not rouse much resentment, but if limitations are imposed by one who is cross, confused, and struggling with her own feelings of hostility, they will rouse a great deal of negative feeling in the child. The child will want to fight and hurt in return, and these feelings will spill out in many situations against anyone who interferes with him.

Few of us are fortunate enough to have been handled all the time by people who tried to decrease the feelings of hostility and resentment that are part of growing up. Most of us feel more resentment than we can manage comfortably on all occasions. Our feelings spill out in inappropriate ways in many situations. When these negative feelings spill out inappropriately, they may make us feel guilty and afraid without knowing what is wrong. They may keep us from learning things that we may really want to learn.

All of Us Have Negative Feelings That Need to Be Released

All of us have a store of negative feelings. So we may be productive, these feelings need to be released in such healthful ways as through vigorous activity, artistic or musical expression, talking to a friend, or in doing something that makes us feel more adequate. When we have such outlets, we keep our negative feelings down to manageable proportions.

All of Us Need to Identify Our Negative Feelings

If negative feelings are not released productively, they may come out later in ways that are difficult to identify. Feeling very strongly about a thing, for example, is an indication that it is serving as an outlet for extra emotion, especially if most people do not seem to feel as strongly as we do about the same thing. It may be good to stop and ask oneself, "Why do I feel so strongly about this?" We can direct strong feeling more safely when we understand why we feel as we do. The likelihood of our meeting the needs of the child is increased if we understand our own needs and feelings.

For example, a teacher finds herself feeling very indignant that a child is allowed to play with his food at the table and even to leave some of it uneaten. She may feel this way because she was not allowed to play with her food when she was a child. Now that she has accepted adult patterns and identified herself with the adults in this situation, all the resentment that she felt at being denied the delightful experience of playing with food, as well as tasting it, is turned into resentment about seeing a child permitted to do what she was not allowed to do and what she was forced to consider "bad." It is not easy to take on values, and we often pay a heavy emotional price when they are forced on us too early. We cannot bear to see others getting by cheaply.

We shall not discuss here whether or not a child should be allowed to play with food. We are only pointing out that it is important to be able to make decisions about the child's behavior on the basis of its meaning for the child and whether or not it is a good thing for him, instead of on the basis of our own personal conflicts. In other words, it is important to be able to identify the emotional forces that lie behind our reasoning.

All of Us Tend to Resist Change

A characteristic that we all have in common is resistance to change. In spite of ourselves we find all kinds of reasons for avoiding real change in our thinking and in our behavior. New ways of behaving, no matter what their merit, are rejected until we manage to handle our resistances. Most resistances are the result of childhood experiences. Recognizing this, a teacher can handle her resistance more appropriately, saying to herself, "I don't have to feel and behave as I did when my mother (or my big sister or my father) was bossing me. I'm no longer a child. I'm grown-up, and I'm free to use a suggestion, if I think it is a good one, or to reject it, if I think it is a poor one." She can free herself from the control that childhood patterns may still be exerting over her in adult life.

The more insecure we are, the less likely we are to feel that we can afford to change, for change involves uncertainties. Even a too-ready acceptance of a new point of view may mean only a superficial acceptance, in itself a defense against any real change. It is important for us to be aware of this universal tendency to resist the new, the different, so that it will not block us when we try to profit from others' thinking. We must assert our right to use opportunities—whether it is a morning in the school, a discussion period, or the reading of a book—to reach our own conclusions.

We Need to Accept All the Feelings We Have

It is essential for all of us not to feel ashamed or guilty about our feelings. We have been taught so often that we must be "good" that we may be afraid to face our negative feelings. They go unrecognized and thus interfere with our thinking more than they would if we had accepted them.

As adults we can afford to look at our feelings, because we have more capacity for managing them than we had as children. As children, our strong feelings often overwhelmed us. Perhaps anger turned into a violent temper tantrum. We may have felt guilty and afraid, and we may not have had much help from the adults around us. Now that we are grown, we have less need to feel afraid. We are not as helpless as when we were children. We have more ability to handle feelings when we know that they exist. We realize that everyone has negative feelings at times.

We Need to Recognize the Ambivalence of Our Feelings

It is also essential to be aware of ambivalence in our feelings. Feelings are usually mixed. Feeling comfortable or uncomfortable, enjoying and not enjoying, loving and hating are all mixed together, although we may be aware of only the feeling that is strongest at the moment. We may be surprised at sudden changes in feeling, because we have not been aware that other feelings were present all the time. We may want to learn more about people and yet resist learning. We may like and dislike the same person; he, in turn, may have some of both kinds of feelings about us. We seldom feel all one way or all the other way about a person or an experience.

We Need to Try to Understand Rather Than Judge Ourselves and Others

We all have many kinds of feelings, pleasant and unpleasant, and most of us want to make changes in some of our feelings and ways of behaving. Real change is not likely to take place as a result of disapproval or blaming ourselves or anyone else. Change more often takes place as a result of being able to consider feelings and circumstances and to make an effort to understand them.

It does not help to blame ourselves and feel discouraged, for example, when we are unsuccessful in dealing with a child's behavior, or when a child or an adult rejects us for some reason. It does help if we think about how we felt at the time, what we did, what we might have done instead, and what the situation may have meant to the other person. By reflecting in this way we will gain new insights into the situation. It is tremendously profitable to recognize that we can do something to change our ways of feeling and acting if we are willing to try. We can grow in understanding ourselves and others.

Some of the things we may discover about ourselves and others may be confusing or disturbing. Understanding is not a simple task, for human behavior is complex and difficult to understand. Needs differ as people grow. It may be important to talk problems over with someone. Certain questions may be brought up for discussion. Some less clear or more personal matters may be talked over with a teacher whose longer experience has added to her understanding of behavior.

THE CENTER IS A HUMAN RELATIONS LABORATORY

The whole center is thus full of human beings who must understand and accept their feelings and those of others. Each adult shares some common problems.

Students, as they start teaching, have the problem of facing and accepting the almost inevitable feelings of inadequacy that a new situation brings.

Parents whose children are in the center face the problem of being able to leave the child free to take a step toward greater independence.

Teachers must continue their professional growth and deepen their understanding of the ways to meet the needs of children and parents.

The *cook* must share in the center's goals, too. She must find satisfaction in what she is doing for and with the children, as the food is prepared and served.

The *custodian* must be able to understand and accept the needs of children, if she is to see the job as one of making a satisfying place for children instead of merely a good place for a custodian.

The *director* must continue her professional growth and deepen understanding of ways to support children's and teacher's learning. The director must be able to help build staff relationships that facilitate human relations and support the educational program.

For everyone the center can be a human relations laboratory. It can be a place where we learn more about ourselves and others, as we gain skill in guiding children's development.

Projects

1. What were your favorite toys and play activities when you were the same age as the children described?
2. List some of the things that children do that you find annoying. List some of the things that children do that you enjoy watching. Keep this list and check it later to see whether or not your feelings have changed. If they have, how would you explain the changes?

For Your Further Reading

Axline, V. (1964). *Dibs: In search of self.* Boston: Houghton Mifflin. Moving account of a withdrawn but brilliant five-year-old's play therapy and successful struggle for identity.

Caldwell, B. M., & Hilliard, A. G., III. (1985). *What is quality child care?* Washington, DC: National Association for the Education of Young Children. Two presentations on the "true meaning of professional care for young children."

Hymes, J. L., Jr. (1975). *Early childhood education: An introduction to the profession.* Washington, DC: National Association for the Education of Young Children. Discussion of why teaching young children is such a satisfying profession.

National Association for the Education of Young Children. (1984). *A beginner's bibliography.* Washington, DC: Author. Excellent list of recent books on how children grow and learn; updated periodically.

National Association for the Education of Young Children. (1982). *What are the benefits of quality child care for preschool children?* Washington, DC: Author. One of the excellent leaflets published by NAEYC; useful for teachers, parents, students, and people in the community. Single copies free.

UALEAIE

Going to School (girl, 4 years)

2 ♦ Programs and Types of Centers

The word center as used in this book refers to programs in which young children are cared for in groups outside their homes by a qualified teacher and her assistants. They are able to provide adequate care and learning opportunities appropriate to each child's age and interests. These centers may last for a half day or from 9 A.M. to 3 P.M., or they may provide longer day care to meet the needs of parents who work outside their homes. Much of what we will discuss can also be applied to children who are cared for in homes and family day-care settings.

THE NEED FOR CHILD CARE

The need for centers that care for young children has grown rapidly through the last decades. Many more women today are working outside the home than in recent decades; some do so for economic reasons, and others because of the job opportunities now open to women. There are more single parents. In 1984, 52 percent of mothers with children under age six were employed outside the home. As knowledge about child growth and development increases, we are more aware of the extent of learning that takes place in the early months and years of life. Children need a wide variety of firsthand experiences if they are to develop well, and they enjoy and profit from contacts with other children. Because of the educational and social advantages centers give their children, many parents who do not work outside the home also seek a center.[1]

A center caring for young children can be of value because it offers parents and children an opportunity to spend some time apart. There may be a real need for time apart when families live in small homes or apartments under crowded conditions with little or no space for outdoor play. With a child underfoot constantly, a parent is likely to find it hard to be patient and loving all the time. The child who has to carry all the attention and irritation or anxiety will have a heavy burden. Some centers give priority to children who have been abused, knowing that parents under stress need a respite from constant interaction with their children, and the children need experiences with other adults.

Children need quality programs in the centers they attend, but programs differ. All programs should meet certain standards. They should provide an environment that is safe, that promotes health, and that offers learning opportunities adapted to what is known about developmental needs of young children. The adults in a center share with parents the responsibility for promoting sound growth in this period when growth and learning are most significant. The needs of the children should be the main concern of the adults in any center. Respect for the individual child is the basis for a quality program.

CHARACTERISTICS OF QUALITY PROGRAMS FOR YOUNG CHILDREN

Centers for young children can be thought of as laboratories for developing human relationships and learning. Although centers differ in their appearance and their program offerings, universal themes are apparent in all quality settings. These themes include opportunities to play with other children, to manipulate objects and materials, to discover what works, to make mistakes, and to imagine and create. Programs should be planned with these ideas in mind. In this type of program children are seldom all

[1]Children's Defense Fund. (1985). *A Children's Defense Fund budget: An analysis of the President's FY 1986 budget and children.* Washington, DC: Author.

doing the same thing at the same time. An observer looking into such a setting may see one group of children engaged in dramatic play in the homemaking corner; another group building with blocks; a child or two working in the woodworking corner; another child painting at an easel; another small group making play dough; and a child watching others play.

Play is an avenue for learning, so there must be ample opportunity provided for a variety of play experiences. Young children need many opportunities for looking, touching, listening, tasting, smelling, and moving. Young children also use play as a way to discover more about themselves and their world. In play they re-create what they have observed, rehearsing roles and making representations of objects. We see children using blocks to build roads or towers representing what they have seen. We also see them in the housekeeping corner imitating adult roles they have observed by caring for the dolls and setting the table. Discovery of how

Painting outdoors.

Valley College, Campus Development Center

things work, of how to manage feelings and relationships, and developing concepts about the world around them, all are a part of the active process of learning.

In a quality program the environment is planned to support the developmental needs of the children through the equipment and materials supplied and the planning of space and time. (This will be discussed in more detail in Chapter 4.) The teachers encourage and guide children in their use of the environment. They observe carefully and plan to meet the changing needs of the group and of individuals. The teachers are careful observers. (There will be more discussion of the teacher's role in Chapter 11.)

TYPES OF CENTERS AND THEIR FUNDING

Many different types of centers care for young children from infancy to school age, and funding for these centers comes from a variety of sources. Usually nursery schools are half-day programs, and day-care centers are full-day programs. Infants and toddlers can be found in either setting. School-age child care occurs before and after the regular school day and provides care for children ages five to twelve. Within these general classifications are a wide variety of arrangements and complex funding patterns depending on the needs and socioeconomic status of the families.

Many centers are in churches or temples because they have space available on weekdays. Some of these centers are supported by a religious group, but others are sponsored by agencies or private groups. They serve the needs of working parents as well as of parents who want a child to have a group experience. They generally are nonprofit.

There are many types of private early childhood programs. Generally the proprietary centers are run by individuals interested and educated in early childhood education. Some of the private schools such as the Montessori schools have their own methods, materials, and specially trained teachers. Many of the private schools serve the needs of working parents by providing full-day programs.

Many young children are in some kind of home care. While the parent is at work a child may be left with a neighbor, or several children may go to the licensed home of someone who cares for a group of children. There are a variety of reasons for these arrangements, including parents' preference for a home setting, economic conditions, and a shortage of centers. Quality standards for the number of children in the care of one caretaker depend on the ages of the children. (Refer to the table on page 36 for the preferred group size and staff–child ratio.)

Availability of day care for infants and toddlers is one of the fastest growing needs in the field today. Children in this age group need a great deal of individual attention. The standards for quality group care of infants and toddlers recommend that an adult should care for not more than three infants at any one time, and each infant should not have more than two caregivers whenever possible. Most children under the age of three have not developed a large enough measure of trust to feel secure when the caregivers change frequently during a day. Even three-year-olds entering a center usually need to depend on the same teacher for a time before they are able to make a satisfactory adjustment to group life. The care of infants and toddlers is a costly arrangement for parents.

Mother-infant, mother-toddler, and parent education groups are sometimes available. They give young children the opportunity to be with others in an environment with materials appropriate for play at this age. They give parents a chance to observe child behavior and learn more about child development and the needs of their own child. The parent often gains the most from these groups, but the children enjoy play in the company of other children. Some school districts support these groups, charging minimum fees, while other groups are privately operated with fees paid for by the parents.

There are parent cooperative nursery schools in which interested parents form a group and arrange to open a school for their own children, hiring a trained teacher, and acting as her assistants. Generally nonprofit centers with lower fees due to the parents' participation, these are usually half-day programs and may be found in a variety of settings in a community. One early cooperative has operated for many years in Berkeley, California, and has built its own building. Parent cooperative nursery schools became very popular after World War II. Today their numbers are diminishing due to the social changes taking place with more parents working.

Head Start programs enroll children from low-income families usually in the year before these children enter kindergarten. The goal is to help them become successful with school subjects. Head Start is a federally funded program which began in the summer of 1965. The community is required to make a contribution in the running of the center, usually by providing the quarters and some services. Head Start is a comprehensive program which provides social services and medical, nutritional, and educational components. The Title XX Social Services Block Grant funds a variety of social services for Head Start families.

Other day-care centers also receive federal and state support under the auspices of Title XX programs. According to the Children's Defense Fund, Title XX is the largest program providing federal support directly for child care. Most of the families using Title XX programs are headed by single women who need to work out of economic necessity. Title XX provides a variety of types of assistance, one being subsidized care in licensed child-care centers and in family day-care homes. At the present time there are serious funding cutbacks taking place in Title XX programs. These cuts have hurt low-income families, particularly those headed by women.[2]

[2]Ibid.

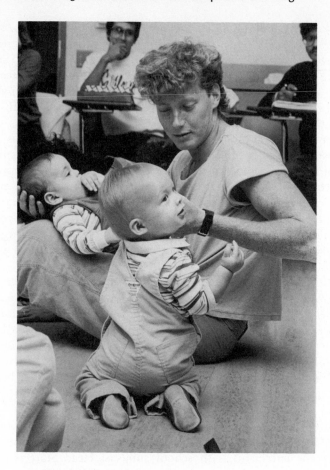

Children and adults together learning about each other.

Santa Monica College

A few state governments fund centers as part of school programs. An example is the state funded Children's Center Program in California. These centers are usually found in or near a public school.

Many colleges and universities have established nursery schools as laboratories for research and for students in classes. State universities with home economics departments usually have nursery schools on their campuses. These are usually half-day programs, and the waiting lists are long. In addition many colleges and universities today have campus child-care programs for the children of students and staff members. Some have full-day programs operating on the campus as well as laboratory nursery schools.

A relatively new trend in the United States in day care is coming from private business that supports different child-care options as part of employee benefits. This may include a center at the workplace, vouchers to help parents pay for child care at already existing centers, or direct

Older children enjoy reading activities.

Valley College, Campus Child Development Center

contributions to centers where employees' children are enrolled. Hospitals have been leaders in providing on-site centers. They find them to be cost effective in attracting employees and in reducing staff turnover. The largest and most comprehensive employer-supported child day-care program in the United States is that operated by the Department of Defense.[3] At military installations across the country there are programs which include a variety of services for children and families.

Kindergarten is the most prevalent kind of early childhood program for young children. It is available in public school systems in most states, and many private early childhood centers offer kindergarten programs. Programs range from those that stress social and emotional growth to settings that emphasize reading and other academic subjects. Some states have also introduced public school programs for disadvantaged four-year-olds and for children who are learning disabled, physically handicapped, or emotionally handicapped.

A new movement in child care is seen in the Burbank Unified School District in California, which has merged with private enterprise to provide day care for employees, using both public and private funds. Still another trend involves franchised child care programs. These are chains of day-care

[3]J. T. Cook. (1985). *Child daycare.* Davis, CA: International Dialogue Press.

Well-organized space invites active involvement.

Valley College, Campus Child Development Center

centers mainly found in suburban areas that are operated as large-scale businesses. In general, franchised child care provides fewer social services and other supportive elements to families than more traditional early childhood programs.[4]

A growing concern today is that of the so-called latchkey child, school-age children who let themselves into an empty house or apartment after their regular schoolday is over. Many school districts are responding to the concern for these children by providing space and materials for the care of children in before- and after-school programs. Local community agencies, such as Boys Clubs and Girls Clubs, city recreation programs, and the YWCA and YMCA also provide programs for this age group. School-age child care often overlaps areas of center-based care and family day care.[4]

Although many different kinds of centers exist, the number of quality day-care centers is still far from meeting the demand that parents have for them. Satisfying the variety of needs of working parents and providing quality settings for young children should be of major concern to our society. The cost of good day care is high, especially for any center that

[4]Ibid.

A child works steadily, sweeping the sand off the cement.

First Step School, courtesy Deborah Hansen

cares for children under two years of age. Budgets in most centers are inadequate.

The Children's Defense Fund, 1985, says

> The availability of child care lags so far behind the demand for it that approximately 7 million children 13 years old and under, or more than one in six, may be going without adult supervision for part of each day. The need for infant care is climbing as is the demand for after-school programs. As more parents of young children work, child care needs will become an even greater problem.[5]

STANDARDS AND LICENSING

Most states set legal minimum standards for the care of young children outside the home. The National Association for the Education of Young

[5] Children's Defense Fund, op. cit.

Children (NAEYC) affirms the importance of child-care licensing as a means of controlling the quality of care for young children in settings outside their own homes. They advocate licensing standards that take into account the nature of the child-care setting and the number of children to be served; set standards for centers, group homes, and family homes; include care of children from infancy through school age; and cover full-time, part-time, and drop-in arrangements. Current research demonstrates the relationship between the quality of care provided and such factors as group size, staff-child ratio, and staff education and experience. The NAEYC believes that standards should be clearly written, enforceable, and vigorously enforced. The standards should deal with patterns of safety and health including nutrition, staff-child ratio, and numbers in a group. Licensing should be administered by agencies that are known and accessible to parents and to the individuals providing care for children. The standards should include written policies and should describe processes for initial licensing, renewal of license, inspections, revocation of a license, and appeals.

Because licensing requirements stipulate the basic necessary conditions for protecting children's well-being, the NAEYC firmly believes that all forms of supplementary care of young children should be licensed and that exceptions from licensing standards should not be permitted. Whenever a single program or group of programs is exempted or given special treatment, the entire fabric of licensing is weakened. Licensing is not mandatory in most states at present.

The public has a responsibility to ensure that child-care programs promote optimal development in a safe and healthy environment. All parents who need child care have the right to choose from settings that will protect and educate their children in a nurturing environment.[6]

SELECTING A CENTER

We believe that a child usually thrives best in a home setting with a consistent caregiver during his first two or so years. In the home he usually has the best chance to build up a foundation of trust and confidence and to explore the world at his own pace. This foundation enables him to cope more easily with a variety of relationships and experiences in the years that follow. Circumstances in homes differ. When parents, from necessity or from choice, decide to enter their children in some form of group care, they must try to select the center that seems best suited to the individual child. Children differ in their needs, just as parents differ.

[6]National Association for the Education of Young Children. (1984). *NAEYC position statements on child care licensing and family day care regulation.* Washington, DC: Author.

The teacher plays an important role in the lives of these children.

Valley College, Campus Child Development Center

What information does a parent want about a center and its policies before entering a child there? In selecting a center parents will need to visit one or more centers before deciding to enter their child. Talking with someone who has had a child in those centers is helpful in making decisions about placement. The adults in the center play the major role in caring for young children. The teachers' education and experience, the size of the group, and the staff-child ratio play important roles in determining the quality of the experience for children.

The head teacher is a very important person. What education and experience has she had? Does she enjoy children? What is her philosophy about learning? What are her expectations for the children and their behavior? Does she respect individual differences among children? Parents will want to ask these questions about other teachers in the center, too.

A child squeezes paint from a tube on to spinning paper while teacher and other children watch and wonder what will happen.

Bakersfield Community College

The size of the group and the staff-child ratio are also important points. Young children profit most when the group is small so that teachers can help individuals. We suggest these guidelines for optimal group size and minimum staff-child ratio for centers.[7]

Age	Maximum Group Size	Staff–Child Ratio
Birth to 2 years	6 children	1 adult: 3 children
2 to 3 years	12 children	1 adult: 4 children
3 to 6 years	16 children	1 adult: 8 children
6 to 12 years	20 children	1 adult: 10 children

[7]Adapted from M. R. Bradbard & R. C. Endsley. (1978). Developing a parent guide to quality day care centers. *Child Care Quarterly,* 7 (4) 279-288. And from National Association for the Education of Young Children. (1984). *Accreditation criteria and procedures: Position statement of the National Academy of Early Childhood Programs.* Washington, DC: Author.

Is there *adequate space* indoors and outdoors? Is it a *safe place*? The space should be free of hazards such as broken equipment, sharp corners, and steep stairs without hand rails. There should be latches, a childproof fence around the outside play area, no fire hazards, and fire extinguishers well placed.

Is there visible concern for *health?* Are the kitchen and bathroom clean? Are toilets and facilities for washing and drying hands and face near the play area and easily supervised? Are the snacks and meals planned with good nutrition in mind? What is done if a child becomes ill?

Is there a wide variety of *equipment* available for active and for quiet play? Is the equipment well arranged with space for block play, props for dramatic play, provisions for children's books, music, and a variety of art activities?

The program evolves through teacher-child relationships. Do teachers value play? Do teachers value books and read often to small groups of children? Do teachers encourage talking with children rather than at them? Is a limited time spent in whole group activities with most of the time spent in small groups with self-initiated activities including projects? How do teachers deal with children's conflicts or a very quiet child?

Parent-teacher relations are an integral part of a young child's experience in a center. Are parents or other caregivers welcome to visit at any time? Are there opportunities for conferences with the teachers? Are there parent meetings?

The *setting* should support emotional well-being of young children. What is the atmosphere in the school? Is it relaxed but alert? Are children happy and busy with activities in an independent way?

These guidelines for selecting a center are elaborated in other parts of this book and are provided here as a beginning guide. The National Association for the Education of Young Children has published a useful guide called "How to Choose a Good Early Childhood Program." The parent will need to take some time observing to find answers to these points and may want to talk and ask questions with the teacher again at some later time. Unfortunately, a parent may not have much choice in the selection of a center for the child, and decisions may be made out of necessity rather than choice.

THE PROGRAM AS IT FUNCTIONS FOR A CHILD

There are many similarities between half-day programs and full-day programs, yet there are some notable differences. Children in full-day programs have needs that differ from children who spend a morning away from their homes. In full-day programs the homelike atmosphere becomes more important, as does the provision for rest. The need for softness, privacy, and perhaps a slower pace of activities should be carefully considered by both the staff and the parents. The child's participation in keeping the room clean and tidy takes on another dimension beyond learning how to put things away. Parent-staff relations become more important due to the longer period of time the child spends away from the home.

We will describe what a child's day is like in an all-day program by following a hypothetical child through the day. Her experience might be something like this.

Jasmine, age three years nine months, and her father are the first ones to arrive at the center. It is 7:30 A.M, and father brings Jasmine to a center near his work. His employer has provided child care as an optional employment benefit. Jasmine holds her father's hand as they walk into the room where the teacher is setting out some puzzles and a lotto game on a low table near the entrance.

Jasmine and the teacher exchange greetings, and Jasmine shows her father the puzzle. Jasmine is a little reluctant to give up his hand this morning. The teacher helps by asking Jasmine's father about when he expects he will be picking Jasmine up. She tells Jasmine her group will be making bread this morning. Jasmine's father tells the teacher that Jasmine's mother is away this week, letting the teacher know that life at home has been disrupted. Other children soon begin arriving, and Jasmine joins the group making bread.

The morning for the children begins in a room that provides a homelike atmosphere. There are cushions in the book corner. The bread-making activity fills the room with the smell of yeast and cinnamon. The block corner is arranged to invite play. Hats, shoes, and dress-up clothes are available in the dramatic play area.

By 9:00 A.M most of the children have arrived. Now Jasmine joins her group for outdoor play. Jasmine runs to the climbing structure, makes it to the top, slides down the pole, and climbs up the rope ladder for another try. After some vigorous outdoor play she joins Michael and Rebecca in the playhouse. A number of props are available, and Jasmine selects the black jacket and boots to become the train conductor. The three of them try on other clothes provided in this area, and the play becomes whatever they want. Snacks are served outdoors at a low table near where the children are playing, and soon Jasmine is enjoying some of the bread she helped to prepare.

Clean-up time comes with an announcement from the teacher. It is almost time to go indoors for group time. Jasmine and Michael are back in the playhouse and continue to play, but Rebecca begins to return the props to their place. The teacher suggests that Jasmine and Michael help Rebecca, and they do so. Jasmine gets the small broom and sweeps the house and says, "Now it's all nice for the next group to use." The teacher nods and gives her a smile.

Jasmine comes inside, puts her sweater in her cubby, and joins her group in the carpeted area of the room for a story. Toilet time is part of this transition from outdoor to indoor time, and Jasmine runs over to the toilet when reminded. She takes a long time washing and soaping her hands in the warm sudsy water.

After checking on who is absent today the teacher and several of the children walk around the room talking about the various activities available. Science, art, dramatic play, music, and books provide the basis for arranging the room environment. Jasmine decides to paint and is joined by Michael and Rebecca. She paints long wide paths of color on the paper. As the paint begins to run, she catches it with her brush and makes circular patterns over the paths. She is completely absorbed in this activity. Michael and Rebecca have moved on to the block corner. Jasmine seeks out the teacher to show her the painting, her eyes dancing with delight as she tells the teacher about the colors she has used. She does not want her name on the front side of the paper but says it is all right to put it on the back. Carefully she takes her finished painting to the drying area. With a very satisfied expression Jasmine looks around the room at what others are doing. She stops at the dollhouse and arranges the furniture for a few minutes. Next she picks up a book and glances at the pages, dropping it on one of the cushions when she hears the music coming from another part of the room. She joins three other children who are moving to the music using scarves from a box from the dramatic play area.

Lunch preparations begin, and the teacher tells the children to get ready for lunchtime. The children begin to fold up the scarves and put them back in the box provided. Jasmine finds her place in the small circle of children with her teacher, who is reading a story about turtles. The teacher unveils three live turtles that have been lent to the school by one of the parents. Jasmine is very upset that the mother turtle in the story does not stay and look after the newly hatched turtle. The children talk about their mothers, and Jasmine says her mother wouldn't ever leave her for very long. Jasmine's teacher is aware that Jasmine's mother is away for the week and that this story has special meaning to her. During the discussion one to three children at a time go to the toilet and wash their hands with a teacher's help. Jasmine tells the teacher in the toileting area about the mother turtle in the story as she washes her hands.

At lunch Jasmine sits near the teacher and helps pass the small bowls of food. Food is served family style with children helping themselves and passing to others. Jasmine spills her milk, and the teacher suggests she get a paper towel from the cart nearby to clean up the spill. Jasmine is table helper today and gets extra food for Michael when the bowl is empty. She clears the table and brings over the tray of fruit. As the lunchtime concludes the children regroup for a story while the cots are set up for nap time.

Jasmine gets her sheet, blanket, and doll from her cubby and goes to her cot. She puts her blanket and doll on the cot next to hers while she arranges her cot for sleeping. Mika tells her to get her doll and blanket off her cot, and Jasmine says, "Wait, wait, I have to spread my blanket." Mika pushes Jasmine's doll onto the floor and throws her blanket on her cot. Jasmine gets very angry over this and hits Mika. Mika protests, "Don't hit, we aren't supposed to hit." Jasmine scolds, "Well, don't throw my things on the floor." The two girls finish with their cots and cuddle up in their blankets. No more is said. The teacher notices what is happening but allows the girls to settle the problem themselves. Lights are turned off, shades drawn, and teachers and children make as little noise as possible as nap time begins.

Jasmine's teacher settles down on the couch in the teacher's room and uses this time for some well-deserved rest. Her day began at 7:30 A.M., and she has been working steadily since then. Her team teacher who arrived at 10:00 A.M. is quietly arranging the room for the afternoon session.

Jasmine wakes up slowly, plays with her doll and blanket for a while and then begins to fold up her sheet and blanket. She moves slowly as she makes her way to the toilet. Other children are waking, and a snack is available at one of the low tables. Jasmine put her things back in her cubby and joins the group at the snack table. She spends the next hour outdoors playing in the sand, riding the tricycle, and trying out the woodworking materials the teacher has set out. She plays by herself and for some privacy seeks out a quiet corner in the play yard under the climbing structure.

The room has been rearranged for afternoon activities that include puppet making. The puppets will be used during story time the next day. Jasmine decides to help the teacher wash the cupboards in the play area as several other children join in the work of keeping the room clean.

A computer center is available, and Jasmine spends some time playing the popular concentration game at the computer with Michael. Jasmine's father arrives and watches her play at the computer from the observation room. He enters the room; and Jasmine beams, runs over to him, and is picked up and hugged. She gets her artwork from her cubby and heads for the door where her teacher is waiting to say good-bye. Jasmine's day at the center ends at 5:30 P.M. Jasmine's parents have been able to select a center that seems to meet Jasmine's needs and their own.

The care of young children is provided in a wide variety of settings reflecting the diverse needs of today's families. Selecting the "right" program is a complicated process due to the variety of choices available. Parents and teachers should consider carefully the choices available if they are to find the one that best suits their needs.

Projects

1. Make a survey of your community and report on the number and types of early childhood programs available. What are the most prevalent kinds of programs? (The yellow pages of your phone book, the local affiliate group of NAEYC, and the day-care licensing department are good resources.)
2. Visit a Head Start program and a day-care center. What are the goals of these groups, and how well are these goals met?
3. Interview the personnel officer of a large company in your area and find out what provisions are made for child care for employees. If child-care provisions are not offered, discuss the possibilities and what other companies are doing. Check your library for information about employer-sponsored child care.
4. Visit your local college campus child-care center. What are the arrangements for students attending school who need child care? What are the goals of the program? How well are these goals met?
5. Visit a school-age after-school child-care program and a first grade classroom. What are the hours of operation? What is the teacher-child ratio? What is similar and what is different in the two groups?

For Your Further Reading

Auerbach, S. (1982). *Choosing child care: A guide for parents.* San Francisco: Institute for Childhood Resources. A detailed, extensive guide to selecting child care.

Clarke-Stewart, A. (1982). *Daycare.* The developing child series. Cambridge, MA: Harvard University Press. Sound, readable book that includes discussion of why American society seems biased against day care.

Cook, J. T. (1985). *Child daycare.* Davis, CA: International Dialogue Press. Comprehensive coverage of day-care history and economic dilemmas, particularly urging advocacy in the day-care crisis.

Day, D. E., & Sheehan, R. (1979). Elements of a better preschool. In L. Adams, & B. Garlick (Eds.). *Ideas that work with young children* (Vol. 2). Washington, DC: National Association for the Education of Young Children. Pp. 219–227. Discusses three dominant features of quality programs: use of physical space, children's access to materials, and adult-child interaction.

Day, M. S., & Parker, R. K. (Eds.). (1977). *The preschool in action: Early childhood programs* (2nd ed.). Boston: Allyn and Bacon. Articles giving a thorough overview of programs, from infant and home-based to center-based preschool programs.

Hendrick, J. (1984). What makes a good day for children? In *The whole child: Early education for the eighties.* St. Louis, MO: Times Mirror/Mosby. Chapter 1 is especially helpful in planning a good day for children.

National Association for the Education of Young Children. (1983). *How to choose a good early childhood program.* Washington, DC: Author. Criteria to help parents or professionals in looking for quality programs. Leaflet; single copies free.

Rutter, M. (1981). *Maternal deprivation reassessed* (2nd ed.). New York: Penguin Books. A review of research about mothering. Day care, foster care, and home care are examined with regard to infants. The evidence (Chapter 8) is supportive of group care of infants.

Lady and Dog
(girl, 3 years)

3 ◆ The Children and the Teaching Staff

The center as we have defined it serves the needs of children by offering them experiences adapted to what is now known about growth needs at these age levels. It shares with parents the responsibility for promoting sound growth and learning in a period when growth is rapid and significant. Respect for the individual child and his needs is the basis for a good program.

In a good center the groups are small. Children are seldom together in one large group, doing the same things at the same time. They work or play in groups of two to four. These smaller groups allow a great deal of talking, for language skills are valued.

THE CHILDREN

Early childhood programs meet the needs of young children, their parents, or both. Some centers mainstream, that is, place in regular classes, children with physical or mental handicaps, while others work with these children in their separate classrooms. All centers, however, are interested in the healthy development of young children.

Centers are fortunate if they can enroll children from diverse backgrounds, because attitudes about race, sex, handicap, and cultural differences develop early in life. Under the guidance of understanding teachers, such diversity brings significant enrichment in the opportunities for all children. Children can develop positive attitudes about people who differ from them and broaden their understanding of the world around them.

Number of Children in a Group

To meet the individual needs of children the group size should be small. As we discussed in Chapter 2, age, range in age, and staff-child ratio are important factors in determining the number of children in a group. Groups for infants and toddlers and groups with special-needs children should be very small. The numbers of children in full-day group care should also be small, because these programs make heavy demands on the staff as well as the child. Too often limits in the size of the group are disregarded for economic reasons. State and federal guidelines have been established to ensure that the number of children being cared for in groups is based upon sound early childhood practices.

Ages of the Children

Most centers are flexible in the range of ages of children in groups. The age span depends on the goals of the program, the needs of the community, and the children served. There is evidence that a narrow age range in a group may increase competitiveness among children and deprive the children of the learnings that come from being with children who are both younger and older. Teachers may find it easier to provide opportunities adapted to each child's needs when the age range is within a year. Chronological age is not, however, the only measure of maturity. The range in levels of development is large in any group, whatever the range in age.

In a family-type or mixed-age group the younger children have the opportunity to learn through watching and playing with older children, and the older children may gain from helping and playing with the younger ones. Cooperative play seems to occur more easily. The mixed age group requires skillful teacher guidance to prevent the younger children

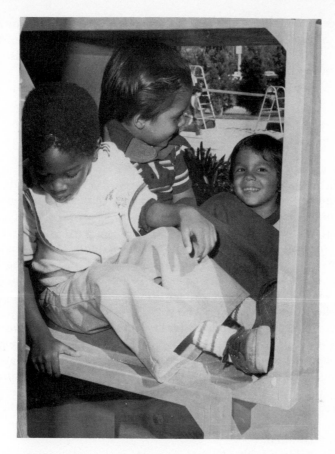

Children learn about each other through their play.
───────
Valley College, Campus Child Development Center

from taking passive roles or the older children from interfering in the play of younger children. Patterns of relating to siblings at home may be repeated and then worked through in the center.

We can conclude on the present evidence that the optimum range in age may depend on the preferences of the teachers, space arrangements, funding constraints, or other needs.

Length of the Day

The length of the day varies in different centers. Young children gain from attendance that supplements their home experience. In day care, where the needs of the family make a longer day necessary, the program will adapt its pace to meet the demands that a longer day makes on the child. Two-and-a-half hours a day spent away from home with other children in the center meets the needs of most children when there is a parent at home. Other children may need to stay longer because parents are working outside the home. Strains in the family situation, such as poor housing, ill health of the caregiver, or stress that might lead to child abuse, also necessitate children having longer days in centers.

THE STAFF

Number of Staff

The number and type of staff members in a center will depend on its size and purposes. A large program will have a variety of staff members—a director, teachers, assistant teachers, aides, perhaps students in training, and volunteers who may or may not be parents. There may also be a secretary, a cook, and a person responsible for the cleaning and maintenance of the building. There may be people from other professions, such as a social worker, a speech therapist, or a nurse, and perhaps a doctor, psychologist, or psychiatrist who act as consultants. In a program planned to meet the needs of young children there will always be *more* than one adult with each group of children, regardless of the size of the group.

When two-year-olds are enrolled in the group, they need attention and individual care from a teacher, such as help in dressing, in using the toilet, and in eating. Two-year-olds also need to have someone to turn to for encouragement or comfort. The teacher must be there when they need her, and she must be a person who enjoys, but does not foster, the dependency of young children.

When children with physical or emotional disabilities are enrolled, the center needs additional staff. A child who is blind or partially sighted, hearing impaired, emotionally disabled, or developmentally delayed requires more help from teachers than do other children. These children with special needs may gain from being mainstreamed in a group of children, and they may contribute to the experiences of the other children when the situation is well planned and well staffed. A balance must be maintained between meeting the needs of special children and the needs of the rest of the group. For the good of all, the group should not be overweighted with children with special needs, or the gains will be less for everyone.

The number of staff needed is also influenced by the physical arrangement of the classroom and the playground. Teachers can direct all their energy to meeting the needs of children if the toilets and the playground are next to the classroom, if supplies are kept adjacent to where they are used, if children can move freely from one area or room to another without needing adults' help, and if there are no blind spots in the rooms or yard.

A two-year-old involved in discovery.

Santa Monica College

QUALIFICATIONS OF TEACHERS

Personal Characteristics

There is ample evidence that the teacher is the most important single factor in determining what a school experience will be like for children. Not only a teacher's skill but also her attitudes and feelings will influence what she does for and with the children.

To meet the daily demands of a group of active young children, a teacher needs to be in good physical health and emotionally stable. She must be able to manage her moods so that they do not interfere with her responses in the teaching situation. She also needs to have confidence in herself and in others, a capacity for warm personal relationships, and a zest for living and learning. A sense of humor and a "light touch" will help her keep her perspective, as she meets the daily crises in work.

A good teacher is flexible, resourceful, independent in her thinking, realistic, and capable of sustained effort. She is sensitive and responsive but able to use authority in constructive ways. She trusts herself enough to experiment and to act with spontaneity. She is not immobilized by her own

The teacher labels this child's construction.
Santa Monica College, Child Development Center

errors but learns from them. In addition, she has a sense of order, an appreciation for beauty and the wonders of life, and a belief that each child can learn.

It takes time for a teacher to grow in understanding and skill, just as it takes time for a child to grow. Becoming a competent teacher is a process that continues throughout one's teaching career. There will be teachers in different stages of "becoming" in any group. A teacher must develop an awareness of what is significant to learn and gain skills in teaching. One cannot skip any stages in growth. The attempt to take shortcuts may preclude the possibilities of growth in later stages.

Professional Qualifications

Becoming a professional teacher of young children is a developmental process. The professional background comes from early childhood education courses with special emphasis in the fields of child development, principles and practices of working with young children, supervised field work experience, curriculum courses in art, music, science, language and literature, and health and safety. Courses in science, social studies, and the humanities provide the breadth necessary to enrich the teacher's own life as

PROFESSIONAL PATH

LEVEL 1. *Early Childhood Teacher Assistant*

The basic educational requirement for this entry-level position is a high school diploma or equivalent. No specialized early childhood preparation is required for entry at this level, but once employed the individual should participate in professional development programs.

LEVEL 2. *Early Childhood Associate Teacher*

To be qualified as an *Early Childhood Associate Teacher*, the individual must complete either an associate degree in early childhood education or child development; or demonstrate competency as defined by the National Child Development Associate (CDA) Credentialing Program. The attainment of these competencies requires supervised field experiences in appropriate settings with young children.

LEVEL 3. *Early Childhood Teacher*

To be qualified as an *Early Childhood Teacher*, the individual must demonstrate all Level 1 and Level 2 competencies. Completion of a baccalaureate degree in early childhood education or child development from an accredited college or university satisfies the competencies required of an early childhood teacher.

LEVEL 4. *Early Childhood Specialist*

To qualify as an *Early Childhood Specialist*, an individual must be able to demonstrate Level 1, Level 2, and Level 3 competencies. The qualifications of an Early Childhood Specialist are a baccalaureate degree in early childhood education or child development from an accredited college or university plus at least three years of successful full-time teaching experience with young children and/or an advanced degree.

The *Early Childhood Specialist* role requires expertise in the areas of curriculum design, supervision of adults, and staff development. This expertise may be obtained through specific administrative course work within the baccalaureate program or may require additional training and experience beyond the baccalaureate degree.

SOURCE: National Association for the Education of Young Children. (1984). *NAEYC position statement on nomenclature, salaries, benefits, and the status of the early childhood profession.* Washington, DC: Author. Copyright © 1985 by the National Association of Young Children and reprinted by permission.

well as the lives around her. "Research demonstrates that a major factor in the quality and effectiveness of programs for young children is the specialized education of the staff."[1]

The assistant teacher should also have or be working toward courses in child development and in methods of working with young children. She should have an understanding of personality development and the learning process in young children. As part of her education, she should have worked with a group of young children under the supervision of a head teacher.

In nursery schools or day-care centers associate teachers may be persons trained as Child Development Associates under a program funded by the federal government in which academic work is coordinated with field experience. Credit is given for previous practical experience. The Child Development Associate (CDA) is a competency-based assessment system. On October 4, 1985, the Head Start Bureau, Administration for Children, Youth and Families, the Office of Human Development Services, Department of Health and Human Services, and the Employment and Training Administration of the Department of Labor signed an Interagency Agreement. The intent of the agreement is to enable more child-care programs, such as day-care centers, to receive Child Development Associate training and assessment leading to the CDA credential. An important feature of the agreement is its emphasis on serving individuals who are economically disadvantaged. The CDA credential is now awarded by the Council for Professional Recognition of the National Association for the Education of Young Children.[2]

The National Association for the Education of Young Children has published a position statement which includes recommendations for nomenclature and qualifications for early childhood educators. The early childhood professional path consists of four levels. The following is a description of the knowledge and skills required for each level and the ways in which these can be acquired.

Volunteers

Volunteers may be very helpful in enriching the program of the center. They may come regularly, carrying out duties similar to those of an assistant teacher, or they come for special purposes. They may be parents or grandparents, real or surrogate; they may be high school or college students; they may be people from the community or "cross-age" tutors

[1]National Association for the Education of Young Children. (1984). *NAEYC position statement on nomenclature, salaries, benefits, and the status of the early childhood profession.* Washington, DC: Author.
[2]Human Development Services. U.S. Department of Health and Human Services, *Administration for Children, Youth and Families.* (Log 85–29.)

from an elementary school. One may come to play a musical instrument, such as a violin, flute, or horn; one may bring a pet to school or invite the children to visit and get acquainted with the animal at home; and someone who has a collection may be willing to bring parts to share with the children.

Volunteers can contribute needed services, too, helping with transportation on excursions, preparing snacks at the center, or working with children on special days. Parents may be encouraged to share cultural aspects of their family life such as food, music, dance, stories, clothes, and toys and games.

Volunteers gain from taking part in the program, and the center is enriched by their participation. Whatever their age, volunteers bring their individual capacities for human relationships. When they are able to offer a warm, loving, caring-type of relationship to children, they bring something of great importance. If volunteers are to be successful, there must be someone responsible for giving them adequate directions and a background for understanding individual children, as well as some knowledge about how children learn and what children need to learn. This guidance should be given without diminishing their spontaneity or interfering with their own style of relating to children. Success with even one child opens up the possibilities for success with other children.

PROFESSIONAL GROWTH EXPERIENCES FOR STAFF MEMBERS

All teachers need continuing opportunities for learning. Some of these opportunities will occur within the center itself. There will be regular staff meetings for planning and for discussing questions that arise about the program, about individual children, about the philosophy of the center, and about planning curriculum. Regular staff discussions are an important part of every program. Brief discussions can be held at the end of half-day programs or during rest time in full-day programs. Longer discussions may be held in a monthly evening meeting or a weekly potluck supper. Staff meetings serve the important function of restoring teachers' energy and interest.

In group discussions staff members may spend time planning for future activities, such as cooking with the children, deciding what supplies may be needed, how they will share the responsibilities, what the goals may be, and how teaching and learning will be evaluated. They may discuss how the budget will be allocated to meet the needs of the center. If a trip is planned, arrangements will have to be made. What and how will these be done? They may evaluate the day's learning opportunities and decide on a change in the arrangement of the housekeeping corner or the placement of the easels. More discussion about professional growth occurs in Chapter 23.

Improving Staff Insights Based on Observations

Teachers' discussions of their observations lead them to greater insight into the needs of individual children. One may ask, "I wonder what happened today when the boys were fighting over the wagon outside?" In describing the incident, another member may suddenly realize more clearly just what did happen and her part in it. Insights into situations and into the needs of individual children grow as a result of such thoughtful consideration.

As they recall a number of incidents about a particular child, the staff members may begin to understand more clearly the meaning of that child's behavior. They may develop a more consistent and constructive plan for helping the child learn, or they may realize that they need to understand much more about the child. They may decide to observe and make notes about this child and to discuss his behavior again at the next staff meeting.

Another staff member may comment, "I realized today that I have never given much attention to Jane. She doesn't seem to need it. Now I'm beginning to wonder if she is missing out somehow. She hasn't changed much since she entered school." The staff can then pool their feelings and observations of Jane, trying to assess her behavior to see whether her patterns are those of independent competence or of passive avoidance of difficulty.

Then someone may comment, "I really felt angry when Jim kicked me today and told me to go away when I was trying to help him." Others assure her that Jim has made them angry, too, and they have felt frustrated and uneasy about their responses to him. In talking about the situation, they feel some relief and can begin to smile at themselves. He is such a little boy, rejecting these big grown-ups. They begin to wonder what the world must be like for Jim, if he sees everybody in it as an enemy. Why does he feel and act this way? What can they do to help him change his perceptions of people and of himself? How is one friendly and firm with such a child?

Staff discussions are one of the ways in which teachers evaluate what is taking place in the center and plan the next steps.

Maintaining Staff Relationships

Staff members become better teachers through such discussions, but discussions like this depend on good staff relationships. The development of good relations may be helped by drawing up some "ground rules" for conducting a discussion such as the following.

It is understood that all members agree to:

1. Respect individual differences in feeling and in "styles" of working and accept the fact that there are many possible ways of reaching a goal.

Staff discussions center around planning, evaluation, and increasing insights.

California State University, Chico. Child Development Laboratory

2. Refrain from passing judgment on what another person does. Instead, they join in looking at questions and in thinking about them, rather than condemning or criticizing. One may ask, "I wonder why you did that?" attempting to understand; or "I wonder what else could have been done?" attempting to seek alternative solutions.
3. Respect, as a matter of "professional ethics," the confidentiality of personal things that are discussed in the staff meeting and not to repeat these outside the professional setting.

In the climate of acceptance set up by such agreement, staff members are better able to be honest and objective in looking at their own as well as at children's behavior. They are better able to function with competence, channeling their energies into common goals, less entangled by the universal problems of jealousy and rivalry. They are better able to work out ways of facing the problems of authority which everyone must face. They are freer to grow in their insights into human relationships, just as they hope to help the children grow in understanding their relationships with others.

Projects

1. In the school where you are observing or participating, check these points:

   a. The number of children in each group.
   b. The ratio of boys and girls in each group.
   c. The ratio of children and adults in each group.
   d. The education and the experience of the staff members.
   e. The scheduling of staff meetings and parent conferences.
 2. Arrange to observe in a family-type group where ages are mixed. Also observe in a group where the ages of the children are within about a year of each other. What differences are there between the two groups? What differences might be due to the difference in age range? What are the advantages and disadvantages? Compare the number of children in each group and the ratio of children and adults in each group.

For Your Further Reading

Allen K. E. (1980). Research in review: Mainstreaming: What have we learned? *Young Children, 35*(5), 54–63. For mainstreaming in preschools to be validated as an effective learning experience, research is essential, both on classroom effects and home effects. This article reviews research and points out future needs.

Dittmann, L. (Ed.). (1984). *The infants we care for* (rev. ed.). Washington, DC: National Association for the Education of Young Children. Practical ideas for operating home- or center-based infant care programs, including staff selection and training, budgeting, facility, equipment, and program planning. T. B. Brazelton and B. L. White contributed.

Freedman, P. (1982). A comparison of multi-age and homogeneous age grouping in early childhood centers. In L. G. Katz (Ed.). *Current topics in early childhood education* (Vol. 4). Norwood, NJ: ABLEX. Pp. 193–209. Examination of research on the interesting question of mixed-age or heterogeneous grouping versus same-age grouping. Language, social, and cognitive effects are considered, along with practical matters like space, planning, and teacher preferences.

Hartup, W. B. (1977). Peer relations: Developmental implications and interaction in same- and mixed-age situations. *Young Children 32*(3), 4–13. Reviews the importance of peer relations, especially in educational settings. How young children behave differently in same- and mixed-age groupings in social behavior and in task performance.

Johnson, H. M. (1972. Originally published 1928). *Children in "The Nursery School."* New York: Agathon. A record of early years in the first genuine nursery school in the U.S. Concerns sound surprisingly contemporary: children exploring freely; importance of play; role of teacher as stimulator not programmer of learning; detailed observations of individual children.

O'Brien, M., Porterfield, E., Herbert-Jackson, E., & Risley, T. R. (1979). *The toddler center: A practical guide to day care for one- and two-year-olds.* Baltimore, MD: University Park Press. Useful guidelines for design, management, and operation of group care for children younger than those discussed in many references.

My Play Yard (girl, 3 years, 4 months)

4♦ **The Physical Environment**

The indoor and outdoor physical environment fosters optimal growth and development through opportunities for exploration and learning.
The physical environment affects the behavior and development of the people, both children and adults, who live and work in it. The quality of the physical space and materials provided affects the level of involvement of the children and the quality of interaction between adults and children.[1]

Children are active doers who learn best through firsthand experiences. This point of view serves as a guide in planning an environment that will enhance development. A good deal of thought should be given in planning this environment, for it extends or limits the experiences of children.

[1]National Association for the Education of Young Children. (1984). *Accreditation criteria and procedures: Position statement of the National Academy of Early Childhood Programs*. Washington, DC: Author.

THE BUILDING

AMOUNT OF SPACE.   The amount of play space per child recommended by the National Association for the Education of Young Children is "at least 35 square feet of free space per child indoors and 75 square feet of space outdoors."[2] The association also suggests that centers with ample outdoor space that are located in warm climates take advantage of the outdoors for activities often conducted indoors. Conversely, centers with limited outdoor space may use their greater amount of indoor space (such as a gym) and conduct an equivalent activity program.

EXPOSURE.   A south exposure is desirable for the playrooms so that they may be sunny and bright. There should be plenty of light coming in through low windows. Children want to be able to look out and see what is happening outside. One school surrounded by a block wall fence was able to have the fence on the street side of the yard replaced by a steel mesh fence so the children could see the rolling hills across the street from their school. This was especially important because occasionally sheep were unloaded there for grazing.

PARKING SPACE.   Parking space near the entrance is not only convenient for parents, but it also reduces the hazards of traffic for children. By providing easy parking arrangements parents are encouraged to have more contact with the staff at arrival and departure times.

RELATION OF ROOMS TO EACH OTHER.   The layout of the center can help to make a program flexible and supervision easier. The entrance should be spacious enough to accommodate parents and children as they come and go. It should look attractive and lead directly into the play areas. At one center a large dollhouse was located at child's eye level near the entrance. This served as a way of helping new children enter the area. As children gained confidence in the new setting, they would arrange the furniture and put the dolls to bed or in the kitchen.

Doors leading outside of the center should have childproof latches. Personal storage spaces for the children should be near the entrance. The toilet and washrooms should open off the playroom, and the outdoor play area should be directly off the inside play area.

ACTIVITY AREAS.   The physical arrangement of space and its boundaries are important considerations in planning a program for young children. There is no one best way to arrange a classroom, but certain criteria should be considered, such as books located in a well-lighted area and blocks

[2]Ibid.

located out of the line of traffic. The space should allow children to move freely and make choices about activities. The room arrangement should suggest the activities available, bounded by low dividers that can be used for storage and for protecting the play from interference. Low room dividers also enable the teacher to see what is happening and to supervise from strategic points. The room and the yard should include places for privacy as well as for company. Materials and equipment should be appropriate for the age level of the children and should encourage independence.

STORAGE SPACE. As every teacher knows, adequate storage space is essential. Individual spaces for children to hang their clothing and store their personal belongings are necessary. Convenient storage space for supplies and equipment is needed both inside and outside. Some storage space

Materials that encourage independence and initiative.

California State University, Chico. Child Development Laboratory

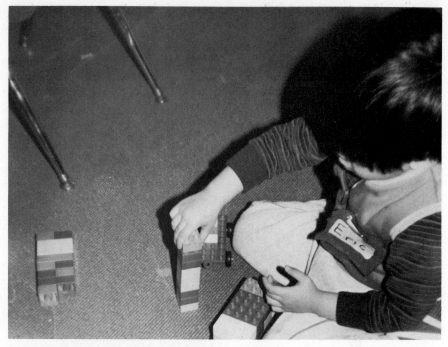

Materials that encourage independence.

Valley College, Campus Child Development Center

should be at the child's level to encourage independent behavior. Paint supplies on low shelves near the easel plus collage materials, paper, and glue located near low tables encourage independence and free choice. There should be provisions for drying wet clothing and for a work space for making and repairing equipment.

Conveniently arranged storage space should include space for collections, space for "junk" of all kinds that may be of use in the future, space for things which can be taken apart and examined, and space for raw materials out of which things can be constructed.

OUTDOOR ACTIVITY.   The outdoor activity area should consist of both sunny and shady areas and should have a variety of surfaces: grass, dirt, and hard-surfaced areas for wheel toys and for play when the ground is wet. A covered outdoor shelter is desirable adjacent to the building so that children can play outdoors even on rainy, cold days. Around the playground there should be a childproof fence with childproof fastenings on any gates. Good landscaping will add interest and variety to the children's experiences. Different kinds of areas, such as a slope, a digging area, and garden space for the children, make different types of play and learning possible.

HEALTH AND SAFETY. Provisions for protecting health are important. The heating and ventilation should be adequate. Shades or blinds may be needed as a protection against glare. The center should be cleaned daily, bathroom fixtures disinfected, and trash removed. Toys that children touch with their mouths should be washed daily.

Toilets, drinking water, and hand washing facilities should be easily accessible to children. Soap and disposable towels should be provided. Electrical outlets need to be covered with protective caps. Cushioning materials, such as mats, wood chips, or sand, should be used under climbers, slides, and swings. Climbing equipment, swings, and large pieces of furniture should be securely anchored. Swings should have canvas seats rather than wooden ones.

The building and all equipment should be maintained in a safe, clean condition and in good repair. Fire hazards should be eliminated and fire extinguishers and escapes provided as recommended by the fire authorities.

Small manipulative toys need a good storage arrangement.

Valley College, Campus Child Development Center

Several levels provide places to see the playground from a variety of perspectives.

Valley College, Campus Child Care Center

The health and safety of the children are a first responsibility for the center. It is essential for every center to carry accident and liability insurance to cover children and staff.

BEAUTY. In addition to being safe and functional, a center should be an attractive place where attention is given to color and pleasing lines and shapes—a graceful arrangement of flowers in a bowl, a picture on the wall, an interesting mobile. Children respond to beauty in their surroundings.

Many centers are in buildings that do not have all of these desirable features. Space may have to be adapted in churches or schools that are far from ideal. Much can be done in remodeling and in the organization of available space, however, to make the facilities serve adequately the needs of children.

EQUIPMENT

Age-appropriate equipment of sufficient quantity, variety, and durability are important ingredients for a quality setting for young children. All age groups need active play equipment, materials which stimulate the senses, construction materials, manipulative toys, dramatic play equipment, art supplies, and books and records. The National Association for the Education of Young Children suggests that children are more likely to play constructively and creatively if these materials are accessible to them. Materials and equipment should be organized to promote independent use by children, and they should be changed periodically to provide variety.

Equipment should be sturdy, safe, and capable of serving a wide variety of purposes. Sometimes equipment seems dangerous at first glance, especially real tools and outdoor climbing apparatus. It must be remembered that children want to gain mastery, and they need adventure in play. Every child should have the pleasure of using a *real* workbench and hammer or digging with a small, real spade. He should have the opportunity to experience the thrill of climbing up high and sliding down a firepole. A child only learns to use equipment by using it again and again. Our concern is with the *safe use* of equipment. Giving a child too much help may result in his doing something that is beyond his ability or level of skill. It is at such times that he is likely to have an accident. Safe use means maintaining certain rules about the use of equipment, such as permitting only one child at a time on a ladder. Safe use means showing a child how to use a piece of equipment safely—placing a ladder in a secure way or carrying a sharp implement with the point downward. Helping children learn to use equipment safely allows them to become competent and to move freely. Learning about safety is an important aspect of learning to use equipment.

No one equipment list is ever complete, nor should it be, because the inventiveness of parents, teachers, and children can make a center's equipment unique. Yet there will be some equipment common to all centers.

BLOCKS.   Every center should have a variety of blocks of different sizes and shapes. Large blocks promote motor development and encourage cooperative and dramatic play. Small blocks offer many opportunities for children of all ages to construct and learn in areas such as mathematics, science, and art. Blocks should include units, half units, and double and quadruple units as well as a variety of basic shapes and sizes. Blocks are useful in different ways to children at different stages of development. It has been estimated that about one-third of the floor space should be devoted to block building. There should be shelves for the storage of the blocks so that they can be organized and stored by shape and size. Large hollow blocks that are multiples of each other should be available, too.

DRAMATIC PLAY.   The dramatic play corner should include a stove, sink, cupboard, small table and chairs, doll bed and chests, and other furniture

Housekeeping allows children opportunities to recreate their experiences.
Valley College, Campus Child Development Center

that allows children to create the world that they know. One center provided a child size couch, play television set, and rocker where much play that happens in the living room of the home could be represented. Racks for hanging clothes, shoe shelves, pegs on the wall for hats, mirrors, and doll buggies allow children to recreate life around them. Clothing, accessories, and props should provide nonsexist choices appealing to both boys and girls.

ART. The art center should have easels with space for two or four children, primary color paints, and a water supply. Racks are useful for hanging paintings to dry, but, if not available, rope and clip-type clothes pins can be used. Low tables and chairs for collage, clay, and other activities should be provided. Clay may be stored in a large crock or small trash can with a tight fitting lid. Crayons, sheets of plain and colored paper, felt pens or marking pencils, paste, and blunt scissors should be available in this area.

BOOKS. The library center should look cozy, soft, and inviting. This is an area where children can sit on large cushions to hear stories. Book racks should allow books to face forward so that children can see what is available. Shelves for books can also serve as dividers. Cool colors such as blue, green, and lavender help provide a quiet setting.

SCIENCE. The center for exploration and experimentation may include low tables and chairs, magnets, magnifying glass, balance scales, cages for pets, shelves with an egg timer, hourglass, abacus, measuring cups in sets, measuring spoons, steel tape, a ruler, and a compass. Smell bottles, sound boxes, and attribute blocks provide opportunities for experimentation and discovery.

PUZZLES AND GAMES. A center for quiet play will consist of low tables and chairs near shelves on which are manipulative toys, puzzles, and games that provide children with much pleasure.

MUSIC. The music center might have a piano, a record player, and perhaps an autoharp. It might also have instruments such as a large drum, smaller drums, bells, large gong, if possible, and smaller wrist bells, xylophone, triangle, tone bars, sand blocks, maracas, castanets, and other sound-making items. Scarves or colored squares of gauze for use in dancing adds to the experience.

"MESSY" PLAY. "Messy" play centers are important! Tables with plain surfaces that can be washed are used for fingerpainting or wet clay with a heavy piece of plastic to be used under the table to protect the floor. A tray for fingerpaint with a roll of butcher paper with cutter on the shelf or wall nearby provide the ingredients for rich experiences.

SAND.   A sand area is an indispensable place in which to dig roads and waterways and to make mountains and tunnels. Water should be available to fill pails and plastic jars so children may discover the properties of sand and water, engage in dramatic play, and make pies, cakes, cookies, and other molded shapes.

CLIMBING.   Climbing equipment of all kinds should be provided, such as a jungle gym, ladders, large crates, rope ladders, sewer pipes, planks, ladder boxes, and tree trunks. Stable bases of support provide challenging learning opportunities for children.

WOODWORKING.   A heavy workbench, several sawhorses, and tools such as a vise, hammers, and saws are also important pieces of equipment. The tools should be real and functional and carefully supervised.

CONSTRUCTION.   Children may construct their own play space with appropriate building equipment. They should have large hollow blocks, boards of different lengths, sawhorses, packing boxes, used tires, and canvas or nylon sail fabric to use as a tent or a roof.

GARDENING.   Gardening and dirt digging areas offer opportunities to explore the properties of dirt and water, to plant a garden, and to find earthworms and insects. Small shovels, trowels, and rakes are useful additions to this area.

MATERIALS

A list of materials could be endless. In general, materials should be selected that directly relate to the program's objectives and to the particular children in the program. The following lists provide some suggestions for basic materials. Some items could appear in more than one list.

BUILDING MATERIALS.   boxes, large and small, carpet pieces, boards, old sheets, blankets, plexiglass pieces, styrofoam packing pieces, string, rope and pulleys, scrap lumber, cardboard.

MATERIALS TO TAKE APART AND PUT TOGETHER.   dump trucks, pickup trucks, barn with animals and people, dollhouse, dollhouse furniture, baskets, cans, buckets, crates, spools, small blocks, stones, small cars, shells, pegs and pegboards, tinkertoys, lego blocks, nuts, bolts, screws, puzzles.

MATERIALS FOR PRETENDING. play stove, sink, refrigerator, tables, chairs, dishes, pots, pans, dolls, doll beds, broom, dustpan, telephones, cash register, dress-up clothes (hats, shoes, purses, dresses, scarves, jewelry, neckties, vests, boots), watches, wallets, briefcases, lunch box, picnic basket, play money, canceled stamps, prop boxes.

OTHER MATERIALS. hot plate, toaster oven, electric frying pan, popcorn popper with see-through lid, blender, meat grinder, food mill.

The chapters on curriculum areas will give further examples of materials related to objectives and to planned learning opportunities.

HOUSEKEEPING

Just as a parent at home knows that order reduces needless frustration, the teacher in the center finds that having a place for materials and equipment and keeping things in their place make for a smoother program. Students, assistants, or volunteer workers in the center find it easier when they know where materials are kept. A neat label on a shelf indicating its contents helps those working in a center to be clear about what to replace there. Children, too, gain from knowing that things have a place. They can expect to find them in this place and to take responsibility for putting them back in the place where they can find them again.

When teachers find material scattered during the day, they will take time to restore order, not in such a way that it interferes with children's activity, but in a way that it adds to the activity by giving a sense of new opportunities. Carmen, a student teacher, started picking up some of the blocks that appeared to be interfering with the construction of a tower that two children were building. One of the children smiled and said, "Now we can build a road to the tower." Carmen enhanced this block building by helping the children clear the way for further building.

Staff must also be alert to wiping up spilled water or paint or washing a table that may need to be cleaned. Keeping the sand swept off the sidewalk is a safety measure as well as a housekeeping task. It will be important to have mops, cleaning cloths, broom, and dustpan nearby for both children and adults to use. Good housekeeping is as important in a center as in a home.

The center should look well lived in, but it should also look attractive. Fresh flowers artistically arranged in a lovely vase; bright-colored autumn foliage; a plant; the children's pictures, mounted and carefully hung at their eye level or fastened to a display board; an interesting mobile; a piece of fabric with lovely colors, pattern, or texture used as a wall hanging—all these add to the charm of a room which should be full of life and color. Children are sensitive to beauty, and it becomes part of them. Their

A teacher helps in the block corner.

Valley College, Campus Child Development Center.

attention is caught by the introduction of something lovely. They are aware of these things even though they may make no comment. The center may often be in disorder while it is in use; but if there is an underlying sense of orderliness and of attention to beauty children will feel it. In fact, all of us are influenced by the atmosphere of a room.

Another important aspect of housekeeping is making sure that materials are available and the equipment is working. For example, paint jars should have plenty of paint in them, and paper should be available for painting.

A piece of broken equipment should always be removed, and it should be repaired, if possible. A child may feel frustrated or discouraged if a toy does not do what it is supposed to. For example, a child who struggles with a toy that is supposed to stand upright but does not because a part is missing may feel that something is wrong with him. As a result, he may carry this frustration into his next encounter with things or people, and it may again interfere with his learning. Difficulties may be avoided by keeping materials in good condition. Keeping equipment in good condition also means keeping surfaces smooth to prevent splinters and renewing chipped paint as it wears off. Equipment kept in order, freshly painted, and stored in a proper place is more likely to be treated with care. We encourage the child to treat equipment with care when we keep it in good order and respect its upkeep ourselves. We are setting a pattern for the child to follow.

THE USE OF SPACE

ARRANGEMENT OF EQUIPMENT. The way equipment is placed in the space available for it influences the use that children will make of the equipment. A housekeeping center with plenty of room in it encourages more children to play there and reduces the amount of conflict. Two or more items of a kind, like two doll buggies, encourage social play. Easels placed side by side give children a social experience as well as an art experience. Even the use made of wheel toys will depend in part on the amount and arrangement of the hard-surface space available. A broad walk

Magazines and art materials within easy reach encourage independence.

Valley College, Campus Child Development Center

that circles the playground will handle traffic in a way that an unbroken block of hard surfacing in one part of the playground cannot.

Storage space where the children themselves can reach the equipment and put it away easily offers opportunity for them to be independent and self-sufficient. These are all ways in which the arrangement of and for equipment influences the children's behavior. By providing materials that have been carefully selected and by offering adequate arrangements for their use, the center helps ensure a rich environment for children.

THE NEED FOR SPACE.   Young children need plenty of space, and the good center will provide enough space for children. They need space for vigorous active play, space for social play, space for "messy" play, and space to play alone and undisturbed. In centers where children stay all day it is especially important to provide for some private or protected boundaried areas. Just as adults need a place to be alone and undisturbed, so do young children. A card table covered with a blanket, a closet with the door removed, and some soft cushions on the floor can achieve this.

THE CONTENTS AND ORGANIZATION OF SPACE.   Our concern is with the quality of space as well as the quantity of space. In a study entitled *Planning Environments for Young Children: Physical Space*,[3] Kritchevsky, Prescott, and Walling present a useful analysis of play space, based on a three-year study made in day-care centers. According to their analysis, quality depends on the content and the organization of the space. They classify contents into simple units, such as a swing or a wagon; complex units, such as a sand table with digging equipment; and super units consisting of three or more play materials combined, such as a sandbox with play materials and water. Complex and super units allow for more types of activities and for use by more children at one time.

Using such a classification, the teacher can check her play areas to see whether or not there are a sufficiently wide choice of activities and enough activity for each child. Is there a sufficiently wide choice of things in the units available, or are there a lot of tricycles and no wheelbarrows or wagons, for example? Are the number of play spaces sufficient to provide a place for every child to be doing something and also to permit a change of activity? For example, a housekeeping center equipped with a table and dishes, a stove and cooking utensils, dolls and doll bed, doll clothes and an iron and ironing board will accommodate four children at one time. If there are three children using this "super unit," they can shift activities or make room for another child to enter.

[3]S. Kritchevsky, E. Prescott, with L. Walling (1977). *Planning environments for young children: Physical space.* (2nd ed.). Washington, DC: National Association for the Education of Young Children.

These boys create a private space by climbing inside a crate.

John Adams Children's Center, Santa Monica

The study also says that when space is well-organized it will have (1) sufficient empty space, (2) a broad, easily visible path through it, (3) ease of supervision, and (4) efficient placement of storage units. Based on their observations, the authors conclude that not less than one-third and not more than one-half of the play space should be empty. The empty space should be capable of being used in different ways, such as for setting up a store or for building with blocks. It should be easy for a child to see how to get from one place to another without interfering with any activities. It should also be easy for the teacher to see what is going on in the room without having to walk through the room. Low room dividers that separate play centers make this possible.

The authors point out that the advantage of well-organized space is that the teacher has more "discretionary time" or "time to act out of her own choices made in terms of her knowledge, experience, and sensitivities, just as the children are acting out of theirs. . . . It is not necessary for the staff to provide directed activities as a compensation for spatial inadequacy. . . ."[4]

[4]Ibid.

By proper organization of space, the teacher can make the available space serve the needs of the group most effectively. She can eliminate points where activity is likely to be unproductive or full of conflict. She will give herself more time to observe and to work with individuals or small groups. Using space well is an important aspect of good teaching.

THE USE OF TIME

Decisions about the length of the day or year are usually made on the basis of money, facilities, precedent, and how long parents are at work. A day-care center that serves the needs of children of working parents may be open from early in the morning until evening each working day in the year. A college or university laboratory nursery school may follow the institution's calendar and have morning sessions only. Most nursery and kindergarten children attend school two-and-a-half to three hours a day.

Within the given time of each day, teachers will work out a schedule for the day that meets the needs of the particular children in a particular group. Schedules will consider the children's interests and involvement and will revolve around such "givens" as arrival, snack, and departure in a part-day program and snack, lunch, sleep or rest, and departure in a long-day program. The availability of special staff or facilities may also determine a daily schedule. Large blocks of time between these "givens" should be planned, so that children have freedom and learn to use it to make choices within the structure.

There are some generalizations that can be made about a schedule, because all children have some needs in common. Any program for young children should provide for the following:

1. active involvement in work and play outdoors
2. quiet involvement in work and play indoors
3. opportunities for not being involved and for rest and relaxation
4. toileting and washing
5. nourishment of some kind

Children also need an order in the events of the day. Those children who have known little order in their lives at home may be especially in need of order in their school day. A fixed sequence to parts of the program gives a child confidence in himself, because he knows what to expect. He can predict the order of the day. The order should be flexible, and it should be modified, from time to time, for a trip or a special event. Flexibility can be predictable, too. Children should be a part of this planning for flexibility.

A SCHEDULE

A schedule will include:

Arrival. Children like to know what to expect when they arrive at school. They like to know that the teacher will be there to greet them, that she is waiting for them to come, and that she expects them to greet her, too. Then they go on to hang up their coats in their lockers or to proceed outdoors.

Snack Time. A midmorning snack for a morning group, with a snack after naps for an all-day group.

Mealtime. A fixed point of time when the meal is served, preceded by toileting, washing, and toothbrushing after meals.

Rest or Nap. A short rest or quiet period before lunch, a longer rest period on cots after lunch in the all-day program (not over an hour if the child does not fall asleep).

Group Time. This may be a period before the end of the morning in a half-day program, or before lunch and at the end of the day in a full-day program. Teachers will read to small groups or they may have something to show to the group such as an interesting plant or a special picture or game. It may be discussion, making plans or talking over what has happened or reporting on experiences. It will be a period for thinking, talking, learning.

Picking-up Time. A time for putting away materials at the end of the morning and at the end of the afternoon in the all-day program.

Departure. After preparations for ending the day are completed, the time comes to say "good-bye" to the teacher, something to give a sense of an ending before welcoming the arrival of the parent.

Children should have large blocks of uninterrupted time for play between these regularly occurring points in the program. Someone has said, "No child has enough time for play." The center should make sure that children have plenty of time for play, especially for dramatic play. The teacher will make some of her most significant contributions to children's development by extending and enriching their play, skillfully and unobtrusively, and by observing them at play so she may come to understand them better.

Over a period of days children should have the chance to participate according to their individual interests in:

Music and Movement. Teachers should be ready to sing with children frequently, to make music together using simple instruments, or have music and movement experiences.

Art. A variety of art materials should be available for use every day.

Books. Teachers should be ready to read to a child or to small groups. Children should have available plenty of books, displayed in an attractive manner, and soft cushions to sit upon while using the books.

These boys share information in this magazine.

Valley College, Campus Child Development Center

Language. Teachers should be ready to talk with children, answer questions, listen, and encourage children to create with words.

Exploring and Discovery. Teachers should plan to introduce new materials and experiences for discovery in the school as well as plan walks and excursions to broaden the children's experiences outside the school.

A flexible schedule for activities encourages initiative on the part of children and teachers and sustains interest. It allows for planning individual and group experiences and includes time for review of what has happened during the day. It permits the group to develop projects over a period of time. A schedule exists as a framework only. It gives a sense of sureness and order to the day.

Projects

1. Consider one learning center of the classroom and list all of the equipment and materials located there to enhance young children's development.

2. Draw a diagram of the indoor space and a diagram of the outdoor space in the center where you are. Indicate where a teacher is needed if the areas are to be adequately supervised. List five things you see children playing with in the various areas of the setting.
3. Show on your diagram where those things are located. Considering the units of equipment as simple, complex, and super, check to see if the number of play units or "spaces" is adequate for the number of children who may be using them.
4. Describe the closed play materials, that is, those that require attention to constraints for a correct solution, such as puzzles, geoblocks, and lotto. Describe the open play materials that have no one particular "right way" to play (i.e., blocks, paints, clay, housekeeping).
5. Comment on the organization of the play space. Are the pathways clearly visible? Does supervision appear to be easily given? Is there enough but not too much empty space?

For Your Further Reading

Frost, J. L., & Henniger, M. L. (1979). Making playgrounds safe for children and children safe for playgrounds. *Young Children, 34*(4), 12-24. Also in D. W. Hewes (Ed.). (1979). Pp. 101–108. *Administration: Making programs work for children and families.* Washington, DC: National Association for the Education of Young Children. Serious playground injuries can be lessened by eliminating hazards and by helping children to play safely. Statistics and practical tips.

Harms, T. (1979). Evaluating settings for learning. *Young Children, 25*(5), 304–306, 308. Also in D. W. Hewes (Ed.). (1979). Pp. 187–190. *Administration: Making programs work for children and families.* Washington, DC: National Association for the Education of Young Children. A useful tool for evaluating a center, with emphasis on opportunities for learning.

Harms, T., & Clifford, R. (1980). *Early childhood environmental rating scale.* New York: Teachers College. How to evaluate all aspects of a center's environment, with a helpful rating scale that results in a profile.

Kritchevsky, S., Prescott, E., with Walling, L. (1977). *Planning environments for young children: Physical space* (2nd ed.). Washington, DC: National Association for the Education of Young Children. How program goals relate to outdoor and indoor space, with practical ideas for arranging play areas.

Moyer, J. (Ed.). (1985). *Selecting educational equipment and materials: For school and home.* Wheaton, MD: Association for Childhood Education International. The best resource on equipment selection for programs from infant through school age; comprehensive lists for several acquisition stages; addresses.

PART TWO

◆

BASIC TEACHING SKILLS

Cobweb (boy, 4 years)

5 ◆ Observing Children

If understanding a child is like unraveling a mystery, then taking records is the gathering of clues. Like experienced detectives we must recognize the significant clues, we must develop special skills.[1]

All teachers need to develop skill as observers. They need to see and record what is happening as accurately and as objectively as possible. Teachers learn most about children by studying their behavior directly. By learning to observe with objectivity, making careful notes, and going over them thoughtfully, a teacher increases her understanding of a child's behavior.

The teacher as an observer is someone who is, herself, part of the situation. She is an "involved observer" or "participant observer." Hers is

[1]D. Cohen & V. Stern. (1983). *Observing and recording the behavior of young children* (4th ed.). New York: Teachers College.

not an easy task. She is interested in the meaning behind the behavior. To achieve even a measure of objectivity takes practice and self-discipline. The teacher's accurate observation record can make a valuable contribution toward understanding a child's behavior and planning for his learning.

Objectivity means seeing what is actually taking place. It means observing without being influenced by value judgments like "bad," "good," "right," or "wrong." It means trying to reduce the distortions that are the result of biases, defenses, or preconceptions.

Beginning teachers need to develop their skills in making observations before they undertake the role of "participant observer." As a part of their education for teaching, they need to spend a great deal of time observing and recording their observations of young children.

Teachers need to continue making observations as a part of their teaching. Teachers can carry a pad and pencil in a pocket to make notes describing behavior as it occurs. They should jot down the words said by the child, for the exact words are hard to recall later, note the date, and add a word or two about the circumstances. Such notes are valuable. They are the raw material out of which understanding grows. When written up more completely later and then filed, notes become part of a record about a child. This record should be reviewed and summarized at intervals. It can be used in evaluating a child's progress, in making plans for him, and in preparing for a conference with his parents.

Teachers should try to manage time during the week when they can step aside and do more sustained observing. They may have a special purpose in mind, such as trying to discover how a certain child approaches other children, or why there is trouble so frequently in the block-building corner, or how the setup for finger painting might be improved. If the staff feels that a particular child is having difficulty, they may all try to observe him throughout a week, making notes on what they observe. One of them may take time to do a longer observation in order to add still more information. Pooling these records, they can discuss his behaviors in a staff meeting. They will have more accurate information about his strengths and vulnerabilities and be better able to plan for him. The use of a video camera provides another way of observing what is happening.

TYPES OF RECORDS

There are many types of observational records. The *informal, random notes* that a teacher makes are of value in understanding a child's behavior. They usually record characteristic behavior, or significant behavior, or examples of a particular type of behavior. The *diary record* or *running record* is an observational record covering a period of time, including all that can be recorded in that time interval. *Sampling records* are observational records repeated at intervals. *Selected observations* may be made of certain types of activity, such as observations of a rest period or of children's skill in making parquetry designs or a child's behavior on the first day at school.

A useful reference on the subject is the monograph by Cohen and Stern (1983), *Observing and Recording the Behavior of Young Children.* Two books by Susan Isaacs, *Intellectual Growth in Young Children* (1966) and *Social Development in Young Children* (1972) contain a wealth of examples of situations involving children individually and in groups, recorded with interpretive comments.

A good teacher will spend time observing, making records, and using these to increase her understanding of young children and their behavior. Here are some examples of different kinds of records.

Informal Notes

5/12 Bruce, constructing a building, tried to enlist the help of Marvin, saying, "You can be a roof helper," and then turned to me, "You are so

The quality of a child's involvement is an important part of an observation record.

Valley College, Campus Child Development Center

tall you can help with the roof." Example of Reasoning and Social Skill,—
K.R.

Report of a Single Incident

10/6 As I came out onto the playground, Joe ran up and asked me to tie
his shoe. I bent over and did it for him. Off he ran, and then Betsy, who
had been sitting on the step, said, "Wait." She reached down, carefully
untied her shoelace, and stuck her foot out, asking me to tie her shoelace.
I smiled at her, tied it, and patted her; off she went.—K.H.

Comment and Interpretation

In this record one is struck by the *un*self-conscious way in which Betsy
asked for a share of the teacher's attention. The teacher seemed willing to
accept her request and give her an extra bit of attention. It appeared to
satisfy Betsy, and she moved away into activity rather than just sitting. It
would be worth observing Betsy further to see whether she may be an
"easy" child, who is not getting much attention, or whether she has a real
problem with jealousy or with finding her place in the group. At least she
is showing that she has ways of coping with the situation.

Ten-Minute Running Record

10:30 Billy is kneeling in front of a low blackboard, carefully drawing
diagonal lines of scallops across the board, pursing his lips as he draws.
Kim comes up, kneels beside him, and draws a heavy dark line through his
scallops: and then she sits back with a pleased expression. Billy looks at
her in surprise and then back at the board. He picks up the eraser and
carefully erases both lines. He appears to ignore Kim and begins to draw
scallops again, tracing the lines of the previous scallops, which are still
faintly visible. As he draws the fourth scallop, Kim reaches out and draws
another dark line intersecting the scallops. Billy sits back on his heels and
looks at the board, but not at Kim, frowning slightly. Then he reaches
forward and erases the board, glancing at Kim. He begins to draw the
scallops again, this time looking at Kim each time he makes a scallop. Just
as he begins the fourth one, again Kim reaches out and scribbles over his
drawing. Billy turns to her, raises his hand with the eraser over his head,
and then lets it fall. He turns back and uses the eraser to erase the board
very thoroughly.

10:35 Billy draws a line down the center of the blackboard, saying as he
finishes, "There," and pointing to the side nearest Kim, "Use your own
spot," He sits quietly back on his heels and says with determination, "I'm
going to be a good boy." Kim, bringing her eraser across the entire board,

says, "Now we got to race." Billy says, as though to himself, "I don't care." Then he says to Kim, "Do you want to erase your name?" "OK," Kim answers. Billy draws a "B" on the board.

10:39 Just then a teacher calls to Kim to tell her that it is her turn to have the swing. She jumps up and runs off. Billy goes back to work on his scallops. When he finishes he leans back on his heels and, with apparent satisfaction, says, "There's my monster."

Comment and Interpretation

The observation seems complete, giving details that enable us to reconstruct what has taken place. The descriptive phrases that are used, such as "looks at the board, but not at Kim" and "diagonal lines of scallops," are clear. It is objective, free of interpretation. The impressions are clearly labeled as "with determination" or "with apparent satisfaction." We have an objective picture of Kim's and Billy's behavior, relatively unclouded by what the observer thought.

Billy seems wholeheartedly involved in his own purpose. He copes with the problem of Kim's interference in an unusual way. First, he tries to ignore it. He almost seems to want to pretend she isn't there. As she persists, he repeats his attempt until it obviously is unsuccessful. He feels like hitting her with the eraser, but he controls the impulse. Perhaps he feels better after he drains off some of this feeling by erasing the board vigorously (as he would like to have wiped her out).

Then Billy moves on to another level of coping. He divides the space, one side for Kim and one for himself; he probably hopes he will be undisturbed. His internalized adult conscience comes out in the words, "I'm going to be a good boy." He is trying to exorcise the monster with these often heard words. Kim, however, is operating on a different level. She feels aggressive and competitive, and she suggests a race. At this point Billy tries to persuade himself that he doesn't care. This device doesn't seem to work, and he then comes up with a remarkable solution. He decides to give her something to erase, her own name, a wonderfully positive suggestion with significant overtones. It is in line with her interests at the moment, and the "B" he draws is the first letter of his own name, probably the only name he knows how to write. As she has been intent on destroying his product, erasing the "B" seems significant. When Kim leaves at this point and Billy is able to finish his drawing, it becomes a "monster," probably carrying the load of frustration and resentment that he feels. It seems to satisfy him.

Billy's control over his impulses seems to be very strong. His strengths lie in his ability to put his feelings into words and finally to express them in his drawing. One might wonder whether or not this control is almost too great for a four-year-old boy and may interfere with his standing up for himself with other four-year-olds. "I'm going to be a good boy" is not an easy thing when one is with others who have not "internalized" this concept. It leads him into some unusual problem-solving actions: dividing the board with Kim and giving her something to erase. These actions demonstrate his capacity to cope with a situation on a high level and, later, his capacity to use drawing as an avenue for finally expressing the feeling that he has not allowed to come out more directly.

How effective his defenses are, where they will lead him, and what they really mean to him can only be understood after further observations of Billy. Billy is the third child in a family of four children. One suspects that Billy has had a lot of help in coping with the interferences of a younger sibling in a family where standards are high and relationships are good. What help does he need in the center?

We also meet Kim in this record, the minor character in the drama, at a moment when she has been thwarted in carrying out a purpose. She wants to swing, and she has had to wait for a turn. She begins to frustrate someone else, teasing and annoying Billy, but not in an unfriendly way. She is apparently an active child; she does something rather than wait. She is also sociable, and she turns to another child rather than to an object. She tries actively to get Billy's attention. In making a line through his drawing, she is also probably draining off some of *her* frustration. She is persistent, but she is not concerned with trying to be a "good girl." She, too, can make a suggestion. Her suggestion, "We got to race" is a vigorous, competitive one, but she is flexible. She accepts Billy's different suggestion about erasing her name instead. She quickly returns to carry out her original purpose when the teacher calls her. She seems to be a normal, healthy four-year-old.

Kim's behavior is a reminder to us that any child who has to "wait" may need some of the teacher's help. To be left at loose ends, frustrated in the immediate carrying out of a purpose, is not easy for a child. As teachers, we need to be alert to the child's need for a suggestion about what to do while waiting. Perhaps the waiting time can be used for a conversation with the child. At least we need to keep an eye on what the child does in the waiting period. Kim needed some help in coping with her problem. She put a burden on Billy in this case.

CONTRAST IN OBSERVATIONS

Just as detectives look for clues in trying to reconstruct a scene and solve a mystery, let us look for clues to understanding a child by observing and recording the child's behavior. What clues do we look for? How well does the description of the child's actions enable us to get a clear impression of what the child may be like? Is the record objective rather than subjective? Are impressions clearly labeled as such? Is the record free of obvious bias?

A sense of mastery!

Hill an' Dale Family Learning Center, Santa Monica

Is the setting or the circumstances, or both, included when these play a part in the child's responses? Are clues to the way the child feels included? How much can we learn from a record?

Becoming a competent observer takes time and much practice. It is a skill well worth the effort if one is to understand and guide young children. Here are three records of observations made by different observers. What does one learn about Jasmine from reading each record?

Observation 1

Jasmine helped the teacher set up the cots for nap time. She got her basket of bedding from her cubby and made her bed. The teacher helped her straighten the sheet. She covered herself with the blanket and went to sleep.

COMMENT. In this record we have an account of what Jasmine did. There are no details about the way in which she helped the teacher, how she seemed to feel about helping, or about the way she managed making her own bed and settling herself for sleep. Jasmine might have been any child. There are no clues to help us see Jasmine as an individual. What is she like? We do not know from the record.

Observation 2

Jasmine seemed to enjoy helping the teacher set up the cots for nap time. She had no trouble getting the legs of the cot into position and putting the cots in place. When she had finished helping the teacher, she went to her "cubby" and got her basket with its sheet and blanket and doll. She had a little trouble getting her sheet on the cot because she had it going the wrong way. The teacher helped her, and soon she had her sheet just the way she wanted it. She got her doll and blanket, crawled into bed, and pulled the cover over herself. She fell asleep quite fast.

COMMENT.   This observation tells us more about Jasmine, but details are missing. Some statements are subjective, for example, "Jasmine enjoyed helping the teacher." What did Jasmine do or say that made the observer come to this conclusion? The clue is missing here. Jasmine "had no trouble with the legs of the cot" is not a description of Jasmine's behavior. It suggests that she is a competent child, but next we find she "had a little trouble" with her sheet and needed help from the teacher. Did Jasmine ask for help? Was she aware the sheet was on the wrong way? Many of the clues are missing in this account. We still do not know much about the child who is Jasmine.

Observation 3

Jasmine is helping the teacher set up cots while the rest of the children listen to a story. Jasmine walks purposefully, attending to her task with a happy expression on her face. She seems to feel important and confident, as though helping the teacher was something very special. Jasmine carefully pulls the lightweight cots out of their storage corner without bumping the wall. She proceeds to open the cots and secures the legs by applying a little pressure, probably imitating the way she has observed the teacher doing it. She sets up three cots in their places, adjusting the positions slightly until she is satisfied.

She is now ready to make her own bed. She gets a basket from her locker which has her sheet, blanket, and doll. She carefully places the basket on the floor next to her cot. She puts the blanket and the doll on the cot next to her cot and starts spreading the sheet. Her movements are quite deliberate now. As she pulls the sheet to one end of the cot, she sees that it is not covering the other end. She goes to the other end and pulls the sheet so that it covers that end, and again she notices that the sheet is not covering the other end. Again she goes to that end and pulls the sheet toward her. She repeats the same action again, apparently unaware that the sheet is on the wrong way. Lynn, one of the aides, comes over. She points out to Jasmine that there is a long and a short side to the sheet just like there is to a cot. Jasmine looks at her with a puzzled expression but continues to pull on the sheet. Lynn puts the sheet on the right way, unobtrusively holding one corner so that it will stay in place as Jasmine smooths it out. Jasmine seems satisfied with her cot making now. She grabs her blanket and doll from the other cot, hastily opens the blanket which is slightly rumpled by now, and crawls in under it. Her movements are no longer deliberate. She quickly cuddles up with her doll, puts her thumb in her mouth, and closes her eyes. In no time she is sound asleep.

COMMENT. In this record we have a much more detailed account of Jasmine's behavior. We can begin to see Jasmine as an individual and what an engaging little girl she is. The observer gives us clues to Jasmine's feelings in recording her "purposeful walk," the expression on her face, her careful efforts with the cots. These all suggest a child who is feeling important and confident, enjoying what she is doing. She is likely to be an observant child, too, as shown by the way she imitates the teacher's actions and later notices that the sheet does not fit. The observer is careful to label impressions by using such words as "seems to feel."

The bed-making experience is recorded in detail with descriptive words such as "carefully places the basket" and "deliberate" movements. Jasmine's persistence is apparent in her efforts with the sheet. She does not appear to expect help. She looks puzzled at Lynn's explanation about the sheet. Her puzzled look may indicate that she does not understand the reason for her difficulty. Jasmine's change of pace from deliberate to hurried may be a clue to her feelings. She hurries to get into bed, cuddling her doll and sucking a comforting thumb. She may be somewhat upset about the sheet even though Lynn had helped her succeed. She fell asleep almost immediately.

We know much more about Jasmine than we did from the first two records. There are still many questions to ask. What are Jasmine's relations with other children like? Does she do much exploring and discovering on her own? How does she usually meet difficulties? These questions can only be answered by more observations, if we are to begin to understand this child. It would help us if the record included the child's age and the length of time of the observation.

Projects

1. Observe one child for a ten-minute period, keeping a record of what the child does and says in this time. Comment on what you have learned about the child or what questions the observation has raised.
2. Select a piece of equipment and observe and record which children make use of it through a period of 20 minutes. Summarize your observations. Of what value is this equipment?

For Your Further Reading

Almy, M., & Genishi, C. (1979). *Ways of studying children: An observation manual for early childhood teachers* (rev. ed.). New York: Teachers College. The meaning of child study for teachers; and observation as the most basic way to study children, ages two to eight; treats teachers as well as children as developing learners.

Bentzen, W. R. (1985). *Seeing young children: A guide to observing and recording behavior.* Albany, NY: Delmar. For observing children from ages 0–8; includes methods and ethics.

Cohen, D., & Stern, V. (1983). *Observing and recording the behavior of young children* (4th ed.). New York: Teachers College. A classic little book; useful and practical tips with illustrative anecdotes.

Isaacs, S. (1930. Reissued in 1966.) *Intellectual growth in young children.* New York: Schocken Books.

Isaacs, S. (1933. Reissued in 1972). *Social development in young children.* New York: Schocken Books. These two books are still sound and are helpful in observing children; contain many observation examples.

Raskin, L. M., Taylor, W. J., and Kerckhoff, F. G. (1975). The teacher as observer for assessment: A guideline. *Young Children. 30*(5), 339–344. Guidelines for teacher observations when a child may need referral for special help: visual, motor behavior, use of writing tools, listening and remembering, social-emotional behaviors.

Richarz, A. S. (1980). *Understanding children through observation.* St. Paul, MN: West Publishing. Intended to help develop an understanding of children's behavior through observation; learning observation techniques is a secondary goal of this guide.

Trains (boy, 3 years, 7 months)

6 ◆ Initial Support Through Guides to Speech and Action

We have described the center itself. Now we turn to the question of how we will fit into a center as teachers. What guides are there to speech and action? How can we best meet the demands made on us by the situation while we are increasing our understanding?

FEELINGS OF INADEQUACY

Each of us will respond somewhat differently to the experience of beginning to work with children. Some of these responses may interfere with what we do, while others may be helpful.

We discussed in an earlier chapter the necessity of accepting that we may feel uncertain and uncomfortable in the center at first. Too frequently we only increase these feelings by struggling against them, making it more difficult to develop constructive ways of acting. Sometimes we try to defend ourselves against feeling inadequate in a new situation by plunging into action as though to take our minds off the way we feel. We may do unnecessary things like talking to children when talking serves no useful purpose for the child. We may offer help that is not needed or try to start activities that have no real place at the moment in the child's pattern of play. Sometimes we may defend ourselves against feeling inadequate by withdrawing and taking no action at all. Sometimes we may fight against the necessity for direction by being very critical of the direction given; and at other times we may seek reassurance by trying to be completely dependent on instructions, insisting that these be specific and detailed so that there is no room for uncertainty.

These adjustments or defenses are part of a resistance to change that all of us feel and that is sometimes a protection and frequently a limitation on growth. Growth is often an uncomfortable process. But growth is rewarding and satisfying when we have mobilized our resources and reduced the conflicts that interfere with our growth. Instead of spending energy trying to deny feelings, we can make constructive use of them.

GUIDES GIVE SUPPORT

When one feels inadequate, one needs support of some kind. What are the supports available in the situation? What help can one get from the experienced teacher? What help can one find in one's own past experiences in related situations, in books, or from discussion? In any new experience we begin to gain confidence when we assemble the useful, appropriate supports and build a framework in which to operate.

In this chapter we will list some techniques and principles that can be depended on as guides to action. These can be applied in an increasingly individual way with added experience. The success of some of these techniques depends in part on the relationship built up with individual children. Time is required to build as well as to understand relationships, but during the process these "rules" will give clues to appropriate action. In time, with experience and increasing insight, each one of us will make her own generalizations and add new interpretations. There is always more than one "right" way.

Set down alone, these statements may seem somewhat like letters in an alphabet. Only when they are combined by experience into larger units will they have much meaning. At this point they must be accepted as part of the alphabet that goes to make a "language" used in guiding behavior.

These fifteen points can serve as guides to speech and action in the beginning when the situation is an unfamiliar one. Here they are.

In Speech

1. State suggestions or directions in a positive rather than a negative form.
2. Give the child a choice only when you are prepared to leave the choice up to him.
3. Use your voice as a teaching tool. Your words and tone of voice should help the child to feel confident and reassured.
4. Avoid trying to change behavior by methods that may lead to loss of self-respect, such as shaming or labeling behavior naughty or selfish.
5. Avoid motivating a child by making comparisons between one child and another or by encouraging competition.
6. Redirect the child by suggesting an activity that is related to his own purposes or interests whenever possible.
7. Give a direction or suggestion at the time that it will be most effective.

In Action

8. Avoid making models in any art medium for the children to copy.
9. Give the child the minimum help in order that he may have the maximum chance to grow in independence; but give the child help when he needs it.
10. Make your directions effective by reinforcing them when necessary.
11. Learn to foresee and prevent rather than mop up after a difficulty.
12. Define limits clearly and maintain them consistently.
13. Be alert to the total situation. Use the most strategic positions for supervising.
14. Make health and safety a primary concern at all times.
15. Increase your own awareness by observing and taking notes.

GUIDES IN SPEECH

1. State suggestions or directions in a positive rather than a negative form.   A positive suggestion is one which tells a child what to do instead of pointing out what he is not to do. If a child has already done what he should not do or if we think he is about to do something he should not, then he needs help in getting another, better idea. We give him this kind of help when we direct his attention to what we want him to do.

It has been demonstrated experimentally that directions stated in a positive way are more effective than the same directions given negatively. This can be subjected to proof informally in many situations. For example, a teacher in nursery school demonstrated it in this situation. She was finding it difficult to weigh the children because almost every child reached for support when he felt the unsteadiness of the scale platform. When the teacher asked them not to touch anything, she had very little success. She changed her negative direction to a positive one, "Keep your hands down at your sides," and the children did just that. Telling them what to do, instead of what not to do, brought results.

A question is *not* a statement. We may find ourselves putting something in the form of a question instead of a statement because of our own uncertainty. We may say, "Don't you want to pull the plug?" when we mean that we want the child to pull the plug, but we are not at all sure that we can persuade him to do it. What we should say is, "Pull the plug now and dry your hands."

A positive direction is less likely to rouse resistance than a negative one. It makes help seem constructive rather than limiting and interfering. Perhaps the child is doing the thing because he thinks it annoys us. By emphasizing the positive we reduce the attention and thus the importance of the negative aspect of his behavior. We usually help rather than hinder when we make a positive suggestion.

In addition, when we make suggestions in a positive way we are giving the child a sound pattern to imitate when he himself directs his friends. He is likely to be more successful, to meet with less resistance, if he puts his suggestions in a positive form. We give him a good social tool to use. One can tell something about the kind of direction that a child has received as one listens to the kind of direction that he gives in play.

More important still, having clearly in mind what we want the child to do, we can steer him toward this behavior with more confidence and assurance—with more chance of success. Our goal is clear to us and to him. We are more likely to feel adequate and to act effectively when we put a statement positively.

To put directions positively represents a step in developing a more positive attitude toward children's behavior inside ourselves. Our annoyance often increases as we dwell on what the child should not be doing, but our feelings may be different when we turn our attention to what the child should be doing in the situation. We may have more sympathy for the child's problem as we try to figure out just what he could do under the circumstances. It helps us to appreciate the difficulties he may be having in figuring out a better solution.

An experienced teacher will often say, "Keep the clay on the table, not on the floor," thus letting the child know what he should avoid doing, but first her emphasis is on making it clear what he should do. It may be wise to use only the positive part of the statement in the beginning. It is easy to slip into old habits and rely on the negative. Making only positive suggestions is a hard exercise because most of us have depended heavily on negative suggestions in the past and have had them used on us. It is worth correcting oneself whenever one makes a negative statement in order to hasten the learning of this basic technique. Every direction should be given in a positive form.

For example, the teacher will say:

1. "Ride your tricycle around the bench," instead of, "Don't bump the bench."
2. "Throw your ball over here," instead of, "Don't hit the window."
3. "Leave the heavy blocks on the ground," instead of, "Don't put the heavy blocks on that high board."
4. "Give me the ball to hold while you're climbing," instead of, "Don't climb with that ball in your hand."
5. "Take a bite of your lunch now," instead of, "Don't play at the table."
6. "Take little bites and then it will all go in your mouth," instead of, "Don't take such big bites and then you won't spill."
7. "Play softly on the piano," instead of, "Don't bang on the piano."

2. *Give the child a choice only when you are prepared to leave the choice up to him.* Choices are legitimate. With increasing maturity one makes an increasing number of choices. We accept that being able to make decisions helps to develop maturity. But there are decisions which a child is not ready to make because of his limited capacities and experience. We must be careful to avoid offering him a choice when we are not really willing to let him decide the question. Sometimes one hears a mother say to her child. "Do you want to go home now?" When the child replies, "No," the mother acts as though the child were being disobedient because he did not answer the question in the way she wanted him to answer it. What she really meant to say was, "It's time to go home now."

Questions like that mother's are most often asked when a person feels uncertain or wishes to avoid raising an issue that she is not sure she can handle. Sometimes asking a question is only a habit of speaking. But it is confusing to the child to be asked a question when what is wanted is not information but confirmation. It is important to guard against the tendency to use a question unless the circumstances make a question legitimate.

Circumstances differ, but usually a young child is not free to choose such things as the time to go home or the time to eat or rest. He is not free to choose to hurt others or to damage property. On the other hand, he is free to decide such things as whether he wants to play outside or inside, what play materials he wants, and whether he needs to go to the toilet.

Sometimes a child may be offered a choice to clarify a situation for him. For example, he may be interfering with someone's sand pies and the teacher may ask, "Do you want to stay in the sandbox?" A response of "Yes" is defined further as, "Then you will need to play at this end of the box out of Bobby's way."

It is important to be clear in one's mind as to whether one is really offering the child a choice before one asks a question. Be sure that your questions are legitimate ones.

3. Use your voice as a teaching tool. Your words and tone of voice should help the child to feel confident and reassured.   All of us have known parents and teachers who seem to feel that the louder they speak, the greater their chances of controlling behavior. We may also have observed that these same people often have more problems than the parents and teachers who speak more quietly but are listened to. A quiet, firm manner of speaking conveys confidence and reassures the child.

It may be necessary to speak firmly, but it is never necessary to raise one's voice. The most effective speech is simple and direct and slow. Decreasing speed is more effective than raising pitch.

It is a good rule never to call or shout across any play area, inside or outside. It is always better to move nearer the person to whom you are speaking. Children as well as adults grow irritated when shouted at. Your words will get a better reception if they are spoken quietly, face to face.

This teacher uses her voice and her touch.

First Step Nursery School, Santa Monica

Speech conveys feelings as well as ideas. No matter what words they hear children are probably very sensitive to the tone quality, for example to the tightness in the voice, which reveals annoyance, unfriendliness, or fear. One can try for a pleasant tone of voice, and one may find one's feelings improving along with one's voice.

The teacher sets a pattern in her speech, as she does in other ways. Children are more likely to use their voices in loud harsh ways if the teacher uses her voice in these ways. Voice quality can be improved with training, and every one of us could probably profit from speech work to improve our voices. A well-modulated voice is an asset worth cultivating.

4. Avoid trying to change behavior by methods that may lead to loss of self-respect, such as shaming or labeling behavior naughty or selfish. We need to learn constructive ways of influencing behavior if we are to promote sound personality growth. Neither children nor adults are likely to develop desirable behavior patterns as the result of fear or shame or guilt. Improvement will be more apparent than real, and any change is likely to be accompanied by resentment and an underlying rejection of the behavior involved when these methods of control are used.

It takes time to learn constructive ways of guiding behavior. The first step is to eliminate the destructive patterns in use. We must discard the gestures, the expressions, the tones of voice as well as the words that convey the impression that the other person should feel ashamed of himself. In passing judgment on another, we make the other person feel that we do not respect him. It is hard for a person to change his behavior unless he feels some respect for himself. The young child is especially dependent on feeling that others respect him.

If we believe that there are reasons why a person behaves as he does, reasons for his patterns of reacting, we will not blame the individual for his behavior. We may see it as undesirable or unacceptable and may try to change it, but we will accept and respect him. We will not add to his burden by passing judgment on him. Labeling behavior, for example, by calling it "selfish," means we are passing a judgment which is undiscriminating and fails to take circumstances into account. It often prevents us from observing closely. It does not build self-respect.

A child will be helped if we accept him as he is and try to make it possible for him to find some success, rather than if we reprove him because he does not meet our standards. Here is an example.

Mark, an active child with a short attention span who often acts destructively, sits down and starts to put a puzzle together. He whines when a piece does not fit in the first place he tries and throws the piece on the floor.

The teacher says, "Does it make you mad when it doesn't fit right away?" She puts into words the feeling he appears to have, thus indicating her acceptance of it and him. This probably helps him to relax.

She reaches down and gets the piece and passes it to him, and he completes the puzzle successfully. She says, "That's fine. You did it." She does not reprove him for throwing a piece on the floor or expect him to pick it up. He is not ready to meet such an expectation. It is more important for him to have some success. She helps him be successful and respects him for what he can do.

5. Avoid motivating a child by making comparisons between one child and another or by encouraging competition.   Comparing one child with another is a dangerous way to try to influence behavior. We may get results in changed behavior, but these changes may not all be improvements. Some of these results are sure to be damaging to the child's feeling of adequacy and his friendliness.

Competitive schemes for getting children to dress more quickly or to eat more of something may have some effects that are not what we want. Children who are encouraged to be competitive are very likely to quarrel more with one another. In any competition someone always loses, and he's likely to feel hurt and resentful. Even the winner may be afraid of failing next time, or he may feel an unjustified superiority if the contest was an unequal one. Competition does not build friendly, social feelings.

Competition not only handicaps smooth social relationships but also creates problems within the child himself. We live in a highly competitive society, it is true, but the young child is not ready to enter into much competition until his concept of himself as an adequate person has developed enough so that he can stand the strains and the inevitable failures that are part of competition. On the one hand, constant success is not a realistic experience and does not prepare a child well for what he will meet later. Too many failures, on the other hand, may make him feel weak and helpless. Both are poor preparation for a competitive world. For sound growth it is important to avoid competitive kinds of motivation until children have developed ego strength and can balance failures with successes.

This raises a question about what is sound motivation, anyway. Do we really get dressed in order to set a speed record or to surpass someone else? Is it not true, rather, that we dress ourselves because there is satisfaction in being independent and that we complete dressing quickly in order to go on to another activity? There may be a point in spending time enjoying the process of dressing if there happens to be nothing of any greater importance coming next. We may be better off when we get pleasure out of the doing of a thing, not just in getting the thing done. It is wise to be sure that we are motivating children in a sound way even though we may seem to move more slowly. We ensure a sounder growth for them and give them a better preparation for the years ahead.

Children should not feel that their only chances for getting attention and approval depend on being "first" or "beating" someone or being the "best." They should feel sure of acceptance whether they succeed or fail. One has only to listen to children on a playground to realize how disturbing highly competitive feelings are to them. Statements like "You can't beat me," or "I'm bigger than you," or "Mine is better than yours" increase friction and prevent children from getting along well together.

6. Redirect the child by suggesting an activity that is related to his own purposes or interests whenever possible.   What does this mean? It simply means that we will be more successful in changing the child's behavior if we attempt to turn his attention to an act which has equal value as an interest or outlet for him. If he's throwing a ball dangerously near a window, for example, we can suggest a safer place to throw it. If he's throwing something dangerous because he's angry, we can suggest an acceptable way of draining angry feelings—like throwing against a backstop or using a punching bag or pounding at the workbench. In the first case his interest is in throwing, and in the second case it is in expressing his anger. Our suggestions for acting differently will take into account the different meaning in his behavior. We will always try to suggest something that meets the needs he is expressing in his behavior.

Bobby, for example, stands up in the sand and throws a pan at Susan who is startled and cries. Bobby has been playing in the sandbox for some time. The teacher assumes that he has lost interest and needs a suggestion for doing something more active. She says, "Bobby, Susan didn't like that. If you want to throw something, there's a ball over there. Let's fix a place to throw." She turns a barrel on its side and suggests to Bobby that he try throwing the ball through the barrel. He tries it and is successful. They throw it back and forth. Another child joins and takes the teacher's place in the game. It involves a great deal of running and chasing, which both children enjoy.

If a group is running around wildly after a long period of quiet play, its members may need a suggestion about engaging in some vigorous and constructive play like raking leaves outside. Their needs will not be met by a suggestion about sitting quietly and listening to a story. The meaning of their behavior lies in a need for activity. The teacher's part is to help them to find some acceptable expression for this need. If they are running around wildly, on the other hand, because they are fatigued by too much activity and stimulation, a suggestion about listening to a story will meet their need for rest.

Effective redirection often requires imagination, as in the following example where the teacher gave a suggestion which captured the interest of these particular children.

Donnie and Michael are at the top of the jungle gym and notice a teacher nearby who is busy writing. They shout at her, "We're going to tie you up and put you in jail." They have a rope with a heavy hook on it. Donnie climbs down with it saying, "I'm going to tie you up!" He flings it toward the teacher and stands looking at her. She says, "You don't quite understand what I'm doing here, Donnie, do you? I'm writing down some things I want to remember," and she continues, "I wonder if you could use the hook to catch a fish from the jungle gym. It would take a strong man to catch a big fish from the top of that jungle gym." He picks up the rope and climbs up the jungle gym and the teacher ties a "fish" on to the hook. The boys have fun pulling it up and lowering it for a fresh catch.

Effective redirection faces the situation and does not avoid or divert. The teacher who sees a child going outdoors on a cold day without his coat does not give him help when she stops him by saying, "Stay inside and listen to the story now." She is avoiding the question of the need for a coat. She helps him by saying, "You'll need a coat on before you go outside." On the other hand, in another situation, suggesting a substitute activity may help the child, as in the case of two children wanting the same piece of equipment. The teacher helps when she says to one, "No, it's Bill's turn now. You might rake these leaves while you're waiting for your turn." Redirection should help the child face his problem by showing him how it can be met, not by diverting him.

7. Give a direction or suggestion at the time that it will be most effective.   The timing of a suggestion may be as important as the suggestion itself. Through experience and insight one can increase one's skill in giving a suggestion at the moment when it will do the most good. When a suggestion fails to bring the desired response, it may be due to the timing.

Advice given too soon deprives the child of a chance to try to work things out for himself. It deprives him of the satisfaction of solving his own problem. It may very well be resented. A suggestion made too late may have lost any chance of being successful. The child may be too discouraged or too irritated to be able to act on it.

Help at the right moment may mean a supporting hand *before* the child loses his balance. It may mean arbitration *before* two boys come to blows over a wagon or the suggestion of a new activity *before* the group grows tired and disorganized. Effective guidance depends on knowing how to prevent trouble.

Douglas says to Robert, "There's Pam. Let's hit her." They run over and hit Pamela and run away. The teacher comforts Pamela and goes after the two boys. They are already interested in digging and appear resentful that she interfered with their digging. If the teacher could have stopped them firmly and quickly as they started toward Pamela, she might have made it clear to them that she expected them to control their impulse and that she was there to help them control it. She might have asked them what other possibilities there were for action. They were readier to learn the lesson before they hit rather than afterward. Timing is important.

GUIDES IN ACTION

8. Avoid making models in any art medium for the children to copy. This may seem like an arbitrary rule. We hope that it will seem justified later. Of course, this rule takes away the teacher's fun of drawing a man or making little dogs or Santa Clauses out of clay for an admiring crowd of preschoolers. All this may seem like innocent fun, but we must remember that art is valuable because it is a means of self-expression. It is a language to express feelings—to drain off tension or to express well-being. The young child needs avenues of expression. His speech is limited. His feelings are strong. In clay or sand or mud, at the easel, through finger paints, he expresses feelings for which he has little other language. If he has models before him, he may be blocked in using art as a means of *self*-expression. He will be less likely to be creative and more likely to be limited to trying to copy. Art then becomes only another area where he strives to imitate the adult who can do things much better than he can.

Notice what happens to a group at the clay table when the adult makes

A student helps a group of children make pancakes.
Santa Monica College, Child Development Center

something. The children watch and then ask, "Make one for me." It isn't much use to say, "You make one for yourself." They can't do it as well and they feel that the adult is uncooperative. Most of them drift away from the table, the meaning gone from the experience. It is no longer art or self-expression.

You may see children cramped over a paper with a crayon trying to make a car like the one the adult made, or children who will not touch the paints because they are afraid that they can't "make something." They may well envy the joy of the freer child who splashes color at the easel, delighting in its lines and masses, and who is well content with what he has done. He has had no patterns to follow.

The need for help with techniques comes much later after the child has explored the possibilities in different art media and discovered that these can be used as avenues of self-expression. Then the child will want to learn how to use the material to express better what *he* wants to express, but not to imitate better.

The skillful teacher will avoid getting entangled in "pattern making" under any guise. She may sit at the clay table, for example, feeling the clay, patting it and enjoying it as the children do, but she will not "make" anything. It is possible, of course, for children to watch adults who have found in art a means of self-expression as they work in their favorite medium. This may be a valuable experience for the children. Being with an adult who is expressing himself through an art medium is valuable for any child, but it is a very different experience from having an adult draw a man or a dog to amuse the child. Avoid patterns!

9. Give the child the minimum help in order that he may have the maximum chance to grow in independence; but give the child help when he needs it. There are all kinds of ways to help a child help himself if we take time to think about them, such as letting him help to turn the door knob with us, so that he will get the feel of how to handle a door knob and may be able to do it alone someday; or putting his boots on him while he sits beside us instead of picking him up and holding him on our laps, a position which will make it hard for him ever to do the job himself someday. Too many times the child has to climb down from the adult's lap when he might have started on his trip to independence in a more advantageous position.

Giving the minimum help may mean showing a child how to get a block or box to climb on when he wants to reach something rather than reaching it for him. It may mean giving him time enough to work out a problem rather than stepping in and solving it for him. Children like to solve problems, and it is hard to estimate how much their self-confidence is increased by independent problem solving. To go out and gather a child into one's arms to bring him in for lunch may be an effective way of seeing that he gets there, but it deprives him of the chance to take any responsibility for getting himself inside. It is important to give a child the minimum help in order to allow him to grow by himself as much as possible.

In leaving the child free to satisfy his strong growth impulse to be independent, we support his feeling of confidence in himself. "I can do this all by myself," or "Look what I can do," he says.

We must remember, however, that looking for opportunities to let the child do things for himself does not mean denying his requests for help. When a child says, "Help me" as he starts to take off his coat, he may be testing out the adult's willingness to help. The adult does not meet the test if she replies, "You can do it yourself." She reassures him if she gives help freely, with a full measure of willingness, or if she cannot, answers like this, "I'd like to help you but I'm busy just now," giving whatever real reason she has for not being in a position to help. A child may say "Swing me," and he may be wanting assurance that the teacher really values him enough to do extra, unnecessary things for him. He seeks a relationship with the teacher. We should avoid giving unwanted help, but we should give the help which the child feels he needs.

10. Make your directions effective by reinforcing them when necessary. Sometimes it is necessary to add several techniques together in order to be effective. A glance at the right moment, moving nearer a child, a verbal suggestion, actual physical help are all effective techniques.

A verbal direction, even though stated positively, may not be enough to get a response. "It's time to come in for lunch," may need to be reinforced to be effective. We need to add techniques in sequence until we get compliance. We must assume more responsibility at each stage in the sequence when the child avoids his responsibility.

The first stage may be to restate the direction, adding the reason for it. "Lunch is ready, and everyone needs to put things away and come inside." If there is no response, we may suggest some active participation such as, "I'll help you put your wagon in the shed, and we can go in together." A conversational approach usually makes it easier for a child to cooperate and avoid a confrontation. Young children often get interested in the action and forget to be negative.

The next step may be to discover why the child is ignoring or refusing to comply. "What is the matter?" The child may have a reason that he can communicate. We can work together with him in explaining or reassuring, but the necessity to go in remains. He may feel differently about going in for lunch, however.

If nothing reasonable emerges, we need to make the consequences clear to the child. In this case it will be "no lunch" and a hungry child, and we must make sure that the consequence follows. This is probably a child whose behavior should be discussed in a staff meeting.

The final stage in the sequence means that we must assume all the responsibility. We can bring the child in, picking him up or taking him firmly by the hand. Eating is up to him! This step should seldom be necessary. If it is a situation where there is any danger, of course, the teacher will immediately take over and act, explaining why she did so to the child later.

The sequence in using techniques differs in different circumstances, but we need to remember that we have more than one tool to use. There is a reasonable sequence to follow when one gives a direction to a child. When children are playing together in a group, some of them are likely to respond to a direction more readily than others. We are wise if we approach these children first when we need to interrupt the play. Success with one child will reinforce our chances of success with the others.

A common fault with teachers and parents is to use too many words in giving a direction or to give two or three directions at once when one is enough. Anxiety and insecurity may take the form of oververbalizing, showering the child with words. Children develop a "deafness" on hearing too many words.

It is important to have confidence in the child's ability to respond to a reasonable request or direction, given once. It is better to use different techniques in sequence until one is successful. Reinforce when necessary.

11. Learn to foresee and prevent rather than mop up after a difficulty. We are all aware that an ounce of prevention is worth a pound of cure. This is true in working with children. The best strategy depends on foreseeing and forestalling rather than mopping-up operations. Success in forestalling problems comes with experience. It takes time to learn what to expect in certain types of situations or with particular children or combinations of children.

Learning to prevent problems is important because, in many cases, children do not profit from making mistakes. The child who approaches others by doing something annoying may only learn to feel that people don't like him, and, in time, this may become a reality. He may learn acceptable ways of approaching others if the teacher, knowing his past behavior with groups, suggests suitable approaches to him when she observes that he is about to go up to a group. She may say to him, "If you'd like to play with them, you might knock first," or "Ask Michael if he needs another block." She may move into the situation with him to give him more support, or to interpret to the group what his intentions are, or even to help him accept his failure and find another place where he might have a better chance of success. If she waits until he fails he may be unable to learn anything constructive. He may only retreat.

Sometimes children tell us what they are going to do. In these cases we need to listen and prevent what may be undesirable, rather than wait until the damage is done and there is little chance to learn from the experience.

12. *Define limits clearly and maintain them consistently.* There are some things which must not be done. There are limits beyond which a child cannot be allowed to go. The important thing is to be sure that the limits set are necessary limits that are clearly defined. / Much of the difficulty with adults' discipline of children is because of confusion about what the limits are. In a well-planned environment there will not be many "no's," but these "no's" will be clearly defined. The child will understand them, and the adult will maintain them.

We are very likely to overestimate the child's capacity to grasp the point of what we say. Our experience is much more extensive than his. Without realizing it we take many things for granted. The child lacks experience. If he is to understand what the limits are, these limits must be clearly and simply defined for him.

When we are sure that a limit is necessary and that the child understands it, we can maintain it with confidence. It is easy to feel unsure or even guilty about maintaining limits. We may not like to face a child's unhappiness or his anger. Our own feelings bother us here. We may be afraid to maintain limits because we were overcontrolled, and we turn away from the resentment and hostility that limits arouse in us. Because of our past experiences we may not want to take any responsibility for controlling behavior. Gradually we should learn to untangle our feelings and handle situations on their own merits with confidence and without hesitation.

The adult must be the one who is responsible for limiting children so that they do not come to harm or do not harm others or destroy property. Children will feel more secure with adults who can take this responsibility. They will feel freer because they can depend on the adult to stop them before they do things that they would be sorry about later.

13. *Be alert to the total situation. Use the most strategic positions for supervising.* Sometimes one will observe an inexperienced teacher with her back to most of the children as she watches one child. On the other hand, the experienced teacher, even when she is working with one child, will be in a position to observe at a glance what the other children are doing. She is alert to the total situation.

Turning one's back on the group may represent, consciously or unconsciously, an attempt to limit one's experience to a simple situation. It is quite natural that one should feel like withdrawing from the more complex situations at first or that one should take an interest in one particular child because other children seem more difficult to understand. It is a natural tendency, but one should guard against it. It is important to develop skill in extending one's horizons. Observation of the total situation is essential to effective guidance. It is essential if the children are to be safe. Safety requires alert teachers who will see that all are supervised.

Enrichment of experience will come when a teacher is observing all the children, not just one child. The teacher who is reading to children, for example, may encourage a shy child to join the reading group by a smile, or she may forestall trouble by noticing a child who is ready for a change in activity. She may encourage him to join the group before his lack of interest disrupts others' play.

Sitting rather than standing is another technique for improving the effectiveness of one's supervision. One is often in a better position to help a child when one is at the child's level. Children may feel freer to approach the adult who is sitting. It also makes possible more unobtrusive observation.

In a group where there may be many adults, it is important that the adults avoid gathering in groups, such as near the entrance or in the locker room or around the sandbox. Grouping calls attention to the number of adults present. It may increase any tendency children have to feel self-conscious or to play for attention. Too many adults in one place may also mean that other areas are being left unsupervised.

Where one stands or sits is important in forestalling or preventing difficulties. A teacher standing between two groups engaged in different activities can make sure that one group does not interfere with the other and so can forestall trouble.

"Remote control" is ineffective control in the nursery school. Stepping between two children who are growing irritated with each other may prevent an attack, but it cannot be done if one is on the other side of the playroom. Trouble in the housekeeping corner, for example, may be avoided by a teacher who moves near quietly, as tension mounts in the "family," and suggests some solution. Her suggestion is more likely to be accepted if her presence reinforces it. Trouble is seldom avoided by a suggestion given at a distance.

Choose the position for standing or sitting which will best serve your purposes. Study a diagram of the center where you are teaching, and check the spots that are strategically good for supervision. List places where close supervision is needed for safety, such as at the workbench.

14. Make each child's health and safety a primary concern at all times. The good teacher must be constantly alert to the things that affect health, such as seeing that drinking cups are not used in common, that towels are kept separate, that toys which have been in a child's mouth are washed, that the window is closed if there is a draft, and that jackets or sweaters are adjusted to changes in temperature or activity.

The good teacher must also be alert to things that concern the children's safety. Being alert to safety means observing and removing sources of danger such as protruding nails, unsteady ladders, or boards not properly supported. It means giving close supervision to children who are playing

The teacher helps.

Santa Monica College, Child Development Center

The child succeeds!

Santa Monica College, Child Development Center

together on high places or to children who are using such potentially dangerous materials as hammers, saws, and shovels. The point is familiar but clear-cut and important: the skillful teacher never relaxes her watchfulness.

15. Increase your own awareness by observing and taking notes. Underlying all these guides is the assumption that teaching is based on ability to observe behavior objectively and to evaluate its meaning. As in any science, conclusions are based on accurate observations. Jot down notes frequently, statements of what happens, the exact words that a child uses, the exact sequence of events. Make each note at the time of the event or as soon after the event as possible, always dating each note. Reread these notes later and make interpretations. Skill in observing and recording is essential to building understanding. Improve your ability to select significant incidents and make meaningful records.

Projects

1. Observe and record ten positively stated directions that you heard a teacher use with a child. Indicate the effectiveness of each statement you recorded, giving the reasons why the statement seemed effective.
2. Observe and record five questions asked by the teacher. Classify the reason for asking a question as (1) to get information about a fact, (2) to discover an opinion or preference, (3) to suggest a possibility, (4) to clarify a situation, or (5) for another purpose. How effective was the question in each case?
3. Listen to the quality of the voices around you. What feelings do the tones seem to express when one pays no attention to the words spoken? Note the differences in pitch, in speed, and in volume in the teachers' voices. Report a situation in which you feel that the tone of voice was more important than the words in influencing the child's behavior.
4. Report a situation in which the suggestion or help given was well-timed. Why? Report a situation in which the suggestion or help given failed, apparently because of poor timing. Why?
5. List ways in which you have observed a teacher protecting the health and safety of the children in the nursery school.

For Your Further Reading

Briggs, D. C. (1970). *Your child's self-esteem: The key to his life.* Garden City, NY: Doubleday. Excellent guide to skills which adults can use to strengthen self-esteem in children. Contains helpful developmental information.

Coopersmith, S. (1967). *The antecedents of self-esteem.* San Francisco; W. H. Freeman. An important review of factors with negative or positive influence on self-esteem.

Lickona, T. (1983). *Raising good children: Helping your child through the stages of moral development.* New York: Bantam Books. Ways to help children become responsible people; excellent guide for moral development.

Spock, B., & Rothenberg, M. B. (1985). *Dr. Spock's baby and child care.* New York: E. P. Dutton. Dr. Spock has chosen Dr. Michael Rothenberg as collaborator for this new edition, which includes topics like day care, teenage pregnancy, divorce, and single parenthood.

Warren, R. M. (1977). *Caring: Supporting children's growth.* Washington, DC: National Association for the Education of Young Children. Chapters on self-esteem building, dealing with separation, transition times, and some of life's harsh realities.

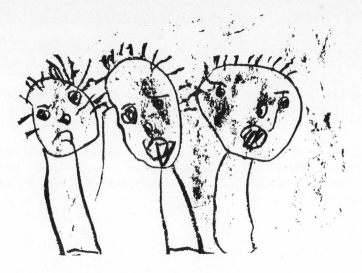

Three Naughty Girls (girl, 3 years 6 months)

7 ◆ Using Discipline: Setting Limits

DISCIPLINE

No subject is likely to be of more concern to a parent or teacher than that of discipline. Normal, healthy children misbehave at times. Their behavior must be controlled for their own good as well as for the good of those around them. Adults must make decisions about the actions to take when a child's behavior is unacceptable or unsafe for himself or others. Discipline is a necessary part of guidance.

Some adults think of discipline as synonymous with punishment. What is discipline? What is punishment? What are some essentials for sound discipline?

Defining Discipline

Discipline refers to actions adults take to help a child change his behavior. Adults identify for him what kinds of behavior are acceptable to the people whose approval he wants and help him to understand the possible consequences of his behavior. Discipline may involve stopping a child from a certain action and taking responsibility for helping him change his behavior.

Our feelings probably matter more than the methods we use in our discipline. If we expect that children will sometimes misbehave, disrupt a story period or the play of other children, or destroy and defy, we are not surprised by their actions. We find it easier to respond to their behavior in ways that help the child. We are helped, too, if we understand that it is often not our failure that has brought about the behavior, but that it is a result of the ordinary conflicts in growing.

Growing up is a complicated process that takes a long time. Children have a right to a certain level of irresponsibility during the process. If the adults around them are loving and firm and permit only what does no harm and produces no real anxiety, children will learn to master their impulses. We must have confidence in children and in ourselves. If we lack this confidence, we may respond to the misbehavior in a punishing way that can be very damaging.

Defining Punishment

Punishment refers to the actions taken by an adult to change a child's behavior by making him suffer physically or emotionally. A young child often does not understand why he is being punished. He may be confused about what behavior is acceptable to the punishing adult. As a result, punishment may leave the child feeling angry, resentful, and guilty. He may only learn that he is "bad." Such feelings contribute to a child's sense of self-doubt, and the child who lacks confidence is less ready to assume responsibility for self-control.

We know from research that punishment, when it is used at all, must follow misbehavior closely; it must be appropriate in degree of severity, and it must be focused on the specific behavior. For example, a child on an excursion who runs away from the group and even goes into a street must be dealt with promptly. The child must immediately be taken back to the center, even if it means the entire group is taken back. He must understand that he cannot go on an excursion until his actions change.

Effective consequences are restrictions in space, such as where the child can play or be, and restrictions in use, such as what he can use. *Consequences should not be restrictions in activity*, such as being made to sit on a chair. A child's thoughts during the time he is sitting are likely to be of questionable value.

Some Essentials For Sound Discipline

In infancy and early childhood normal, healthy children use all kinds of behavior to test the world. They need to discover how the framework of their world will stand up to what they can do to it. They need to find firmness and strength and love in the adults around them. Not all adults can stand up against such testing. An adult who refuses to allow *any* testing behavior gives a child little chance to discover what is acceptable and what is not. The child does not learn what may happen as the result of misbehavior. The adult who lets a child do anything he pleases, on the other hand, gives this child little chance to learn about acceptable limits. "Testing out" behavior leads to learning when the discipline that is used is sound.

Parents or teachers who discipline very strictly or even harshly and those who avoid any disciplining are not likely to help children in learning to control their own behavior and to show consideration for others. As a result these children may become unhappy, unloved people. Children are helped when adults act with firmness, love, and the tolerance that comes with confidence and a sense of responsibility.

The word *permissive* is sometimes used to describe a kind of non-guidance that permits a child to do anything he wants to do. Allowing a child to act impulsively without guidance is neither realistic nor helpful to his self-regulation. This kind of care-giving does not help the child to control his impulses. Such behavior by an adult can be a sign of irresponsibility or ignorance.

An environment that permits, freely and generously, all legitimate activity for a child in his particular stage of development is *not* a permissive environment. It is a supportive and encouraging environment.

CHANGING PATTERNS OR STANDARDS

We live in a society that is not, on the whole, a giving one with children. The emphasis in childrearing is frequently on restriction: not touching, staying dry and clean, and being quiet. Human relationships are often given less consideration than material objects. The child's needs to assert himself and find avenues of autonomy, initiative, and self-expression are often not accepted. The child may suffer a debilitating loss of self-confidence as a result of such patterns. As we shift to a more giving attitude, we should not bear a burden of guilt when we sometimes act in a way that is not giving. In changing our patterns of discipline it becomes all the more important to remember that limits have a positive value if they are appropriate for the child and are wisely maintained. Sound discipline promotes healthy social, emotional, and cognitive growth.

A teacher helps this child regain control.

Santa Monica College, Child Development Center

WAYS IN WHICH THE ADULTS HELP THE CHILD DEVELOP SELF-CONTROL

Accept the Child's Need to Assert Himself

The young child is in the process of becoming an independent person. He has the urge to assert himself and thus prove that he is independent. At times he will assert his independence by *not* doing what he is told. He is testing out what it is like to be an autonomous person, a person in his own right. The urge to assert oneself is important and necessary to healthy development. A child needs to feel that it is possible to assert himself safely, just as he also needs to find that he can live with restrictions and limitations. The kind of discipline that he receives will determine how well he learns to be assertive, as well as how he learns to limit his own behavior. For example, as an infant, the child may have closed his mouth tightly, refusing the food his parent offered. Instead of interpreting this behavior as defiance, the wise parent waits, giving him time to assert his independence, knowing that he will soon be ready to continue with the feeding.

Take Action When Action Is Needed

We may have to *restrain* a child who is about to hurt another by holding him with firmness. In taking action we respond as a confident authority. Although the child may be very angry with us at the time, he will ultimately feel safer and less anxious. We can acknowledge his feelings by saying something like, "I know you are angry with me, but I cannot let you hurt John." Understanding and sympathy can accompany firmness. We should never act aggressively toward the child or try to lower his self-esteem by calling him not nice, bad, or naughty. When he can listen, we explain why the behavior is not permitted and what other action he might take to channel his feelings more constructively and competently. We act as responsible adults who can help him learn to control his impulses.

This boy listens as the teacher explains the limits for safety.

John Adams Children's Center

We may need to *remove* a child from a situation that is too difficult for him to manage acceptably on his own. The child who keeps disturbing the play of other children in the sandbox must play somewhere else. We should isolate a child only when he cannot control his own behavior. Such behavior may be due to fatigue or overexcitement. We should be honest with the child about the reasons for his separation from the group. We want him to view the time away from the group as a relief, rather than as a punishment. He can have an opportunity to play alone quietly with something he enjoys until *he* feels ready to be with others.

We may need to *deprive* a child of an object or from participating in an activity as a consequence of his behavior. A child who knowingly uses a hammer in the wrong place should be deprived of the hammer for a time.

Set Reasonable Limits

There are not many prohibitions in a favorable group environment for young children. The important limits relate to safety, general welfare, and the protection of the rights of others. These limits must be clearly defined and consistently maintained for each child.

For example, a child is not permitted to leave the premises on his own. Teachers put this in a positive way to children, saying, for example, "Stay where the teacher can see you, so she can keep you safe." If a child does go beyond the limits of the play yard, he meets with disapproval and suffers a consequence, such as being restricted to a specific area in the yard. We explain the reasons why his behavior must be limited; however, we know that he does not fully understand why the act is dangerous. We also know that his control over his impulses is too weak to be reliable at all times. We must be responsible to watch and take care of him. He usually obeys us, because he trusts that we care about him and set limits for his protection. He needs the support of our limits.

Children often need help in respecting the rights of others, such as the right to keep possession of an object while using it or the right to be free of disturbance in carrying out an activity. For example, two three-year-olds playing together in the sand may come to blows over the possession of a spoon. The teacher steps in, putting her arm around the one who has taken the spoon by force and saying, "No, Bill was using the spoon. Please give it back to him. I will help you find another one." She may add, "Hitting hurts. Next time, ask him to give you the spoon when he finishes using it." If there are tears, she comforts the one who is crying and says, "I'm sorry you were hit. It hurts, I know." As a teacher is observing the children, she may be able to step in with a suggestion before the hitting occurs and prevent the struggle.

Learning to control impulses is difficult for the child. Time and experience with both freedom and control are necessary if the child is to learn self-control. On the part of the teacher it requires knowledge about how all children learn and develop, as well as insight into the individual child. This understanding and insight will grow out of many careful observations of a child and of children, as they work and play together.

Use Timing and Time Effectively

There is a right moment for stepping into a situation if guidance and redirection are to be most effective. The new teacher will find it helpful to observe experienced teachers, making notes when possible, and thinking over what she observes as well as relating her observations to her own experience. The impulsive child, for example, will need help more quickly than the placid or slow-moving child.

Every child needs to have the opportunity to help himself as much as he can, even in settling disputes. The teacher must study each child until she can decide the timing of assistance and what help will be most useful to him. Children's temperaments and styles differ, and so do the kinds of help they require and can accept. The guidance given must fit the child at a specific moment. The teacher's relationship with a child will be a factor in determining when to step in to prevent a conflict that is beyond a child's ability to manage. Success in timing of help comes with experience and reflection. New teachers will make mistakes in judging when to step into situations. Risking errors is a part of learning to teach.

A child sometimes just needs to be given time to accept directions. When we say to a child, "You will need to put your boots on before you go out. The grass is wet outdoors this morning," we do not have to see that he marches right over to his locker to put on his boots. He may have to protest a bit until he convinces himself that here is a demand with which he must comply. We may have to stop him if he starts to go outdoors without his boots, but we give him time to accept the limit and then comply or stay inside.

A conversational approach may help. Here is an example. Eric is outside playing in the sand and has pulled off his shoes and socks. A teacher decides it is too cold outdoors for bare feet. She goes over to Eric, and sits on the side of the sandbox quietly. Then she says, "It feels good, doesn't it, Eric," and smiles, enjoying it with him. She continues, "I wish I could let you play in your bare feet in the sandbox, but I think it is too cold to be outdoors without your shoes on. You'll have to put them back on this time. When the weather is warmer, you can take them off outside." She adds, "I used to like to be barefoot when I was a little girl. Now I'll help you put your shoes on." Together they get the shoes back on while Eric tells her about what he was doing. Eric is a very independent child who has often resisted directions. Because his teacher takes time to enjoy the moment with him and let him know she understands, Eric is able to accept the necessary limit and cooperate. There was no need for the teacher or for Eric to act quickly in this situation.

Develop Skill in Defining and Explaining Limits

Every teacher needs to develop skill in using language that the child can understand, as she explains the behavior expected of him. The teacher first explains clearly what *can* be done before she defines what *cannot* be done in a specific and concrete way. It takes practice to use language effectively with young children as well as an understanding of each individual child's stage of development.

When a child hits another child, for example, the teacher must stop him, and she must also help him to understand the reasons for her actions. She must explain how the other child feels (hurt and unhappy) and how she feels (disapproving) about this behavior. She should also make a positive suggestion about what can be done in the situation. "Next time *tell* him what you want," or "Next time tell him you want him to move his truck." In some situations the teacher may state the consequences if the child does not change his behavior. To a child who is throwing sand, she may say, "You will have to leave the sandbox unless you stop throwing sand."

The teacher may help two children who are in conflict by interpreting the actions of each, thus helping them begin to think about behavior rather than to act on impulse. Children can begin early to understand that there are reasons why people behave as they do. Guided by a teacher, four- and five-year-old children often benefit from discussing the reasons why a conflict occurred, and what might be done at another time. Talking over problems is an important step in learning about social relations for four-year-olds. Children need to learn to become aware of their own feelings as well as those of other people.

The Physical Environment and the Schedule

Careful planning of the environment and the schedule will often prevent the occurrence of conflicts or issues and reduce the need for discipline. Adequate and well-arranged space, where supervision is easily managed, will promote positive relationships among children and enable them to work and play together with a minimum of conflict. Making available a wide variety of carefully selected materials will also help to reduce conflict, because the teacher has planned something to interest each child. When conflicts are frequent in any particular area, the teacher should observe carefully and try to determine if a different arrangement of space or equipment might create a more favorable situation.

Keeping the subgroups small is also a preventive measure. A rule of thumb for a teacher is that the number of children in a subgroup should be about the same as the age of the child, that is, three three-year-olds, four four-year-olds, and so on. When planning options or choices for children in a period of the day, there should be about twice the number of work and play spaces as children. Small groups give each child an opportunity to participate and receive needed help from a teacher or another child. Such planning minimizes the potential for conflict.

A schedule that calls for little waiting by children reduces the need for discipline. Sometimes moving snack time to an earlier hour or making group times shorter can reduce stress. Children can take much more responsibility for their behavior if the environment and events are well planned to meet the changing needs of individuals and the group.

Model Acceptable Behavior

The word *discipline* derives from the word disciple or follower. It suggests an important element in self-control, that of following an example. The child wants to be like the adults who are important to him. Teachers are important people to children. If the teacher is calm, speaks quietly, and manages her own feelings acceptably when she encounters difficult situations, she gives the child a positive example to follow. If she can meet frustrations without piling up feelings of irritation and if she can respond to defiant behavior without anger, she gives the child a model for dealing with his own feelings and with similar situations he will face.

Children in a group are aware of how the teacher responds to a child who is disruptive. If that child is handled with firmness and understanding, other children are reassured that the teacher is trustworthy. They learn about limits of behavior, and they see a demonstration of an appropriate response. Anger should not be met with anger. It can be coped with reasonably and channeled in constructive ways.

Even the most competent teachers are not always successful models. Everyone has stress and strain to cope with at times, so we should try to understand our own needs and meet them. For example, we can try to avoid fatigue. Rested, satisfied people are more likely to model acceptable behavior. There will be times when stress will cause us to be less sensitive to and thoughtful of others or to respond with irritation. This is a time to model ways to accept the responsibility for our behavior and to apologize. Children are remarkably resilient and forgiving.

Projects

1. Observe and report a situation in which a limit was set for a child's behavior. How did the adult define the limit? How did the adult

maintain it? What was the child's behavioral response? How do you think he felt about himself in the end?

2. Report a situation in which the statement of a limit was well timed. Why did you feel the timing was good? What was the result? Report a situation in which the timing was poor or the teacher failed to maintain the limit set. What was the result?

For Your Further Reading

Brazelton, T. B. (1984). *To listen to a child: Understanding the normal problems of growing up*. Reading, MA: Addison-Wesley. A positive approach to help adults understand how children's developmental needs are revealed through common behaviors such as fears and tantrums.

Faber, A., & Mazlish, E. (1980). *How to talk so kids will listen and listen so kids will talk*. New York: Avon. An enthusiastic action approach to communicating with children and helping them solve their own problems.

Haswell, K. L., Hock, E., & Wenar, C. (1982). Techniques for dealing with oppositional behavior in preschool children. *Young Children, 37*(3), 12-18. Also in J. F. Brown (Ed.). (1982). *Curriculum planning for young children*. Pp. 221-227. The development of techniques for dealing with negativism.

Marion, M. (1981). *Guidance of young children*. St. Louis, MO: C. V. Mosby. Deals with short- and long-term goals in guidance, including discipline, aggression, prosocial behavior, positive self-esteem, and theoretical bases for guidance.

National Association for the Education of Young Children. (1985). *Love and learn: Discipline for young children*. Washington, DC: Author. Single copies of this helpful leaflet are free.

Riley, S. S. (1984). *How to generate values in young children: Integrity, honesty, individuality, self-confidence, and wisdom*. Washington, DC: National Association for the Education of Young Children. Treats topics such as discipline, toilet training, security blankets, early reading.

Soderman, A. K. (1985). Dealing with difficult young children: Strategies for teachers and parents. *Young Children, 40*(5), 15-20. Reviews the issue of individual temperament, which affects others' reactions to children; offers positive strategies to replace those often used with difficult children.

Tree (boy, 4 years)

8 ✦ Teaching Strategies Need a Theoretical Base

Our observations of the behavior of young children hold more meaning for us if we see a bit of their behavior not as one isolated incident but in relation to a stage in the individual's total development. We can recognize, for example, that the two-year-old who refuses our proffered hand on a steep slope is exercising an urge to independence. His behavior is evidence of an achievement in a growth process. The two-year-old who always clings to our hand may be revealing a blocking in his growth. A group of four-year-olds arguing in the housekeeping corner are using language as a tool to work out compromises with others. A year or so earlier the same children would probably have been pursuing their own purposes in parallel play and might have resorted to blows to settle a conflict.

THREE PEOPLE WHOSE THEORIES HAVE INFLUENCED EARLY CHILDHOOD EDUCATION

As teachers we need to understand these stages in growth so that we can respond appropriately. Sound teaching strategies need to be based on a framework of theory about human growth and development. Among the many investigators in the area of child growth and development we have selected three whose thinking has contributed to our understanding of human behavior: Sigmund Freud, Erik Erikson, and Jean Piaget. Many other investigators have, of course, made important contributions, but they have not developed such comprehensive theories. The theories of these three men were based on careful observation of human behavior, much of it done under natural rather than laboratory conditions.

Contributions of Sigmund Freud

The theories of Sigmund Freud have greatly influenced our understanding of personality development. His work in the late-nineteenth and early-twentieth centuries has become part of our thinking about personality. It must be remembered that his work reflected his time and place. It has been criticized today as sexist. Even if some of his concepts are considered dated, Freud was a germinal thinker who gave us the concept of the unconscious, that great reservoir of universal feeling within us which we can never be aware of directly but which influences what we do.

Freud's work with disturbed adults convinced him of the great significance of the individual's earliest experiences in determining later attitudes and behavior. He described the early stages in young children as the oral, the anal, and the phallic, with their respective sources of excitement and satisfaction, followed by a latency period lasting until adolescence. He pointed to the male and female components in the personality of every individual and the process a child goes through in establishing his or her sexual identification.

Freud developed the method known as *psychoanalysis* for gaining insights into the defenses built up by an individual that block the creative use of energies. Psychoanalysts working with disturbed young children have used *play therapy* as a method of treating children's emotional disturbances. Play therapy is based on the principle that in play children often reveal indirectly or symbolically the conflicts they are feeling. Among these therapists is Anna Freud, the daughter of Sigmund Freud, who has made important contributions to our understanding of children.

The process of discovering and accepting one's sex, according to Freudian theory, takes place in the first years of life and becomes the basis for normal sexual adjustment later in life. In the beginning, all infants relate closely to the primary caregiver. Later, the infant moves toward identification with the parent of his or her own sex, male or female. The struggle of the male child to shift identification from the mother to the father is known as the *oedipal conflict* and is most acute in the third, fourth, and fifth years. We see boys of this age asserting themselves in vigorous, aggressive ways, imitating males and needing to have their father's attention and approval.

Young boys in families in which the father is absent may have a serious problem; they have a real need for contact with a man from whom they can learn male attitudes and behavior. Centers should have men as teachers and caregivers to meet this need, either as regular staff members or as volunteers. The staff in centers for young children may be predominantly female, but it should not be exclusively so. Girls, also, need contacts with males in order to develop their femininity. Girls shift to a new relationship with their mothers, that is, identifying with the mother as a female. The shift to identifying with the same-sex parent is more gradual for girls than for boys.

In the center we observe the interest that children have in each other, as they use the toilets together and observe differences in the sexes. A girl may be interested in the boy's penis and wonder why she lacks one. All children are interested in the subject of babies and where they come from. They have many misconceptions, which can slowly be cleared up by offering the correct roles in their sociodramatic play, as they seek to discover more about what these roles are like in the grown-up world.

Contributions of Erik Erikson

Erikson's interest in personality development led him to observe people in different cultures. From his studies he formulated a theory of stages in personality growth, with each stage having a major *task*. He presented an outline of these stages at the 1950 White House Conference on Children and Youth in Washington, DC.

According to Erikson, a task consists of resolving in a favorable direction the conflicting impulses that characterize the stage. For example, in the first stage, during the first months of life, the major task in personality development is to ensure a sufficient balance of trust over mistrust. The task of establishing a large measure of trust rather than mistrust in feeling is not completed in the first months of life, but its most significant growth takes place during this period, the critical period for this task. We will consider the crises and tasks of the preschool years as Erikson has outlined them.

Personality Tasks in Childhood as Formulated by Erikson

The *first and most basic task in healthy personality development* is achieving a *sense of trust outweighing the sense of mistrust*. In the first year or

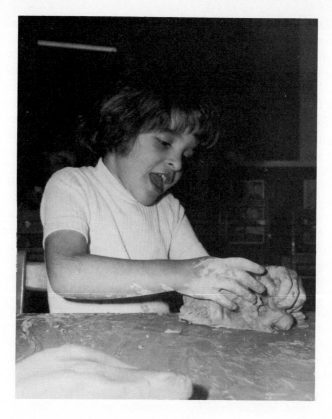

This child explores a new material, clay.

San Diego State University. Courtesy Sam Hollander

more of life the infant needs to feel that the world is a trustworthy place and that he himself is trustworthy. This sense of trust will grow out of the experiences the infant has with his mother or primary caregiver and later with other significant people in his world. Out of many experiences of having his needs met, being fed when hungry, being kept warm and safe, and being handled with loving care, he begins to trust the world. This feeling enables him to meet the new, the unexpected, the frustrating experiences that come later. Because of these good experiences, the individual learns to trust his own capacity to meet what comes.

The importance of early good mothering and its influence on personality development has been studied further by D. W. Winnicott, an English pediatrician who later became a psychoanalyst. Winnicott pointed to the importance of a mother's adaptation to her infant in the first weeks and months when, by her sensitive management, she adapts completely to the infant at first and then gradually withdraws this complete adaptation as she senses that the infant is ready to tolerate delays and frustrations—in other words, when he has developed sufficient trust. By presenting the world to him "in small enough doses," she enables the infant to build a sense of trust over mistrust which is the cornerstone of a healthy personality.

All through life we continue to need experiences that contribute to our feeling that the world is a place where we can feel comfortable and trust ourselves. But the most critical point, the crisis point for the development of this trait, is in the earliest months of life. The infant needs protection then from experiences that produce mistrust which may overpower him. Separation from the care-taking person, for example, may be overwhelming to an infant even when it is brief. It may seem an eternity to him because of his undeveloped sense of time.

Mutual adaptation is an important element here. As the weeks and months go by, the infant under favorable circumstances builds up a large "bank account" of trust on which he can draw. His mother or other caregiver can then expect him to make adaptations to her needs and the needs of others. In doing this she shows her trust in him and in his growing capacity to delay satisfaction.

Infants differ in their responses. Some seem to grow to trust easily and others find it more difficult, but it is the mother's sensitive management that enables each to succeed in developing a healthy balance of trust over mistrust. We can see the results in children's behavior when they reach nursery school age. The task of continuing to build trust remains important throughout the preschool period. In fact, all our lives, as we suffer disillusionment, we need at times to restore our faith in ourselves and in the trustworthiness of others.

The *second task in healthy personality growth* is that of developing a *sense of autonomy outweighing the sense of shame or doubt*. Already toward the end of the first year we can see evidence of the child working on this task. It becomes the major task of the second and third years. The mother or other caregivers must be sensitive to the great need of the child to assert his independence at this time. It is the "Me do it" stage, and if he is permitted to "do it," the child has the chance to begin to take steps in organizing himself as a learner. It is the stage in which Benjamin Spock says the child asks himself, "Am I a man or a mouse?" It is the age of "No" and frequent "contrariness," but out of this is born an independent individual capable of feeling "I *am* someone."

Mutual adaptation is again important here, if this task is to be accomplished with sufficient autonomy to balance the necessary dependence and doubt. It is a period when the discipline should be mild and reserved for the most necessary points. If we can accept the self-assertion, we find the child usually does what we want because he can feel that *he* is deciding to do what we have asked. Giving him choices, avoiding confrontations, and introducing a play element all work better than issues at this stage. In this way we are protecting him in his task of beginning to feel himself an autonomous person, "I *am* and I am important and powerful," in his own small world. Feeling autonomous is better than feeling helpless as one faces life.

The *third task in personality growth* as outlined by Erikson is that of developing a *sense of initiative outweighing the sense of guilt*. It is the important personality task of the child of three, four, and five years, although we see many signs of initiative earlier. In this stage the child is more actively exploring and investigating. He is beginning to ask questions, to think new thoughts, to try himself out in all kinds of ways, in other words, to take the initiative. He is also developing a conscience, a sense of being responsible for actions as an autonomous person. A conscience is necessary and valuable, but it should not carry too heavy a load at this point in healthy personality growth. A four-year-old can easily feel *too* guilty for some transgression or guilty for the wrong things. It is important that his sense of initiative, of being able to forge ahead and try, should outweigh his fear of wrongdoing. Understanding guidance is needed in this period if the child is to emerge with a large measure of initiative outweighing but still maintaining his capacity for guilt.

In this stage the child has an urge to make and to do things. It is a creative period in personality growth. A four-year-old who may be helping to carry the blocks back to the shelves where they belong may suddenly discover the interesting patterns they make as they tumble from his wagon or the way in which they can be stuffed into the holes in the fence. He begins a new and imaginative form of play. He will need a reminder about the job in hand and perhaps some help in getting on with the task. We can give these with an appreciation for what he has discovered and for the excitement he feels for his discovery. Life should be made up of such experiences in discovery when one is four.

This period is an important one for intellectual development. The groundwork is being laid for the child's learning in school. With a firm foundation of trust and a sense of being an autonomous person, he exercises his initiative, taking hold of experiences as they are offered and making something out of them.

He uses all of his senses as he explores and discovers and makes things happen. It is a period of learning by doing. He discovers interests as he explores and creates. Initiative thrives on opportunities for play in a favorable environment. There will, of course, be unfinished business left over from the earlier stages for almost all children. We need to give help with all these tasks if sound personality growth is to continue, but the major task of the period is to encourage and support the child's sense of initiative.

The *fourth task in healthy personality growth*, the development of a sense of industry outweighing the sense of inadequacy or inferiority, is the important task of the school-age child. It continues to adolescence. At this stage the healthy child sees himself as a worker and a learner. Games with rules, skill in sports, and group activities become important. He is a schoolchild ready to accomplish learning under favorable circumstances. He is in the intellectual stage of "concrete operations," to use Piaget's words.

As we work with children, we will keep in mind these personality tasks and the help we may be able to give children in order that the crises may be resolved in ways favorable to healthy development. We will adapt our methods so we can support the balance of trust over mistrust, the balance of autonomous feeling over doubt, and the balance of initiative over guilt. We will value the child's developing sense of industry over inferiority as he becomes more of a learner and worker.

Contributions of Jean Piaget

Jean Piaget, a scientist, became interested in observing the behavior of his own children and devoted himself to studying their behavior. He was interested in how children learn, and he continued his work by observing and interviewing many children. He developed a theory about how children reason and learn. He was well known in Europe before he was "discovered" by American educators in the late 1950s.

Piaget concluded that young children learn by constructing their own knowledge. They do this by moving from one level of understanding to another, correcting earlier inaccurate perceptions. *Constructivism* is central to Piaget's theory. He felt that knowledge is not taught but must be constructed through an active mental process. Learning does not depend on maturation, which is a biological process. It comes from within if it is true understanding. In constructing knowledge, children move through different stages. In the first stage, for example, the child constructs physical knowledge out of his experiences with objects. He constructs knowledge or "learns" about objects and their properties. The more experiences he has with objects, the more he "learns." His learning is an active mental process. It is not taught but has been constructed by the child.

Social-conventional knowledge is another type of knowledge. Communication with others, either through body language or oral communication, is part of this knowledge. We might note here that the child structures his acquisition of language without being "taught." Logical-mathematical knowledge, another type, is constructed by the individual in a later stage of development.

We can help the cognitive or constructive process by providing activities that stimulate thought, the discovery of the properties of objects, and the putting of objects into relationships. Among activities that do this are block building; painting; playing with sand, water, and clay; and pretending.

On the basis of his detailed observations of children, Piaget has described the following stages children go through as they construct knowledge. Central to these stages is the concept that the child constructs his knowledge through assimilation and accommodation. The "taking in" (assimilating) of information complemented by an intellectual reorganization (accommodating) when previous information does not "fit" with what is "known" is one way of explaining the construction of knowledge.

Stages In Constructing Knowledge

1. Stage one, from birth to around two years, Piaget calls the *sensorimotor stage*. In this stage, the infant or toddler is looking, listening, touching, smelling, tasting, and moving in response to stimulation of his senses. He learns in sensorimotor ways. Thought consists of patterns of action or sensorimotor schemata. These schemata are ways of behaving that he can apply to a variety of objects or situations, behavior like grasping, shaking, banging. As previously stated he develops these schemata through *assimilation*, or taking in of sensory impressions, and through *accommodation*, or modifying his action patterns to fit changes in the situation such as a rattle presented in a different position. He comes to "know" an object like a rattle by having many different experiences with it, fingering it, mouthing it, banging it. Through all these experiences he stores up impressions and nourishes this zest for exploring.

During this stage he becomes aware of the permanence of objects. He begins to look for the rattle he has dropped. He realizes it still exists even when he no longer sees it. His mother is somewhere even when she is not within his sight. His mother is important to him because good relationships with her, her attention and care, enable him to feel enough trust to reach out for new experiences. Her interest and encouragement support his learning and may be as necessary for learning as the experiences themselves.

2. Piaget calls the second stage, from about the age of two to about the age of six or seven, the *preoperational stage*. In the preoperational stage the child continues to construct physical knowledge, but he now constructs much more social-conventional knowledge. He makes things happen in purposeful ways. He has mental images and uses symbols. He does something and watches to see what will happen. He is no longer so surprised by what happens. He is extending his thought processes. He extends his social knowledge by participating in such events as birthdays and holidays. He has experiences with relatives and learns more about relationships among people. He likes some people more than others. He becomes aware that people respond differently to his ways of behaving.

There are steps in the growth of his perceptions. He perceives differences, but it is some time before he can grasp logically that an amount

The child is giving whole-hearted attention to investigating a sponge.

San Diego State University, Courtesy Sam Hollander

is the same whether it is in one piece or divided into parts. Piaget calls this the *conservation of matter* and says that children at the preoperational stage of development are nonconservers. The child "centers in" on one aspect and is unable to consider such aspects as reversibility. Young children have no problem with the concept of big or small, but they cannot yet arrange objects in a serial order from largest to smallest. Seriation tasks, in general, are not a part of the preoperational child's understanding.

In the preoperational stage the child continues to construct knowledge out of his experiences. He reconstructs his thinking to fit a new level of understanding. For example, he may know that a dog and a cat are "animals." His concept of animal at this point may be of something that has a furry feel, that runs around, that makes a variety of sounds. Then at the center he meets the large, hard-shelled turtle. It has a very different feel. It moves very slowly or hardly moves at all and does not make any kind of noise. He is told that it is an animal too. He must "accommodate" these perceptions, changing his concept of "animal" to include this new dimension. He learns by making mistakes.

The development of speech gives the child a new tool for remembering and storing impressions. He can begin to learn from the experience of others, when it fits into what he has already constructed from his own experience. He can understand simple explanations if they are put in terms of what he already knows. He is asking questions and seeking answers to "why?" but he continues to assimilate and accommodate, to adapt what he perceives or experiences to new patterns of action.

Reaching a level of competence in a field of thought seems to depend on having completed necessary experiences. The young child may know how to count to ten or twenty, but he may have constructed a true concept of numbers only as far as four. He has internalized his knowledge only that far.

3. The third stage Piaget calls the stage of *concrete operations*. Piaget defines *operations* as "a means of organizing facts already internalized about the real world so that they can be used selectively in the solution of new problems."[1] School-age children are in this stage. Now the child can deal with properties of matter or their stability or invariance in spite of changes in appearance. He gradually expands this understanding to length, weight, and volume. He is now a "conserver," able to "decenter." He is no longer locked into believing only what he sees.

4. The fourth and last stage is *formal operations* and begins around the age of eleven or twelve, or later. In this stage, formal or abstract, as well as concrete, operations can be carried out. Some individuals may never construct knowledge by formal abstract operations because they have not experienced problems that require abstract thought.

Summary

Piaget's work has value for teachers because he has shown "the fundamental connection between action and learning and the extent to which true learning is dependent on the activity of the learner. 'Activity' is no fanciful addition to the curriculum to give children more enjoyment (although it does) but the necessary element in all learning. Piaget has helped us to understand what we mean by activity, by revealing its role in the genesis of mental structure and therefore of 'mind itself.'"[2]

All teachers are concerned with cognitive development. We believe that young children must be active in any learning process. It is a process of constructing knowledge based on incomplete experience, making errors, and constantly reconstructing with added experience. As we have said, Piaget calls this constructing knowledge from within. It is a thinking, not

[1]M. Brearley and E. Hitchfield. (1966). *A guide to reading Piaget.* New York: Schocken Books.
[2]Ibid.

This girl plans with care and constructs.

Bakersfield College

a passive, process. Neither is it a matter of giving correct answers. As Piaget has pointed out, knowledge does not develop from "all wrong" to "perfectly correct." Teachers should take into careful account the knowledge children have constructed from previous experience if the teaching is to be effective.

Piaget's preoperational child is the same child Erikson describes in the stage of developing his sense of initiative outweighing the sense of doubt and guilt. He is the child Freud describes in the process of discovering and accepting his sex and moving toward an identification with the parent of the same sex. He is the child we meet in centers for two-, three-, four-, and five-year-olds.

BASIC TENETS IN EARLY CHILDHOOD EDUCATION

We will present some tenets common to most early childhood programs. They embody principles we will use as we work with young children individually or in groups. The overall goal of early childhood education is to provide a child with an environment that will promote his optimum development in a period when growth is rapid and the child is most vulnerable to inappropriate experiences and to deprivation of appropriate experiences.

All aspects of growth are considered in a quality program: *physical* development; the development of *social* relationships, or the capacity to enjoy and get along with other people; *emotional* development, including confidence in and understanding of oneself as a person and growth in ability to express thoughts and feelings and to manage impulses; and *intellectual*, or cognitive development, including language competency, nourished through guidance in a stimulating environment.

Some of the basic assumptions and tenets underlying a program are these:

1. *Every child is an individual* with his own rate and style of learning and growing, his own unique patterns of approach to situations, and his own innate capacities. His genes and his experiences have made him unique. His family experience is different from that of any other individual, with its strengths and its vulnerabilities. Some of these differences may seem "deficiencies" if aspects fail to fit the expectations of a particular situation. A child from a Spanish-speaking home, for example, may seem "backward" when compared with children in an English-speaking group. We need to accept each child as an individual in his own frame of reference and values, without employing any limited or preconceived standards. A child skillful in cooperation with others may not be successful in competitively motivated situations, for example; a child with manual skills may be considered "deficient" in an academic setting. To do justice to individuals we need to broaden our horizons to include respect for the strengths of individuals.

Every child needs experiences adapted to his individual needs, with respect for his individuality. For example, Juan, described in Chapter 1, waits and watches before entering an activity, while Jean plunges into new experiences without waiting to watch what others are doing. Guidance for children takes into account their differences and their varying backgrounds of experience.

2. *The genetic constitution and the environment together determine the course of development of an individual.* We may say that the genes determine the limits of development and the environment determines how much of what is possible will be achieved. A normal person is born with

the capacity for developing speech, for example, but he does not learn to talk unless he is with people who use speech. The kind of language he learns and how well he uses the language depend on his environment.

A normal person is also born capable of a range of feelings. What he will feel, his biases and prejudices, his loves and hates, grow out of his experiences. In the nursery school we influence the direction and the extent of development in the children we teach.

3. *Intelligence develops as it is nurtured.* Cognitive development depends on adequate and appropriate physical, mental, and social nourishment supplied by the home, the school, and the community. The "critical period" for nurturing intelligence seems to occur early in the life of individuals. The individual needs a range of suitable experiences and opportunities to act on these. He needs to feel secure and valued by people who also value learning.

Intelligence is not just a single entity, although it is part of the whole child. There are varieties of intelligence. Among the children we meet in the center, there will be some who have been well nurtured intellectually and others whose nurture has not been adequate. Making up for deficiencies may be an important part of the program for many children. Play, both the informal and the more organized types, is significant in nurturing intellectual growth.

4. *All aspects of development are interrelated*, physical, social, emotional, intellectual. The child develops as a whole, with each area influencing and being influenced by what takes place in other areas. In planning a program, we consider the child as a whole, not just one aspect of his development. For example, in planning equipment for developing body skills we are also interested in how these build self-confidence and increase opportunities for contacts with other children and add to the child's knowledge of physical forces.

5. *Growth means change.* Changes take place not only in a child's height and weight but also in his capacities and characteristics. Changes are often accompanied by conflicts or disturbances until a new equilibrium is reached. During these periods of change the child is likely to respond well to appropriate guidance or help. Our role is to influence growth changes in positive, healthy directions, physically and psychologically.

Children's behavior changes as circumstances change. When a child is tired or ill, for example, he behaves differently than when he is rested or well. When we say that a child is "dull" or "lazy" or "selfish," we are reporting *only* what we interpret at the moment. In time, or under different circumstances, or in someone else's view, the child might be described very differently. We change too. With more experience and more understanding, we perceive different meanings in children's behavior.

6. *Growth takes place in orderly sequences or stages*, with each successive stage depending on the outcome of previous stages. No stage can be

skipped without handicapping the child. Rates of growth differ for individual children, but the sequence of stages is uniform. A child sits up before he walks; he laces his shoes before he can tie his laces. Age gives only a general indication of what to expect because children differ in the time they take to complete a stage, but not in the order in which the change takes place. For example, most six-year-olds and some five-year-olds can tie shoe laces but very few four-year-olds can.

Having time to complete each stage, with a variety of experiences appropriate to the stage, enables the child to leave one stage behind and move on, fully prepared for the next. Pressure or "nudging" to move on before a stage is completed inhibits sound growth, just as blocking the forward movement does.

In every stage there are certain aspects of development that are "critical," most vulnerable to deprivation at this point, and most likely to benefit from optimum conditions. Severe protein deficiency in the diet of the twelve to twenty-four-month-old child, for example, will impair physical and intellectual development, but the same deficiency may have only a temporary effect on an adult. Between six months and twelve months, for example, the infant is at a critical stage in his development of a feeling of trust. He is more disturbed by an extended separation from his mother at this point than he will be later.

7. *Play is an important avenue for learning and for enjoyment.* Children learn through active experiencing in play, using all their senses; through doing things to and with materials; through representing concepts in play, rehearsing roles, and thus clarifying them. Children test out, explore, discover, store up impressions, classify, organize, assimilate, and accommodate to experience.

Discovery and mastery are part of play, as are sustained attention and effort, the characteristics needed in learning. Play calls for initiative, imagination, purposefulness. It calls for motor skills and for social skills. Beginnings of symbolic thinking occur in play. Play with other children is considered essential for healthy personality development. The values of play are increased by informed guidance and a wide variety of appropriate materials and equipment, as well as space and uninterrupted time.

8. *Attitudes and feelings are important in learning and in healthy personality growth.* The attitude of the child toward himself, the way he feels about himself, is an important factor in his learning and in his mental health. If he is to develop well, a child needs to feel that the significant people around him like him and feel that he is an able person. A positive self-concept or self-image enables the child to use his capacities well.

Becoming aware of one's own feelings and those of others and finding avenues for expressing feelings in constructive and creative ways are other important aspects of learning. They can be fostered by understanding guidance. Self-control results from being aware of one's impulses and having avenues into which negative impulses can be channeled. Imagination and its expression in art and language and its use in problem solving can also be stimulated through a favorable environment.

9. *Behavior is motivated by extrinsic and intrinsic factors.* Extrinsic forms of motivation consist in giving attention, approval, or reward for a specific behavior or in withholding attention, in disapproval, or in punishment to reinforce behavior or to make it more likely that the child will repeat or desist behaving in some way. The effectiveness of the reinforcement will depend in part on the relationship existing between the child and the one who reinforces. Personal relationships play a large part in motivation.

Intrinsic motivation comes from inside the child, arising out of his curiosity, his drive towards competence, his past experiences in finding satisfactions or in not finding them. In using a hammer or a saw, for example, the child may persist because he has an end in mind or because he finds satisfaction out of the increasing competency he feels in doing the job.

Timing of reinforcement and type of reinforcement used at any point are important. The child who is doing something because he wants to do it does not need reinforcement in the same way as a child who is doubtful about himself and his ability. The first child may want to be sure of the teacher's interest, but the second child is dependent on her external reinforcement.

10. *Understanding, responsible guidance is necessary* if the child is to develop his potential. In his early years the child needs caregivers who like him, who are generous and warm in feeling, who can assume responsibility for setting limits, who are informed and resourceful in providing him with a favorable environment, who enjoy learning themselves, who can feel respect for the child as well as for themselves, and who can communicate with children. Learning is personal for the child and is influenced by his relationships with those who provide for him and guide him. Personality development depends, too, on personal relationships with caregivers who serve as adequate models for the child.

Parents are the child's most important teachers. Teachers need to work with parents. Teachers and parents learn from each other. Early childhood education programs respect the parent-child relationship. Teachers have responsibility for interpreting programs to parents as well as understanding the expectations of the parents about the education of their own child.

11. *The development of a young child suffers if there are deficiencies* in nutrition and health care; in attention and loving care; in opportunities for play which nourishes social, emotional, and intellectual growth; and in richness and variety of appropriate firsthand experiences. Some apparent "deficiencies" are only differences in experience, such as those in language

competency where English is not the first language. When real deficiencies do occur, they can best be compensated for by going back and supplying what was lacking in earlier stages, giving the chance for sound growth to take place, rather than pushing a child on to the next stage.

12. *A healthy environment is the right of every child and the first responsibility of the community, the state, and the nation.* A healthy environment provides adequate health care, food and shelter, and community services including schools and services that offer support to families. It includes a family life free from excessive burdens of economic insecurity, deprivation, and discrimination, and with adequate provision for satisfaction and stimulation for all members of the family. A child development center is one of these community services. It contributes to the child and the family at a critical point in life.

As teachers we may know that a certain procedure is useless or even harmful to a child's learning, but we may be required to use such a procedure by pressure from politicians and the public who are interested in what they consider correct answers or the call to go "back to basics." We need a rigorous scientific explanatory theory about how to construct knowledge in order to explain and defend our practices. Constance Kamii, whose early childhood research focuses on learning, feels that educators are now in a position to make a statement about teaching as a profession using a scientific basis and specific objectives. Our goal in the future should be to "prepare people who have the knowledge and the originality to build a far better world than we ever imagined."[3] The teaching profession itself should be engaged in a reconstruction of teacher education. Children deserve this effort from the teaching profession.

Projects

Prepare a written or oral report on Sigmund Freud, Erik Erikson, or Jean Piaget. To prepare your report include the following.

1. The bibliographical source for your report.
2. A brief description of the period of history in which the theorist lived or lives, and the forces which have influenced him.
3. Some highlights of the person's life.
4. Two or three major ideas and/or contributions made by the person.
5. Close with a statement or reaction to the person's ideas.

[3] C. Kamii. (1985). Leading primary education toward excellence: Beyond worksheets and drill. *Young Children, 40*(6), 3–9.

For Your Further Reading

Braun, S. J., & Edwards, E. P. (1972). *History and theory of early childhood education*. Worthington, OH: Charles A. Jones. Traces evolution of early childhood education in western civilization, discussing theorists from Plato to Piaget.

Brearley, M., & Hitchfield, E. (1966). *A guide to reading Piaget*. New York: Schocken Books. Quotes from Piaget's experiments followed by discussion; to aid practicing teachers in scientific justification for teaching by theory and intuitive judgment.

Erikson, E. H. (1963). *Childhood and society* (2nd ed.). New York: W. W. Norton. This book has had an indelible impact on thinking about development with its eight stages of psychosocial development and emerging ego qualities from each stage.

Kamii, C. (1985). Leading primary education toward excellence: Beyond worksheets and drill. *Young Children, 40*(6), 3–9. Makes a strong argument against pressures to produce higher test scores and use of workbook drills, which are erroneously based on "what did not work before" in education. Defines constructivist teaching and learning, and pleads for reform in teacher education to include Piaget's theory.

Maier, H. (1969). *Three theories of child development*. New York: Harper & Row. The theories of Erik Erikson, Jean Piaget, and Robert Sears, and some of the implications of these theories on current practice.

Phillips, J. L., Jr. (1981). *Piaget's theory: A primer*. San Francisco: W. H. Freeman. Very easy to read explanation of Piaget's theory. Clear illustrations of tasks to determine child's stage of cognitive functions.

PART THREE

◆

GUIDANCE IN EXPERIENCES COMMON TO EVERYONE

Fun to Go to the Store (boy, 4 years)

9 ◆ Helping Children Adjust to New Experiences

WE ALL KNOW WHAT IT IS LIKE TO BE IN A NEW SITUATION

We suggested earlier that one of the first steps for us to take in the center was to accept our feelings because we were in a new situation. We may have tried to defend ourselves against the inadequacy we felt because we were new. Some of our defenses may have handicapped us in learning. We needed to learn to feel comfortable about being new in the situation.

The child faces feelings similar to those of the adult when he meets new situations, such as entering a center or accepting the approaches of unfamiliar people. He may try to defend himself against the uncertainty and fear he feels by inappropriate behavior, rejecting the strange people, crying, or withdrawing. Because we know what it is like to feel new and strange, we may find it easier to understand the child's behavior. We may be better able to help the child as he tries to cope with a new experience.

Each Child Has Characteristic Patterns of Responding to New Experiences

For the child, as for the adult, new experiences call forth defenses, tendencies to retreat or to explore. What the child or the adult does will depend on his individual makeup and on his past experiences.

What kind of adjustment is a "good adjustment"? Fear is obviously very limiting to any learning in a situation. Uncritical acceptance sometimes reveals a lack of awareness that may lead to undesirable consequences. Desirable behavior includes a readiness to accept differences, the capacity to pick out familiar elements in the situation, and the ability to relate the known to the unknown.

Each Child Brings His Past to the New Experience

What lies behind differences among children in their adjustment to the same situation? We can be certain that the same situation does not seem the same to all children. Demonstrable differences in responsiveness to stimulation are present at birth or soon after. One child, for example, will be more disturbed than another by a sudden loud noise or a difference in the intensity of light. New people, places, and events will have different meanings for each child depending on the sensitivity that is part of his constitutional difference.

Each child brings his own past experiences to a new situation. These experiences have prepared him differently. It does not matter if we do not know specifically what these past experiences have been as long as we accept the child's behavior as having some meaning. Being taken to a new place may mean pleasant possibilities to one child and disturbing possibilities to another. We should expect and accept different behavior from different children.

The many daily experiences a child has are probably of more importance in influencing his adjustments than any single disturbing event. In other words, the sum total of the child's experience is usually of greatest importance. It is desirable, therefore, for the child's daily life to contribute to making him feel more secure and more adequate. We are not likely to gain strength by being hurt; we are certain to acquire scars.

A child who is forced into making adjustments for which he is not ready is less prepared for further adjustment. He may try to conceal his feeling, as is sometimes the case with the child whose mother declares, "He doesn't

This child found a safe place for group time.

Valley College, Campus Child Development Center

mind being left anywhere." The strain this child suffers may be evident only in indirect ways, as in a loss of creativity, an inability to play, greater dependence, or increased irritability. Too many experiences of feeling strange or frightened can add up to a total that may be disastrous for sound adaptation and adjustment.

Entering a center means that the child must leave his familiar home and depend on adults other than his parents. It means finding a place for himself in a group of other children about his own age. There are new toys, different toilet arrangements, and a strange play area. He meets a variety of responses from the other children, some of them apparently unreasonable responses. He must trust the teachers to understand him and keep him safe in these new situations.

The child's feeling of confidence in himself will be strengthened if he can make the adjustment successfully. For many children, attending a center confirms a feeling of trust in others and in himself which has already been fostered in his home and neighborhood. For other children, entering a center gives them a valuable opportunity to "work through" earlier problems and take steps in building feelings of confidence and trust. Some children can be helped to recover from fears left from earlier experience.

What makes a child ready for a group experience? Why do some children enter eagerly and others hold back from this new experience? What do we do to reduce the difficulties to manageable proportions for each child?

Children who are cared for by loving people feel safe. They are likely to feel secure and friendly. There are many reasons why one child may not feel as safe or secure as another. Many moves that leave little in the way of familiar physical surroundings or frequent separations from parents or caregivers may interfere with a child's feeling secure. Separations coming at sensitive times in development are likely to make it harder for a child to develop a sense of trust. He may take more time to feel secure.

It is important to reduce the stresses of entering a center. The experience should add to, rather than threaten, the child's feeling of trust and security. Safeguards include avoiding starting the child in school shortly after a new baby arrives, after the family has just moved, or after there has been an upsetting event such as the mother starting to work outside the home. It is better, for example, for the child to enter the group well before the mother starts to work. If it is necessary for a child to enter a center under unfavorable circumstances, he must be given more time and support by the staff in making the adjustment. Parents can help prepare their child through talking about the center, describing what it may be like to enter a group, or asking, "What do you think the center will be like?"

Entering a Center Is a Significant Experience for a Young Child

The experience of entering a group can contribute to growth in important ways. We will try to understand its significance for the child and for his parents. Then we will outline the steps to follow that may best promote healthy personality growth. We recognize that these steps are not always possible, but our goal with every child will be to use the experience to promote the child's confidence in himself and his ability to cope with the world around him.

The tasks facing a child entering a center are twofold. First, he must feel secure enough to be able to go out to meet the new situation, rich with possibilities for learning and social contacts but full of the unknown for him. The second and perhaps more significant task which the child faces is one inherent in growth itself. He must resolve the conflict inevitably felt when one enters something new and strange. The conflict to be resolved in this case is lessening the close dependency on his parents or other caregivers in order to live in the world the center offers. In going forward, he must leave behind a measure of dependency in order to take a step in the direction of independence. He must resist his desire to cling to the relationship with his caregiver, which has been the main source of his satisfaction and security up until now. He must act on the wish to separate himself and be ready to explore new relationships that may also prove to be sources of satisfying experiences.

For some children who may have found their sources of satisfaction in a number of other people, as with children from large families, there may be less conflict. These children have already found security in a variety of relationships and have less need to hold on to dependency. There are children, too, who have not known closeness to any one person and who do not appear to need any support. They have other needs which are likely to come out later in other ways. For the child from a small family with mainly positive relationships, there will still be some degree of conflict to resolve, as he enters a group and leaves his family for even a short time.

Each Child Has His Own Strengths and Vulnerabilities

In meeting these tasks each child brings different strengths and vulnerabilities with him. His constitutional endowment will differ as will his tempo of living and the intensity of his response. One child may delight in sounds, another in color, another in movement. One child will respond quickly, reacting to a variety of stimuli; another may be content to experience more slowly. What each child has known in the past may differ even more. Some children will enter having had limited opportunities for sensory experiences, while others have had many opportunities to touch, taste, smell, see, and hear. Some children will come having known much uncertainty and fear in the past. Others will have felt secure. Cultural differences will mean differences in experience for children. Each child will come with his own expectations about the center and with his own special interests.

Relationships with His Caregiver and His Teacher Are Important

The relationships with his mother or primary caregiver will probably have the most effect on the way the child proceeds toward independence. If his caregiver has been able to help him develop a sense of trust, she will have satisfied in large measure his pressing infantile dependency needs. He is now free to move on to develop new relationships which will meet new needs.

The teacher plays a significant role because of the help she gives the parent as well as the child. They both face a new kind of experience. The teacher can give support to the parent's desire to leave the child free to separate as well as to the child's desire to move toward independence. The teacher will give this support best when she sees clearly what the significance of entering a group may be for both child and parent.

It is not simple for a teacher to move with certainty because each child and each parent will differ in what she or he brings to the situation and expects from it. In addition, the teacher herself may be handicapped by set patterns in the way school entrance is handled, by her own fear, her own need to control, or the way her own dependence needs have been met. As she develops in sensitivity and skill, she will find satisfaction in helping children and parents work through the problem of separation. It is here that the center can make one of its most significant contributions, one that will be of value in future separation experiences.

THE PROCESS OF GIVING SUPPORT TO THE CHILD AND HIS PARENTS

How does the teacher proceed as she helps the child face separation and an experience with groups of other children? How does she help the parents face separation from the child for part or all of the day?

We will suggest a series of steps that may be taken to help a child enter a group successfully. In outlining these steps we need to recognize that, in many situations, the steps will necessarily have to be condensed, as in the case of a parent who is employed. Attending school for an hour with his mother, father, other relative, or caregiver may be all that can be managed as a first step for the child. It should be emphasized that no young child should ever be left at a center without any preparation. The mental health of a child is too important to put at risk. He should have someone staying with him on his first day, and the first day should never be a long one. Attending for only part of the time for the first week helps the child make

Homemaking play is important for both boys and girls.
———
Bakersfield College

the adjustment more easily. It saves time in the end, and the child is less likely to get overtired.

STEP 1: A PARENT-TEACHER CONFERENCE. A conference between the teacher and one or both parents is a necessary first step. In this conference the teacher explains the policies of the center to the parents and makes clear the matter of fees, health regulations, hours, and steps in admission. She tells them something of the program and their part in it and tries to answer their questions. She learns something of the child's interests and skills and some of the parents' expectations for this child. She will ask the parents to fill out a developmental history and home information form to be kept in the center. One of the important parts of the conference will be a discussion of the steps to be taken in enrolling the child. These steps will need to be clarified in subsequent conferences, but it is essential for the parents to understand that someone well known to the child must be there for the child to turn to in the first days at the center.

In discussing the kind of help the child will need from the parents, the teacher will point out that the child needs to feel that his parents are glad to have him go to the center and that the center is a good place to be. The child also needs to feel, not that the parent is leaving him, but that the parent is letting the child do the leaving and will always be glad when he returns.

STEP 2: A VISIT TO THE CENTER. The next step is to give the child some concept of what "school" is like through a visit to the center. The child needs a picture in his mind when he hears the word *school* or *center*. He needs to anticipate what lies ahead in as realistic a way as possible.

When possible the teacher will arrange to have the child and his parent or his main caregiver visit the center when other children are not present. The situation then is simpler and easier for the child to manage. He can become familiar with aspects of the physical setup and discover areas where he feels secure. He is protected against what may seem to him unpredictable behavior in other children. He has an opportunity to enter into a relationship with his teacher without the competition from other children to divide her attention. She has an opportunity to become acquainted with him and to take a step in understanding what his needs and interests are likely to be and what role she may play as his teacher.

Following the initial visit or as a first visit for some children, the child will come with his parent or caregiver when the center is in session. The child can watch, make contacts with others if he wishes, and participate if he feels ready. The visit will be a short one, probably not over an hour. The teacher will decide with the parent the most convenient time in the day for the child to visit, for it is important to give consideration to the family's schedule. The mother or caregiver will stay with the child. Before entering the center, every child should visit it with his main caregiver while it is in session.

Children will differ in the way they use this visit. Some will make many contacts with children. Others will follow, watching from a distance. Still others, who have already visited, may return to the play materials that they enjoyed on the earlier visit, seeming to pay little attention to the other children around them.

The teacher will add to her understanding of a particular child by observing him in this new situation. Seeing his interest in something, she may place this material near him, bringing it easily within his reach. If he looks at a child painting at the easel, she may walk nearer with him and say a few words about the paint, the colors, and so forth. She does not push him into activity. She only moves with him, if she feels this action makes him feel more secure. He may find the piano, and together they may share some music with other children joining them. If he is more interested in watching what other children are doing, she may comment on what is happening, mentioning the children's names. Some children may be made anxious by too much attention from the teacher until they feel more at home. The teacher can limit her help to a reassuring smile when such a child looks in her direction and be ready with more active help later.

When a new child enters a group, he holds a special place as a visitor. Other children have a chance to become aware of him as a "new" child. They may become aware of "newness" and the fact that there are steps in proceeding from being "new" to feeling familiar and at home in a group. A wise teacher may use the opportunity to support growth in individual children already in the group. She may say, "Remember when you were new and visited?" She may recall some special incident and add, "Now you know where things go and what we do. You have friends." In this way she points out and strengthens the movement this child has made toward independence and greater security.

There should be opportunities to develop a relationship with the teacher. Through observation and interactions with the child during his visits, the teacher makes an effort to establish a relationship with the new child. Her task is to help him discover a teacher as a person who is there to be depended on and who cares for and about him. It is important for the teacher to spend time with the child or to be available to him. He needs a person he trusts and to whom he can turn, if he is to make the adjustment in a constructive way.

The teacher will bring only *one* new child at a time into the group because it is difficult to give the needed reassurance to more than one new child at a time. We are speaking here of bringing children into a group. A group that is just forming represents a different situation.

The teacher may plan to bring perhaps four children together for an hour with their parents. Four new children are not likely to enter into sustained relationships with each other or to demand a great deal from the adult immediately. She can be available to them all. Another group can come at another hour to go through the same process, and in a few days several such groups may come together to become a larger group entering school. In this way, each child begins in a small group first and is with children he knows when he enters the larger group.

A clear understanding about the length of time the child is to stay helps in the adjustment. The wise teacher will have a clear understanding with the parent as to the length of time the child will stay on his first day at the center. More than an hour spent in an environment that demands so much responsiveness is fatiguing for most children. The child needs to be protected from fatigue. Some children can, of course, stay longer, and many children will wish to do so; but there are advantages in setting a definite length of time for the first visit and maintaining it.

During these first days it is advisable for the child that his parent or caregiver come without bringing other children in the family. Entering school is a significant event in the life of the child and his parents. If the parent is free to give him all her attention, she may reaffirm for him his sense of being valued by her. This attention may be especially important to him if there is a baby at home who has necessarily been taking much of the parent's time. It may help the child to realize that his parent cares for him at this moment of approaching separation.

The parent's feelings influence the child's adjustment. The way the parent feels about sending the child to school will have a profound effect on the way the child adjusts. If the mother feels reluctant, unsure, or overanxious, she hinders his ability to meet the new situation and grow more independent. Both parent and teacher may not realize how completely a child senses what they may be feeling.

There are many reasons why a parent may feel uncertain. She inevitably feels some conflict between wanting to hold on to the child, to prolong his dependence, and wanting the child to be strong and independent. If the mother is working outside the home, she may have a feeling that she is deserting her child. The teacher needs to stand ready with reassurance. She needs to strengthen the parent's acceptance of the reality of what the center offers and the parent's confidence in her child's readiness for it. A parent may both want very much to have a child in the center and yet still not want him there. She may be afraid of the disapproval of other people or feel guilty about her own sense of not wanting him home all the time.

The mother who is working outside the home may not be able to take more than one day away from her job. In this case the teacher has special responsibility for meeting the child's need for closeness and reassurance. Much will depend on the child's own capacity to cope with change and how well the parent or caregiver has prepared the child.

If the parent or caregiver is present she can help the child by saying, "I will be right here. I am staying with you. I won't leave." She may find a chair where she can see and be seen easily by the child and stay there. She does not push him away from her with words like, "Why don't you go play with the blocks or with that boy over there?" It is the teacher's and not the parent's responsibility to encourage the child to move from his parent. The parent indicates her pleasure in whatever he has done on his own. If he is hurt or rebuffed by another child, she gives him the comfort he seeks; but she accepts the incident as part of the reality of existence with others, trying to look at it in the way she hopes he will. She should show confidence in his ability not to be upset, just as she will not be unnecessarily upset herself. When employers realize the importance of a mother's relationship with her young child, they will be more likely to give the mother time to help her child with his adjustment to life in a day-care center.

The teacher finds ways to help both the child and the parent. The teacher is also the one to take the responsibility for helping the child to participate when he is ready. She is always alert to the need to give him support in the efforts he makes to move toward greater independence. When he does leave his parent, the teacher stays near him to give him the protection he needs at first. By staying near him the teacher is also demonstrating to both him and his parent that she is there, looking after him. She makes it easier for the parent to leave the child free to participate.

Some children are helped to make the adjustment if they bring something from home to keep with them at first. While it may not be the usual

Watch how carefully Nicole pours the pretend formula.

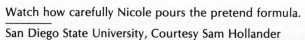

San Diego State University, Courtesy Sam Hollander

practice of the school to encourage children to bring their own toys, it may be desirable during the initial adjustment period. It is unlikely that the child will be able to "share" this possession if he is depending on it for support, and he should be protected against having to do so. A simple explanation by the teacher such as, "Mary is new here and needs to keep her doll. Later, when she knows us better, she may let you play with it, too," will serve to deepen understanding.

Parents respond in different ways. Some parents find the time spent at school interesting; others are restless, finding little to interest them. If a parent is interested, she will find it easy to respond to the child's request to come and look at things; but she also needs to make him feel that it is his center. She looks at what he shows her, but she will avoid trying to point out many things to him. The teacher, for her part, will look for ways to help the parent to appreciate the significance of what is occurring. When possible, she can sit with the parent, pointing out and explaining what is happening. Some people have had little background for understanding the development of children. They lack interest in it because they know little about it. Parents are almost sure to be interested if they are helped to see the significance of the children's play. The teacher and the school may open up possibilities to parents for growth in understanding that will be valuable through the years.

STEP 3: REGULAR ATTENDANCE FOR PART OF THE SESSION WITHOUT HIS PARENT. The next step for the child in entering school is to attend regularly for part of the session and to begin the process of having his parent leave him. The point to keep in mind is that a relationship of trust in the teacher and interest in the program itself are the sources of support which will enable the child to be successful in staying by himself with confidence and a sense of achievement. The first visits have been steps in preparing him for the separation. Most children will need their parent with them for only a few days until they feel at home in the center and with the teacher.

One mother reported to the teacher on the second day that her three-year-old son had told her on the way to the center, "I want you to go home today, Mummy." Wisely, they decided to follow his request. She went home for a short time and then returned. He was telling them clearly that he felt ready to be left for awhile, and they showed him that they had confidence in him. He did not need her the next day. He was ready to stay without his parent.

It is interesting to note that most parents overestimate their children's capacity to adjust. One cannot depend on a parent's assurance that "He'll be all right without me; I've left him lots of times." He may be a child who stands quietly and withdrawn, the very child who needs his parent most because he cannot express his insecurities. He may have had too many experiences of being left! Entering the group experience with his parent may mean the chance to overcome some of the past, to reassure himself by this present situation that his parent really will stay with him when he needs her. This may be the feeling that he needs if he is to be free to explore and enjoy the new setting.

The tendency on the part of most parents to expect too much of their children in the way of adjustment probably indicates how universally adults fail to realize what is involved in learning and growing. We are not accustomed to observing behavior for cues to feelings. We look for what we want to see and not for what is really there.

The teacher plays an active part in helping the child separate from his parent. It is usually necessary for the teacher to take an active part in the process of separation. Some sensitive teachers, concerned about the danger of forcing a separation, lose sight of the growth potentials in the child. They fail to pick up the clues he offers for his readiness to move toward independence, provided he has some help. Prolonging his dependency in the new situation may interfere with his growth toward independence, which is the task at hand developmentally. The skillful teacher will help the child reach his goal *in the shortest time possible.*

The parent helps with her understanding. As soon as the parent and teacher agree that the child is feeling comfortable at the center, the parent will prepare the child by saying, for example, "Today, I am going to do some errands while you are here. I will be gone a little while, and when I get back, I'll see what you are doing." If his response is, "I don't want you to go," she may answer, "I won't go for a while after we get there, not until I know you are ready. I will tell you and I'll only be gone a very little while."

The teacher can prepare the child for what he already expects by saying quietly, "Your mother is going now, John. She will be back very soon." With the teacher there, the parent can say good-bye to the child and leave for a short time. If they have estimated the child's readiness correctly, the teacher will be able to help the child handle the anxiety he feels until his parent returns.

The first separation should be a very short one if the child is finding it difficult to let his parent leave. Even 15 minutes may seem a long time when one feels unsure of oneself and under some strain. When the parent returns, she will speak to him and then stay for a while, giving the child time to enjoy his play, before they go home together. In this way his parent is showing him the pattern that she will follow. She goes, but she comes back. He is discovering the satisfaction of feeling more and more comfortable about being able to stay at the center on his own. In this way he looks forward to returning. If a child seems to be finding the separation very difficult, the teacher may visit his home to help him gain confidence in her.

STEP 4: FULL-TIME ATTENDANCE. When a parent is able to leave the child almost as soon as they arrive at the center and stay away for as long as two hours without his becoming uneasy, the child is ready for the last step—that of full-time attendance by himself. Most children need a week or more before they are sufficiently secure to attend for the whole session.

Few two- or three-year-old children reach this step in less than a week. Some take much longer. Sleep disturbances, toilet accidents, and increased irritability may be the result of trying to move faster than the child is ready. Good adjustment requires time, and relapses are less likely if the adjustment has not been either hurried or prolonged unduly.

The four- or five-year-old child will probably be able to feel safe at the center more quickly than the three-year-old. He has had more experience and more time to develop confidence in his own resources. Sometimes the struggle to make the separation may be unduly prolonged because the parent finds it hard to leave the child. The parent may lack confidence in herself, the child, or the center. It is important that the teacher be aware of the point at which the separating has "bogged down" and that the child really wants to stay. The teacher needs to take positive steps in this case to resolve the conflict. She will talk with the parent, indicating her feeling that the child is ready to stay by himself, and they will plan together how this step may be accomplished. The teacher will act with firmness and confidence in carrying through the plan. She may need to hold the child in her arms when the mother goes, giving him time to cry, putting into words the fact that she knows he wants his parent and that his parent will be back. Then the teacher will help him find his place in the center, sitting with him, watching with him, finding him a familiar toy, or perhaps taking him to visit the homelike kitchen which he enjoyed seeing earlier. While his parent is gone, the teacher will make sure that she is always available if he needs her. She will try to see that the first separation is a successful one. Through it, the child gains confidence to continue separating himself from his dependency on his parent or other caregivers.

It often happens that a child who is disturbed by some event at home or at school will revert to an earlier level of dependency, wanting his parent again. It is important that his real needs be accepted and met. If his adjustment is sound, he is usually quickly reassured by his parent's willingness to stay with him for a time, and it does not take long for him to become independent. Again, the teacher helps him by accepting him and by giving all the support she can to his desire to be more self-sufficient.

Summary

We may summarize the steps in entering the center in this way:

1. The teacher has a conference with the parents in which, among other

things, the procedures to be followed as the child enters the center are defined.

2. The child and his parent may visit the center when it is not in session to become acquainted with the physical setup and to establish a relationship with the teacher. Next he visits the center when the children are present.

3. The child begins attending regularly for part of the session and begins the process of separating himself from his parent or caregiver. The teacher takes the responsibility for planning with the parent the time and method of separation.

4. The child attends without his parent for increasingly longer periods until he is coming for the full session.

The stages we have described are those best suited to the needs of a child as he enters a group and separates from home care. The optimum procedures are not always possible. But in every case both parent and teacher should recognize the importance this experience holds for a child. They should give the child as much support as possible as he copes with the new experience.

If the step of moving toward independence and away from the dependency on his parent is taken so that it does not produce more anxiety than the child can manage easily, he is free to enjoy and profit from the group experience. He gains in self-confidence. We may wonder whether children who have had this kind of help in separation will be as likely later to suffer from panic in strange situations or to be disorganized by feelings of homesickness.

Here are some examples of the ways in which different children make the adjustment to entering the new group experience.

MIKEY, WHO WAS READY TO STAY BY HIMSELF.   Mikey, three years old, was brought to school by his grandmother on the first day. He was the next to the youngest in a family of six children and one of the youngest children in the group. His reaction that day seemed to be one of complete amazement. He darted from area to area and toy to toy, touching everything and exclaiming, "Oh, no! Oh, no! Look at all these toys. All kinds of toys. So many toys!" He could hardly bear to leave when the time came. He wanted to touch everything all over again, even though the teacher explained that he could come back the next day. Finally he was persuaded to go and he left saying, "Good-bye, I hope I can come back some day."

On arriving with his grandmother the second day, he made a check to see if everything was still there. He spent most of the time dashing from place to place and exclaiming with wonder at all the things for children. He commented on the fact that there were "little tables and little chairs just for children." When his grandmother tried to leave for a short time,

Mikey stated emphatically that she was to stay at the center. On Mikey's third day he asked why he had to go while some of the other children could stay. The teacher explained that when he could let his grandmother go and stay at school by himself, he could stay with the others for lunch. The next day he told his grandmother that he was ready to stay with "his teacher" now, and she was to go home and come back after lunch. He showed the same pattern of amazement and delight at his first lunch period. He seemed entirely comfortable with the teacher. At the end of the day he said, "I hope I can stay for lunch again someday."

Here we see a child who manages his dependency needs easily but who is almost overwhelmed by the stimulation of an environment new to him. Mikey made an excellent adjustment very quickly. His friendliness, lack of defensiveness, and his delight in the new were a source of help to many children less sure of themselves.

RALPH, WHOSE MOTHER COULD GIVE HIM TIME TO GROW IN FEELING SECURE.   Ralph, three and a half years old, was an only child, with a father and mother who were very fond of him. Although they were gentle and kind, they were very anxious to have Ralph meet all their expectations, perhaps because they were not too secure themselves.

On his visit to the center before he entered, Ralph enjoyed playing with the cars and blocks, but he called his mother's attention to everything and referred to her constantly. It was apparent that he depended on her and would not be ready to have her leave for some time, even though he was eager to go to the center and was friendly with the teacher.

When he came on the first day, he held his mother's hand tightly. She went into the playroom with him and sat down near the block corner. Ralph immediately began playing. When other children approached, he seemed pleased and made attempts to join their play. One of the boys took a block from him in spite of his mild protest. Tears came into his eyes as he relinquished his hold on the block. He turned toward his mother but did not go to her. She smiled sympathetically and encouragingly, not quite sure what to do. The teacher quietly reassured him, "That was your block, wasn't it? I'll ask Bill to give it back. There are other blocks for him. There are plenty for both of you to build with." It was easy to get Bill to return the block, and under the teacher's watchful eye the two played satisfactorily side by side. Ralph returned to his mother's side finally, flushed and happy.

Ralph was inclined to stutter when he became excited. The disfluency showed that he was sensitive to strain and was further evidence that it was especially important to proceed slowly in introducing him to newness. It was also apparent that there would be some strain for him in adjusting to the realities of three-year-old behavior because of the somewhat "adult" standards to which he had been accustomed. He had shown some strengths on that first day in his ability to enjoy not only the play materials but also the other children, and to accept help from someone other than his mother.

Ralph and his mother went home at the end of an hour, and returned the next day, both eager to be back at the center. Ralph's mother watched the things that went on in the center with interest. After Ralph and his mother had been coming for a week for two hours each day, both his mother and teacher agreed that Ralph no longer needed his mother, but that he still needed a short day at the center. He came happily the next morning, knowing that his mother was not staying. When she started to leave, however, he asked her to go to the store and not to go home without him. Apparently he could not quite bear to think of his mother at home without him. She went shopping, and he had a good morning at the center. It was nearly a week later that he decided he would like to stay for lunch, like the other children, and did. His adjustment had proceeded smoothly. His mother smilingly remarked one day that she missed being there, adding, "It was such fun and I learned so much. They're all different, aren't they?" The days had been worth almost as much to Ralph's mother as to Ralph. She had gained confidence in the center, too.

Not long after Ralph entered, he ran back as he was leaving one day and threw his arms around the teacher's neck and gave her a kiss. It probably showed that he felt he belonged at the center and to the adults who helped him feel comfortable there, as his mother did at home. As the result of his success in adapting, he had probably grown less tense and felt himself to be a more adequate person, more secure because he now knew he could proceed at his own pace.

ALL NEW EXPERIENCES NEED TO BE HANDLED THOUGHTFULLY IN ORDER TO INCREASE A CHILD'S CONFIDENCE

Entering school is a big adjustment, but it is not the only new situation that the child may face. When the children go on walks, for example, they may see unfamiliar or even frightening things. New people, places, and events, wherever they are encountered, need to be handled thoughtfully. They may build up confidence or decrease it. A visit to the fire station may mean strange noises, unfamiliar people, as well as the sight of the huge fire engine itself. Some children will need to proceed slowly. One child may be able to watch the fire engine comfortably if he holds the hand of the adult. Another may need the safety of being held in the adult's arms. Others may need the reassurance of knowing that they can leave the situation wherever they want.

The necessity of keeping each opportunity within the level of the child's ability to participate in it without anxiety means that at least two adults must go with any group from school to all but the most familiar places. On a walk to the barns, for example, a child may show signs of fear about going inside. An adult will need to stay outside with him, accepting the fact that for some reason he is not ready to go inside. They both can have a pleasant time together outside the barn. Later the child may want to go inside, or he may be willing to return at another time. With his fear accepted and with time to proceed at his own rate, a child will gain confidence in himself as he succeeds in handling the fear. If he is pushed into entering the barn when he is still afraid, he may only learn to conceal his fear or to depend on adult support. In such a case if anything happens which startles him while he is in the barn, such as a cow mooing, he may be thrown into a panic because of the feelings of fear inside him which are released by the sudden noise. He may become more afraid and lose confidence.

Trips to a fire station or to a barn are only two examples of new situations. Children are continually meeting new situations. For one child it could be a piece of climbing equipment on the playground; for another child an encounter with a small furry animal; or for another it could be seeing a worm. It is important that teachers respect children's reluctance and fears and help children to cope with these gradually.

The Adult's Feelings Influence the Child's

The attitude of the adult influences the child, and in any emergency it is imperative that the adult meet the situation calmly for the sake of the child. A group of four-year-olds were visiting the fire station one day when the fire alarm sounded. One of the firefighters directed them calmly, "You all stand right against the wall and watch this fire engine go out." His composure steadied the teachers; in a matter of seconds everyone was against the wall, and the fire engine pulled out before the eyes of the thrilled line of children. It was the best trip to the fire station they had ever had. The reports of bombings in World War II showed that children reacted in the way the adults around them reacted. If children were with calm people, they were not likely to be upset even when the situations were terrifying; children became hysterical for much less cause when they were with hysterical people.

In planning any experience for the children, the teacher must always be familiar with it herself. If the event is to be a trip, she should have made the trip so that she can prepare the children for what they may expect. What will it be like? What will they do? What will they see? Will they hear a noise? If there is much that is unfamiliar, it helps to go over it in words

A new place for a routine can enhance adaptive behavior.

Valley College, Campus Child Development Center

so that the children have some framework into which to fit the situation. Often a lively review of what each child saw will help to place the experiences among the "known" things. The review can take place on the way back to the center and again later at an appropriate time.

It is usually important to talk to the volunteers and parents about what will help the children enjoy the trip more. Not all adults understand the needs of young children. For example, on a trip to a fire station, a firefighter may think it is fun to startle children by turning on a siren unexpectedly or ringing a bell. If the adults are not helpful, it may be better not to visit the fire station, or at least to be very careful to take only the children for whom such events will not be frightening. People who work with animals can usually be counted on to be gentle and quiet and to help rather than hinder the children's pleasure in the experience they are having.

Observing a Child Meet a New Experience Gives Us Insight into His Feelings

Observing the way children explore the world outside the center is one way to become aware of the different patterns of behavior that children already have. Some children go out to meet the new with confidence. There are others whose areas of confidence are limited, and there are those who are disturbed by the smallest departure from the familiar. Opportunities offered to children must be adapted to what they are ready to accept.

When a child stops to watch something, the wise adult will wait. It is a sign that the child is absorbed in the new, attempting to relate it to what he can understand. He may or may not ask questions. Moving on before he is ready will only mean leaving behind unresolved ideas. The habit of exploring the new fully is a sound one and builds feelings of adequacy.

In the first few months at the center most children need to be limited to the center itself, before going on any trips. There are many new people, objects, places, and events in the school. By watching, questioning, and participating, the child becomes familiar with the new, whether it be a wasp's nest brought in by the teacher, a visitor in a foreign costume, or just a new toy. When he repeats an activity over and over, he is assimilating it, making it his own. He is adding to his feeling of being an adequate person as he masters the activities in the environment.

CHILDREN HAVE DEFENSES WHEN THEY FEEL UNCERTAIN. Children, like adults, have defenses that they are likely to use when they feel uncertain because the situation they are in is new and strange. When children feel unsure of themselves, they may withdraw or retreat from any action and play safe by doing nothing, thus running no risk of doing the wrong thing. This behavior is a type of denial of the situation—like turning one's back on something.

For example, when Helen, a three-and-a-half-year-old, entered the center she made no protest at her mother's leaving her. She simply stood immobile on the spot where she had been left. If an adult took her hand and led her somewhere, as to the piano, she went passively. She had had many new situations to meet in her short life and much unfriendliness. A frail child, she had protected herself in the only way she could—by being passive. The teachers made no attempt to push her into any activity but gave her friendly smiles, often sat near her, and sometimes took her to the piano or the finger-painting table. Very slowly she began to show some responsiveness.

It was interesting to observe that it was only after Helen had been in the center for some months that she began to make a fuss over her mother's leaving and to beg her to stay. It seemed likely that she was just beginning to feel free enough to dare to make some demands on her mother—to indicate how she really felt. Unfortunately, her mother could not accept her demands and refused to "baby" her. Helen stopped this behavior, but she continued to make progress, making some demands on the teachers and occasionally joining another child in play. When the situation changed in any way, as when there were visitors, she became quite passive. One wonders whether Helen would have been less passive if her mother could have accepted the child's demand that she stay. Would she have felt less helpless? Would she have been less likely to retreat into passive behavior?

Sometimes a child who feels strange and uncomfortable will suddenly begin to play for a lot of attention or act "silly," as though seeking reassurance by surrounding himself with attentive adults. Another child will be aggressive. He may bully others as though to prove to himself that he is big and strong and not as weak and helpless as he fears. These children are doing something active about their problem. They give us an opportunity to help them with it.

Steven, three years old, on the second day at the center, appeared disturbed by all the strange children and teachers. He suddenly picked up a toy horse and said, "This horse is going to kill all these many bad people around here." His teacher replied quietly, "I think you don't like finding so many people here. They will be your friends someday." Because they were strange to him, they seemed bad. He was actively trying to cope with his anxiety through projecting onto the horse the wish that he could dispose of them all. He was also communicating to an understanding teacher his need for reassurance.

CHILDREN NEED HELP WHEN THEY ACT DEFENSIVELY.   It is not uncommon to see a child, who has been frightened by something startling or unusual, turn and hit a companion with almost no provocation. In this way he releases the feeling of fear which is uncomfortable. The adult's role is to help him face the feeling and find some acceptable outlet for it. Fear is a less uncomfortable feeling when one is not ashamed of it. It may help if the teacher can say, for example, "Lots of people feel afraid when they hear a big noise like that. It's all right to be afraid. Take hold of my hand and let's walk farther away, then it won't sound so loud. There's no need to hit Billy. He may be afraid, too." The other child will need some explanation such as, "I think he hit you because he felt afraid. I'm sorry." This kind of handling will help each child to understand why people behave as they do.

Often children will actively reject a situation or some part of it because they feel strange and insecure. In the laboratory nursery school the number of adults present may increase any difficulty a child has in accepting adults. Frequently he will meet a friendly advance with the words, "Go 'way, I don't like you." It's like getting in the first blow when you're expecting the worst. For the child's sake, it's important to recognize the real feeling behind these words, to understand its meaning as "Go 'way. I'm afraid of you." It usually *is* better to go away until the child has had more time to make an adjustment. It is sometimes possible for a teacher whom the child does know to interpret his feelings to him in such a case, saying, for example, "I think that you don't like her and want her to go away because you don't know her yet. When you know her, you may like her. Her name is_____. She might help you find a shovel for digging."

It is important to be able to identify children's defenses and to help them make adjustments that are really appropriate to the situation or to help them discover how to release their disturbed feelings in acceptable ways. It is equally important to see that children have experiences in which they feel adequate, so that they will have less need for defenses. When adults can do these things, they offer real help to the child.

Projects

1. Record a situation in which a child was faced with a new experience in the school. Summarize your observation, noting the child's significant reactions and the help given by the adult (if any). Estimate what the experience may have meant to the child.
2. Observe two children of different ages in a grocery store or on a playground, and note the degree to which they seem to feel safe and comfortable in the situation. How do they show their feelings? What defenses do they seem to use against the feeling of being strange and unsure? Is the experience building up or breaking down the degree of confidence the children feel?

For Your Further Reading

Bowlby, J. (1982). Attachment and loss: Retrospects and prospect. *American Journal of Orthopsychiatry, 52*(4), 664–678. A summary of Bowlby's important contribution to our understanding of attachment and separation.

Bowlby, J. (1975). *Separation anxiety: A critical review of the literature.* New York: Child Welfare League of America. Relates observations of children to traditional theory, proposing that separation anxiety, grief and mourning, and defense are phases of a single process.

Dunn, J. (1977). *Distress and comfort.* The developing child series. Cambridge, MA: Harvard University Press. Outstanding readable book on the topic, with practical suggestions as well as research background.

Hazen, N., Black, B., & Fleming-Johnson, F. (1984). Social acceptance: Strategies children use and how teachers can help children learn them. *Young Children, 39*(6), 26–36. Guidelines for teachers to help children who are not socially accepted.

Jewett, C. L. (1982). *Helping children cope with separation and loss.* Harvard, MA: The Harvard Common Press. Excellent book deals with stages of coping with losses of many kinds: divorce, moving, death, hospitalization, military service.

Street (girl, 3 years 6 months)

10 ♦ Helping Children in Routine Situations

We have seen how new experiences can contribute to building confidence and security in a child if we accept and respect the child's level of readiness for the experience. The need to understand and accept the child's readiness for an experience is as important in everyday events as in new or unusual ones. Daily events may contribute to feelings and set patterns in ways that influence growth even more significantly than do the new or the unusual. Teaching in routine situations should be based on an awareness of the child's degree of readiness.

Routines such as toileting, resting and sleeping, dressing, washing, and eating are everyday events. They serve as a framework around which the child's day is organized. They satisfy biological needs and are closely tied to his interest in his body. The child gains assurance from knowing that there are familiar aspects of the day that he can anticipate and understand. They enable him to get a sense of the passage of time and of order in life. These routines are also part of the procedures or rituals of individual families and their cultures.

The National Academy of Early Childhood Programs, a division of National Association for the Education of Young Children, has set a criterion for the management of routine tasks in programs that care for young children. It states, "Routine tasks are incorporated into the program as a means of furthering children's learning, self help, and social skills. Routines such as diapering, toileting, eating, dressing, and sleeping are handled in a relaxed, reassuring, and individualized manner based on developmental needs."[1]

TOILETING

Some of the best opportunities for teaching young children occur in the toileting situation, for elimination is a significant part of the young child's life. It is one about which his feelings are sure to be strong. It offers the possibility for growth in autonomy and mastery.

For the child, toileting is associated with many intimate experiences with a parent or caregiver, with her care of him, with his efforts to please her, and perhaps with conflicts over her attempts to train him. Toileting may even be related to his ideas about good and bad behavior. One parent used to leave her child at school with the admonition, "Be a good girl today." What she really meant by these words was, "Stay dry today." This kind of morality is confusing.

When children enter a center at about three years of age, they have probably only recently been through the period of toilet training. They may not have emerged from this training period completely unscathed. Many children now enter group programs when they are one- to two-and-a-half years old. Teachers of toddlers must assume more responsibility for the accomplishment of toilet training than teachers of three- to five-year-olds. We will suggest ways to help teachers foster children's feelings of mastery and comfortable acceptance of the elimination process. A child's behavior tells us something about what the experience means to him, whether he is a two- or four-year-old.

TRAINING FOR TOILET CONTROL MAY HAVE AN EFFECT ON MANY AREAS OF BEHAVIOR. Excessive negativism is one common result of toilet train-

---

[1] National Association for the Education of Young Children. (1984). *Accreditation criteria and procedures: Position statement of the National Academy of Early Childhood Programs*. Washington, DC: Author.

ing that is not based on a child's readiness. The child who says no to everything and who looks on contacts with adults as possible sources of interference and restriction may have acquired this attitude during his toilet training period. A most resistant, hostile child in one center had been subjected to an early, rigid period of toilet training. She defied adult suggestions and could not share with children. The quality of the relationship she had with her earnest parents can be pictured in the note which her mother sent one day, "Pearl has *refused* to have a bowel movement for four days."

If the child has been forced to achieve bowel and bladder control before he is ready, his "control" may include the inhibition of spontaneity and creativity in many areas. We may see some children who were trained early to stay "dry and clean" and are now unable to use play materials in creative ways. They cannot enjoy play in mud and wet sand, use finger paint, or savor the ordinary joys of childhood and the social contacts that occur in such sensory play.

According to pediatrician T. Berry Brazelton, this kind of early pressure for toilet control has decreased dramatically in his thirty years of practice. However, some parents still feel pressure from so-called experts to train early with reward or punishment systems and may feel like failures if the child is not successful.[2]

The child whose parents have treated the acquiring of toilet control in the same way as any other developmental step, such as walking or talking, is likely to be a comfortable child. After he has started walking, he may show an interest in the toilet and in imitating the behavior of the people he observes there. His parents encourage his efforts and make it easy for him to use the toilet in the way they do. They can show the same satisfactions in his success here as they do in his other developmental accomplishments. They should be ready to accept any resistance as a sign that he is not ready yet and drop their efforts for a time. They should not make an issue of learning toilet control any more than they would of learning in other areas. When there is no undue pressure, the child usually begins to take on the patterns of adults some time between the ages of eighteen and thirty months.

ADULT ATTITUDES AND STANDARDS MAY COMPLICATE THE TOILETING PROCESS. Toileting is sometimes complicated for the child by parental anxieties. A parent may give a great deal of anxious attention to the child's elimination. She may undertake training early, in a determined way, to prove herself a good parent. She may impose standards about toilet behavior before the child can understand them. Separation of the sexes, demands for privacy, and disapproval of many kinds of toilet behavior can

[2]T. Berry Brazelton. (1984). *To listen to a child*. Reading, MA: Addison-Wesley.

Toileting is a significant part of the young child's life.

Jean Berlfein

have little meaning to the young child. These standards may add feelings of fear or guilt to the situation. It becomes hard for healthy attitudes to develop under these circumstances.

Parents should examine their own feelings of pressure from society for early toilet training, according to Brazelton. "Success in the toilet area should be the child's own autonomous achievement, not success by the parent in choosing the right technique to 'train' him. Unless he feels it is something he wants to achieve, parental efforts will always be seen as pressure."[3]

CHILDREN GAIN FROM INFORMED HANDLING OF TOILETING AT THE CENTER. The important thing for us to remember as teachers caring for young children is that the children come from homes with many different beliefs and practices about toilet control. Some will have healthy, matter-of-fact attitudes with no doubts about their ability to handle the toilet situation competently. They will expect to meet friendly, accepting adults and will not be disturbed about toilet accidents. Other children will be tentative and insecure. They may be upset by failures to control their elimination. Some will use the toilet situation to express their anxieties or

[3]Ibid.

defiance. Some will not be able to use the toilet at the center until they feel comfortable there. They must be helped according to their different needs. All of them will gain from informed handling of toileting at the center.

If the handling is to be sound, the children must meet adults in the center who are themselves comfortable in the situation. To feel comfortable is not always easy, for many of us have had experiences in our past that have included being ashamed or embarrassed about the subject of toileting. Being with children and adults who have matter-of-fact attitudes will often help us to free ourselves from conflicts generated by our own past experiences.

The interest that children show in the subject of toileting can be seen in the frequency with which it appears in their dramatic play. Again and again they will act out with their dolls what is for them the drama of the toilet. This play is a desirable way of expressing any conflicts they may feel and making them seem more manageable. The center designed to meet children's needs will provide bathroom fixtures including toilets among the dollhouse furniture and dolls.

WHAT THE ADULT DOES ABOUT TOILET ACCIDENTS IS SIGNIFICANT.

Toilet accidents are likely to be common in the child's first weeks at the center and may be indications of the strain that he is feeling in the new situation. The child is reassured when he realizes that he does not need to fear having a toilet accident. He gains confidence if he finds friendly, accepting adults to help him if he has a urine or bowel accident.

Another child may react to the new situation by withholding his urine and feces. He may be unable to use the toilet for some time. This behavior may be one indication of the way he feels. It is hardly necessary to say that no pressure should be put on a child to use the toilet until he is ready.

Sometimes a child who has been attending the center and successfully using the toilet will suddenly have a series of toilet accidents. These accidents may be a sign of emotional strain or impending illness and should be regarded as a significant symptom. It is helpful for the teacher to talk with the child's parent to try to discover any possible sources for the changed behavior. We should not increase the strain by disapproval.

It cannot be emphasized too strongly that adults' matter-of-fact attitudes about toilet accidents is exceedingly important. If a child knows that accidents are not condemned, he feels much freer and safer. He can proceed to acquire control at his own rate and to feel pride in his own achievement.

While we can show pleasure in his successes, we must not value success too highly. If success is overemphasized, the child may also overemphasize the occasional, inevitable failures. Under no condition should a child ever be made to feel disapproval or shame for his toileting behaviors. It is the child's feelings about success or failure which must be considered, not the parents' or society's.

TOILET PROCEDURES THAT ARE CONSTRUCTIVE. The physical setup plays a part in building positive feelings. If the toilet room is a pleasant, light, and attractive place, the child is more likely to feel comfortable there. Small-size toilets are desirable because they make it easier for the child to manage independently. If they cannot be obtained, a step can be placed in front of the toilet and a hinged seat provided to make the opening smaller. A door to the room or in front of each toilet can be a handicap. It may interfere with the children's self-help efforts and the teacher's ease of supervision.

Interest in the plumbing usually rises to a peak around the age of four. Observation of the toilet while it is being flushed, with discussions about water pipes, sewer systems, and the destination of the products of elimination, are of absorbing interest. These discussions have value. Attempts to hurry the child out of the situation or to discourage his curiosity will make it harder for him to develop a healthy attitude. The wise adult will be prepared to spend time and feel comfortable in the toileting area with the child.

Children from about the age of three can be expected to handle their clothing independently at the toilet if they are properly dressed. Some parents need to be urged to dress children in self-help clothing such as pants with elastic tops. Boys can be reminded to raise the toilet seat before urinating. Children can be expected to flush the toilet. The teacher might say, "Now it will be fresh for the next child." When an occasional child refuses to flush it, we can safely assume, as we can with any refusal, that there is some meaning behind it. Children are sometimes frightened by the noise and movement of water in a flushing toilet. They will be reassured in time as they watch others. Their refusal should be respected.

Handwashing should be encouraged after toileting. It is a desirable habit, and a child usually enjoys the washing process. Handwashing is necessary before food preparation or eating. Children pattern their judgments after what they see. Often their hands look clean to them. If the teacher washes her hands and tells the children it is important to wash hands after going to the toilet as well as before eating, they are likely to follow her example.

In the center boys and girls use the toilets freely together with an adult present. Children usually are very accepting of this arrangement. They value their ability to manage toileting independently more than they are concerned about who else is using a toilet. If an occasional child seems surprised or uncomfortable, the teacher can explain, "Here all children use the toilet together." Adults sometimes ask, "But won't this practice make it harder for a child when he has to learn a different custom?" The teacher may reply that children are able to accept the custom that is appropriate for the time and place. Toileting on a picnic differs from that at home. Boys accompany their mothers into public restrooms when they are young but learn to make a distinction when they are older. Patterns of behavior differ with age, gender, and society. The child learns to accept differences.

ACCEPTANCE OF CHILDREN'S INTEREST IN EACH OTHER PROMOTES HEALTHY ATTITUDES. Sound handling of toileting includes a matter-of-fact attitude in situations in which children show an interest in each other at the toilet. Children need a chance to satisfy their curiosity about bodies and processes. The center offers casual opportunities for this healthy curiosity. Girls will be interested in the fact that boys have penises and stand when they urinate. Boys may wonder if girls used to have penises. A girl who has no male family member at home may want to watch boys urinate until her interest is satisfied. It may help if the teacher verbalizes in some way, such as, "Bill has a penis. He stands up at the toilet. Boys stand up, and girls sit down."

Psychiatrists tell us that an important factor in sexual adjustment is the acceptance of one's gender. In the toileting situation a boy may feel important because he possesses a penis. Sometimes a girl will try to imitate the boy by attempting to stand—with not very satisfactory results! She learns from her own actions, and no particular comment is needed. Girls may need help in feeling that being a girl is desirable. The teacher may remark, "Mothers sit down, too," or "Boys have a penis, and girls have a vagina."

ESTABLISHING A SCHEDULE FOR TOILETING. When a very young child enters the center, his teacher soon discovers how frequently he needs to go to the toilet by talking with his mother and by observing his behavior. The teacher can establish a schedule to fit the child's rhythm. She will take most of the responsibility at first, saying to him, "Time to go to the toilet now," and attempting to time her interruptions to a shift in his activity. In this way she will avoid building resistance in him. If she is pleasant and friendly, he will welcome this opportunity for adult contact and attention. A new child may adjust more easily if he has the same adult helping him each time. He feels secure more quickly and may begin to come to her when he needs to go to the toilet.

As a next step the teacher may ask the child, "Do you need to go to the toilet now?" rather than simply telling him that it is time to go. This question begins to shift the responsibility to him. If the number of his toilet accidents shows that he is not ready to take this much responsibility, the teacher can go back to the earlier stage. Many factors change a child's rhythm, such as cold weather, excitement, or drinking more liquids than usual.

A set schedule for going to the toilet has the disadvantage of not meeting individual needs or changing needs. Nevertheless it is possible to have a framework within which to expect toileting, and this routine simplifies management. If we remember that the goal of any toileting schedule is to help the child go to the toilet when he needs to go, and not when the teacher wants him to go, we can work out a schedule that will be flexible. Younger children will need reminders at the normal transition times in the day, such as snack time, lunch time, and before and after rest time. The more mature children, those who have taken over responsibility for their toileting, will follow their own schedule; but the teacher will find it wise to suggest toileting before lunch or before taking a walk.

EXAMPLES OF PROBLEMS IN THE TOILET SITUATION.   Let us consider some specific problems that may arise.

Mary, a four-and-a-half-year old, was a delightfully imaginative child. She loved music and often played and sang at the piano or danced when music was played. She was friendly with other children and enjoyed homemaking play in the dramatic play area. She was curious about many things, played actively outdoors, and enjoyed expeditions outside the center. However, she responded to adults in a very negative way. She resisted suggestions and was likely to become self-conscious and show off. At the table she seemed to concentrate on behavior that she knew would not be acceptable, like putting her fingers in the food, throwing it, or running away from the table. She found rest difficult. She was wet several times a day and consistently refused to go to the toilet. She always changed her underpants immediately, leaving the wet ones on the floor in the toilet room. Her mother reported that she had been toilet trained early and then suddenly began wetting again within the last year. They had "tried everything" to make her stop, even shaming her and making her wear diapers. At first she would stay wet; but they had succeeded in impressing on her how "dirty" that was, and now she wouldn't stay in her wet clothes a minute.

It was easy to see where Mary's negativism came from. It seemed likely that she was an able child trying to assert herself. The methods of training and disciplining that her parents had used with her more docile older brother had only increased her resistance. She was defiantly insisting on being independent.

Since Mary was out to defeat "bossing," it seemed evident that pressure for conforming to standards, no matter how desirable the standards, needed to be reduced before she could be expected to change. The whole matter of toileting was dropped at the center. No comment was made on her need to use the toilet or her wet clothes. It was hard for her parents to accept the idea that she must be convinced that she could be wet if she chose before she could accept adult standards. However, they were cooperative, intelligent parents; and somewhat reluctantly they followed the teachers' suggestion of saying nothing, perhaps because they had tried everything else. It was several months before Mary began using the toilet at the center. It might have happened sooner if her parents could have been more wholehearted in turning the responsibility completely over to her. Whenever she felt dominated, Mary would revert to a series of wet pants. It was the area in which she felt she could win in the battle to assert her independence. When left to accept things at her own rate, she was an unusually social and capable child who thoroughly enjoyed the activities available.

A child does not always express resistance to pressure as directly as Mary. In a less friendly and understanding home a child may have to conceal his feelings of resentment. Jethro was a little over four years old. His mother reported that she had felt that "the sooner I started him on regular toilet habits, the better." She began when he was six months old, and he responded "perfectly." Now however Jethro often sat passively instead of playing. He chewed on his blanket, sucked his finger, and was very inactive. His mother said, "He doesn't enjoy anything that I can see." This child did not feel strong enough to protest in a direct way as Mary was able to do. With many other strains in his life added to the pressure to be clean, his position was far less favorable. He was dry but not free. Spontaneity and the ability to play were sacrificed to conformity.

MEALTIME

Eating is also important in the development of feelings and behavior. When children enter a group they come with a long past as far as eating goes. They have had many previous experiences with food. These experiences have been satisfying in varying degrees. The child's attitude may consequently be favorable or unfavorable toward the meal situation.

ADULT BEHAVIOR AND ATTITUDES INFLUENCE THE CHILD. From the very beginning the child is affected by the way the adults act and feel about his eating. If his first days are spent in a hospital nursery, the infant may be fed on a schedule because this schedule is part of the many routines in hospitals. The infant's hunger pangs are an individual matter and usually do not fit into a regular schedule. They are acute and distressing to him. If they are not relieved by food, he is miserable and helpless to meet his own needs. Even being awakened to be fed constitutes an intrusion which may be annoying to a baby. The more experienced a parent is in caring for children, the more likely she is to trust her child and feed him when he indicates he is hungry. This experience may account in part for the easier adjustment that is frequently seen in later children in families.

Many hospitals today have a plan whereby mother and baby are together, and shortly after his birth the mother can begin taking care of her baby and can feed him according to his needs. She can thus not only meet the baby's needs for food, comfort, and reassurance but also satisfy her own need to be close and to care for him.

Today most mothers leave the hospital one or two days after the birth of a child. The newborn infant may have been put to the breast soon after birth, and the mother may have been able to feed the infant according to his needs. She was also able to meet the infant's need for close bodily contacts and her own need to know the infant and care for him.

In many hospitals today fathers may be present at the birth. Fathers, too, find it satisfying to become acquainted with their child from the first moment of birth. Sharing the experience may strengthen the bonds among the three.

BASIC ATTITUDES APPEAR IN THE EATING SITUATION. From the child's behavior in the meal situation at the center we can get cues to his feelings and to the kind of adjustment he is making. Appetite is a sensitive index to emotional adjustment. Mary, mentioned earlier, who resisted efforts at toileting, also defied every convention at the table. This behavior was part of her effort to assert her right to be an independent person. It is important, not only from the standpoint of nutrition but also from that of personality development, that the child's behavior at mealtime be managed with understanding.

EATING WITH OTHERS. The ordinary, healthy child enjoys eating. Unless he has had unpleasant experiences in connection with food, he enters the group ready to enjoy the mealtime there. He usually has a conservative attitude about food and prefers those foods he already knows. He has his likes and dislikes, and probably he has not done much eating with groups outside his family. At first he may be distracted from eating by having other children around him. The implements, the dishes, even the chairs are likely to be different from those he has used at home. He will probably meet quite a few unfamiliar foods. The expectations of the adults may be different, too. There is a great deal for him to adapt to in the new situation.

GOALS FOR MEALTIME AND SOME WAYS TO SUPPORT THE CHILD'S LEARNING. Just as there are goals for learning in other opportunities provided, there are goals for mealtime. We want the child to continue to enjoy his food, to learn to like a variety of nutritionally desirable foods, and to practice acceptable ways of eating and behaving at the table. Achieving these goals will take time. Pushing or forcing a child will not help and is almost sure to lead to problems.

The teacher should start by making sure that the child enjoys his meal. She can find out from his parents what the child likes and dislikes, and she will try to make sure that some of his familiar well-liked foods are served.

Eating with friends.

Valley College, Campus Child Development Center

She may suggest that he taste all the foods, but she will not insist. She will also consult his parents about the mealtime arrangements at home, so that she can help the child understand the differences at the center. She may invite his parent to have a meal with the child, so that his parent is in a better position to help the child understand the differences and similarities between mealtimes at home and at the center.

A young child should not be expected to sit at the table until everyone is finished. He should be able to leave when he has finished his meal. She does not insist on a "clean plate." There are slow eaters and fast eaters. No one should be hurried. It is another example of how individual differences can be accepted and provided for.

In addition to staying at the table while they are eating, children of two, three, four, or five can be expected to pour their own milk or juice if it is in small pitchers on the table. They can use a fork as well as a spoon and later a knife. They can serve themselves "seconds" in most cases, sometimes with the teacher's help. They can be expected to wipe up any spilled milk or food if a cloth or sponge is readily available. They can clear the table when they finish eating. All these tasks promote their growth in independence and responsibility.

There are *individual differences*, too, *in the amount of food that children eat*. Some children eat much more than others. The same child will eat different amounts on different days, or he may eat a great deal of one food and very little of another. It is a good thing if we avoid any preconceived notions about what or how much a child needs; then we will find it easier to accept the fluctuations in appetite, which are common to all children.

The best practice is to serve very *small* helpings and leave the child free to take as much more as he wants. A child is likely to eat more when he is served small helpings rather than large ones.

Children should have the right to refuse a food and to make choices, but the main meal should precede dessert, and at least some of the main meal should be eaten before the dessert. Drinking milk should be encouraged. With a good mealtime atmosphere, a skillful teacher helps the child live up to her expectations most of the time.

Finger foods, such as toast sticks and carrot sticks, should be served often. Green beans, for example, are often more popular than peas because of the ease with which they can be eaten as finger food. We are primarily interested in nutrition and only secondarily interested in table manners at this point, although table manners are not neglected. The teacher models good manners and gives approval to the child who says, "Please," or uses his utensils properly.

A child will usually continue to use his fingers at times long after he has begun to use a spoon. He may revert to an earlier level when he is tired or not feeling well. If we believe that it is important for him to enjoy his food, we will not interfere. Gradually he will depend more and more on a spoon and fork. The kind of manners he will acquire in the end will depend on the example set by the adults around him and not on how much pressure they have exerted on him to meet their standards. On the other hand, his interest in food will be adversely affected by their pressure. We need confidence that the child will acquire the eating patterns of those around him *as he is ready*, just as he acquires their language.

If we move too fast in teaching manners, we may interfere with the child's appetite. Being "messy" with food normally precedes being neat in eating. We remember a three-year-old who ate like an adult, but who ate practically nothing at the table. She did eat between meals when she did not have to conform to the very high standards expected of her at home and the pressures to eat more than she wanted.

Introduce new foods gradually and do not expect the child to learn to like too many foods at one time. Extending food horizons too rapidly does not bring good results in most cases. As he watches others enjoy different kinds of foods, the child will be ready to try them himself.

How a child feels influences his appetite. There are important emotional factors and emotional consequences to what we do in the eating situation. A secure child, for example, may be able to accept a variety of new foods more easily than a less secure child who may need to cling longer to familiar foods, as in other things, to gain reassurance. The emotional balance of the insecure child may be threatened if he is pushed into eating too many new foods. Feelings of security and confidence will influence the child's ability to accept new foods.

What the child eats will often depend on who is offering him the food. Infants seem to be sensitive to the likes and dislikes of the person feeding them. They are also sensitive to other feelings in the person feeding them. A baby may take his bottle well or accept his cereal when the person who gives it to him is relaxed and enjoys feeding him. He may refuse the same food if it is offered by someone who dislikes the "messiness" of his eating and is tense and uncertain in her relationship with him. Some children eat very little when there is a new teacher at the table, for example, but will taste new foods or eat everything on their plates when the familiar teacher is there with whom they feel safe.

Because feelings and appetite are so closely related, we must recognize that any emotional disturbance will affect the appetite. We all probably have had the experience of losing interest in food for a time because of upset emotional balance. The child who is suffering from anxiety or some other emotion may have little appetite even though he may be physically well. When the emotional problem is solved, his appetite will respond to the normal demands of a growing organism.

Attacking the loss of appetite directly may do a great deal of harm. The immediate effect on the child may be vomiting or storing food in his mouth. The more serious and lasting result may be a strong aversion to food. Being made to eat when one is not hungry is a very unpleasant thing. If eating is to be a pleasant experience for the child, we will avoid forcing him in any way.

Frequent demands to be fed may be regarded as part of a pattern of dependence. Perhaps the standards for eating behavior have been set too high. Often a child will ask to be fed when he grows tired because of the demand on his coordination that eating makes. As his motor skill improves, he will need less help. Sometimes a child asks to be fed because he wants to find out if the adult is willing to help, to be reassured about his ability to get help when he wants it.

There are many direct and indirect ways to help a child enjoy eating. An attractive-looking table appeals to children. Bright-colored dishes, flowers, a neatly laid table, all add to the child's pleasure and interest in food. Food that "looks good," with a contrast in color, is important. Chocolate pudding, for example, usually disappears faster than colorless pudding.

Children's tastes differ from adults' in that children usually do not care for very hot or very cold foods. They do not like mixed flavors, either. A casserole or loaf may be unpopular even though each individual flavor in it may be relished separately. They care less for creamed foods or sauces over foods than adults do, which can be a welcome advantage to a busy cook. Strong flavors or unusual textures in a food are usually less acceptable to a child.

Children usually enjoy foods they have helped to prepare. Many centers include cooking activities as a regular part of their curriculum. Children who cut up raw vegetables for a mixed salad and sample the vegetables as they prepare them are more likely to eat the salad for lunch. The use of "real" cooking utensils like knives with cutting boards, graters, food mills, egg beaters or blenders, and even electric skillets and hot plates provide learning as well as enjoyment. Children learn about safety by using unsafe things. It goes without saying that an adult is needed in these preparations.

A child will enjoy eating more if he is comfortable at the table. He needs a chair that will permit his feet to rest on the floor and a table that is the right height for him. He needs utensils that are easy to grasp. A salad fork rather than a large fork, a spoon with a round bowl, and a small glass add to his comfort and his pleasure. He will also enjoy clearing away his own dishes when he finishes eating. He is more comfortable if he is not crowded too close to others at the table. A name card at his place at the table avoids uncertainty about where he is to sit and helps the teacher in planning suitable combinations of children.

Companions can be distracting at times. Eating with other children is fun, and one good eater will influence others, but sociability may need to be kept within bounds by thoughtful spacing and placement of the children. The main business at the table is eating, although conversation has an important place.

The teacher may need to help children by influencing the amount of conversation taking place. Conversation sometimes interferes with eating, for children have not mastered the art of talking and eating. In his enthusiasm for communicating with others, a child may forget about eating. If he is a child for whom the teacher estimates that talking to others has more value at the moment than eating, she may give him time to finish later, as in the case of a shy, withdrawn child who is just "blossoming out" and needs to be encouraged to continue. A different child or a five-year-old who is already socially skilled may need to be reminded at some point to "eat now and talk later."

There may be *practical time limitations* inherent in the situation that determine how much time a child can be permitted to spend at the table. Eating should not proceed by a clock. Just as a "set" toilet schedule does not meet the needs of children, so a "set" length of time to eat cannot mean the same thing to all children. Some are deliberate, and some are quick. These differences are reflected in the time they take for their meals. Meals are served because we need food, and we enjoy eating. There is no special virtue in eating to get through a meal.

REST AND SLEEP

Rest is something children need but often resist, both at home and at the center. Many children find it hard to settle down for a rest or nap because it comes as an interruption in play. It may hold special difficulties when children are in a group and distract each other. The teacher herself must feel very sure that rest and sleep are important if she wishes to communicate this conviction to the children.

Every program should include a rest or quiet period if the children are to avoid getting overtired. In a morning program rest may be before snacks or before lunch. There may be music to listen to or the teacher may read a story. Sometimes a child will need an extra rest. There should be a quiet corner with a cot in it for use whenever a child wishes to rest.

In the full-day program a nap period will follow the lunch period. The children may be expected to leave the table, go to the toilet, brush their teeth, and go directly to rest, or they may have a period of quiet play until the whole group is ready for rest. The schedule will depend on the physical arrangements of space and on the number of staff available. It is desirable, but not always possible, for children to rest in a room other than the room where they have played actively. Whatever the arrangements, the children should sleep or rest on comfortable cots or mats with a sheet and with adequate covers over them.

The teacher can set the stage for naps by seeing that the room is in order and everything is ready for rest, with the room darkened. She will create an atmosphere which suggests rest. She will move quietly herself and speak in a low voice. She will make her expectations clear—that is, she will *expect* the children to come in quietly, remove their shoes and perhaps other garments, and settle down without disturbing others. Her expectations will be reasonable ones. She will give each child time to settle down, with perhaps a whispered word to his neighbor. A child may bring a favorite toy, perhaps, or a picture book to help him relax. The children who do not fall asleep can rest quietly for at least half an hour. Many children will sleep for about two hours after an active morning.

A rest period usually proceeds most smoothly when the children know the teacher well and have confidence in her. The children are more likely to be restless if the adult is new and strange to them or if there are too many adults present. The new teacher must accept the children's restlessness and not let it disturb her unduly. The experienced teacher will give the children time to settle down in their own ways. Teachers are often tired by the time a rest period comes and may be eager to get the children settled. They may find themselves pushing the children into resting. A more relaxed teacher will be better able to help children make the transition from wakefulness to sleep.

Brushing teeth after eating.

John Adams Children's Center

DEPENDENCY NEEDS ARE GREATER AT REST TIME. One can expect the child to make demands on the teacher at rest time because resting is closely associated with experiences with his parents and their care. His need for them may come closer to the conscious level. He reverts to earlier dependencies. He may want the teacher's attention; he may want to have a blanket straightened just to have some contact with her. Failing to get attention, he may be noisy, which is another way of getting attention. He may be less able to bear the teacher's disapproval at rest time than at other times.

At rest time children are likely to be jealous when the teacher's attention goes to other children. The teacher must be able to make each of them feel that there is enough attention for all. If an individual child needs an extra amount of attention, she will make it clear to other children that this child needs particular help today. Prolonged back rubbing is not a desirable way to give attention because it interferes with real resting. Children can accept the fact that at some times a child *needs* particular help. Each child has

171

needed special help at some time. The confident, nurturing person will be most successful in helping the children relax and perhaps sleep.

INDIVIDUAL NEEDS DIFFER.   There are individual differences in the amount of rest children need, and these differences should be respected. Children who fall asleep will probably sleep for varying lengths of time. As each one awakes, he can get up quietly and put on the clothing he removed. Here is an opportunity for children to grow in independence, with the teacher giving only the help that is needed.

After resting, some of the older children who do not take naps have an opportunity for play in small groups before the younger children are up. The teacher may use the period to provide these children with individual learning opportunities and individual attention. There may be opportunities for trips that are not appropriate for younger children or for games and "work" periods that challenge these children.

The teacher will want to consult with the parents about the child's patterns for resting and for naps at home. Knowing what is customary for him at home will help her adapt the schedule at the center to his needs or to allow him the ritual that helps him rest, as she tries to help him develop good patterns for rest and relaxation in his group setting.

We have discussed some of the meanings that toileting, eating, and resting may have for children. We have indicated some of the problems that arise in connection with these routine activities and how the teacher facilitates learning. Now we will look more closely at transition points in the day's program and the meaning these hold for children and for teachers.

TRANSITIONS

Many of the difficulties a teacher faces occur during transitions, the time when the teacher interrupts the child's activity to direct him into a routine activity. Children may delay, resist, or defy directions. Their behavior is appropriate to their developmental level. They want to be independent. They need to assert themselves to test how independent they really are. Everyone finds it hard to face leaving an activity one has enjoyed, but it is often necessary to do so.

Clean-up time is a transition period that often presents difficulties. Children do not always feel ready to put materials away and help with straightening the playroom. It is a challenge to the teacher to devise ways of helping them feel and act like independent, responsible people at this point. The teacher sets an example with her own actions. She reinforces whatever steps they take in helping by her attention and approval. As the

This child sees that the sand is swept off the pavement.

First Step Nursery School

teacher and children work together they talk about what they are doing or about the day's events. Sometimes singing together or making up games will help lighten the task. Some children will give more help than others, but the teacher makes no comparisons.

Some of the problems that arise in connection with routine activities may be related to the physical surroundings in which they occur. A crowded locker area creates problems when children are putting on their outdoor clothing. Cots set up in the playroom may make resting more difficult. A change in the situation may be possible. Sometimes making a change in the schedule itself, the time or the sequence as well as in the physical arrangements, may reduce the difficulties which have been arising.

The National Association for the Education of Young Children has set a criterion covering transitions in quality programs for young children: "Staff conduct smooth and unregimented transitions between activities. Children are not always required to move from one activity to another as a group. Transitions are planned as a vehicle for learning."[4]

Young children are always learning from both planned and unplanned activities. Transitions between activities are integrated into the program as learning opportunities. The emphasis is on procedures that will help prevent problems and conflicts. Teachers will plan carefully for transitions. They will give children advance notice of the coming change, and they will make the transitions gradual rather than abrupt. They will encourage the children to help during the transition. Any waiting should be short. Lining children up is a poor procedure and should be avoided. By using these procedures the teachers help prevent problems and conflicts during transitions.

IT IS IMPORTANT TO RESPECT CHILDREN'S NEEDS TO FEEL INDEPENDENT. Children find great satisfaction in doing a task unaided. Shoes laced in irregular ways, a shirt on backwards, hands only partly clean may be sources of pride to a child because these accomplishments were achieved independently. The drive to be independent, which every healthy child feels, may come up against one of our own needs—the need to help. This need is especially strong when we feel least sure that we can help. By helping, by doing things for a child, we try to prove to ourselves that we are in fact competent, able, and needed. The child's dependency on us reassures us that we have a place in the center.

Watch what happens in the locker area. The teacher who is unaware of the situation's potential for a child to learn is the one who steps in and expertly buttons the button which the child has been fumbling with intently. She takes the child's coat from its low hook and holds it for him. Then she may be surprised when he runs away instead of putting it on. In the washing area she may put the plug in the sink when he is ready to wash his hands, push up his sleeves, and hand him the soap. She deprives him of many opportunities to perform tasks that he can do for himself. She is acting out of her own need to help. If she is to handle her feeling about wanting to help, she must be aware of this feeling as well as aware of the values for the child in being independent. Keeping his need in mind, she will plan the situation so that he has a maximum opportunity to do things for himself. She will keep from helping him needlessly.

---

[4] National Association for the Education of Young Children. (1984). *Accreditation criteria and procedures: Position statement of the National Academy of Early Childhood Programs.* Washington, DC: Author.

When we have recognized the importance of the child's need to be autonomous, as well as the likelihood that we will feel a need to offer help unnecessarily at times, we must still be ready to accept the fact that there are times when the child does need to be dependent on us. Erikson makes it clear that no development is completed at any one stage; we carry on to the next stage the uncompleted tasks of earlier stages. A child may ask for unnecessary help because he wants reassurance that he can still be dependent if he wishes. It may be important to help him with his coat if he asks us, or to tie his shoe when we know he can. In routines we must be certain only that we do not deprive the child of the opportunity to be independent when he is ready.

Projects

1. Observe children during the following transition times. Note the different responses shown by the children and discuss the possible inferences.
    a. toileting
    b. mealtime
    c. nap time
    d. story time
    e. indoor to outdoor time
    f. outdoor to indoor time
    g. clean up time
2. Observe a transition period recording the behavior of the children. What differences in individual needs did you observe? What help did the teacher give? What goals did she seem to have in mind?

For Your Further Reading

Alger, H. A. (1984). Transitions: Alternatives to manipulative management techniques. *Young Children, 39*(6), 16–25. Also in J. Brown (Ed.). (1984). *Administering programs for young children.* Pp. 89–97. Washington, DC: National Association for the Education of Young Children. Classroom management at arrival, group times, clean up, meals, toileting; emphasizing learning and appropriate expectations.

Brazelton, T. B. (1984). *To listen to a child: Understanding the normal problems of growing up.* Reading, MA: Addison-Wesley. Warm, helpful discussion of topics like bedwetting, feeding, and sleeping problems.

Cherry, C. (1981). *Think of something quiet: A guide for achieving serenity in early childhood classrooms.* Belmont, CA: Pitman Learning. Chapter 5 on rest times is particularly helpful.

Davidson, J. (1980). Wasted time: The ignored dilemma. *Young Children, 35*(4), 13–21. Poorly planned transition times may waste as much as one hour each day for children in waiting and boredom. Contains ideas for enrichment of routines and transitions.

Fraiberg, S. (1959). *The magic years: Understanding and handling the problems of early childhood.* New York: Scribner. Includes helpful discussion of physiological routines like sleep, toilet training, and feeding. A psychoanalytic approach.

Mugge, D. (1976). Taking the routine out of routines. *Young Children, 31*(3), 209–217. Routines in classrooms can aid children to understand democratic principles and to feel competent, rather than the negative learnings which often result from routines.

PART FOUR

◆

UNDERSTANDING BEHAVIOR

Miss Annie in School (girl, 2 years 6 months)

11 ♦ The Role of the Teacher

In a center for young children the teacher has a stimulating and challenging role. No two days are ever the same. Each child is unique and has his own individual needs. Childhood is a period when learning is more rapid than it ever will be again. Basic personality patterns are being established. There is an excitement about learning, and the environment is one in which everyone is learning, both children and teachers. The teacher may be tired or discouraged at times, but she is seldom bored. She is rewarded by the growth and the changes she observes in the children.

The teacher's goal is to help each child grow as a person, gain the ability to enjoy and profit from opportunities for learning, and develop his or her potential as an individual and as a member of a group.

In this chapter we will look at the teacher as a person, her skills, and the quality of the relationships she has with children as she guides them in the center. In later chapters in Part 5 we will consider ways in which the teacher may facilitate learning.

THE TEACHER PLAYS AN IMPORTANT ROLE IN THE CHILD'S PERSONALITY DEVELOPMENT

The teacher is an important person to the young child. Her relationships with him will influence both his learning and his development as a person. What she is like as a person may be more important than what she teaches. What she is like determines to some extent what the child is able to learn under her guidance.

Learning is a very personal experience for young children. They learn through experiences with people who are significant in their lives. The first attachment bonds are with parents, their first and probably their most important teachers. From them a child learns a great many things such as language and patterns of behavior. He also begins to learn to trust people and himself, the first task in personality development, according to Erikson. The development of a sense of trust must outweigh mistrust if the child is to achieve healthy personality development. The first task of the teacher when a child enters the group is to start building a relationship of trust with the child. Most children entering a center will have learned to feel a measure of trust in adults and are ready to begin to relate to the teacher with feelings of trust. For her part the teacher needs to show them that she is a trustworthy, reliable person. In some cases the teacher may need to help restore a sense of trust in a child who has not succeeded earlier in building much trust.

The next task in the development of a healthy personality is the achievement of a sense of autonomy or independence outweighing the sense of dependency. To help the child to achieve this task the teacher will give him many opportunities to be independent, to do things his way, and to make choices when possible. She will encourage him to master skills like climbing, riding a tricycle, fitting puzzles together, or building with blocks. By her approval and encouragement she helps him see himself as someone able to do or make things independently while still using the help that may be needed for success. The teacher is in a position to add to the child's confidence and respect for himself as an independent person because of the relationship of trust they have built together.

The teacher also plays an important role in helping children with the third task in personality development, that of encouraging a sense of initiative that outweighs feelings of doubt and guilt. In order to learn and grow children need to feel free to explore, discover, imagine, and create, without being afraid of making mistakes or doing wrong. Developing initiative is the most significant task of healthy three-, four-, and five-year-old children. They are active and eager to explore, make discoveries, and play with their peers. They are also beginning to develop a conscience and feel a sense of responsibility. At this age they sometimes feel too responsible for what happens because of their inexperience. It is very important that the teacher or the parent be aware of the child's feelings. The adult needs to make the situation clear to the child and not to add to his burden of guilt feelings. The adult should define what is acceptable and what is not acceptable, in any case, so that the child can grow in his understanding. The teacher in the center will provide many opportunities for a child to explore his interests, enlarging and enriching them, and she will give him many opportunities for experiences with his peers. She will also make sure that he has opportunities to create with materials and with words and in play with others, such as in dramatic play. At the same time, the teacher makes sure throughout these explorations that she keeps the child safe, so that trust and confidence are not damaged.

The Teacher Accepts and Respects Each Individual Child

A good relationship between a teacher and child makes it easier for the teacher to discipline in constructive ways and easier for the child to respond in desirable ways. The teacher will be friendly and firm in setting realistic expectations for behavior. She helps the child face the consequences of his behavior, without resorting to punishment that stirs resentment but not repentance.

Sand and water allow for active exploration.

Valley College, Campus Child Development Center

The significance for the child in having a teacher whom he likes and who, he feels, likes him is tremendous. Young children see the world subjectively and are influenced by their relationships with people even more than adults.

The child is influenced, too, by his teacher's expectations of his abilities. He tends to behave and achieve accordingly. He needs to have a teacher who appreciates his strengths and who helps him make the best use of his capacities.

We must remind ourselves that the environment from which a child comes has both favorable and unfavorable factors in it. Deprivation of some kind exists in every background. While one child may have experienced poverty in material things, he may be rich in the quality of his personal relationships. Another child may have had poor personal relationships, even though he has lived with material abundance. Each child has had some favorable experience from which he draws strength. It is important that a teacher respect and make use of these strengths.

We are responsible as teachers for accepting and respecting each individual child as another important human being who is trying to cope with difficulties, find satisfactions, and learn. Every child is worthy of the best we have to give him.

The Teacher Helps Children Face Failure in a Positive Way

The teacher gives approval and attention to the child when he achieves or behaves acceptably, but she also can accept his failures and try to turn these to constructive use. She may say to the child at the workbench, "Next time hold the hammer this way, and it may be easier to make the nail go in straight." In saying this the teacher helps the child look for causes, consider what has happened, and improve his performance. His errors become a means of learning and not just a failure. He gains a new perspective and approaches situations more positively.

Sometimes the teacher will say, "I wonder why that happened," if she thinks the child is ready to discover by himself the remedy or reason. In doing this she is helping him take a "problem-solving" attitude, which is very necessary in learning. If he is successful in finding the reason, he gains new confidence in his own capacities. He may discover that the tower he built fell down because the base was not broad enough, or because it was not on a level surface. It is often easy for a child to want to blame someone or to blame himself when something he does fails to work out. He can learn to take a less personal way to face failure. He can learn to look for reasons.

THE TEACHER SERVES AS A MODEL FOR CHILDREN

Every teacher serves as a model for the children in her group. They imitate her actions and attitudes, which become part of what young children learn.

Children sometimes imitate the teacher in unexpected ways. A teacher, looking around the playground one morning, was puzzled to see two boys with jackets thrown over their shoulders. She suddenly recalled that she herself had been wearing a jacket thrown over her shoulders whenever she had a short time to spend outside.

Because children imitate so readily, teachers must be careful not to set models in areas where self-expression is the goal, as in art and music.

The Teacher Serves as Model in the Way She Gives Directions or Suggestions

The teacher who is accustomed to guiding children by positive directions, telling them what they can do or may do, sets a model for children to use as they play or work together. Positive statements are more effective than negative ones. They make it clear to a child what he can do or what he should do. They help children succeed. The teacher's goal is to help children be successful in what they undertake. If children are with teachers who use positive rather than negative statements, they are likely to imitate the teacher's way of giving suggestions. If we listen to these children as they play together, we may be surprised at how often we hear positive directions given. They have gained an important skill in social relations.

In the following situation the teacher emphasized what she felt was the correct response. Three children were playing with picture lotto under the direction of their teacher. Pat was the first to complete his card. He excitedly yelled out, "I win. I win." The teacher, wishing to emphasize the positive rather than the competitive element, said quietly, "You covered your card. Yes, you covered your card." She suggested to Pat that he might help Tyrone and Felicia to cover their cards. Pat was delighted to do this, and his help was accepted willingly. The lotto game was very popular. When it was brought out the next day, Pat happened to be the first to cover his card again. This time he yelled out, "I covered my card. I covered my card." Pat knew what he should say.

The Teacher Serves as a Model in the Way She Meets Frustration

The teacher sets an example for the children in the way she meets the frustrations that are an inevitable part of teaching. Her best efforts in teaching fail at times. She is not always successful. If she accepts this state of affairs, she helps children build a concept of how to live with frustra-

The teacher is sympathetic to the child's grief.

First Step Nursery School

tion. One does not need to lose faith in oneself or in others but can have patience and confidence that the next time will be better.

If the teacher can leave the children free to doubt and question, and sometimes *not* to respond to her suggestions, she is helping them, too. There is uncertainty, and there is flexibility. Both serve purposes which can be constructive. The children can build more trust in themselves as well as in the teacher when frustration and doubt are accepted and acceptable.

THE TEACHER NEEDS TO FACE HER ATTITUDES TOWARD RACIAL AND SOCIAL CHANGES

We have become a multiracial and a multicultural society. Many changes have taken place and are still taking place in social attitudes. The old inequalities of sex, class, and economic condition are no longer acceptable. Racial and cultural biases are not acceptable. The teacher needs to understand these changes, and she needs to be aware of her own biases.

All of us have some biases from the past. These may lie deeper than we realize, but it is important for the teacher to model attitudes that are as free from biases as possible. Every individual has the right to expect to be accepted and judged on his or her own worth as an individual.

In most groups in a center there will probably be children of more than one nationality. They may come from families with different cultural patterns or structures. The teacher is helped in understanding these children if she tries to learn as much as she can about the ethnic and cultural backgrounds of the children in her group. The children may be from African-American, Asian-American, Native-American, or Latino heritages or other cultural settings. She may find it possible to attend celebrations or festivals arranged by one of these groups. She may learn from talking with parents or other people belonging to the cultural group. She may find as a result that some of her attitudes are changing, revealing a bias that she hardly knew she held. The children may look, speak, believe, and behave differently from ways she expects. The teacher may find herself responding negatively to a child or expecting poorer achievement from a child who does not use or speak correct English or does not behave in ways she thinks appropriate. Many so-called deficiencies of children may be simply a difference in cultural background and experience. The teacher may misunderstand the meaning of the child's behavior until she understands more about the culture he comes from, just as the child or the parent may misunderstand hers.

Attitudes of acceptance and understanding may not be enough to overcome all discrimination and bias. The teacher may need to promote positive attitudes of acceptance in children toward persons of all colors, languages, and cultures. She must stop all racial slurs and stereotypes that perpetuate attitudes of discrimination. In Part Five we will consider ways that the teacher may help young children in this area.

Families represented in the groups may include many nontraditional occupations. It is acceptable for women to enter the same range of occupations as men in most cases. The old sex-role stereotypes are changing. Men and women share the tasks at home. More women work outside the home. Family structures are changing. Children of the single or divorced parent, the career mother, and the traditional family may all be represented in the center. The teacher needs to be aware of these changes and to respect them. Her relationship with the children and the families is the same. Each is an individual to be accepted and respected.

THE TEACHER GIVES CHILDREN OPPORTUNITIES TO MAKE DECISIONS

Making decisions for oneself is a part of taking responsibility for one's behavior. In guiding children we look for situations in which they can make their own decisions. We give a child a choice whenever choices are possible. We look for alternatives in action where a child can select what he prefers to do. There are many matters about which the child is not yet ready to make judgments, but there are other situations in which he can make decisions. These opportunities are important for his growth in autonomy. If we give the child a choice or ask for an opinion, we must be sure that it is a legitimate choice or question. If we ask the child, "Are you ready to go now?" or "Are you through painting?" we must be in a position to accept his answer. Here are two examples of a situation that often occurs. Note the different ways in which two parents manage the same situation: Henry is a roly-poly, somewhat immature little boy. His father comes in and says to him, "Are you ready to go?" "No," says Henry sturdily. His father answers, "Well, even if you're not, you're going anyway. Put your things away and come along." His smile relieves his words, but the words suggest a reason that Henry remains immature. He is treated as a much younger child. One senses that he feels helpless. Dick, the same age as Henry, says to his mother when he sees her, "I don't want to go home." His mother answers with a smile, "I know you like it here and you want to stay, but we have to go now. We'll be back in the morning." Her words show that she accepts his feeling. It isn't difficult for Dick to leave.

There is, of course, a danger in giving the child responsibility or authority for which he is not ready. We must remain the confident authority, while we present the child with reasonable alternatives from which he can make his own choices.

The Teacher Provides Many Opportunities for Exploring and Learning

The teacher creates a physical, social, and emotional environment that invites learning through exploration and discovery. She encourages children by the questions she asks and by her own zest for finding out about things. She encourages individual initiative and supports the excitement of discovery, an excitement that begins in early childhood and should be preserved through life.

Here is an example of learning by discovery in a group of four-year-olds, which would not have taken place without guidance from the teacher. A potential conflict, with the teacher's help, became a social studies investigation.

> In a block scheme, a boy had built a fish store. . . . Every time [a girl] went to his store to buy fish, he closed it. Finally, in great irritation she yelled at him, "You can't do that. A store has to sell—that's what it's for, stupid." The teacher approached the children and entered the conversation, first by listening and then by asking, "Can you go shopping in a store anytime you feel like it?" Discussion led to the following conclusions: (1) you do not shop late at night because you have to sleep; (2) stores do have hours for

shopping to which people must pay attention. . . . It was decided that the boy and the girl plus two other children who had joined the discussion would take a walk around the block with the teacher in order to find the answer to her question, "How do you know when a store opens and when it closes?"

They returned from their trip and as they entered the classroom, their newly gained information exploded; "It's on the door," "It's not the same for all the days," "They have a sign." Information was explored and shared. Signs went up on several buildings posting store hours. One child posted times for visits to her house, fixing the hours around the baby's sleeping schedule.[1]

It is worth noting the way in which the teacher guided this opportunity. She "entered the conversation, first by listening and then by asking." She took time to find out what the argument was about and then asked the right question. She guided the discussion and supplied information that the children did not have by making a suggestion about how to find out. The children returned from their trip, excited by their discovery. The results of what they learned appeared in many forms, even the imaginative one of posting a schedule for visiting. It was a social studies and language opportunity with meaning for the children. They gained information and, more important, they had models for problem solving and answering questions. One talks over the solutions to a problem; one investigates; one reorganizes his ideas. Learning can be exciting!

THE TEACHER PROVIDES OPPORTUNITIES FOR SELF-EXPRESSION. An important part of teaching young children is helping them become competent in expressing thoughts and feelings. Language is an important means of expression. A child needs to be able to put his thoughts and his feelings into words if he is to have satisfying social relationships. Teachers must be aware of the many ways in which the excitement of language can be developed.

There are other avenues of expression. For the young child, art media offer important avenues for expressing feelings and for communicating. He uses art media such as paint, clay, pencils, and marker pens freely when they are available. Construction with blocks, manipulative toys, and wood are other ways of expressing ideas and concepts. Body movements and dance are also forms of expression that children enjoy.

All of these avenues of self-expression should be developed in a program for young children. We will discuss the skills needed by the teacher to encourage expression of thought and feeling in Part Five.

[1] Harriet Cuffaro. (1974, 1984). Dramatic play—the experience of block building. In E. Hirsch. (Ed.). *The block book.* Pp. 69–87. Washington, DC: National Association for the Education of Young Children.

These two boys share a quiet moment with their books.
Santa Monica College, Child Development Center

The Teacher Provides Many Opportunities for Experiences with Peers

The social environment created by young children playing and learning together is enhanced when the teacher sets the stage for it. As children play with each other they begin to define relationships, sometimes taking on the role of leader, sometimes of follower. These roles tend to change depending on what the child brings to the activity. A block-building project may find one child directing the others to bring the long blocks from the shelf and the children following these directions, delighting in the camaraderie of belonging to the block-building project. Another time the leader in this activity enjoys the role of being the follower. The teacher observes and rearranges either the structure of the setting or the relationships in the group depending on what will most benefit children's play together.

Young children often need to be taught how to interact with others in a friendly and acceptable manner. Some children need to learn how to be a part of a group of peers and how to enter the group. Emily, a four-year-old who was starting nursery school for the first time, didn't know how to enter the group. She would pick up a handful of sand and throw it at other children as she entered the outside area of the school. Some children ran when they saw her coming; others ran and told the teacher. Emily needed help in entering the group. The teacher first made sure that Emily was met at the gate when arriving and later added another child to the welcoming committee. Slowly Emily began to move into the group.

As children move throughout their day, talking, playing, and working on projects, the teacher plays an important role in helping them to have meaningful experiences with each other. Her role is one of watchful observer, mediator, and comforter when social situations break down.

PLANNING FOR THE USE OF TIME

There will be a structure in the schedule the teacher plans. There are some events that occur every day at regular times, such as snack time, mealtime, rest time. There are other events in the schedule that will change with the seasons or with children's changing interests. The teacher will make sure that opportunities for art, music, and science experiences are always available along with reading to children, looking at books, and storytelling.

The teacher will also plan for blocks of uninterrupted time in order to give children the chance to develop and carry through to completion their projects. Dramatic play lends itself to acting out many themes. Block building may become more and more complex when there is enough time. Both dramatic play themes and block play may develop over many days with changes in the themes in play and increasing complexity in building structures. Some activities soon come to an end. Successful completion of a project gives children a feeling of accomplishment. When a child or a group of children finish a project, they understand something about beginnings and endings and something about efforts that bring results. One can move on to new projects. The sense of completion comes after many repetitions. Maria loved to play with puzzles. She fitted them together time after time, and each day she returned to the puzzles. The satisfaction she felt was apparent in her expression of delight at times. She concentrated on her task. It took some time before she moved on to new activities. Other children may find satisfaction in fast moving dramatic play in small groups. The play evolves and calls for resourcefulness. The play changes each day. All children need blocks of uninterrupted time if they are to carry on self-initiated activities in which the teacher plays only a supporting role.

There will often be situations in which time runs out. Children terminate their play because it may be time for lunch or time for a scheduled activity. The teacher helps children if she gives them the reason, for example, "I'm sorry, but it is time now to get ready for lunch. There is no more time for painting." By stating the reason, the teacher helps children learn that there is a structure in a day and a limit to time. The teacher will avoid saying, "You've played with blocks long enough now." This statement adds nothing to children's understanding. It is misleading and suggests that they have no control over time and what they do in it.

A teacher needs to be sensitive to the times when activities should be terminated because of fatigue, lack of interest in them, or impending trouble. Activities that are initiated by adults should be of a short duration. In one school a young volunteer brought his guitar for a song period with the children. They were delighted and almost all of them gathered around him. The opportunity to have a man in the teaching role was new to them. He adapted his songs to their level, and they participated eagerly as he taught them the words. He continued with song after song, enjoying their close attention. By the time he stopped singing, some of the children were very tired, although only a few had left the group. The children could not settle down for a while after he left. Several children cried, and others were disorganized before they became involved in other activities. Several shorter sessions would have benefited the children much more than the one long session.

THE TEACHER'S ROLE IN USING AUTHORITY

"You're the boss of the whole school," remarked Susan to the teacher as they sat eating lunch together, and she added with deliberation, "Last year the school was all the bosses itself." Susan had evidently been trying for some time to figure out who was "boss" at the center. Her parents were still trying to show her who was "boss" in their house. She must have been puzzled about the center situation at first, until she selected the teacher as the source of authority.

For many people, as for Susan, the problem of authority is a confusing one and remains so all through their lives. As children these people have been made to feel that the role of boss is the most important one. When they are grown, they struggle to do some bossing themselves or to resist being bossed by others. This struggle interferes with their solutions to other problems. They hurt themselves and often the people they love in their efforts either to boss or to resist bossing.

Discipline that leads to a struggle over who is going to be "boss" is damaging to a child. It does not help children respect themselves or others. Like Susan, people who have met this kind of discipline have little concept of what it means to be a responsible member of a group. They are not ready for the self-discipline that democratic living demands.

Authority takes many forms. Some people have experienced authority mostly as a succession of commands or "don'ts." They associate authority with punishment. All of us at some time have met with authority that was needlessly harsh, restrictive, and not based on respect for individuals.

Children develop best when they experience authority based on love and a caring attitude. This kind of authority enables a child to feel safe and free to be himself. Then the problems of authority can be worked out in a way that has positive values for the individual. Our goal is to help children to take increasingly more responsibility for their own behavior until, in the end, they alone are responsible.

Our Own Feelings Are Important When We Use Authority

If the authority we experienced as children was mainly reasonable and sympathetic, we will be able to exercise authority ourselves with more confidence and with more respect for individual needs. Our goal is to help children to take more and more responsibility for their own behavior, that is, to be their own authority. To prepare them adequately for this role we must be clear about our feelings on the subject. We must be aware of the adaptations we have made. Our feelings about these adaptations will facilitate or interfere with the exercise of discipline that benefits the child.

When a child defies us, for example, how much threat do we feel because of his behavior? Are we secure enough to see the child's defiance in the light of what it represents to the child rather than what it means to us? Do we face this behavior by overreacting, because we identify with the rebellious child or because we feel a threat to our own autonomy? Can we be responsible adults, no longer little and helpless, who can support a child in his struggle for independence while maintaining necessary limits for his behavior? Can we be confident, responsible authorities capable of acting with respect and understanding? Let us look at two teachers whose feelings made it difficult for them to exercise authority.

Ms. X was a teacher who had difficulty in helping the children in her class control their behavior. The children often lost their control and engaged in a great deal of destructive behavior. She was a sympathetic person with insight and at times was skillful in turning the group's energies back into constructive activities. After they had overturned the furniture, for example, the children usually did complex block building. They were often creative and played well together, but some of the timid children in the group suffered. They were frightened by their own anxieties after participating in or watching an episode of uncontrolled behavior.

Ms. X had never been able to accept discipline herself. She had grown up as an only child in a strict household. She conformed outwardly but expressed her resistance in indirect ways. She was never on time; she never quite finished a task; she was absentminded. As soon as she was grown, she had left her home. In her work with children she was determined that they should not suffer from the "boss" type of authority, as she had. Because she had not experienced authority as a help, she found it difficult to use it constructively with her group. A sensitive, creative person herself, she gave her group freedom but was not able to meet their needs for the support of limits in their out-of-bounds or destructive behavior.

Ms. S was another teacher who bitterly resented the way in which she had been treated at home as a child. As a child she had too often experienced a form of discipline that served only as an outlet for hostility and aggressive feelings. Her feelings against authority were very strong. She could not limit the children in her group because she would have disliked herself too much for doing it, or she might even have disliked the children for "making" her act that way. She was thus unable to discipline in a constructive way.

It is true that aggressive feelings may come out in the use of authority. People may punish, because they wish to hurt; in punishing they may pour out their aggressive, hostile feelings. At times all of us release feelings in inappropriate ways and with the wrong person. If we face the hostile, aggressive feelings we inevitably have, we are better able to cope with them and find appropriate and constructive avenues for their expression. We can keep or direct them where they belong, and they need not spill out in inappropriate places. We can act with confidence when the limits we impose are meeting the child's needs rather than serving as an outlet for our own feelings.

When we enforce a standard of behavior that interferes with a child's impulse to act as he wishes, we may expect the child to be angry with us or at least to feel resistant or resentful. He has every right to feel this way, but he does not have the right to act out these feelings if the action is destructive to himself or others. We are acting responsibly when we stop this type of behavior.

It is important that we accept and not deny his feelings and help him express his feelings in words. We can say, "Tell me about it." Expressing a feeling in words helps drain off some of the anger the child feels. He is then better able to listen and talk things over with the teacher. He can take a step toward identifying and understanding feelings. This step leads to better control over impulsive behavior. With his feelings identified and "off his chest," the child is ready to channel his energies more constructively. Having a sense of humor and imagination helps in these situations.

We have a right to our feelings, too. In the school a teacher may say to a child, "I feel very cross when you do. . . ." Her words help the child to perceive her feelings and understand the impact of his behavior on another person. We ourselves get angry or annoyed at times, and we must acknowledge our negative feelings and cope with them. It may often help to talk over the kinds of feelings we have with our colleagues or others who can reflect on them with us. As we share our feelings, we may discover new aspects of ourselves as teachers. We may feel more self-respect, and perhaps we can manage our feelings in more mature ways as we work with children.

The child is less bewildered when the feelings he arouses in others are identified directly. Putting feelings into words makes them more manageable. If we as teachers face and manage our own feelings, we help create the kind of climate in which a child can learn to recognize feelings in himself and others and learn to cope with them in ways that are constructive and even creative. He will then be less afraid of his own feelings and those of others.

The Role of Guilt

Feelings of guilt are a necessary part in changing behavior. We must feel sorry about our behavior if we are to make any real change. We can only be truly sorry because we *care*. Fear of punishment does not make this kind of change in a child. As the child develops trust and a sense of autonomy and moves on to the stage of initiative, daring to do things on his own, he begins to feel a sense of responsibility for his acts. Doubt and the fear of being wrong bring feelings of guilt. His conscience is developing. But he is inexperienced, and too often his feelings of guilt spill out over too many actions. The child who said, "I didn't do it" when his mother crashed the car into a tree was feeling that he must be responsible in some way. A measure of guilt may be the first step in changing behavior, but a heavy load of guilt is damaging for a child. He may feel so much guilt that his impulse controls break down. He no longer cares about the consequences of his actions. Authority that relies on increasing a child's guilt may have serious effects on his personality development. As adults we should avoid adding to a child's burden of guilt and shame by the way we use authority, just as we do not interfere when a child must face reasonable consequences and feel guilt that is within his capacity to bear if he is to learn.

THE TEACHER'S ROLE WITH PARENTS

The relationship between the teacher and the parent or caregiver is an important one for them both. The teacher needs to learn about the child from the parent. The parent needs to share with the teacher information about the child, his needs, and what the parent's expectations for the child are as he enters the group. The teacher needs also to know more about the parent's point of view, for parent and teacher must work together for the good of the child.

As we discussed in Chapter 9, in the first interview the teacher will explain the steps taken for the child in entering. She will outline the program and the policies of the center. She will also answer any questions the parent may have. She will encourage the parent to visit and to feel welcome at any time to talk with her again. It is important to begin to develop a relationship of confidence so that the parent feels trust in the teacher, and the teacher begins to understand the parent and her reasons for entering the child. The teacher will need to maintain a relationship with the parent or with the caregiver in which they keep in close touch.

Parents have strong feelings about their children. They may be anxious or uncertain about the separation. They may have little understanding about what the center is really like. Parents may not be in touch with present practices in the care and education of young children. The early childhood education movement is relatively new. Many questions are sure to arise, and the teacher should welcome the questions. She should listen carefully and thoughtfully if she is to understand the meaning of the question fully. She is responsible for helping the parent feel more comfortable and satisfied about having the child in the center. The teacher may be able to make some changes if they are needed while still maintaining the standards of the program. She accepts and respects the parent's viewpoint.

The teacher's relationship with the parents is a professional one in which the teacher offers her knowledge and experience to the parent in the interest of the child. It is not a social relationship as with personal friends. The teacher treats all information the parent gives as confidential. It is never discussed with anyone outside the staff. Confidentiality is the first tenet in professional ethics and must be strictly observed.

When there is a relationship of trust between teacher and parent, both find themselves learning and growing in understanding of young children.

Summary

The teacher of young children needs to be interested in *understanding* people, experiences, and events, rather than in passing judgment on them. The teacher also needs to be *sensitive* and *responsive*, able to "listen with the third ear" to what the child may be trying to say through his behavior. The teacher should know the satisfactions of learning and be able to *appreciate the child's accomplishments* as he masters each stage in development. With the help of such a person the child can grow comfortably as a whole person.

The child also needs a teacher who can *communicate* with him, both in language and in expression and gesture, with a smile or a nod, as well as an approving word. He needs a teacher who is aware of his or her own feelings and is able to *express feelings* as well as ideas in constructive and clear ways. The child needs a teacher who *values spontaneity* and yet is able to maintain an *orderliness* in activities and in the setting. In addition, the child needs a teacher who is *imaginative* and *resourceful* and who has a *sense of humor*. Few of us show all these qualities in all situations or all the time. We have our weaknesses as well as our strengths, but we grow and change with experience.

Projects

1. Observe the teacher in a nursery school or day-care center and record incidents in which she did any of the following:
   a. created a climate for discovery
   b. extended and enriched an interest or purpose initiated by a child
   c. allowed time for a child to complete a task
   d. played a supportive role in building a child's self-confidence
   e. helped a child to solve a problem for himself
   f. helped two or more children to cooperate

For Your Further Reading

Ashton-Warner, S. (1963). *Teacher.* New York: Simon and Schuster. A remarkable account of a young and unconventional teacher working with Maori children.

Jones, E. (1978). Teacher education: Entertainment or interaction? *Young Children, 33*(3), 15–23. Innovative look at learning environments for those learning to be teachers, using the same dimensions as children's learning environments: mobility, softness, intrusion, complexity, and openness. Considers what actually happens in some quality teacher education classes.

Jones, E. (Ed.). (1978). *Joys and risks in teaching young children.* Pasadena, CA: Pacific Oaks College. Unusually valuable contribution in chapter "The Invisible Child" as well as others on emergent curriculum and teachers' roles.

Katz, L. G. (1978). Challenges to early childhood educators. In L. G. Katz (Ed.). (1978). *Talks with teachers.* Pp. 57–66. Washington, DC: National Association for the Education of Young Children. Four "generic teaching principles" that apply to all teacher-learner encounters, whether children or adults are the learners.

Phyfe-Perkins, E. (1981). *Effects of teacher behavior on preschool children: A review of research.* Urbana, IL: ERIC Clearinghouse on Elementary and Early Childhood Education. ED211 176. A brief summary of research findings on direct teacher effects and indirect teacher effects, which supports the idea that behavior of adults in early childhood education does indeed have an impact on children.

Spodek, B. (1985). *Teaching in the early years* (3rd ed.). Englewood Cliffs, NJ: Prentice-Hall. Intended for those preparing to teach preschool through primary grades, covering curriculum, teaching, and evaluation. Curriculum chapters integrate many sources, practical and theoretical.

I Like to Play with My Friends (girl, 4 years)

12 ◆ The Role of Play in Social Relationships

The whole panorama of life is lived over again in the play of children. If there is any way of gaining knowledge particularly suitable to this stage of development, it is in the play which they spontaneously devise but which needs nevertheless an attentive teacher for its support and nourishment.[1]

THE VALUES OF PLAY

Susan, not quite three years old, was in the kitchen with her mother who was preparing for a tea party. "You may put the cupcakes on this big

[1] B. Biber. (1967). *Young deprived children and their educational needs.* Washington, DC: Association for Childhood Education International.

plate," said the mother in answer to Susan's wish to "help." Pleased at the task, Susan carefully placed the cakes one by one on the plate until it was covered. Then she faced a dilemma. There were several cup cakes left but there was no space left on the plate. She stood looking, uncertain and thoughtful, and then she began placing each remaining cup cake exactly on top of one of those already on the plate. Susan exclaimed with delight, "Look, caps!" The incident illustrates how a young child can use an experience in a playful way and in the process solve a problem imaginatively and enjoy her achievement.

From infancy on, all healthy children enjoy play. Play is at the heart of any program for young children. Play makes a major contribution to the physical, social, emotional, and intellectual development of children. Children explore, discover, and learn in play. Children make contacts with others in play and begin learning about relationships with their equals. Children use play as a means of reducing their fears, anxieties, and aggressive feelings. Spontaneous dramatic play, alone or more often with others, fosters imagination, resourcefulness, and reasoning. Play brings its own reinforcement, and the child puts wholehearted effort into it. Healthy children in favorable environments spend a great deal of their waking time in play.

In our somewhat compulsive society play is often not respected, because it does not seem directly productive. Yet the creative achievements of scientific thought depend on sustained attention and imaginative ways of perceiving and dealing with reality, the very qualities that appear in children's play. We need to appreciate the tremendous significance of play for children. Teachers who observe children as they play can gain important insights into what children are thinking and feeling. Children need teachers who value children's play.

In this chapter we will consider the ways in which play contributes to social learning and personality development. In later chapters (17–20) we will discuss ways in which play fosters learning in a variety of areas: motor, language, music, art, mathematics, and the sciences.

Early Play

The beginnings of play appear in infancy when the baby starts to be aware of people and objects. First the baby plays with his fingers, moving them and staring intently at them, and later with his toes. We notice the concentration that goes with any satisfying play activity. As his coordination improves, he fingers an object, bangs it, grasps it tightly, only to let go when another attractive object presents itself. He is learning about the "me" and the "not me," about objects and their qualities and what he can do with them. He smiles, and his mother or other caregiver responds. There is mutual play between them as the adult is caring for him. He is learning about relationships.

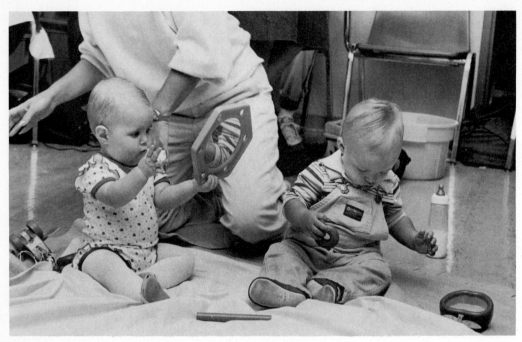

Jennifer and Sam explore, discover, and learn in their play.

Santa Monica College

The playful modes of responding begin early in the games parents play with infants, such as in peek-a-boo and dropping and picking up objects as well as in smiling, repeating sounds, and bouncing on the knee. These are games that have no rules. They are forms of relating to people, of finding mutual responses, and of playing together. These kinds of responses will later be elaborated in play with other children.

Playful Behavior Depends on a Capacity to Trust

Being able to play freely implies a sense of trust. Building up a sense of trust, as Erikson points out, is the first and most basic task in healthy personality development. Its foundation is laid in the child's early experience in being cared for by a loving, responsive caregiver.

A mother or caregiver who is reliably present when the infant needs her and who can regulate her giving to his needs, who sees and responds to him as an individual, enables him to move into spontaneous playfulness. He can test out and discover his enlarging world. He can become involved in relationships with other people. Playing is a sign of health, made possible by a favorable environment.

As a toddler the child still plays best in the presence of an adult whom he knows and can trust. Even three-year-olds who are playing together need a responsible person nearby and readily available, someone on whom they depend but not someone in a "managerial" capacity. The adult's role is to provide the setting and to assist by enriching and extending the play as she observes a need, giving guidance and the techniques for play.

Transitional Objects

Sometime during the first year most young children find a favorite object. It may be a cuddly toy or a blanket to which they become attached. It becomes their first possession and serves as a comforter, a defense against anxiety. It seems to represent the early security of contact with the mother. It stands in place of the mother as a symbol to tide the child over when she is not present or when the child is under strain. This transitional object has properties for the child that ordinary objects do not have, standing as it does between his inner world of feeling and fantasy and the outer world of realities to be faced. Possessing this object, he is freer to proceed with playing. We see the use made of such a symbol by children who bring an object from home in order to make the adjustment easier as they enter a group. We, for our part, need to respect the special qualities with which

Mother and baby play together.

Santa Monica College

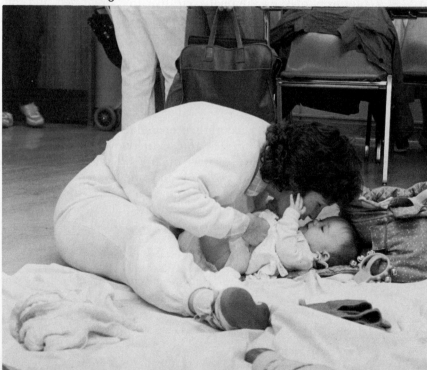

such an object is endowed. The attachment weakens as the child becomes more secure and is involved in a wider variety of play relationships.

Settings for Play

We discussed some of the equipment and materials needed for a favorable play environment in Chapter 4. We also considered the adequacy and use of space and time provided for play. There should be spaces where one child or a small group of children can play without being disturbed, open spaces for activities like block building, space where buildings can be left and worked on over a period of time, outdoor space that is full of variety and interest. Every group can use supplementary "bits and pieces" or "junk" as well as the standard equipment and raw materials that have many uses. A schedule should provide both flexibility and a framework for ordered activities. These are all considerations that promote a rich play experience.

Children need to play often with materials in what appears to be random play, "messing about," before they can use the materials to the best advantage in problem solving. It is a kind of "as if" or "what if" exploration of the materials in play to discover what their possibilities are before they can make use of them. Watch a child at play and observe how he tries out possibilities, finds new uses for objects, arranges, combines, pretends, and through these activities comes to understand more about the materials.

The teacher's "ingenuity and resourcefulness in providing the necessary equipment must be combined with understanding of the value of different forms of play, e.g., dramatic, creative, free, organized, and constructional."[2] All these forms of play have a place in a center for young children.

Children Play to Master Feelings

"In the preschool years play is the child's principle means of solving the emotional problems that belong to development."[3] Children have many fears, the fear of being left or deserted, the fear of being hurt and helpless, and sometimes the fear of their own violent impulses. Children use play as a way of reducing and gaining mastery over these fears and anxieties. As we watch children at play we observe how often they take the role of the one who punishes and controls and who does the going away and leaving. By reversing roles they are helped to deal with their feelings in these situations. We also see this in the frequency with which "doctor-nurse" play appears when a child has had a painful experience with doctors or a hospital.

[2]D. W. Winnicott. *The child and the outside world*. (1957). New York: Basic Books.
[3]Ibid.

Play is also a way for children to handle the problem of being "little" in a world of big people. In play they can identify themselves with "big" roles and lessen the inevitable frustrations of growth. Notice which child wears the helmet or goggles. It may be a child unsure of his place in the group. Children may use gun play or "superhero" play to help them feel big and powerful. Whatever we may feel about the use of guns and this kind of play we need to accept the fact that it meets a need for the child. Freer of fear or anxiety, children can go on to master other problems with more confidence.

Children Play to Make Contact with Others

It is in play and only in play at first that children make contact with other children. Through play with others a child begins to be aware of the feelings of other children. He is better able to understand that others may be sad, happy, afraid, or frustrated or that they may want to possess or be first. These feelings are not his alone but belong to others as well. They can be dealt with in an outer world and managed with help.

In playing together, children share ideas and extend the range of one another's experience. They make friends through play. In their dramatic play they re-create and rehearse roles and seek to understand better their common problems in family life. Play with other children seems to be essential to healthy growth.

RELATIONSHIPS IN GROUPS, LIVING AND LEARNING THROUGH PLAY WITH OTHERS

Children's relationships in a center will differ from their relationships at home because the group in the center consists of contemporaries. Playing with a group of equals is significantly different from being a member of a family. We can add to our understanding of what relationships mean to each child as we observe them in their group living.

Readiness for Social Experience

Readiness for social experience with groups will depend on the child's earlier experiences in his family and the kind of group the child enters. If the adults the child has known in his home have enjoyed play with him and have treated him with respect, the child is readier for experiences with other adults and for the give and take of play with others. If he has felt secure at home in possessing love which has seldom been withheld, he will have confidence when he enters a group. If he has experienced a conditional kind of love, "Mother won't love you if . . . ," he is likely either to

Putting on grown-up clothes.

Hill an' Dale Family Learning Center

make heavy demands for attention in a vain search for satisfaction or avoid or resist contacts with others. This child is fortunate if he enters a group where the teacher has the understanding, the patience, and the time to help him feel respected and valued.

Children are individuals, and they reveal some of their differences in play. The same situation has different meanings for each child. Here is an example: Patty and Lois had been playing house together when they decided to take their babies for a walk. They each pushed their doll buggies to the far end of the playroom. Lois looked back and saw two boys in their playhouse. "Someone's getting into our house," she said anxiously. Patty turned around. "Oh, we have company," she exclaimed joyfully and hurried back to welcome the boys. Patty expects friendliness, while Lois seems to expect nothing but trouble.

Children May Gain a More Realistic Concept of Self through Group Play Experience

One of the most significant values for the child in being a member of a group of equals lies in his chance to find out more about what kind of person he really is through his play experience. He has an opportunity to build a more realistic concept of himself as a person apart from his membership in a family.

In the family group each member is valued or should be valued because he or she belongs to that particular family, regardless of what one may be or do. We do not need to prove our worth in order to belong to the family group.

In a group of contemporaries, on the other hand, the place each one of us holds depends more on our skill and what we have to offer the group. We must measure ourselves against others who are like us, finding our strengths and facing our weaknesses, winning some acceptance and meeting some rejection. When we experience success, it is based to a great extent on achievement. The limitations we face are likely to be real rather than arbitrarily imposed. A favorable family situation helps us to feel secure, but experiences with our own age group help to develop an awareness of ourselves and of social reality which family experience alone cannot give. Playing with age-mates provides this self-awareness.

We should mention the effect of discriminations of any kind on the development of the sense of self. When our position in the group does not depend on our worth to the group or the contribution we bring, we are likely to build a distorted sense of self. We may fail to value ourselves or others. The distortions about self that result from discrimination and prejudice are reflected in a loss of potential contributions to society and in diminished individual growth.

A realistic sense of one's individual identity, of who one is, is important to everyone. For example, twins have some special problems in establishing this sense of individual identity. The adult can help twins by avoiding thinking of them or referring to them as the twins. She can call them by their individual names and, although she will respect the special relationship they have with each other, she will arrange separate experiences for them whenever she can. She may place them at different tables at lunchtime or take them on trips at different times.

Self-Confidence

Besides building a more realistic picture of who he is, the child begins to feel less helpless and little in a group of other children. In the world of adults the child really is helpless. When playing in a group of children he is among equals. He may feel able to act in ways that he would not dare to on his own.

It may be difficult for a teacher to accept group defiance unless she appreciates what it may mean to the child. A small group of four-year-olds, for example, may climb to the top of the jungle gym when they are told it is time to come inside. They are playing a new role, doing the thing they may have wanted to do many times in the past. They are no longer helpless children, dragged away from play by a powerful grown-up. They are powerful people, high above the adult, asserting themselves in their play.

The teacher in such a situation does not need to panic or feel threatened in her authority, although it is easy to have this feeling. She can allow them their brief moment of power in their play. Inside themselves, they know they are children and she knows that she is an adult, responsible for bringing them inside. She may perhaps manage the matter in a playful way, pretending they are spotters for people from outer space, or she may say, "I'm ready to pull you home in the wagon," or she may seriously discuss with them, "I wonder why it is that you don't want to come in now." To this question she may get some replies that give her a lot of insight into how things look to them and what they dislike. Teacher and children will learn from this method of resolving the situation to their mutual satisfaction. Everyone is the better for reaching a solution together.

Children Find That They Can Share Attention and Like Teachers

Children in groups have the opportunity to face and manage the feelings they have about wanting a big share of the adult's attention. Sharing the teacher's attention with others is less difficult than sharing the attention of one's mother. If the teacher gives her attention freely and generously when children ask for it, she helps them feel that there is enough for all. They are less likely to feel deprived at the times when they cannot have attention. They are more likely to be satisfied. It may be easier to learn this lesson in a center group than at home.

The teacher helps a child feel secure by giving freely to him what he may need in the way of attention and materials for his play. The child who experiences a generous giving by the teacher will be more likely to give freely to others himself.

The Teacher Helps with Techniques for Getting Along with Others in Play

We can help children by suggesting good ways of approaching others or by helping them to understand the feelings that lie behind the approaches of other people, however clumsy these approaches may be.

An approach is usually more successful if the approaching child has some suggestion about what he might be or do or if he makes some contribution to the play in progress. A straight request, "May I play with you?" is often doomed to fail even if it is accompanied by the adult word "please." In helping a child the adult offers more help if she can suggest something specific to the child that he might be or do. Another advantage in this technique is that if one is rejected in one role, one can always find another role or a different activity to suggest. This way there is more protection against failure.

Sometimes the teacher may need to enter the play, taking a role herself, to help the less skillful child and withdrawing when she is no longer needed. She may demonstrate a technique by saying the words for the child, "Doctor, I think my baby needs a shot," to help carry on "doctor" play. She may forestall difficulty by suggesting, "There will be more room for the building over there," when two builders are encroaching on the territory of others.

Children are often very realistic and successful. Terry calls to Tommy, "Say, Tommy, you'd better let Doug play with us because he won't let me have the rope unless he plays, and I want it."

Possessing something desired by others is as much of a social advantage at three as at thirty-three. A wise teacher may utilize this fact in helping the shy child. Letting the child introduce a new piece of equipment or bring something from home for the group to use may help him feel more accepted and give him added confidence. Obviously, such a technique should not be depended on too heavily or for too long, but it can sometimes be the basis for a social start.

Offering something in return for something else one wants is a successful device. Some children have amazing skill in making a second object desirable when they want the first. Even secondary roles can be made attractive by an imaginative child.

Regan, for example, wanted to join the group playing police officer mounted on tricycles, but there were no other tricycles. Terry encouraged her to join anyway, saying, "You can be a walking policeman, Regan. They have walking policemen. You can play if you are a walking policeman." He made it sound worthwhile, so Regan became a "walking policeman."

Terry is already a past master at working out compromises. On another occasion he was busily building with blocks when Regan wanted him to play house with her again. He satisfied her by saying, "I'll live over there with you, but I'll work here. And I'm working now." He went on with his building. Terry has had many successful experiences of getting along with others. He has confidence, and his confidence shows in the way he meets his problems.

As we listen to children in their play, we find that they approach others in friendly ways far more frequently than we may have been aware. We may not have noticed their consideration for each other, because our attention is more likely to be directed to the times when they hit or grab. We will find, too, that there is more friendly behavior in a group in which the children are receiving courtesy and consideration from the adults.

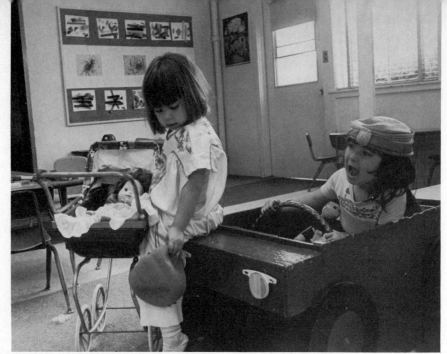

"You are in my way." Children in centers gain experience in living together.

Jean Berlfein

SOCIAL CONCEPTS ARE LEARNED THROUGH PLAY

Children in Groups Learn About Sharing and Taking Turns

An area in which children often need help from the adults is in learning about property rights and "taking turns." Playing in a group of equals provides many opportunities for learning in this area, and the child's concepts develop from his experiences in the group.

Since property rights are considered very important in our society, the child must begin early to learn about possession. In his home he discovers that some things are not his to touch. The wise parent helps him accept this fact by giving him something that is his when she takes away something that he cannot have. She teaches him that some things are his, and she does not insist that he share the things that are his until he is willing and ready to share. She will find that he can share first with people he knows and likes, and then slowly he can broaden his ability to share in most situations.

The child in a group continues his learning about sharing, taking turns, and possessions. Equipment at the school does not belong to individuals but to the group as a whole. No child feels as threatened by a sense of loss when he shares group objects as he might in sharing things that belong to him personally. Two simple principles can be established to cover most of the situations. First, when a person is through using a piece of equipment like a tricycle or swing, it "belongs" to the next person who may wish to use it. One does not continue to claim a thing one is no longer using. Second, after one has used a piece of equipment for a time, one may have to let someone else use it even though one is not through; but one can expect to get it back again.

When we teach children about "turns" we must be sure to follow through in the situations. If a child gives up a swing so that another child may have a turn, we must see that the first child gets it back afterward if he still wants it. Even if he isn't standing there waiting, it may be wise to say, "Johnny, Jane has had her turn now and you can have the swing again if you wish." This clarifies the concept and prevents the child from feeling that taking turns really means losing something.

A group of four-year-olds were playing with boats in a large pan of water where there were also two play turtles. Michelle had a boat but wanted a play turtle. She picked up the turtle that Davy was playing with. "Hey, that's mine," said Davy, and he quickly grabbed it back.

The teacher accepted his assertion of his right to the play turtle, but she commented to Michelle, "It's hard to want a turtle and find that someone else is playing with it."

Davy then turned to Michelle, "Here, this one will be for both of us. I'll share it with you," and he shoved it across to her. It often happens that the child who can assert himself freely can also share easily when he perceives the situation. He can feel good about sharing.

Special Cases Arise under This Concept of Property Rights

An interesting situation is sometimes created by the children themselves. An aggressive child may prefer a certain piece of equipment. Almost before the teacher is fully aware of what is happening, he may establish that it is "his," and the other children, fearing his attack, may prefer to leave it for him and give up their turn with this piece of equipment. The teacher must be alert to such situations and protect the other children in their right to use all equipment equally. Charles, whose aggressiveness was making him unpopular, preferred a red tricycle. With his usual lack of awareness of the needs and feelings of others, he proceeded to take it when he could. It became important for the teacher to accept responsibility for maintaining the right of others to use the coveted red tricycle. It was important because Charles needed to have other children feel friendly toward him. No one in the group was more eager to be liked. It was also important for the teacher to watch this situation because the other children needed to be successful in standing up for themselves in the face of the threat Charles offered them.

Bill was a quiet, thin child who stayed aloof from the children and the teachers. One day he discovered the large red wagon. It may have been like one he had at home. Whatever the reason, he began to play with it almost exclusively and could not bear to share it with another child. The teacher felt that it was important to protect Bill in his use of the wagon for a time. She helped the more secure children find a substitute whenever possible and allowed Bill time to grow more sure of himself at school before she expected him to take turns with the wagon. The time comes, of course, when a child like this should be ready to accept the standards of the group. The teacher must watch for this readiness and, for the sake of his relationships with others, not prolong needlessly the child's dependence on one piece of equipment.

CHILDREN ADJUST TO THE GROUP THROUGH PLAY

Children Find Their Place in the Group Step by Step

In the center most children have temporary or shifting relationships with other children. Two children may play together for a morning or for a few days, drawn by a mutual interest in digging a hole, playing firefighter, or setting up housekeeping somewhere. Then each will have an equally close but short-lasting friendship with someone else. But even in these shifting relationships there are likely to be certain children who are rather consistently antagonistic to each other or attracted for reasons we may not fully understand. We can help children better if we are aware of their feelings of liking and not liking, so that we can be careful to use the one wisely and not to add to the other.

Rivalry Creates Problems

One of the least helpful things that the teacher can do is to encourage direct competition among children. Competitive situations breed ill will. Comparing children, holding one up as an example to others, is unfair to all because of the hostility it arouses. "See who will finish first," or "See how much faster Jane is dressing," or "See how quiet John is"—all these comments are likely to make children like each other less rather than more. They make others appear to be rivals or competitors rather than friends.

The teacher must be aware that young children, in part because of their dependency, will be competing for her attention. Comparisons increase the rivalry they feel. She should be very careful to do nothing to increase jealous feelings. These feelings can cause real unhappiness. Often a child will misbehave at rest or at the table because he wants the attention that the teacher is giving another child. His teacher must be ready to reassure him with a word or a smile that she cares about him too.

Close friendships evolve in group life.

Hill an' Dale Family Learning Center

Close Friendships Are Often a Source of Strength

Sometimes children discover one particular friend, and from this close friendship they develop confidence and assurance. There is nothing much better at any age level than having a special friend. The confidence and assurance that comes from feeling that one is liked by an equal, sought after, and depended on make possible a great deal of development. Such friendships are worth encouraging, even though at one stage they may mean that the pair excludes others. The friendship is likely to lead later on to a growth in friendliness. As friends, they can show consideration for each other's feelings.

Stephen and Francis were friends. Stephen ran out to the playground one day carrying a fireman's hat and yelled, "Francis, here's a fire hat. Put it on fast." Francis replied, "I don't need it. I'm an astronaut." Then he added, "But I'm your friend," and the two ran across the playground together. In rejecting the hat, Francis was careful not to let his friend feel rejected.

Mickey can assert himself but remain friendly. Lisa had bumped her truck into Mickey's dump truck. Very angrily he said, "Hey, you can't bump into my truck. I don't like that; you can't do that," and almost in the same breath he added, "But you're a nice girl," and he blew her two kisses!

Children who are not aggressive may still fail to find close friends. Beth was not aggressive at all. In fact, she sought affection from children and adults. She would run after any teacher saying, "Lady, I love you." In spite of Beth's words her relationships with people were superficial and lacked warmth. Beth had not received the love she needed from her parents. The quality of the relationships each child has experienced in his home influences and limits the kinds of relationships he is able to establish outside his home. Sometimes a teacher can supply the child with a relationship sufficiently warm to make up for a deficit so that the child can achieve an adequate measure of social satisfaction.

If we were to sum up our goals as we work with children in groups, we might say that they all lead in the direction of helping the children like each other more rather than less because of what we do. We might use this as a yardstick. Will the children like each other better if we do this? If children are friends, they will find it easier to get along together. If the techniques they use are constructive ones, they will find it easier to live with others.

As teachers we may have to redirect children as they try to unload hostility onto other children. Louise and Stevie were washing their hands side by side. Louise carried a heavy load of hostile feeling and was always attacking others in a critical way. She said, "Stevie's a bad boy." The teacher replied casually, "Oh, he's my friend, and you're my friend. Isn't it nice that I have two friends?" Stevie beamed, and Louise picked up the idea with, "and Anne's your friend and Mike and Jim." "Yes," said the teacher, "there are lots of friends here."

Isolation Should Not Be Used As Punishment

We sometimes see a parent or teacher isolating a child as punishment for not getting along with others. We have come far enough in our discussion to be aware that punishment may be undesirable because of the load of resentment and hostility that may accompany it. While the child may not repeat a particular act after being punished, he is not likely to feel more friendly toward others or to get along better with them because of it. Isolation or being made to sit on a chair deprives him of the chance to have other, and perhaps better, experiences. It also labels him as "bad" in the eyes of the group and thus adds to his difficulties in getting along with others.

Isolation may be desirable when it is used with a child whose difficulties are the result of overstimulation and fatigue because of too many experiences. In this case, the teacher may accept the child's need of a simpler environment. She will try to achieve it without giving him a feeling that isolation is a form of punishment. She may suggest a story alone or a walk, or she may put him in a room with his favorite toy for a rest, explaining that he will get along better with the others after a rest. She may remove a child who is disturbing other children and put him where he can be free to do as he wishes, but she will not do it as punishment for his failure.

Judy is a tense child, very jealous of her twin brother whom she feels her parents prefer. She has trouble getting along with other children because she seems to see them as rivals. She put it this way to the teacher one day.

> JUDY: "I want to be a wicked witch."
> TEACHER: "I wonder why you want to be a wicked witch?"
> JUDY: "Because they cause spells on people."
> TEACHER: "You mean there are really too many people around and you would like to get rid of them?"
> JUDY: "Yes, there are too many, and I'm going to be a witch and get rid of them."
> TEACHER: "Sometimes it is hard to have so many people around. When you feel like that, we could go off by ourselves where it is quiet until you feel better."

They went into the teacher's office where Judy played with clay. By the time she had finished, she was quite relaxed. Her voice was pitched lower, and she said she wanted to go back with the others.

As we observe children in the center, we are aware that the satisfaction they find in all activity is enhanced by the fact that other children are sharing it, just as we ourselves enjoy experiences that we can share with others. Whether children play cooperatively or merely side by side, they show us that each experience has more meaning for them because it is a group experience. Children belong together.

Kay expressed in her own way what should be our goal in group relationships. She and another child were on a walk with their teacher when they met a stranger who stopped to inquire whether the girls were sisters. "No," replied the teacher, "just friends." Kay smiled at him. "We make friends out of people at our school," she said.

DRAMATIC PLAY—AVENUE FOR INSIGHT

Dramatic play is of absorbing interest to children. In it they relive and try to clarify situations they have met. By observing dramatic play we increase our insights into how children see the world and how they feel about relationships among people. Dramatic play is an important source of satisfaction and learning for children.

With time, with freedom from interference, with props, the children act out what is important to them. Because of all its values the good center encourages dramatic play by careful planning.

Children Play for Many Reasons

There are many reasons why children play. They play because it gives them *pleasure*, as was the case with the child who was delighted with her creation of "caps." They play because they have an *urge to explore and discover*. The infant discovers his fingers at one stage and spends time moving them and gazing at them intently. The preschool child is absorbed as he pours water into the sand, watching how it runs down the channels he has dug. Children also play because of an urge to *master a skill* or *solve a problem*. A toddler will return again and again to a stairway, climbing up and coming down until he does it easily. Another child will persist in riding a tricycle until he rides with skill. Children play *to make friends* for it is one important way that young children form relationships with one another. Play also serves as a means of *mastering the emotional problems* that inevitably come with growth. It is essentially *creative*, involving all the child's capacities.

Dramatic play may occur as part of any activity. It is most likely to occur when children are playing together, trying to understand and make sense out of what they see and hear, and mastering feelings of fear, anxiety, or anger.

Family dramas are among the themes most frequently enacted. Relationships of fathers and mothers and of mothers and children are an almost universal theme in dramatic play. Cooking, setting the table, washing, ironing, caring for the baby, going to the store, carrying on telephone conversations, disciplining children, entertaining friends, dressing up, and going to the doctor are activities that are carried on day after day as children strive to clarify for themselves the grown-up world. They may act out roles they have seen on television. These roles change frequently, and they often reflect the confusions and anxieties that result from television viewing. Some of the roles that children are familiar with that may be included are firefighter, bus driver, and gas station attendant. One has only to listen to a group playing in the housekeeping corner or building a structure on the playground to realize how much talking there is among children at play.

PLANNING FOR DRAMATIC PLAY. In planning it is important that the program be flexible, so that there is a chance for dramatic play to continue once it has started. Children need uninterrupted time for developing their dramas—not just bits of time between scheduled activities. Supervision that is casual and unobtrusive is important too, if the play is to have meaning to the children. They often need suggestions, but they do not need direction.

Heading the list of desirable props that encourage dramatic play are materials for homemaking play. Dolls, doll carriages, beds, tables, chairs, dishes, an iron and ironing board, and telephones are among the things

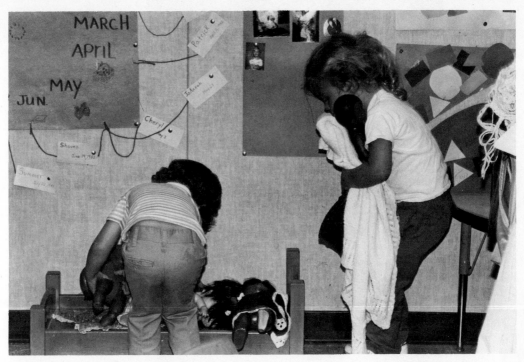

These girls put their dolls to bed.

Valley College, Campus Child Development Center

which will be used. The doll family should be large and should include several "babies." In one group, the most popular doll was a baby doll with eyes painted shut as though she were sleeping. Black and brown dolls should be included. Many centers include anatomically correct dolls, both male and female.

Group play is promoted by having at least two things of a kind—two beds, two telephones, two or more doll buggies, and plenty of dishes and chairs for company. All the equipment should be simple in construction and substantial so that it can take hard usage without the need for limits to save the equipment and perhaps lessen the value of the play for the children. If a bed is strong enough to hold a child, he can use it to act out the part and thus enter more directly into the play and gain more from it.

Variety results from the introduction of materials that can serve many purposes, such as boxes and boards. These things can be used by imaginative children in many ways. Cardboard cartons will serve for a morning of play in endless ways. A ladder and a short piece of hose may suggest a whole fire department and all its activities. A bicycle tire pump and a short piece of hose may be the beginning of a gas station, where wagons and

Hammering a piece of hard plaster helps this child deal with frustration.

Bakersfield College

tricycles are serviced by eager attendants. Empty cereal boxes, butter cartons, cans with smooth edges, paper, and string may transform a house into a store, with the wagons turning into delivery trucks. Raw materials, such as squares of brightly colored cloth for costumes, bring variety into the play. The resourceful teacher will provide materials which suggest uses limited only by the imagination of the children themselves. With the guidance of an observant teacher, dramatic play situations can contribute significantly to the children's learning.

CHILDREN USE DRAMATIC PLAY AS A WAY OF COPING WITH AGGRESSIVE, DESTRUCTIVE FEELINGS. As mentioned earlier, children are helped to deal with their feelings by reversing roles. Here is an example of a child's play that shows us his efforts to master conflict by reversing roles. David, a three-and-a-half-year-old, is playing by himself with some small doll figures and furniture, while the teacher sits nearby. He talks to himself as he plays. A comfortable, happy child, his words nevertheless reveal something of the conflict all children feel during the process of socialization. He puts the smallest doll in a bed, saying, "She has to stay right in her bed. If she makes a noise, I'm going to spank her little bottom—spank her

214

little bottom—spank her little bottom." He turns to the teacher. "She's a nasty little girl because she got up and made a noise, didn't she? She's a nasty little girl. She has to go sound to sleep." He turns back to the doll and continues as if two people were talking together. "Quit doing that. I'm just going to stay downstairs all day. Shut up. It's not daytime. It's still nighttime. I want to stay up all day. Do you want to peepee or not? You're not going to peepee. Stay right in your bed."

In his play David appears to be coping with feelings of resentment about the inevitable issues in conforming to adult standards and resentment of being little and unable to express his feelings. David's parents were comfortable and friendly people. It is unlikely that they were severe in their discipline. This may have made it possible for David to play out this drama. A child from a less favorable background might be unable to express the resentments that all children experience in the process of growing up. He is probably reassured by the teacher's presence, although she makes no comments. He feels her acceptance. She is there to steady him if the play should become too disturbing.

In discussing this issue of expressing resentments one parent described her doll play as a child. She could remember spanking her doll and saying "You must eat all of your spinach," even though she had no recollections of her parents spanking her and making her eat foods she disliked. In fact, she recalled her childhood as one of happy family life. Yet she distinctly remembered being quite punitive with her dolls.

In dramatic play children often act out aggressive, destructive feelings. It is important to accept them in play, being sure only that the children are safe and that the impulses are under control and kept on the pretend level. An adult may need to remain near to "steady" a group that is acting out negative feelings, as in a war game or a fire play. It is important to the children to know that they can stop or that they will be stopped before they do real harm. Without this help the play may not serve the purpose of draining hostility and keeping it within manageable proportion. It may only increase the anxiety of some children about their ability to handle their impulses. As adults we should have no hesitation about making a suggestion, redirecting or limiting play that we can see is going "out of bounds."

In redirecting play, we do not want to deny expression to negative feeling. We must avoid an adult tendency to want only "good" behavior. Here is an example. Ruth, Marilyn, and Gordon are pretending they are lions. Marilyn, who is an inhibited child, says, "I'm a good lion." Gordon says, "Don't eat me up." Lions seem to fascinate him because of their dangerous possibilities. Marilyn changes her role. It's safer. "Don't eat me up," she says. Ruth boldly says, "I'm a mean lion," and chases Gordon. Then she stops and asks him, "Are you a mean lion?" When he answers "Yes," Marilyn feels braver and says, "I am too." "Pretend you can't get us," says Ruth. Gordon answers with, "I'm going to eat you up." Unfortunately, at this point a teacher steps in and tells them to be "good lions," and they drop the lion play. It no longer serves a purpose for them. Marilyn, who has conformed to high standards of good behavior and has paid a price in loss of creativity, had just reached the point of joining Ruth and Gordon in daring to be a "mean" lion. The teacher's words close this avenue of escape from adult demands for Marilyn. It is interesting to get further insight into what Marilyn is seeking by watching her subsequent play. A few minutes later she climbed up high in the jungle gym and says, "This is dangerous."

Play that individuals and groups repeat is almost sure to have meaning for them. We need to try to understand what its meaning is if we are to offer sound help. It is probably neither accident nor perversity that makes a child knock over things or throw them down. We must remember that he himself has tumbled many times. He has been startled, and perhaps hurt, by falling in the course of learning to walk. He may recover some assurance by making other things fall and thus reduce the threat which falls have offered to him. We know that children are frightened by sudden, loud noises and yet as soon as they are able, they pound and bang, making all the noise they can. In this way they may be better able to handle the fear they have felt. Because they can make noises themselves, they are less disturbed by noise.

Being little and often helpless, and being unable to comprehend fully what is taking place inevitably creates some degree of anxiety and resentment in every child. Life becomes more manageable for the child because he can escape at times into play. Donald Winnicott tells us that, "In the preschool years play is the child's principal means of solving the emotional problems that belong to development."[4]

MANY KINDS OF FEELINGS ARE REVEALED IN PLAY.   It is always interesting to note what children consider funny. Understanding humor is one cue in understanding the kind of adjustment a person is making. Children's dramatic play often has a humorous quality, but underneath the humor may lie disguised meanings. We must be aware that feelings of many kinds are likely to be expressed under the acceptable guise of a joke.

One child tickles another with a leaf that he is carrying. They both laugh, for his gesture expressed friendliness. Another child tickles a companion with a leaf, and the child objects. He senses the attacking quality which exists under the apparent playfulness of the gesture and resents it.

Simon, who is struggling hard to establish a masculine role in the world, is making a mask at Halloween. He says, "I want a *man* witch. I don't like girls." His father is a withdrawn person, defensive and aloof.

[4]Ibid.

His mother clings to Simon and is overdirective and possessive. But Simon is valiantly making the effort to identify himself with male things, even male witches. At times he dresses up in skirts and then tries to defend himself by rejecting all girls. His conflicts are revealed in his play.

It has been clearly established that dramatic play has therapeutic value for children. We need to recognize and accept this fact. Such acceptance does not imply that teachers are in a position to undertake play therapy in the more technical sense of the term. In school, however, children need to have plenty of opportunity to play out feelings, try out roles, clarify concepts through spontaneous dramatizations, and thus benefit from the therapeutic values of dramatic play.

Through his dramatic play the child may also be communicating feelings and ideas. With only limited ability to express himself in language or words, he uses actions to represent in symbolic ways what he is feeling and thinking. The child's struggle with jealous feelings after the arrival of a new baby, for example, may be expressed in his destructive behavior with some object which he uses as an outlet. His apparent fascination with covering up objects may be a communication about his concern over the disappearance of people important to him or with finding an answer to something hidden from him. We should look carefully at play behavior that occurs repeatedly and try to understand what the child may be trying to tell us.

CHILDREN WHO ARE UNABLE TO PLAY.   Sometimes we find a child who seems to be unable to enter into play, whether on his own or with others. He is likely to lack a basic sense of trust in some respect. He may be overwhelmed by the anxieties or the anger he feels. One child whose parent sometimes acted with violence, shouting or throwing objects, was unable to engage in much play at home or at school. In the center his play was limited to riding a tricycle around in circles or just watching other children. He seldom explored materials, and he had not developed much speech. He seemed to feel the world was a dangerous place. He trusted no one, including himself. His teacher's first task was to establish herself as a completely reliable person who accepted him in every way, whatever he did. After many weeks he began, hesitantly, to play near other children when his teacher was with him. Then he began to use materials more aggressively and to act out some of his fears. Before many months, he was playing with other children although he needed "his" teacher with him at first. He had learned to trust in this situation and had begun to reach out to play with others. He also began to communicate with speech.

There are times in the lives of all children when they are not free to play because they are overwhelmed by the new, the strange, or the feared. A child may become overwhelmed at times of illness, accidents, death, or family problems. Demands to perform beyond his ability or teasing can overwhelm him. It is important that all children who cannot play or whose play is disorganized and aggressive find a trustworthy, reliable adult in their center. They need a teacher who will not push them to be busy, but rather one who will take time to build a trusting relationship and will help them find ways to cope with their particular stresses.

FANTASY AND IMAGINATION IN DRAMATIC PLAY

Fantasy and reality are often confused in young children's thinking. What they think seems true to them whether or not it is true in reality. Children need help and time to make the distinction between reality and fantasy without having to reject their fantasies. They have a right to imagine and to create fantasies as well as a need to learn to identify reality.

> Francis is at the table playing with the playdough. He rolls it with a rolling pin and pats it. He talks softly to himself. "Is that a birthday cake? Where are some candles?" He reaches and gets some cut straws and places them on the playdough. He then turns to a teacher sitting near and says, "I don't want to sing." The teacher assures him that it is all right to have a birthday cake and not sing. He blows two very hard puffs and says, "I blew it out," adding, "Where is the knife?" The teacher hands the knife to him. He says, "A *really* birthday because I'm cutting the cake. It must be real because I'm cutting it. I blew out the candles and I'm cutting it."
>
> TEACHER: "You pretended to blow out the candles, didn't you?"
>
> FRANCIS: "Yes, but I'm really cutting it." He hands the teacher a piece, and he keeps a piece.
>
> TEACHER: "You really cut it, but we'll have to pretend to eat it."
>
> FRANCIS: "Ya." A slight frown comes across his face. He then runs across the room to Jamie, who is building with blocks. "Superman, I cut the cake for you. I pretended it was my birthday."
>
> Jamie smiles but makes no comment. Francis runs back to the table, picks up the clock, and runs to Jamie with it. "See what I got for my birthday?"
>
> JAMIE: "Why?"
>
> FRANCIS: "Because it's my birthday, and it's brand new."
>
> JAMIE: "Not your birthday."
>
> FRANCIS: "I pretended. I made a cake."

Francis, like most three- and four-year-old children, is coping with the problem of the real and the pretend, and is well on his way to finding pleasure in both. He makes the distinction in "I cut the cake. I pretended it was my birthday."

It is sometimes a struggle for children to get the real world and the world of magic into their proper places. A child is fortunate when he has help from a parent or a teacher in learning this. His imaginative tales can be valued for what they are, delightful figments of the imagination, a method of escape which we can all profit from at times. It is fun to make up stories, but one should be clear about the differences between the "pretend" and the factual. Occasionally one meets a child who makes few contacts with other children and who seems to use fantasies repeatedly as a way of avoiding reality. The child who consistently escapes into fantasy is a child in need of professional help.

Self-Initiated Sociodramatic Play

Four- and five-year-old children spend more time in the kind of play called sociodramatic by Sara Smilansky, who studied children's play in Israel and the United States. In dramatic play a child pretends to be someone else. He plays a role imitatively, and he may play alone. In sociodramatic play there must be at least one other roleplayer, and the children interact with both words and actions in their make-believe.[5] In this episode we find three four-year-old girls playing in a house made of two small screens covered by a blanket.

> KIM: "There is a lion outside the house. We are frightened so we stay in."
> BARBARA: "Yes, and we have to take care of baby sister too, or else the bad lion will get her."
> Kim comes out of the house. She finds another child, Bonnie, standing near the tent. Kim goes up to her, takes her hand and says, "You are a bad lion. You frighten people, so they lock you up in a cage. Now you go to your cage"—Pauses, leads Bonnie to the other room saying, "Come, I will make you a cage." She puts four long blocks together and tells Bonnie, "Now you get in there. That's your cage." Bonnie stands in the enclosure and Kim goes back to the house. She says, "The lion is locked in the cage, so we are safe."
> In the meanwhile, Barbara, still in the house, says to Nancy, "Now you better listen to your big sister like a good girl or else the lion will catch you. Mommy will be back home soon." Kim returning home, calls out to Bonnie from inside the tent. "You have escaped from the cage. You have unlocked the cage and you have escaped."
> As Bonnie walks toward the tent, Kim shouts to the others. "The lion has escaped, the lion has escaped." They all three scream and shout.
> KIM: "I must call the zoo and tell the manager." She picks up the telephone and calls. "There is a big lion escaped from the zoo and he is frightening us. Please get him, will you?" She puts down the receiver.
> BARBARA: "Now they will come and get him and put him back in the cage, Ha! Ha!"
> Everything quiets down and the play shifts.

[5] S. Smilansky. (1971). Can adults facilitate play in children? Theoretical and practical considerations. In N. E. Curry, & S. Arnaud. (1971). *Play: The child strives toward self-realization*, pp. 39–50. Washington, DC: National Association for the Education of Young Children.

NANCY: "I am the mother."

KIM (pointing): "No. You (Barbara) are the big sister and you (Nancy) are the little sister. You are eight and she is five. You better mind her while I go out." She goes out for a few seconds and comes back.

KIM to BARBARA: "Did she (Nancy) mind?"

BARBARA: "No, she was a very bad girl."

KIM to NANCY: "Mommy is not mad at you, but next time you must mind."

NANCY: "I will."

Kim goes out for a few seconds and returns. KIM to NANCY: "Did you do what mother said?"

NANCY: "Yes."

BARBARA: "I know. When you go somewhere like downtown, we could play ring around roses."

KIM: "But be careful, big sister, because she is only three and she might fall down and get hurt."

KIM to NANCY: "You didn't behave and we spanked you—not real hard—I'll show you how—It doesn't hurt, does it?"

NANCY: "No—But don't spank too hard, OK?"

KIM: "And then you played with the telephone."

BARBARA to NANCY: "You better not. You are too little to play with the telephone."

KIM to NANCY: "You were playing in the street and we caught you."

NANCY: "I have to go out to pick berries."

KIM: "No, because you fooled us—(pause)—Why do you have to pick berries?"

BARBARA: "I want to call Grandma." Picking up the telephone receiver, dials 1, 2, 5, 8. Puts down the receiver. "I called but the line is busy."

BARBARA: "I am going to pick berries."

KIM to NANCY: "You also go to pick berries. When we are not looking."

KIM: "We must sleep now. Curl up, honey."

Nancy walks out on tiptoe. Suddenly Kim and Barbara rush out shouting, "Where is she? Where is she?" Both of them run out looking for Nancy. Barbara finds Nancy behind the door and shouts excitedly, "Here she is, Mom—Hurry, Mommy." Barbara and Kim hold Nancy's hands on either side and drag her into the house. Kim pretends to lock the door of the house and tells Nancy, "You have been a bad girl. Now you have to stay in all day."

Here we see the children's concern about misbehavior, fears, playing in the street, running away, and taking care of siblings. They cope with the problem of being little and the temptations they face by creating a "bad lion" and dealing with him. They practice being the punishing parent themselves. They show well-informed solutions such as telephoning the zoo director to come and get the "escaped lion." The maternal role is an important one as they reflect a benign discipline and take care of baby sister.

All the elements of sociodramatic play are seen in their imitative role play, imaginative make-believe substituted for real objects, three players, and much verbal interaction.[6] Sociodramatic play builds confidence in them as they master the situations they create. They re-create their world, but this time they are in control.

The Beginnings of Group Games Develop Out of Dramatic Play

We see the beginnings of group games developing in children's spontaneous play, forerunners of the more organized games that they will enjoy later. Four-year-olds enjoy very simple activities in groups. Four or five children and a teacher may join hands in a circle on the grass in "ring-around-a-rosy, and we all fall down" with appropriate action. Marching becomes a group activity with a variety of instruments in the band and frequent changes of leader. We need to guard against too much patterning, or we may lose the spontaneous development of group feeling that holds much value for children.

Playing is a creative experience, an act of the imagination, and one that can be enjoyed alone or shared with others. We have seen that the values found in play can help children to establish relationships with others. Self-confidence is gained as children learn skills for getting along with others in play. Spontaneous, playful behavior is a source of satisfaction and relief. Winnicott writes, "It is in playing and only in playing that the individual child or adult is able to be creative and to use the whole personality, and it is only in being creative that the individual discovers the self."[7] Play brings the inner world of feeling in touch with the outer world of shared reality. Play leads to the integration of personality.

Projects

1. Observe a group of children playing and record an incident:
   a. in which a child seems to be discovering something about the nature of the world through his play
   b. in which the child seems to use play as a way of mastering an anxiety, fear, or conflict
   c. in which the child is recreating a role in the world around him
   d. in which the child is discovering what other people are like

For Your Further Reading

Almy, M. (1984). A child's right to play. *Young Children, 39*(4), 80. Also in J. Brown. (Ed.). (1984). *Administering programs for young children.* P. 68. Washington, DC: National Association for the Education of Young Children. A short, eloquent statement about the important growth that happens when children

---

[6]Ibid.

[7]D. W. Winnicott. (1971). *Playing and reality.* London: Tavistock Publications.

play. The right to play parallels rights like adequate nutrition, housing, health care, and education.

Cherry, C. (1976). *Creative play for the developing child: Early lifehood education through play.* Belmont, CA: Fearon. Along with the author's useful books on creative art and movement, this book offers practical help on facilitating play and children's use of play to deal with feelings.

Garvey, C. (1977). *Play.* The developing child series. Cambridge, MA: Harvard University Press. Play increases the child's capacity for coping, socially and physically. This book helps the reader understand what play with objects, language, social relationships, and rules means.

Segal, M., & Adcock, D. (1981). *Just pretending: Ways to help children grow through imaginative play.* Englewood Cliffs, NJ: Prentice-Hall. Techniques for parents and teachers to encourage children's pretend play.

Winnicott, D. W. (1971). *Playing and reality.* New York: Basic Books. Emphasizes the importance of children's self-initiated dramatic play in helping the child understand reality and its relation to creative thinking in adult life. Useful for those familiar with Winnicott's earlier writing.

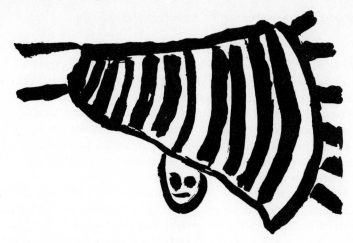

Snail and His House (boy, 4 years)

13 ♦ Feelings of Security and Confidence

"Look here, teacher, I'm bigger than you think. I'm going to have a birthday soon. Let me do this by myself," said Katherine to a well-meaning adult who was trying to help her.

Katherine's words remind us of how often adults handicap children by acting as though children were unable to meet situations. A child has a difficult time developing confidence when he is surrounded by people who "help" him all the time. Children are often more competent than we think! Katherine was able to express her confidence in herself as a person able to do things, but few children are able to do this because they lack not only the verbal ability but the feeling itself.

As adults, most of us probably wish that we had more self-confidence. We realize that we are likely to do a thing better when we feel confident than when we are afraid of failing. We realize, too, that we get more pleasure out of doing something when we feel adequate and are free from anxiety. For all of us, feelings of insecurity and a lack of confidence are handicapping. The person who has confidence in himself may enjoy undertaking something entirely new in which he lacks any skill, but many people are not free enough of self-doubts to feel that the unfamiliar is a challenge to them.

Security refers to the feelings that come with having had many experiences of being accepted rather than rejected and of feeling safe rather than threatened. Security results from a person's having had positive relationships with people. Confidence refers to the feelings that an individual has about himself and his concept of the kind of person he is. This concept, too, grows out of the responses other people make to him. Security and confidence are closely related. The secure child trusts himself and others. He dares to be himself and to discover more about himself. As we work with children, we will seek ways of strengthening their feelings of confidence and security.

FOUNDATIONS FOR FEELING SECURE AND CONFIDENT

Feelings of security and confidence develop out of the way the infant's basic needs are met; his experiences with feeding and, later, with toileting; the kinds of responses he gets from other people; and the satisfaction he finds in exploring the world. Out of these early experiences the child builds a feeling of trust in the world, his first task developmentally. Having learned that he can trust others he is ready to trust and have confidence in himself. The attitudes and feelings of his parents are the most important factors in building confidence because he depends largely on his parents for the satisfaction of his basic needs.

If the child's first experiences have made him feel secure and confident because his needs were satisfied, if he has obtained positive responses from people, and if he has had satisfying sensory experiences, he has laid a firm foundation for confidence and security. If, on the other hand, his needs have not been met and if he has failed to get any response when he needed it, he has already experienced insecurity and felt inadequate. If he constantly heard the words *no* and *don't* when he reached out for experience, he has already grown to distrust his own impulses. The world does not seem to him a place where he can feel safe, and he builds a picture of himself as a person who is not very adequate to cope with the problems it presents. He may begin to think of himself as a person who is likely to do the wrong thing.

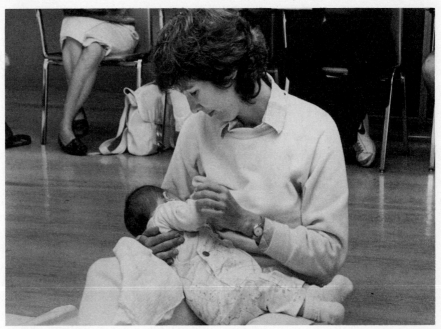

Being fed by her mother, this infant feels secure.

Santa Monica College.

Children Are Influenced in Their Feelings by the Attitudes of Adults

Children tend to behave as they feel they are expected to behave or according to the concept of self they have built up out of people's responses to them. Paul, for example, thinks of himself as a boy who gets into trouble. As he and his father came into nursery school one morning, his father remarked, "See how nice and quiet this place is until you get here!" What is a boy like who hears words like these? He is a boy who is noisy, defiant, and difficult. He lives up to the picture his father paints.

When Stanley's mother brought him to the center, she explained to the teacher as Stanley stood beside her, "Perhaps he'll learn to ride a tricycle here. He doesn't know how yet. He just tries for a minute and then gives up." It was not surprising that Stanley lacked confidence, did not persist, and was unfriendly with both children and teachers.

Three-year-old Ella was timid. She didn't join other children in play, but she did like to paint. She was at the easel painting carefully around the edges of the paper when her mother came for her one day. Her mother saw the picture, and she said half scornfully, "Nobody paints like that!" How can one have much confidence if one is considered a "nobody"? Ella didn't expect to have an important place in the group.

In contrast, we see Michele. Michele was new in the center, eager for new experiences but lacking in skills. Climbing fascinated her. One day she tried very hard to climb a tree even though she was afraid. With some help from the teacher, she finally managed to reach a high limb. Delighted, she called out to everyone, "Look, I'm up here as brave as ever." We see in this incident the element of healthy personality development. Michele sees herself as brave. She has made an effort and mastered a difficult feat. She wants to share her delight. She is sure that there will be someone who cares.

Children who have confidence and do not feel helpless have less need to fight against adults. They can accept adults without feeling threatened by them. Jean, a secure, confident child, seldom felt the need to be defiant or resistant with adults. Some children, on the other hand, never develop sufficient confidence to defy adults but remain anxious and dependent on them. They are "good" children but not happy or emotionally healthy. It takes insight to perceive that resistant behavior may mean growth for the child as a person. It takes insight both into the child's behavior and into our own behavior. It takes skill, too, to guide a child through this stage so that its values are retained and, at the same time, safe limits and a respect for the child are maintained. To understand children who are in this phase of development we must understand our own feelings. Because most of us have many areas of insecurity, we may find it hard not to feel threatened by resistance. The adult who meets children's attacks with, "I won't have that" or "You can't get away with that," reveals herself as an adult who is defending herself against feeling helpless rather than as one who is helping the resistant child.

Leighton and Kluckholn in *Children of the People* make an interesting comment on the attitudes that appear in another culture. They describe the way the Navaho treat young children in these words: ". . . the Navaho toddler is given self-confidence by being made to feel that he is constantly loved and valued."[1] Would Ella and Stanley have behaved differently if they had lived under conditions in which they were "constantly loved and valued"? Many children in our culture are "constantly loved and valued," but many others are treated as "nobodies," like Ella and Stanley, even though there is no conscious intent on the part of adults to treat them this way.

We live in such a highly competitive society that it is often hard for us to recognize the values that may exist outside of achievement. Parents feel the pressure for accomplishment. They want children who will learn to write their names or who paint good pictures. They push their children, even their toddlers. They may have difficulty accepting them as they are.

[1]D. Leighton and C. Kluckhorn. (1947). *Children of the people: The Navaho individual and his development*. Cambridge, MA: Harvard University Press.

Children who have been pushed through a stage frequently have to go back and experience it again before they are free to go on or secure enough to develop further.

Adults May Make Children Feel Guilty

Children sometimes find it hard to develop confidence in themselves because they feel they are to blame for things that happen. A child may enjoy an activity, such as playing in the mud or exploring a bureau drawer, only to find that what he has done is considered very naughty by the adult. With little basis for real understanding of adult values and with a great need to please adults because of his dependency on them, he comes to feel uncertain about himself and his behavior. Many times he thinks that his mistakes are much more serious than we really consider them, and he suffers from a heavy load of guilt. When we blame him for what he does not understand or understands only in part, we damage his feelings of confidence and trust in himself.

By making events conditional on a child's good or bad behavior, we may increase his sense of uncertainty and lack of confidence. He may feel responsible for events that have no connection. Betty said, "Next week if I'm a real good girl, know where we're going? To the beach!" Let's hope that her parents were not too busy or tired that week or that nothing interfered with their plan. If a child can bring about a trip to the beach by being good, he can cause a calamity by being bad.

Pam arrived at nursery school one morning and didn't see the ducks. She was very interested in them and inquired anxiously, "I can't see the ducks." Then she added, "I made a noise. Do ducks get headaches?" She has evidently had to bear a feeling of guilt for causing headaches. Without enough experience to correct his concepts, the child is the victim of his misapprehensions. We may not suspect a child's real feelings or the heavy load of guilt he may feel for events.

Adults May Be Afraid of Spoiling Children

Sometimes adults are afraid to accept children as they are and to meet their needs because they are afraid of "spoiling" them if they do. They needlessly deny and interfere with children because of ignorance of the growth process. They make it hard for the child to think of himself as an adequate person. "Spoiled" children are, in fact, those who get attention *when the adult wants to give it* rather than when the child himself needs it. They are those children who are subject to inconsistent interferences rather than given the support of consistent limits by parents who are willing to take responsibility for limits. Flexible handling that allows the child to live on his own level tends to build secure feelings in the young child rather than to "spoil" him. It reduces to the minimum the denials and interferences that are likely to shake a child's confidence in himself. It accepts him as he is. It helps him feel adequate.

Adults Can Be Caring without Spoiling

Children need limits set for them. The adult who lets a child do anything he wants is an adult who is avoiding her responsibilities. These limits sometimes can be set at quite different points. One person *will not* interfere with a child or stop him in what he does unless she feels sure the child's action will result in undesirable consequences. The child is thus free to explore and experiment with materials, to act in all kinds of childish ways, and to learn for himself. Another person *will* interfere or stop a child unless she feels sure that what the child is doing is desirable. There is much less room for the child to discover and to try out ways of acting under this method. The first person's attitude is "caring," in contrast to the second person's restrictive attitude.

By caring we do not mean indulgence. Instead, we mean leaving children free to explore, to discover, to create, and to find their own way within acceptable limits. We also mean a generous quality in giving to the child, not a meager giving. "Of course you can," rather than, "I guess you can, but I wish you wouldn't"; or, "Take all you need," rather than, "Don't take much"; or, "There's plenty for everyone," rather than, "No one can have more than one piece." When we give generously, children grow less anxious. They need less.

Children are not helped to build confidence by parents who are indulgent, who give in to them rather than face the unpleasant behavior of a thwarted child. They are more secure if there is no lack of firmness when firmness is needed. Both parents and child need to learn to face unpleasant realities in constructive ways, rather than avoid facing them.

Adults Need to Be Secure People

Secure adults find it easier to accept the child as he is and meet his needs freely. A secure person is relaxed, comfortable, and giving. She does not feel much need to make demands on others. Secure people are likely to create the kind of environment in which it is easy for the child to think of himself as an adequate person. Mike, for example, has lived with comfortable parents. He is free of defenses. He looks at the puzzle he worked on the day before and says, "That one was hard for me." He is a secure child, able to try new things and eager to learn.

Insecure people are often defensive and demanding. They are likely to set standards that the child can only meet with difficulty, if at all. They are likely to be very concerned with what other people say about them as parents. There are many reasons why parents have a hard time feeling secure today. They may be handicapped by economic insecurities, tensions and conflicts in the world, by inadequate housing, and limited community resources in health and recreation as well as by an education that offers little guidance in understanding parent-child relationships. Paul's father, who spoke in such a belittling way to his son, is typical of many parents. He wants to be a successful parent, but he is without experience or preparation for his role. Like most people, he values success highly and is striving for it professionally. His concept of a successful parent is one whose child behaves like an adult. He feels he has failed to achieve this goal with Paul. His love for the child is hidden under his constant criticism. He is not a secure parent. He makes Paul an insecure child.

By the time the child reaches the age of two or three, his feelings of security and confidence should outweigh those of mistrust and doubt. He may have come from a home where his parents are too insecure themselves to be able to accept his immaturity. There is clear evidence that the quality of the experience a young child has with his parents is far more important than the amount of time spent together.[2] A mother or father who enjoys spending time with the child can contribute greatly to the enrichment of the child's development, even though the time they have to spend with each other is limited. Both boys and girls profit when the father enjoys being with his young children. He brings a different quality to the caregiving than the mother. It also seems true that the parent who is finding satisfactions in his own life, at work and at home, is likely to give a child the freedom and the encouragement he needs to develop his own interests. The satisfied parent is likely to provide many of the experiences that will enrich the child's intellectual development and increase his confidence in himself.

RECOGNIZING THE CHILD'S FEELINGS

We will raise the question in this section of how we may recognize a child's feelings. How do we identify feelings so that we may be of help to a child?

Children reveal their feelings through behavior. Sometimes they do it openly and directly, and they act as they feel. Sometimes their feelings come out in ways that are more difficult to identify. We must learn to understand what their feelings are; then we can recognize how plainly they speak to us through behavior.

[2] J. H. Stevens and M. Mathews. (1978). *Mother/child father/child relationships*. Washington, DC: National Association for the Education of Young Children.

The first step in understanding the meaning of behavior is to be able to look at the way a child behaves without feeling a necessity to change his behavior. We must learn to look at behavior as it is rather than in terms of what we want it to be. We are likely to confuse the meaning of a child's behavior with our own feelings if we try to judge it or if we decide that the child should or should not be behaving as he is.

Cues in Nonverbal Behavior

We have already pointed out how children differ in the kinds of adjustments that they make to new situations. These differences have meaning. The adult who wishes to understand a child will observe carefully how he responds in a new situation. She will not decide how the child should respond and try to force this pattern of response on him.

Children reveal characteristic attitudes in everyday, familiar situations, too. These cues may be seen in such things as in the way the child walks and runs and holds his hands as well as in his posture. Posture is, of course, influenced by constitutional and environmental factors, but over and above these, reflections of the child's emotional patterns can be seen in his muscle tensions. One child's hands are relaxed, and another's are tense and constantly moving. One child clutches our finger tightly as we walk along with him, a sign of his need for support and the intensity of his feelings. Another lets his hand lie limply in ours, suggesting perhaps the nongiving quality of his relationships with others, in contrast to the warm, responsive grip of still another child who welcomes closeness without clinging to it. These bits of behavior are all cues that help us understand the child's feelings.

Sometimes a conflict the child is feeling is expressed in the movements of his hands, as in the case of the child who is watching finger painting. He may stand at a distance, wiping his clean hands on his shirt or wringing them together, showing us the conflict he feels between his wish to put his hands into the paint and the force of the restriction not to get dirty.

Cues in Speech

Voice quality and language offer cues to feelings. The quality of a child's voice may be strained and tight, or relaxed and easy. It may be loud and harsh, or soft and faint, or it may be confident and well modulated. Even the amount of speech may give some indications of the extent of the child's assurance or of his hesitation. One child talks very little; another chatters almost constantly. These extremes may be reactions to strains and pressures that are making them feel less confident and less secure than they should feel. Insistent, needless questions are sometimes a symptom of insecurity, a seeking for reassurance more than for any specific answer. Too often these questions meet an impatient rebuff, not calculated to satisfy the need they express.

Spontaneous singing usually indicates confidence and contentment. The child who sings at play is probably comfortable, and it is worth noting the times and places when singing occurs spontaneously. We can learn from this behavior in what areas or on what occasions a child feels secure.

The child who asks the teacher, "Do you want to go outdoors with me?" may really be saying, "I'm afraid to go out by myself. It would help if you wanted to go with me." The teacher needs to understand the meaning behind what the child says.

The child who says happily, "Isn't this going to be a good gate? I'm building it all myself," is telling us something about what comfortable feelings he has about himself. This same boy's father once remarked about him, "I think he's one of those fortunate people who like themselves." The child liked himself—and everyone else; he was one of the most likable children one could meet. He had been "loved and valued" in his family.

There is a real consciousness of an emerging self in these words of Katherine—the same Katherine who is "bigger than you think"—when she says, "I'm different from all the other people. When other people laugh, I don't, even if it's silly." Katherine feels secure enough to be different.

Cues in Behavior

Children who feel insecure are likely to face a new situation or a difficult problem by defending themselves. They may retreat, avoid the activity, resist, or attack. Their defensiveness may make it difficult for them in the situation. Children who feel secure, on the other hand, do not feel the need to defend themselves. They are free to look for ways of coping with the situation. They often seek out new experiences.

Three-year-old Ralph bursts into tears when someone knocks against the tower he is building, and then he hits out frantically at the offender. He has little confidence in his ability to cope with interference.

When people lack confidence in themselves, they usually act defensively in many situations. Jane, who is new in day care, begins to cry when the teacher asks her to be quiet at rest time. She is too insecure yet to accept any indication that she is behaving unacceptably. The teacher's suggestion that it was time to settle down and rest would have helped a child who felt at home in the school. The comfortable child can cope with demands. The insecure child tries to defend himself against them.

Sometimes we meet a child who is unable to accept comforting even from a familiar teacher. This child may not welcome a friendly pat, or may avoid an expression of closeness such as an arm around him. He usually is an insecure child who has found close relationships unreliable and unsatisfying. Only slowly does he come to trust adults. Occasionally we find a child striving for autonomy who resents comforting. He has developed patterns for finding his own way and sees the adult's approach as encroaching on his independence. Only careful observation can give us a cue as to each child's needs.

The secure child finds it easy to be friendly. He can share with others because he does not fear loss. He does not need to defend his rights. The insecure child cannot afford to share. His problem is not one of selfishness or unfriendliness, but one of degree of security. We need to handle the real problem, not the symptom, in such cases.

Sometimes the Cues Are Indirect

Peter had a hard time separating from his mother when she started to leave the school. He cried and protested. His mother was distressed and felt she could not leave him. One day he had this conversation with his teacher as she was helping him get ready to go home:

> PETER (half teasingly): Miss Williams, will my locker be here when I come back?
> MISS W.: Yes, Peter, it will be right here waiting for you.
> PETER: If my locker starts to run away, will you hold it?
> MISS W.: Yes, I'll hold it tight and tell it to stay right here because Peter is coming tomorrow.
> PETER: You just hold it. I want it right here.

As the teacher thought about the conversation, she felt that in an indirect way Peter was telling her that although he wanted to run away and go home, he wanted more to stay at school. He needed more help from her in resolving the conflict he felt in separating from his mother. He wanted his teacher to "hold" him, like the locker.

She telephoned his mother and suggested that the mother try leaving, even though Peter protested, for Peter really was enjoying school and might be ready to stay by himself. The mother left him the next day, a bit reluctantly, for he was crying and struggling. Almost immediately he relaxed and was ready for play under the watchful eye of his teacher. She had given him the help he wanted.

John shows us what a name tag can symbolize to a child. He was proud of the name tag he wore and reminded the teacher to put it on each morning. One day one of the teachers reproved him for something he did. John said nothing, but a few minutes later this teacher observed that he had taken off the name tag. She felt that it was as though he did not want his name to be associated with misbehavior. He could remove his guilty self by removing the name tag.

Thumbsucking May Be a Symptom of Insecurity

In the center one may see a child sucking his thumb at rest time or when the group is listening to a story or even during a play period. Like all behavior, thumbsucking is a symptom and may indicate a need in the child for more reassurance and greater security than he has found in his experience. It may be a difficult world for him because he is expected to be more grown-up than he is ready to be. He may be expected to be quiet, to inhibit his impulses for touching things, to take over adult ways of behaving at the table or in social situations, to comprehend and maintain the rules for property rights, and so forth. The strain of living up to all these demands or of failing to live up to them may be so great that the child seeks an infantile source of comfort. He turns to this thumb as a refuge.

The child is telling us something through his thumbsucking, and we need to understand. Adults should not increase his strain by taking away the avenue of comfort that he has found but should try to make his life simpler and more comfortable. They should try to reduce the tensions he is under and offer him a greater opportunity for feeling secure and adequate, so that he may seek other kinds of satisfactions.

Mary Lou Took Her Own Thumb Out of Her Mouth

Three-and-a-half-year-old Mary Lou was a round little girl who sucked her thumb most of the time at the center. She was timid and often held onto the teacher's skirt with her free hand. She didn't venture into activity with other children or even play alone actively.

Mary Lou was the oldest of three children and had always been a "good" girl, according to her mother. She had been easy to care for and could even be depended on to watch out for her little sister while her mother was busy with the baby. She seemed content with little to do and never disturbed the babies. It was not hard to imagine that Mary Lou had had very little chance to have the satisfactions that usually come with being a baby. She had had to grow up very quickly and had had to seek approval by behaving in unchildlike ways.

She remained dependent on the teacher for many weeks, but her interest in the children was plain as she watched a group having fun together. Sitting close to the teacher, she sometimes became part of a group at the piano or at the clay table. She had a real capacity for enjoying what she was doing and a sense of humor which became evident as she felt freer to act. She thoroughly enjoyed the clay, the sandbox, and the mud hole in the schoolyard. She often played alone in the homemaking area after she felt more comfortable at school.

Later she ventured into more active play. She still stood watching activities with her thumb in her mouth part of the time, but she was busy in the sandbox or riding the tricycles more of the time. The most marked change came in her behavior after she gained enough courage to use the slide. Sliding was a popular activity, and Mary Lou would often stand watching, but resisted any suggestion that she join the group at the slide. At last on a day when no one else was at the slide, she tried it, with her favorite teacher near to hold her hand. It was an effort, but she succeeded and went down again and again. She waved gaily to her mother when she came that day and showed off her newly acquired skill. From then on she participated more freely in every group. Mastering the slide seemed to give her a great deal of confidence. She even did a little pushing to hold her place in line at the slide and began to stand up for herself in other ways. She was active and happy. She hardly ever had time for her thumb. By the end of a year some of the adults had even forgotten that she used to suck her thumb. The fact that she no longer needed her thumb told a great deal about the change in Mary Lou.

All Nervous Habits Are Symptoms

Some children may express the tensions they are feeling by biting their nails, twisting on their clothing, or sucking other objects. Masturbation is another means of finding satisfaction and a defense against strain. We may do a great deal of harm by attacking the symptom directly and denying the child an avenue of expression while he is still feeling tension and seeking relief and satisfaction. We need to look on all of these so-called nervous habits as symptoms whose cause must be sought and treated before the symptom itself can be expected to disappear. Treating only the symptom will tend to make some other form of expression necessary for the child and increase the strain he feels. The thumbsucking child may become a nailbiting child or a masturbating child, for example, if the symptom and not the cause is attacked. We must keep in mind the fact that all kinds of behavior have meanings which we cannot afford to ignore.

ACCEPTING THE CHILD'S FEELINGS

In all these ways, a child shows us how he feels. After we have learned to recognize the child's feelings, we must find ways of adding to his feelings of security and confidence and reducing his feelings of insecurity.

What are some of the ways in which we can do this in the center?

We Must Face and Accept Feelings If We Are to Help

The most important step is to make sure that we really accept the child's feelings and that we do not condemn or blame him for them. Perhaps he feels afraid or angry or unfriendly. These may be feelings of which we do not approve, but approval and acceptance are different things. Acceptance means recognizing without blaming. It does not mean permitting the child to act out his feelings as he may wish, but it does mean acknowledging that he has the right to feel as he does without being ashamed of it. We may not approve, but we must accept the child's feelings if we are going to help him with them. Our very acceptance often reduces the feeling and makes the child less defensive about his insecurity, fear, or anger. Instead of hiding his feelings, he can bring them out where he, and we, can do more about them.

Accepting Our Own Feelings May Be Difficult

We usually find it difficult to accept feelings that we have had to deny in ourselves. When we were children, we often felt jealous, resentful, or hostile, but we may not have been permitted any expression of these feelings. We had to act as though we loved a little sister, for example, and were willing to share our dolls with her, or we had to let the neighbor boy ride in our wagon because the adults insisted that children must be generous. Now, as adults, we find it hard to be accepting of the child who refuses to share her doll or who pushes another out of the wagon. We feel like punishing this child. This helps us to deny that we were ever like this little girl. If we handle our feelings by denying them, we cannot offer help to children who face problems with their feelings.

The story of what goes on unconsciously is oversimplified by the description we have given, of course, but we can be sure that whenever we strongly reject a bit of behavior, there are deep emotional reasons from our past experience for such a rejection. For some of us there will be more of these emotionally toned areas than for others, and our feelings will be stronger. Few of us will have escaped without some areas of behavior which we find it hard to accept.

If, on the other hand, we were helped to accept our real feelings when we were children, we will now find it easier to be accepting of children as they show their feelings. If the adults with us when we were children said, "It's easy to get angry at someone who takes your things, I know," instead of saying, "She's your sister, and you must love her and share with her," then we would have felt understood and could have faced our feelings with this kind of support. It would have seemed easier to feel and act more generously. This is the kind of help that we want to offer the children we are caring for today.

It is important if we are to help children in this way that we free ourselves of our old defenses. As adults we can now take the step of accepting the reality of any feelings that exist. We know that all of us find sharing and loving difficult at times. Some jealousy is inevitable as children adjust to changing patterns in the family or at school. It is not necessary to deny the existence of feelings. Hostile, aggressive feelings exist in all of us.

Acceptance Helps the Child

The child who refuses to share a toy is not helped by disapproval and shaming. Neither is the child who is afraid. All these children need to be accepted as they are if they are to feel secure. There is always a reason for their behavior. As we work with the little girl who refuses to share her doll or who pushes her companion out of the wagon, we will accept her feelings and use her behavior as a cue to understanding. We will ask ourselves some questions. What kind of child is it who is trying to keep the doll? Is she craving affection and substituting the doll for the love she seeks? Does she depend on possessing things to give herself a feeling of security? How can we help her?

We Can Voice Our Acceptance of Feelings

We can express our acceptance in words: "I know how you feel. It makes you cross because it's Timmy's turn on the swing and you want it to be yours," or "You feel mad when your blocks tumble over," or "You're pretty angry with me right now because I can't let you play outdoors." Words like these help if they express a real acceptance of the feelings that exist. They are different from words like, "You didn't mean to hit Bobby, did you?" that are untrue, as the child's reply, "I did, too" tells us. We must be honest and state what is true.

CONFIDENCE THROUGH EXPRESSION

Next comes the question of what can be done about a feeling after it has been accepted. The answer is that feelings must be expressed in some way if we are to be secure and confident. If feelings are not expressed, they remain with us to be carried around until they come out unexpectedly in ways that may make us unhappy and less sure of ourselves.

Feelings must be expressed, and they are best expressed at the time they occur. The child who says, "I'm afraid," is already less troubled by the feeling of fear. The child who says, "I don't like you," to someone who frightens him may be managing his feeling better than the child who says nothing but then bursts into tears when the person tries to make his acquaintance. The child who is angry needs to do something about the way he feels at the time, rather than keeping his anger hidden where it may

Children who are friends can discuss plans freely.
_____
Santa Monica College, Child Development Center

come out in more damaging ways later; by that time, his anger may have grown and spread.

When we can do something about the way we feel, we are more confident. Psychiatrists tell us that the child who has been aggressive in his early years and whose behavior has been met with understanding has a better chance to make a good adjustment in adolescence than the submissive child. The aggressive child has done something about his feelings and has had an opportunity to identify them and to learn how to manage them.

It Is Essential to Express Feelings in Words

There are many ways in which feelings can be expressed. Most important, it is essential to learn to put negative feelings into words if we are to manage them constructively. When children can use language to release negative feelings, they have taken a step toward being able to control feelings. Their later responses will be more reasonable.

As adults, we often put our feelings into words to ourselves, silently, and then we know how we feel. We may feel even better if we have an opportunity to talk to a friend about our feelings. Putting a feeling into words makes it clear to us, and thus it seems more manageable. It helps drain it. Knowing how one feels is tremendously important. It is a dangerous thing to try to fool ourselves about our feelings. We must understand and face our feelings if we are to be secure, comfortable people.

The child needs help in understanding what he feels, and he also needs help in putting his feelings into words. We should welcome his verbal expressions of feeling, for this way of expressing feelings means a step in his growth toward maturity and control of feelings. Children usually find it easy to talk things out directly, on the spot. They call people names or shout insults to one another. They may be using the best means of handling feelings that they have at their disposal, for they are not grown-up people yet. They are controlling the impulse to hit or attack, and they are expressing, not hiding, their feelings.

Jill, who is almost five, gives us *an example of what putting feelings into words can do for a child*. Jill had been in the center about six months and had been developing very well. She was a friendly, active child who enjoyed play with other children, and she was eager and curious.

During one holiday period Jill had an experience in the doctor's office that had left her very frightened and upset. Her parents had comforted her as well as they could and tried to interest her in other things. Since they were very disturbed themselves about the affair, they preferred not to talk about it. They did not mention it to the teacher when Jill returned to the center after the holiday. The teacher noticed a change in Jill's behavior. She was quiet and passive. She clung to the teacher and cried easily. Her teacher felt sure that something was wrong and asked the parents for a conference. They were glad to come and talk with her, and they told her about the incident. They, too, had felt that Jill was acting differently, and they were eager to help her. The teacher pointed out that it was important for Jill to feel able to talk to someone about her fears. Jill's mother seemed understanding, although she felt it might be hard for her to talk with Jill about the matter. The teacher suggested that the next time Jill got upset and cried, her mother might tell her that she, too, had been upset in the doctor's office, that she understood how Jill had felt, and that it was good to talk about the matter.

A few days later the mother telephoned to report that she had had a talk with Jill the night before. The parents were preparing to go to bed and had found Jill still awake. She seemed unhappy. The mother had gone into the room and, sitting on Jill's bed, she had begun to talk with her about the frightening experience. She said that at first Jill did not seem able to put anything into words, but as they continued talking, she became freer and finally went over all the details. Her mother told Jill that whenever she felt unhappy and afraid, she could come and talk with her, that she would understand, for she felt the same way sometimes.

At rest time that day in school, Jill said to the teacher, "You know what happened? Last night I was unhappy, and I told Mummy." The teacher asked, "And Mummy understood?" "Yes," said Jill, "she asked me why I was unhappy, and I couldn't say, but she knew it was about the doctor." The teacher answered, "Mummies do understand and know, and you can tell Mummy when you feel that way again." Jill went on, "And she said that at night when I am unhappy to come and tell Mummy and Daddy, but I wasn't unhappy anymore. I was just a little unhappy, and now I'm happy." The teacher repeated, "Mummies and daddies do understand, don't they! You can always tell them."

That evening the teacher telephoned Jill's mother to tell her about the conversation. Jill's mother could hardly believe that Jill had repeated this conversation, even using the same words that the mother had used to her. She realized that it had made a deep impression on the child. She felt that she herself could talk to the child more easily now.

At the center and at home Jill's behavior began to change rapidly. She had played and laughed that day, jumping in and out of a box with two other children. She began to assert herself more and to take her place in the activities of the center. She became more like her old self. It seemed wonderful to the teachers, too, that a conversation with a mother who understood could do so much to relieve a child. Putting her fears into words with the help of someone she trusted had drained much of the disturbing feeling and had left the little girl free to grow as before. Her mother had learned from the experience. It gave her confidence. She knew better how to help her child.

There Are Other Ways to Express Feelings

Crying is another good way to express feelings, yet many times we hear people say to a crying child, "That didn't hurt. You're too big to cry." Whatever the reason, the feeling of wanting to cry is there and needs to be accepted, not denied. No one can handle with wisdom feelings he isn't supposed to have. Words like "I know how you feel," when they are said by a person who really accepts the feeling, help a good deal more than words like "You're too big to cry."

Motor outlets are common ways to express feelings. A young child may kick, hit, or throw. Our job is to help him use motor outlets in a way that will not hurt others. He may even need to be put by himself so that he can act in these ways without hurting anyone. If he is older, he may be able to take a suggestion about using a punching bag to advantage. Vigorous physical activity, such as pounding or throwing a ball hard against something, will serve as an outlet for feelings.

If there is a warm, understanding relationship between child and adult, the child can accept many types of suggestion for releasing negative feelings. The teacher may be successful when she says, "You feel just like hitting someone, I know, but you must not do it. Try hitting the target

Digging a hole.

California State University, Chico. Child Development Laboratory

over there with these beanbags. See how many times you can hit it. I'll count the hits." The child may be able to handle his feelings with the help of an understanding, accepting teacher. Our first job is to see that he does not use destructive outlets. Then we can direct him to outlets that are possible and acceptable.

Creative expression can be used to release feelings and make them more manageable. Finger painting, painting at the easel, working with clay, or playing in water, the sandbox, or a good old mud hole will help a child to relax as he expresses feelings through these media. Making music offers still another possibility and is often used this way by children.

Creative materials should be freely available to children because of their value in the expression of feelings. Adults use these same outlets. The child who has found he can turn his feelings into such creative channels has discovered an outlet which will serve him all his life. A child is more secure if he has many avenues of expression open to him. He grows when he can express himself and his feelings through art media. If he is denied self-expression in art media because models are set for him, he loses a valuable avenue for the relief of feelings.

The Timid Child Can Learn How to Express His Feelings

We will often see a timid, inhibited child swing over into unduly aggressive behavior as he begins to gain confidence in himself. This may be the first step in gaining confidence. He must first express his feelings and find acceptance for them. Then he can proceed to modify them. The child who has been inhibited may express his feelings in clumsy and inappropriate ways in the beginning. His first expression of feeling may seem exaggerated. This expression may belong at a much younger level than his present chronological age. With understanding guidance he will come through this stage quickly, but he must "live out," for however brief a time, a period of expression at the less mature level. He must try out being "bad" and discover that he is accepted and that his "badness" does not frighten the adult. It can be managed.

"Transitional Objects" Give Security

As we saw in Chapter 12, children sometimes use "transitional objects" to help themselves *feel more secure* and better able to cope with new or difficult situations. For some children it may be a blanket they have had from babyhood. For others it may be a cuddly toy. Carrying it or knowing that it is easily available may help the child weather the strains he feels. The object is a device for coping with a difficult world. It has symbolic value for the child.

Transitional objects help in the "weaning" process that is part of growing. They are useful in periods of change when the child must let go

Talking on a play phone.

Bakersfield College

or leave behind his old sources of security. They signal to us the child's need for support, as well as indicate the effort he is making to deal with change. One two-year-old in a group could not part with his sweater for several weeks after he entered the group. It may have represented his mother or his home. He wore the sweater or carried it, and became very anxious if it was out of his sight. The way a child uses a transitional object gives us insight into his feelings.

A Child Feels More Secure When He Is Having Satisfying Experiences

Having his needs met applies to the child's experience in the center as well as to his experience at home. If the center is providing satisfying, stimulating opportunities, it makes it easier for the child to be happy and secure. The whole program as well as the equipment provided will contribute to the child's growth in feeling more secure and more adequate. Learning opportunities adapted to the child's level of development, equipment that fits him and makes it easy for him to solve problems, support from adults who understand what his needs are, all make it easier for a child to gain the feeling of security and adequacy that he needs.

Most important of all, in the center the child is with others who are on about the same level of development. He can have fun doing things with other children. Among this group of equals he does not need to feel inadequate, for he *can* keep up with them. He can do things as well as many of the others. He gains strength from the feeling that he is like others, from being able to identify himself with people who are at his stage of growth. Belonging to a group of equals constitutes one of the best forms of insurance against feeling little and helpless.

The child needs to find teachers in the center who will accept his positive feelings, too. As teachers, we must be ready to return his smile, to take his hand when he slips it into ours, to take him into our arms, or to talk with him when he seems to feel the need for such closeness. We must respond to his warm, friendly feelings. If it is his need and not ours that we are meeting in responding, we can be sure that he is helped to be more independent by what we do. He will gain confidence as he feels sure of having a warm response from us when he wants it.

GOOD TEACHING CONTRIBUTES TO DEVELOPMENT OF CONFIDENCE

By the techniques we use as teachers we will help the child grow more secure and confident. Let us take as an example the situation of a child climbing on the jungle gym and see what it may mean.

Joan, who is almost three, is just learning to climb; she cautiously and awkwardly manages to get halfway up in the jungle gym and then calls for help, "Help me! I want down!" An adult comes to her rescue and answers the cry by lifting her down. Joan is on the ground, safe, but with all feeling of achievement lost! On another occasion a different adult comes to the rescue. She stands beside the child and says reassuringly, "I'll help you, Joan. Hang on to this bar and put your foot here," thus guiding Joan's climbing back to the ground. Safe on the ground, Joan is elated. She starts right up again and this time is successful in reaching the top. When her mother comes, she can scarcely wait to show her this new achievement.

If, when Joan starts to climb the jungle gym, her mother says in a disgusted voice, "Come on, Joan, you've had all morning to play. I'm in a hurry. You can show me tomorrow," Joan may again lose the feeling of confidence. If her mother is eager to share the experience and watches her, exclaiming, "That's fine, Joan, you've learned to climb way up high," Joan takes another step in growing confident.

Let us summarize briefly some of the things that we can do in the center to increase a child's feelings of security and confidence.

1. *Accept him* as he is, his feelings and his behavior, knowing that there are reasons for the way he feels and acts. Recognize that hitting and other forms of motor expression of feelings are normal for the young child. Stop his unacceptable actions without blaming him or shaming him. We can expect him to change his behavior, but he has a right to his feelings. We want him to respect himself and have confidence in himself. We want him to feel that we have confidence in him.

2. Help him find *acceptable outlets for his feelings*. Help him put his feelings into words, not only as a way of identifying what he feels but also as a step toward control. Help him use many avenues for the expression of feelings, especially the creative avenues, but be sure that feelings are expressed. The really destructive feelings are those that have no recognized outlets.

3. Try to *meet the child's needs* as he indicates what his needs are and leave him free to develop in accordance with his own growth patterns at his own rate. Thus, we will give him confidence and the feeling that he is an adequate person. Refrain from "nudging" him. Instead, try to understand him.

4. *Acquire skills in handling him* that will increase his confidence, making suggestions to him in a positive way, reducing the difficulties of the situations he faces, adjusting demands to fit his capacities, and forestalling trouble when possible.

Projects

1. Observe and record three situations in which the guidance given by the adult was directed toward helping the child to feel more secure and confident. Estimate how successful it was in its effect on the child.

2. Listen to the quality and pitch of the children's voices. List the names of children whose voices are high pitched or strained, soft and indistinct, loud and somewhat harsh, and easy and pleasant. How would you relate what the child's voice seems to reveal with what you know of the child's adjustment and his feelings about himself? Do the same with motor forms of behavior such as posture, hand movement, or body tension.

3. Make a list of emotionally loaded words sometimes used in describing behavior of a child, such as spoiled, stubborn, selfish. Indicate briefly how the use of such words may influence objective observation of behavior. Give an example of some descriptive terms which might be used to describe the same behavior in the case of some of the words listed above.

For Your Further Reading

Elkind, D. (1981). *The hurried child: Growing up too fast too soon.* Reading, MA: Addison-Wesley. Discusses the effects of the schools, parents, and television in hurrying children's development.

Gonzalez-Mena, J. (1979). What is a good beginning? *Young Children, 34*(3), 47–53. Discusses ways of achieving a good relationship with the young child.

Hyson, M. C. (1979). Lobster on the sidewalk: Understanding and helping children with fears. *Young Children, 34*(5), 54–60. The origins of children's fears, plus useful ways for adults to help children cope with fearful situations.

Jervis, K. (Ed.). (1985). *A guide to attachment, separation and loss: Strategies for helping two to four year olds.* Los Angeles: Edna Reiss Memorial Trust. A simple book, growing out of a conference, with helpful tips for adults; beautiful photographs capture the mood of the book.

Knowles, D. W., & Reeves, N. (1983). *But won't granny need her socks? Dealing effectively with children's concerns about death and dying.* Dubuque, IA: Kendall/Hunt. Helps adults respond appropriately to children's questions and concerns about death and dying.

Provence, S., Naylor, A., & Patterson, J. (1977). *The challenge of day care.* New Haven: Yale University Press. Chapter 5 deals helpfully with separation for very young children.

Yamamoto, K. (Ed.). (1972). *The child and his image: Self-concept in the early years.* Boston: Houghton Mifflin. Deals with the developing self through communication and nurturing and the "bruised" self.

Fire (boy, 4 years 4 months)

14 ◆ Feelings of Hostility and Aggression

The problem of what to do about feelings of hostility and aggression is a difficult one for individuals and for groups. It is not likely to be solved by avoidance or by denying the existence of these feelings. As we have pointed out, the existence of a feeling must be accepted before it can be handled constructively. Only when we have accepted our hostile, aggressive feelings can we discover (1) the best ways to handle them and (2) the best ways to prevent them from multiplying.

We can use the center as a laboratory to study the problems of hostile and aggressive feelings and to try to understand them. Resentment and hostility expressed aggressively are evident in the behavior of children whenever the situation is one which is not rigidly controlled by adults,

245

whenever children are free to show us how they feel. A child who is angry may address the teacher as "You dummy," and this teacher will be the one in whom he has some confidence. He is likely to be more polite to the teacher with whom he does not feel as safe. "We don't like you," sing out two children to a third. Occasionally, a chorus of "name calling" greets the visitor to the center. Some children do not reveal hostile feelings by such direct expressions, but they may have these same feelings anyway. We can learn to recognize their less direct expressions, too. We can learn how to prevent more hostility and aggressiveness from developing.

HOSTILITY AND AGGRESSION ARE TIED UP WITH GROWTH

A certain amount of hostile feeling in all of us results from the growing-up process. As infants we were helpless and often our needs were not met. We felt threatened by the greater strength of the people around us. There were many frustrations and interferences for us all. Frustrations breed resentment when the frustrated person is little and helpless.

Some aggressiveness is necessary, for growth itself is a going-forward process which demands it. Lawrence Kubie states, "The acquisition of positive, self-assertive, commanding and demanding attitudes in the first two years of human life is an essential step in the development of every child."[1] However, much unnecessary aggressiveness, as well as hostility, is aroused by some of the traditional methods of handling children at home and at school. Healthy aggression becomes unhealthy. Resentments develop that interfere with healthy growth. As our knowledge and understanding grow and we use better methods of guiding children in the growing-up processes, we should be able to reduce the amount of hostility and unproductive aggression in the world with increasing effectiveness.

Resentment Is Increased by Inconsistencies in Guidance

The amount of resentment and aggression as well as the amount of confusion and guilt over these feelings is perhaps greater in our society than in some others because the child meets many inconsistencies in guidance. The child when with his parents at home is supposed to be obedient. On the playground he is expected to "stand up for himself" and come out ahead in highly competitive types of situations. The same bit of behavior is wrong in one place and right in another. These inconsistencies make learning difficult for the child and may increase the number of mistakes he makes and the resulting guilt that he may feel.

[1] L. S. Kubie. (1948). The child's fifth freedom. *Child Study*, *25*, 67–80, 88.

Children in our culture also carry a handicapping load of resentment when parental management is harsh and when standards are rigidly or inconsistently enforced. Such methods may arouse a great deal of hostile aggressiveness in individuals. We have usually refused to acknowledge the extent of these feelings and have gone on multiplying them—in children and in ourselves. The result is that they spill over in all kinds of unsuspected ways in our personal and group lives. Few problems are more important than those of facing and reducing the hostility we feel.

Patterns of Violence in a Society Make Control of Aggression Difficult

Managing feelings of hostility and aggression in constructive ways is made more difficult for the child who is exposed to patterns of violence in behavior in the society. Children watch programs on television that are full of brutal attacks on people, cruelty, and disrespect for the dignity of human beings. The example set by these patterns of behavior in television programs as well as their existence on the street makes it only too easy for children to follow these patterns themselves when their own controls break down.

There are uncontrolled, violent ways of expressing the negative feelings within us, and there are more "civilized" ways that require understanding and control. Feelings must be expressed, but they can be expressed in words, in art forms, or in actions that do no harm to others.

Children Need to Express Hostile Feelings

It is safe to say that *all* children at times feel aggressive and hostile but that not all children act out these feelings. In the past we have tended to give approval to the children who did not act out their negative feelings. From what we now know about mental health, we realize that it is essential that feelings be expressed, and expressed on the spot if possible, if a person is to remain mentally healthy. The problem is to discover avenues of expression that are not destructive rather than to deny expression to these feelings. It is unlikely that we can have a peaceful world when individuals in it are carrying around a load of hostility with the added guilt that having such feelings and denying them is sure to create. We must help children to face and to express their hostile feelings.

It is worth quoting Kubie again:

Repeatedly in the early years of life anger must be liquidated at its birth or it will plague us to the grave. . . . If we are even to lessen the neurotic distortions of human aggression, then it seems clear that the anger must be allowed and encouraged to express itself in early childhood, not in blindly destructive acts but in words, so as to keep it on the fullest possible level of conscious awareness. Furthermore such conscious ventilation of feelings must be encouraged in the very situations in which they have arisen, and toward those adults and children who have been either the active or the innocent sources of the feelings. Only in this way can we lessen the burden of unconscious aggression which every human being carries from infancy to the grave.[2]

Adults Must Accept Hostile Feelings in Themselves

The important job of parent and teacher, then, becomes one of encouraging expression of feeling in nondamaging ways and of diminishing the number of situations in which negative feelings are developed. Our ability to do this will depend in part on our ability to accept our own feelings, or we will find ourselves meeting aggression by aggression and hostility by hostility. When a child calls us "You dummy," we must be able to accept the child's feeling of anger without getting it tangled up with our own angry feelings. This will be easier as we realize that his words offer no real threat to us, as such words might have in the past or under other circumstances. We happen to be the recipient of his anger and hostility at the moment, but these feelings have been generated by many factors in his past experiences, just as our own have been.

To the extent that we were punished or shamed for the expression of our own hostile feelings, we may find it hard to accept that the child needs to express such feelings. If our own defenses against such feelings are strong or if we have permitted ourselves little expression, it may be

[2] Ibid., pp. 70, 89.

Running in a play field is an outlet for energy and aggressive feelings.

Valley College, Campus Child Development Center

difficult for us to permit expression for others. It remains important for us to achieve this acceptance if we are to be of help to the child.

MARVIN COULD COPE WITH STRONG FEELINGS BECAUSE HE COULD EXPRESS THEM. Let us look at an example of the steps one child took to master his anxiety and resentment as he prepared himself to cope with a situation. The year before, Marvin had attended a child-care center for five days. He had objected to going and had cried each day. His parents had not stayed with him, but the director had reported he was "a nice quiet little boy." However, the parents learned that on the fifth day he had climbed into a chair and stayed in it all day, clutching his teddy bear. He had not eaten lunch or taken a nap. As he was a lively, active three-year-old at home, the youngest of three children, they realized that he had really been unhappy and arranged for his care with a caregiver in the neighborhood while they were at work.

They talked over plans the next year and decided to try the center again. Marvin was now four, and there was to be another teacher, whom they knew, in charge. Here is the father's report of what happened when he broached the subject to Marvin.

> Marvin was eating his breakfast. He was in his usual exuberant mood while eating his cereal. He was dive-bombing his spoon into the bowl with appropriate sound effects.
>
> "Marvin," I said, "one of Daddy's friends is going to be working in the center you went to with Tommy. Would you like to visit her with me sometime?"
>
> Marvin stopped eating, his spoon poised in midair. His eyes grew wide with alarm. His body tensed and he almost visibly drew into himself. He continued to stare at me and his lower lip began to tremble.
>
> "If you take me to that center again I'll throw a bomb at it and break it all up!" he blurted.
>
> "We could go just for a visit," I said somewhat uneasily, not at all prepared for the impact the idea still held for him.
>
> "They're bad there! Those children don't like me! That lady doesn't like me!"
>
> "You liked Tommy. Didn't Tommy play with you?"
>
> Marvin was breathing heavily. After a pause he said, "Tommy could come to my house and play with me. I won't go there again!"
>
> "You didn't like that center?"
>
> "No! I will take my axe and chop it all up!"
>
> "You don't want to go there again?"
>
> He was a bit more relaxed. "No." A pause. "No. They don't have good toys. Or good boys and girls. Or good people."
>
> "You didn't have fun there?"
>
> "No." He became quite agitated again. Then, in a quiet voice, he said, "I'm tired of eating." He put down his spoon, climbed down from his chair

and walked into our bedroom. He climbed into our bed and covered himself up.

I sat down on the bed beside him. "Pat me," he said.

I patted him and told him we would not visit the center until he wanted to and that I would stay with him while he visited when we did go.

"But not today?" he asked.

"No, not today," I agreed.

"Not for this many days?" He carefully arranged his fingers so that he could hold up three.

"Not for many days," I agreed.

He lay still for a moment. "I better finish my cereal," he said, throwing back the blankets. He climbed out of bed and went back to the table. "Not for *many* days," he said to himself as he climbed into his chair.

We see that Marvin's first response is a rush of strong feeling. Then he mobilizes his forces and asserts himself. He attacks aggressively, "I'll throw a bomb at it and break it all up." He will solve the problem by destroying it. Wisely, his father does not resist but retreats a bit. Marvin then tries to think of reasons why going to the center must not happen. He does this effectively. Not only is the center "bad" and the lady there "doesn't like me," but his friend could come to his house to play. His father tries to put Marvin's feelings into words more directly, "You didn't like that center." Marvin's aggressiveness returns, "I will take my axe and chop it all up." His father then states the heart of the problem, "You don't want to go there again." Marvin seems a bit more relaxed as it is put into words by his father. He can count on his father's understanding. This time he is less negative. He says they don't have good people there rather than saying they are bad.

His acceptance begins, but his appetite has gone. He leaves the table and goes to his parents' bed, climbs in, and covers himself up. He goes to the most comforting place available to him and hides himself. His father follows silently, taken aback by the intensity of the child's feeling, appreciative of the difficulty of the problem that the child must struggle with. "Pat me," says Marvin, needing and able to use the support he knows an understanding father can give. Now the father suggests a compromise. They will not visit until Marvin feels ready and he, the father, will stay with him. We see the "mutual regulation," the working out of a problem together which brings good solutions and good relations when there is understanding. Marvin tests it out, "But not today?" and his father agrees. Then Marvin asserts himself again, but this time it is in having a share in the decision. "Not for this many days," holding up three fingers. When his father says, "Not for many days," Marvin's response is, "I better finish my cereal." He climbs out of bed and returns to the table, saying, "Not for *many* days," as he climbs into his chair. He has coped with the situation actively and constructively. His self-respect and confidence remain. His father has stood by him in the steps he took to master his anxieties. One suspects there has been a mutual growth in understanding, and both will be able to meet the situation when the "many days" are over and it becomes a reality. They are better prepared. Marvin did enter as planned and he liked the new teacher. She was "good," and he made friends at the center.

SOURCES OF HOSTILE FEELINGS

Let us discuss some of the common situations in which resentment is felt by children, how feelings develop in these situations, and how they may be liquidated.

Feelings of Jealousy

When a new baby arrives in his home the child may feel jealous and hostile. Parents are often afraid that the older child will be jealous and may reassure themselves that he "doesn't seem the least bit jealous." Yet it is inevitable that an older child will resent in some respects the coming of a new baby, however much he may also enjoy other aspects of the changed situation. Julia, a well-adjusted child, was not eager to receive a baby sister into her home. She was at the center when her grandmother came with the news of the arrival of the long-awaited baby. After hearing the news and asking some questions, Julia reassured herself, "She won't come home today, will she?" When her grandmother affirmed this, she added, "I don't want her to," and returned to her play.

If parents ignore the child's jealousy it may come out indirectly in his too rough hugging of the baby, in "accidentally" hurting it, or in an increased cruelty in his play with other children. These indirect ways are not so healthy as a direct expression in words. They are less understandable and less likely to drain the child's feelings of guilt and may even add a burden of guilt feeling. There is less need to be afraid of hostile feelings themselves than of what they do to us when we try to hide these feelings and thus lose control over them.

Liquidating Hostile Feelings at the Center

When there is a new baby at home, the child's feelings often spill out in his behavior at the center. He will act them out in the doll corner, perhaps, spanking the dolls frequently, smothering them with blankets, or throwing one on the floor and stamping on it. In this way he relieves himself by releasing some of the hostility he may be feeling, making it easier to face the real situation. A center should have some dolls that can stand this kind of treatment. A direct "draining off" of feelings in this way may be about the only means some children have of expressing the conflict they feel. Many parents do not, as Julia's parents did, understand and accept expressions of feeling.

If our interest is in sound personality development, it is not hard to see how little real value there would be in emphasizing the proper care of dolls at this point. If one did insist that dolls were not to be treated in this way, one would block for the child this avenue of expression, leaving him in an emotionally dangerous situation. There might be a good deal of trouble ahead for him in his relationship with the real baby. It is worth noting that anthropologists report that certain very gentle tribes of Native Americans permit young children to show great cruelty to animals, which, they suggest, may serve the purpose of draining off some of the hostility children feel, and account in part for the friendly behavior among these Native Americans.

Rubber dolls and other rubber toys serve as a good medium for the release of hostile aggressive feelings. They can be pinched and bitten with a good deal of satisfaction. Jeremy, whose relationships at home had been tense and strained, had felt his position in the family threatened by the return of a father who was almost a stranger to him, and then even more threatened by the arrival of a new baby. His insecurity and hostility came out in the readiness with which he attacked and bit other children in the center. The teacher had to watch him constantly to prevent his attacking others. She found that she could substitute a rubber doll and that he seemed to find relief in biting it. Biting is usually done by a child who feels helpless. He can see no other way to meet his problems. She carried the doll in her pocket for a time so that it would be instantly available, and she gave it to him when she saw his tension mounting, saying, "I know! You feel just like biting someone. Here's the doll. It's all right to bite the doll." The least interference or the smallest suggestion of a rejection filled his already full cup of negative feelings to overflowing. He had to do something, and biting on the doll served to reduce the feeling to more manageable proportions. The teacher's acceptance and her understanding of the way he felt gave him confidence. The day came when he ran to her himself because he knew that he needed to bite the doll. He could recognize his feelings and handle them in a way that was not damaging to the other children. He began to have more success and find more satisfaction in his play. Steadily he had less hostile feelings to handle.

During this time, Jeremy had also been engaging in a great deal of verbal aggression against the adults in the center. When he was faced with the necessity of limiting his activity during the rest period, for example, he would lie on his bed and attack the teacher verbally, "cut her up, her legs, her head, her arms," and would sometimes, "put her in the garbage can," or sometimes, "put her in the toilet." His words revealed the extent to which he himself had been hurt and felt angry and fearful. Very slowly, with many avenues of expression open to him, he released some of his resentful feelings, and the acceptance and success he had in the center helped him to build other kinds of feelings. He discovered other kinds of relationships, and the warm, supporting relationship he had with his teacher left him free to find friends among the children.

Another Source of Resentment Is the Necessity for Keeping Clean

Another source of resentment in children, in addition to changing positions in the family, lies in the demands made on them to "keep clean" and the fear and guilt they often feel when they yield to the impulse to play in dirt.

Ruth was a child whose mother had emphasized cleanliness and proper behavior, including a strict toilet-training regimen. Ruth showed as much hostility and resentment toward adults as did any child in the group at first. She refused requests or suggestions which came from an adult, even though they might be ones she really wanted to carry out. Her mother characterized her behavior as "just plain stubbornness." Their life together had been a succession of issues over one habit or the other. The following incident occurred after she had been at the center a year and had begun to participate in activities with confidence; at this point she was even affectionate with the teachers she knew, saying, "I like you," with real feeling. Even then she still grew disturbed and anxious when faced with a little dirt.

Ruth happened to be on the playground with a student teacher. She was swinging. It was muddy, and as Ruth's boots swept through the puddle under the swing, they splashed mud on her and on the teacher. Ruth looked disturbed. "What will your Dad say?" she asked the student teacher anxiously. The teacher assured her that he wouldn't say anything and that it was just an accident and couldn't be helped. But Ruth answered darkly, "Oh yes, he'll say something."

She again tried swinging but once more they both got splashed. Ruth said warmly, "I'm sorry," and she repeated, "What will your Dad say?"

This time the teacher replied by asking Ruth what she thought he would say. Ruth answered, "He'll say you're all dirty and will have to clean up and take a bath," and then she added, "I'm going inside and stay in, if you don't mind." She went in and did not come outside again during the morning.

Even though she expected no punishment for splashing the mud in this situation, it was a "bad" thing to her. It meant disapproval from the adults on whom this insecure little girl had to depend. Standards for behavior were high and punishment severe. Her anxiety was apparent in her words and her behavior. It was not hard to see why she had shown hostility and unfriendliness.

In this situation, a more experienced teacher not only would have recognized the extent of the anxiety the child was showing by her questions, but she also would have tried to help her put it into words so that it might have become more understandable and manageable—she would not have needed to run away from it. She might have verbalized in some such way as this, "Does your Dad get mad when you're dirty? Mothers and Dads often do, don't they, when children get dirty?" This might have given Ruth the help she did not find in the student's denial that *her* Dad would be mad. Ruth knew better about hers! It would have made it a common experience, easier to face. The teacher might have continued, "Sometimes it is all right to get dirty because we can get cleaned up afterward just as we can now. Sometimes it's even fun to get dirty. I used to like to myself," and this might have relieved the child. She might have been able to stay outdoors and have fun. She might have been better able to trust herself.

The Cue May Be a Small One

Sometimes it is harder to identify the feelings that lie behind words or acts. The child may be afraid to express his hostility or his aggression openly. We have to find the meaning from a very small cue. Grace, for example, had always been very "good." This meant that she was not able to be very expressive or creative. In the center she gradually began to find it possible to act with greater freedom. It was clear to anyone watching her that she often wanted to act differently but did not dare.

One day the teacher observed Grace carefully laying several chairs on their sides on the floor. The teacher made no comment, not understanding the meaning of this behavior. The next day Grace's mother asked anxiously about how Grace was behaving at the center. She was worried because Grace had told her that the day before she had "knocked over all the chairs." It was then clear to the teacher that this careful laying of a few chairs on their sides was in reality an aggressive act for Grace. It was as far as she dared to go in expressing her aggressive feelings, and she would have liked to have made it a much bigger act than it was.

Grace needed to be helped to see that she could express aggressive feelings, that she could really be accepted as a little girl who had "bad" feelings as well as "good" ones, that there were safe limits at the center, too. Her parents needed to have more understanding of the importance of accepting all of Grace's feelings.

Henry was very timid and showed much the same kind of need when he declared, "I'm going to make a lot of noise," and then took one block and carefully threw it on the floor. His parents approved of quiet boys. He had few opportunities to be noisy, and he was trying to show that he really dared to be the kind of person he wanted to be.

With children like Grace and Henry it may be important to accept their "acting out" of feelings without limiting or redirecting them at first, provided the behavior does not harm them or others. When the child has an opportunity to convince himself that the "bad" part of him is accepted, then he is ready to take the more constructive step of putting the feelings into words, of talking about the feeling as Marvin did with his father. Then the child can begin to manage such feelings more acceptably.

Failure to Get Attention and Response

Failure to get attention and response will arouse resentment and hostility in children, too, especially in insecure children who are seeking reassurance by getting attention. Their feelings are involved in a way that makes them sensitive to failure. Situations are constantly arising in which children want attention from the teacher or from other children, want to feel important and needed—and fail. They are resentful and hostile as a result.

The teacher helps solve the problem.
Santa Monica College, Child Development Center

Whenever the situation is competitive, there is more likelihood for failures. A child may want the attention of the teacher and, not getting it, may attack either the child, whom he feels is his rival, or the teacher, whom he feels is deserting him. A child like this needs to have his confidence built up so that he will see others as less of a threat to him. He needs help in accepting and finding better outlets for his feelings. When it is all right to admit wanting the teacher all to yourself, it becomes easier to work out a better solution than attacking others.

As teachers, we should be aware of the strong need most children have to feel sure of their place and to receive a share of our attention. When we give attention to one child, we need to remember that other children may be feeling left out. We saw an example in Betsy, who untied her shoe so that the teacher could tie it for her just as the teacher had done for another child. Not many children can deal with their feelings as directly as Betsy. They may need some help from us. A teacher may say, "I think you'd like me to do something with you sometimes. I've been doing a lot with Helen lately because she is new and isn't sure about what we do. Of course I like helping you, too. Remember when you first came and I had to show you what to do? Now it's different, and you sometimes help the new children." And she can add, "But you tell me when you really want me to do something for you and I'll do it if I can." This attention helps a child feel sure that there is a place for him and that he can have attention, too.

"Nudging" and Harsh Methods of Control

Children who have been "nudged" from one stage of development to the next and who have had high standards set for their behavior may feel a great deal of resentment which they often cannot express directly. One way that these children may try to handle the feeling is by reproving others. They identify with the teacher to escape from the feeling of being helpless. Joshua, for example, has received a great deal of punishment from parents who have never heard of any methods of discipline except the "good old-fashioned ones." Joshua and Larry were building a block tower to dangerous heights. The teacher warned, "Not so high." Joshua immediately turned to Larry and said severely, "The teacher said no more blocks, and when she says something you mind her." Thus he got rid of some of his resentment, but his "punishing" attitude makes it hard for any but the most comfortable children to play with him. Incidentally, in Joshua's behavior we get some insight into the quality of control which harshly disciplined people impose when they themselves are in power and into the need they often feel to identify with the controlling authority. Children who are harshly punished often identify with the aggressor and become punishing people themselves.

Sam Wanted Desperately to Feel Big

Sam is an outstanding example of a child who had been pushed around in many ways without gaining much loving and giving from the adults in return for their heavy demands. He was expected to behave like a little gentleman when there were visitors at home, and he usually came to the center in his best clothing instead of dressing in play clothes like the other children. His speech was more like that of an adult—even his vocabulary of swear words. He was advanced in his development, but he was also burdened with a tremendous load of hostility. It came out in the frequency and the cruelty with which he attacked younger children and animals and in his many verbal attacks against the adults when he discovered that these would not be punished. Instead of trying to identify with the teacher, he fought her on every occasion.

As the group was coming in from the playground one day, he savagely attacked a friendly little boy who got in his way. The teacher separated them quickly and firmly. Sam exclaimed, "That was fun." The teacher merely said, "It wasn't fun for Jim. It hurt him," and told Sam to wait outside. As soon as the others were taken care of, she returned and sat down beside him. They knew each other well, and she felt sure that he could accept her presence without feeling threatened by it.

"I wonder why it makes you feel good to hurt Jim and the other children," she speculated quietly, not knowing whether he could give her any clue. He immediately launched into a description of how his uncle had brought him a toy gun, and he and his "little friend" (an imaginary friend) could use it.

Again the teacher answered, "Sometimes it makes children feel big to have a gun and it makes them feel big to hurt someone. Do you ever feel that way?"

With apparent relief the child answered, "Yes." They discussed how people wanted to feel big and how sometimes it wasn't fun to be little. The teacher mentioned that being friendly sometimes made people feel big. Sam stuttered as he talked and was near tears, something that almost never happened with him. He seldom dared to relax his defenses enough to cry.

At last the teacher told Sam that it was about time for them to go inside. He said, almost crying, "I could stay out here until afternoon." "Yes," she said, "you could." She busied herself picking things up and then asked, "Well, now you can either come in with me or stay outside. I wonder which you are going to do?"

He got up and said rather sadly, "I don't know." At that the teacher knelt down and put her arms around this hurt, bewildered little boy and for the first time he could accept her loving and nestled close against her, no longer "tough." She said, "I know how it is," and then suggested, "You might paint a big picture inside." He nodded and took her hand,

and they went inside. He went straight to the finger-painting table where there was an opportunity for him to express more of what he felt.

Sam gained at the center and became better able to play with others. He was imaginative and resourceful and found a place for himself as his hostility decreased. When he left the center, he was a less hostile child but still needed sensitive understanding. Although his mother had gained some insight into the child's problems, his father would accept none of this "sissy stuff" and continued to rely on repression and a generous use of the rod to bully his son into "good" behavior. It is interesting to note that when Sam was in high school some years later he excelled in athletics and became a person of importance there. He also received several awards for his artwork. He seemed to have found outlets for some of his earlier hostile aggressiveness.

To the Child, Even Friendly Adults May Seem to Be a Threat

All children, to some extent, are struggling with feelings of being little and helpless. Even friendly adults are so much stronger and more powerful than the child that they represent a potential threat. Children handle their feelings in different ways. When they are together in groups, they are quick to blame the adult for things that happen. We may overhear the following when Ricky comes out on the playground and says to Nate, "Who covered up our holes?" "Oh, some teacher probably," replies Nate. Both these boys are friendly with teachers, but they recognize in them the source of many interferences and frustrations as well as the source of needed support. They are glad to identify with each other against the teacher at times.

Craig gives us another amusing example. He happened to throw some sand, which got into Celia's eye. Celia had to go inside and have the sand washed out of her eye. When she came back on the playground, Craig was very sympathetic and wanted to look into her eye. He said to her comfortingly, "I should have thrown it in the teacher's eye and then it wouldn't have hurt you, Celia."

As adults we are concerned with helping children to express these feelings in ways that will not be damaging and yet will serve to reduce them or turn them into constructive channels. We need to understand the possible avenues of expression.

WHAT ARE POSSIBLE AVENUES FOR EXPRESSION OF FEELINGS?

Motor expressions, of course, offer the simplest, most direct means of releasing feeling for children. That is why hitting, pushing, and biting are common among young children. However, other more acceptable forms of expression can be utilized instead. Pounding at the workbench, hitting a soft material like clay, using a punching bag, biting on a rubber toy, throwing a ball against a backstop, or even running and digging can serve as an outlet for feelings in ways that do no damage to anyone. Some children give vent to their resentment at adult interferences by the hard pats they give each piece of paper they paste or by pounding clay.

The skillful teacher will accept the feeling and put it into words: "I know you feel like hitting him because he has the tricycle you want." She will channel the expression into acceptable behavior. "When you feel like that, you can hit our punching bag or pound the clay."

Language Is Another Avenue for Expression

Language is another type of outlet. The crying child relieves himself of a lot of feeling; so does the child who hurls angry words at an offender.

Young children may verbally destroy the teacher in all kinds of ways and tell her "to get dead." Such verbal expressions relieve their feelings. They can see that it results in no harm to the teacher. She remains their friend. It is a satisfactory way for a child to "liquidate" feelings that might otherwise be a source of trouble. Later, as adults, these same children may use fantasy rather than verbal expression and be helped in relieving serious irritations.

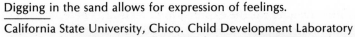

Digging in the sand allows for expression of feelings.
California State University, Chico. Child Development Laboratory

Dancing allows feelings to be expressed.

Santa Monica College, Child Development Center

Art and Music Are Avenues, Too

Art and music offer avenues for the expression of feeling. These avenues of expression are important because they may extend into the adult years and serve as a protection against the emotional load that adults must carry. If opportunities with art are to have value as a means of release for feeling, they must be experiences in which the child uses the medium in his own way. The child who paints the same motif or theme again and again is saying something about the way he feels through his pictures. He may do this through his work with clay or music, too. We need to conserve the values of art as an avenue of expression of feelings. These values are lost if art consists of copying patterns or models.

HOW THE TEACHER MEETS AGGRESSIVE BEHAVIOR

When feelings have many avenues of expression, they do not pile up and become so unmanageable. The teacher encourages expression even though she may face problems within the group situation. How can the teacher meet the needs of individuals and of groups?

The Teacher Helps the Children by Her Example

The teacher helps all children when she remains undisturbed in the face of aggressive behavior and does not meet anger with angry feelings in return. Because of her example, the children will find it less disturbing to meet the inevitable aggressions that occur in their world. The child who is most disturbed over being called a name is probably a child who has been severely reproved for name calling himself. Adults have attached importance to this kind of behavior. Children are likely to meet some rejection and some angry responses wherever they happen to be. If their own aggressive behavior has been met casually, they will find it easier to accept unruffled the attacks they receive. They are less afraid and better able to take the world as it is. In responding to aggressive behavior, the teacher can say, "We all feel this way sometimes." She is not upset by it because she does not accept it as a personal attack.

The Teacher Helps When She Accepts and Interprets Behavior

An important way to help is by interpreting to one child some reasons why another child is behaving as he is. She may reassure the first child by saying, "He's calling you names because he's mad. It's your turn on the swing and he wants it to be his. It makes him feel better to call you 'dope.' You don't need to let it bother you."

She may help a child by showing him how to meet the rejection by explaining, "They want to play by themselves. It's all right. I'll help you find another place to play and you can look for someone who does want to play with you." She does not say, "But you must let him play," to the angry child who has shouted at another child, "You go away!" The newcomer will not be likely to have a successful experience with a person who feels unfriendly toward him.

There are solutions which protect the group while still respecting the needs of individuals. If the child who is excluding others is monopolizing the homemaking corner, the sandbox, or some other area, the teacher can say, "It's all right if you want to play by yourself, but all the children use the homemaking corner or the sandbox. You can make a house over in this corner and leave the rest for the children who do want to play together."

The Teacher May Need to Help Hostile and Insecure Children by Giving Them Techniques for Cooperating

Children need protection when they are unsure and suspicious of others, not denial of the way they feel. The demands of group life are complex. Children who are hostile and lacking in social skills may not be able to play with more than one child at a time. They may need to exclude others.

The teacher helps when she accepts exclusion and makes it possible for them to be successful at their level.

Helping a child who is insecure and hostile to be successful may mean reducing the difficulties he faces. He may need to play with just one child at a time or with materials that can be shared easily or in situations that make few demands for adaptation. It may mean suggesting a desirable way to approach others before he fails in his approach. The teacher may say, "You might get a block and help John build the road," or, when another child approaches, she may forestall failure by interpreting, "I think he would like to dig with you. I will help him find another shovel." Reducing the difficulty of a situation and forestalling and preventing failure are helpful techniques to use with children who find it difficult to accept others.

The Teacher Helps by Providing a Suitable Environment

The teacher also helps the child handle the problem of his hostility and aggressiveness by a thoughtful planning of the environment and the program in the center. In a physical setup that is designed for him, the child will feel less hostility because he will meet fewer frustrations. He can get his own coat, find the play materials he wants within reach, solve his own problems in many ways, and submit to fewer limitations. The program as well as the physical setup can be designed to reduce, rather than increase, interferences and frustrations. If it is flexible and imposes only essential limitations, it meets individual needs in a way that minimizes hostility. Under this kind of program, teachers become people who help rather than people who interfere with the child.

The Teacher Acts with Firmness

The teacher helps the aggressive, resentful child when she is confident and firm in her management. The child needs firmness not punishment. He may want to feel that someone else is to blame, but his teacher will accept only his need to wish that this were so; she does not accept this as fact. She is sympathetic but firm in dealing with his behavior and in facing the reality of the situation. She states it clearly for him. She has confidence that he will be able to face it, too. She tries to help him deal with his feelings directly, in a constructive way. Her firmness helps steady the angry child and reassure the insecure child.

Punishment does not help a hostile, resentful child. It only increases his burden of feeling. Firm action by the teacher may be essential for him so that he does not hurt others and thus add to his burden of guilt. For example, the teacher acted firmly with Sam, who used biting as a way of attacking. She knew she must prevent his biting children and help him use acceptable means such as biting on a small rubber doll, to relieve himself of the tremendous load of resentment and the feeling of helplessness he carried. If she had punished or rejected this child because of his behavior, she might have offered him no help. The already overburdened little boy would have had to find his way out alone or fail.

We should act promptly to stop some kinds of behavior, but we need not do this in a punishing way. We can remove a disturbing child from the group or hold him firmly, but we do not have to blame him for his actions. We do not try to make him feel more ashamed or even to apologize. Making a child say he is sorry usually means making him say something untrue. Truth is important. Later he may say he is sorry when he really feels this way. Our responsibility is to help him find nondamaging channels to express the resentment he is feeling.

Some Children Need Special Help

When a child is very seriously burdened with hostile feelings, he may need special help. He may be given this help within the group by assigning one teacher or an aide to be with him and to help him manage his feelings. With this kind of individual help, he may be successful. A teacher reported this observation of a child who attacked others on little or no apparent provocation. He had had a great deal of punishment and little real discipline. As he started to hit another child who interfered with him, the teacher caught his arm and held it firmly, while saying, "You must feel very angry." He looked at her in surprise, without resisting, and then nodded in agreement. Suddenly he turned and hugged her. The teacher knew how he felt and he was safe. She returned his hug and added, "Next time you feel angry, I will try to help you."

The child who acts out his hostility may be serving a function for the whole group. They learn what happens by watching him and the way his behavior is handled. If it is handled firmly, without anger, all children feel more comfortable. They have more confidence that their own angry feelings can be managed, if not by them at least by the teacher. The children are learning how to manage their feelings by observing each other and by responding to others.

There is often a "difficult" child in a group. Most children can be helped within the framework of the group to handle their hostile feelings acceptably. An occasional child may need individual therapy outside the group in addition to help within the group.

Participation in a Group Has Special Value for the Timid Child

The value that group participation possesses for many timid children is worth attention. Timid, inhibited children are greatly helped in expressing their feelings by the safety they find within the group. The group provides them with an environment in which it is easier for them to accept their own hostile feelings. These children will benefit greatly from the "freeing" of expression that comes in attending a good center. Children in groups may resort to verbal defiance of the teacher when there is some reason for resisting her. They feel strength in being together, and this feeling is one of the values that group experience holds for them. With people of their own age who are also feeling and expressing resistance, timid children are no longer so afraid of their feelings and behavior. Not as "good" in the conventional sense, they become healthier from the mental health standpoint and capable of achieving more emotional maturity.

Ben is an example of a child who learned to express his real feelings. He was a quiet, timid child who remained dependent on the teacher for a long time after he entered the center. He usually found a place beside her when she sat down, and often held onto her skirt when she moved around the school. When he played, he would select the small toys and take them into a corner. He was not active and vigorous and was never aggressive toward others. Very slowly he began to join the other children in play and to identify himself with the group. He seemed pleased when they shouted names or chanted silly or "naughty" words. Finally he dared to express himself in this way, too. One day he was even a member of a group who defied the teacher from the safe height of the jungle gym.

It was at about this time that a videotape taken at the center was shown one morning. A picture of Ben's teacher appeared on the screen. Laughing, Ben went up to the screen and slapped her image. It was probably no accident that he chose the teacher's image. That act may have symbolized the strength and the freedom to be aggressive which he was feeling. With that slap he proved that he had left his dependence behind. His relationship with the teacher was a friendly one, but he was no longer tied to her skirt as he had been in the beginning. Ben had known plenty of love at home but not much chance to express the resentments that he inevitably felt. As soon as he dared to be aggressive, to express what he felt, he became more active and social. He had no great amount of hostility to release. Soon he was able to maintain and accept the limits which the teachers set for the group. He developed rapidly.

We may summarize what we have been saying about hostility and aggression by pointing out that we must: (1) accept the existence of these feelings; (2) see that they are expressed in some acceptable way, but as directly as possible, so that the individual will be freed from the emotional load that he will otherwise carry; and (3) learn how to handle children without creating in them unnecessary feelings of hostility and resentment which make good social adjustment difficult.

Reducing the amount of frustration a young child has to meet, building up his feelings of security and confidence, accepting him as he is rather than "nudging" him into being something different will all help in the solution of the problems which these feelings present to any individual or any form of group life.

Projects

1. Observe and record two situations in which a child faced frustration (was unable to carry out a purpose). How did he try to cope with the situation? What feelings did he express at the time? Later?
2. Report an observation of a child using an appropriate defense; an inappropriate defense. Give reasons for your evaluation in each case. Describe the different kinds of defenses which you have observed children using. Why were they used?
3. Observe and record a situation in which a teacher helped an angry child put his feelings into words.

For Your Further Reading

Caldwell, B. (1977). Aggression and hostility in young children. *Young Children, 32*(2), 4-13. A comprehensive review of past and present thinking on aggression, with practical guides to decrease aggression and increase cooperation.

Carlsson-Paige, N., & Levin, D. C. (1985). *Helping children understand peace, war and the nuclear threat.* Washington, DC: National Association for the Education of Young Children. A topic difficult for adults to discuss with young children, yet research indicates that children younger than eight are aware of nuclear threat. How we can help children cope with and make sense out of threats of war.

Honig, A. S. (1983). TV violence and child agression: Research review. *Day Care and Early Education, 10*(4), 41-45. Simple summary of strong evidence from over 2500 studies that watching TV violence causes later child aggression. Discusses differences between home or laboratory TV viewing. Practical suggestions for parents and teachers.

Ives, S. B., Fassler, D., & Lash, M. (1985). *The divorce workbook: A guide for kids and families.* Burlington, VT: Waterfront Books. Designed for adults to use with children aged 4 to 12 to help them deal with separation and divorce.

Kemmer, E. (1984). *Violence in the family: An annotated bibliography.* New York: Garland. Useful references on the topic from 1960-82, including many on child abuse.

Murphy, L. B., & Leeper, E. M. (1970). *Away from bedlam.* DHEW Publication No. (OCD) 72-18. Washington, DC: U.S. Department of Health, Education, and Welfare, Office of Child Development. Discusses causes and prevention of bedlam in centers, with suggestions for handling the angry and disruptive child.

PART FIVE

◆

THE PROGRAM EVOLVES FROM EXPERIENCES

Peter in an Apple Tree (boy, 3 years 7 months)

15 ♦ The Early Childhood Education Movement

To understand the nursery school program and the philosophy on which it is based we must see it in relation to the twentieth century and social changes taking place. The roots of the movement are deeply embedded in the past, but the role of education has expanded. Education is adapting to the needs of human beings who are coping with social change. The concept of the family is undergoing social changes.

One of the changes taking place is in the position of women in today's world. More and more women of all classes are working outside the home. Families are smaller. Men are sharing more of the home responsibilities with women. Women are moving toward a more equal status with men in the business and professional world as well as in the general labor market.

Quality child care centers assume new importance under these changing conditions. Women who decide to work outside the home need adequate care for their young children while they are at work. There is evidence, too, that all children may need some group experience outside the home by the time they are four, and almost all parents can use the support that a good child development center can offer.

HISTORY OF THE DEVELOPMENT OF EARLY CHILDHOOD EDUCATION IN THE TWENTIETH CENTURY

In the late nineteenth and early twentieth centuries there had been a growing interest in early childhood education. Among the people who contributed to the earlier thought and the literature in Europe were John Amos Comenius, Jean Jacques Rousseau, and Johann Pestalozzi, as well as Sigmund Freud and later his daughter, Anna Freud. Frederick Froebel opened the first kindergarten in Germany in 1837 and was influenced by the work of Pestalozzi. Froebel is known as the Father of the Kindergarten. He valued the child as a child and saw play as serious and significant. He viewed the child as a unique, creative, and productive person who learned through playful activity. Froebel wrote that "play is the highest phase of child development."[1] He laid an important foundation for what would be a later concept—the child-centered school.

At the turn of the century G. Stanley Hall and John Dewey were among the important American educators who were writing and teaching. Dewey stressed the need for firsthand experiences for young children, as Froebel had done. In order to test his educational ideas Dewey established a laboratory school at the University of Chicago in 1896.

Following the work of G. Stanley Hall, Arnold Gesell made detailed observations of growth and development in the 1920s and 1930s. He outlined norms for physical development. Gesell felt that the first six years of life were the most important for physical development. His normative approach gained great popular acceptance. John B. Watson, the founder of behaviorism, also had a tremendous influence on child-rearing practices during the 1920s and 1930s. His behaviorist theories about habit training were at variance with some of the researchers in the field. After World War II Benjamin Spock's book, *Baby and Child Care*, did much to counter-act the effect of some of Watson's theories.

The first nursery school was established in 1911 in England by Rachel and Margaret McMillan. The McMillans had worked with children in health clinics in the London slums and wanted to prevent the physical and

[1]S. J. Braun and E. P. Edwards. (1972). *History and theory of early childhood education*. Belmont, CA: Wadsworth.

mental illness they found so prevalent among the children in these slums. The nursery school program they planned included opportunities for children to learn to take care of themselves and to assume responsibility for some "housekeeping" chores. It also had some activities in learning language, colors, and forms, and in reading, writing, arithmetic, and science. Grace Owens, a contemporary of the McMillans, believed that the needs of three- and four-year-old children could be met best by programs that provided large blocks of time for play and other unstructured activities such as art, woodworking, and water and sand play. She thought that reading, writing, and arithmetic should not be introduced to three- and four-year-old children.

About the same time that the McMillans and Grace Owens were opening nursery schools in England, Maria Montessori was working with retarded children in Italy and later teaching children in the slums of Rome. She developed sets of materials that were self-correcting, needed little supervision, and could be used in a sequence from simple to complex. Montessori was interested in children's intellectual development and in their development of good work habits.

In the 1920s Susan Isaacs in England had a program for a small group of children, largely from professional families, for the purpose of learning about the development of young children. She provided the children with a rich variety of practical materials and encouraged children to explore these in their play. She kept full notes of her observations of children's responses. She studied social, emotional, and intellectual aspects of development and interpreted her observations with insights from Freud's and Piaget's theories. Her goal was the development of the whole child.

One of the first nursery schools opened in the United States was the Play School, founded by Caroline Pratt in 1913. It was later called the City and Country School and was directed by Harriet Johnson with the assistance of Lucy Sprague Mitchell. This school was the laboratory for the Bureau of Educational Experiments, which later became the Bank Street College of Education, which is still in New York City. Caroline Pratt designed the unit floor blocks used widely today in nursery schools and kindergartens.

About the same time Hull House, the settlement house founded and directed by Jane Addams in Chicago, opened a nursery school for children of the large immigrant population in the area. It was used for observing children by students from the National College of Education as part of their teacher training program.

Although the general public showed little interest in educational programs for young children, after the First World War two nursery schools opened in the Chicago area. One was in the Franklin School in a poor socioeconomic area, and the other in the Winnetka School in a well-to-do area. These schools existed in part because of Rose Alschuler, a benefactor, who was interested in children and their welfare. She gave generously of her time and money to help maintain the best possible educational programs in both of these settings.

In 1922 the Merrill Palmer School in Detroit opened a nursery school under the director, Edna Noble White. She brought two nursery school teachers from England to teach there in the first years. The nursery school served as the laboratory for students interested in preparing for parenthood or teaching. It was used by students from colleges across the country who came for a term to learn about the development of young children. Also in 1922 a day nursery was opened in Boston and later became the Ruggles Street Nursery School under the direction of Abigail Eliot. The programs of both these schools were influenced by the English nursery schools.

State colleges and some private colleges began establishing laboratory nursery schools beginning in the 1920s. In the late 1920s a Rockefeller foundation grant made possible the opening of nursery schools for training and research in the Universities of Minnesota, Iowa, and California at Berkeley.

Some private nursery schools were opened in the 1920s such as Broadoaks, established in Whittier, California. Dorothy Baruch, the director, wrote one of the early books in the 1930s for students and parents, *Parents and Children Go To School*. Broadoaks later became Pacific Oaks College for teacher training.

During the 1920s and 1930s the nursery school movement flourished, but little attention was given to improving the standards of day care in public or private schools. Research in child development from major universities and colleges was the major contribution during this time.

Lawrence K. Frank was active in promoting the field of child development and parent education throughout the 1930s and after. He thought of child development as multidisciplinary and believed it should draw from anthropology, biology, sociology, medicine, psychology, and psychiatry in order to understand the development of the individual.

During the economic depression in the early 1930s the federal government authorized the establishment of nursery schools to provide care for children from two to five years from low-income families. The schools were established under the Work Progress Administration (WPA) to provide work for unemployed people. Unemployed professional people, such as high school or elementary school teachers and social workers, attended short training courses at colleges or universities with laboratory nursery schools before they began teaching. A consultant from each state visited each WPA school in that state giving in-service training. In addition to the nursery school program the programs included health care and well-balanced meals with menus prepared by nutritionists. The federal government covered almost all of the costs. These programs generally were of positive benefit lessening the strains of the Great Depression for families and individuals. The establishment of these schools funded by the government also raised the hope that nursery schools might become a permanent part of the educational system.

The Lanham Act

A change came with the outbreak of World War II. The WPA-funded programs ended, and unemployment almost disappeared. The federal government met the changed situation by passing the Lanham Act. This act provided funds to establish schools for the care of young children whose mothers entered war-related industries. Some Lanham-funded centers were sponsored by war-related industries and some by community agencies. These centers varied in their standards.

One of the most successful of these centers was in the Kaiser Shipyards in Portland, Oregon. Two well-planned buildings were constructed at the entrances to each of the two shipyards. This program met the child care needs of mothers who worked in the shipyards. At the peak of the war as many as five hundred children a day were cared for in a twenty-four hour program six days a week. The centers had nurses on duty around the clock to meet the health needs of infants and children up to school age. Hot meals that could be taken home were available at a modest cost.

The two Lanham centers sponsored by Kaiser were under the direction of Lois Meek Stolz, with James Hymes heading the staff in one and Edith Dowley the other. All the teaching staff were college graduates, some with more experience in nursery school teaching than others. All of them gained valuable experience. While the Lanham schools were closed abruptly at the end of the war with funding withdrawn by the federal government, many of the teachers continued teaching in other schools throughout the country. Day-care centers, nursery schools, and parent cooperatives as well as teacher training programs in colleges and universities gained because of these teachers and because of the equipment the government sold to institutions at minimal cost.

Public awareness of the nursery school movement and early childhood education grew steadily through the 1950s. Parent cooperative nursery schools and parent education programs gained in popularity. Research in the 1950s continued to support the significance of early childhood education for later school performance.

Sputnik May Have Influenced Early Childhood Education

With the Russian success with Sputnik in 1957, many Americans feared that the United States might be falling behind in its educational program. The solution proposed was to begin to teach reading, writing, and arithmetic at the kindergarten and nursery level, a return to academic "basics" in education which has created problems ever since.

As we have emphasized throughout this book, the kind of "basics" we promote are the foundation for learning which we know from research and experience. These "basics" are based on a wide range of manipulating objects, discovering, and relating to people, all under the guidance of understanding adults. Pushing a child may restrict his learning in the end.

Head Start

In the 1960s the federal government again began supporting programs for young children. The Economic Opportunity Act in the Lyndon B. Johnson administration was designed to attack poverty through a number of community action programs. This War on Poverty included provisions for educational programs to give children from families below the poverty line opportunities for learning to prepare them for school. The Head Start program, as it was called, began with a summer program in 1965. The following year Head Start became an all-year program providing a pre-school experience for four- and five-year-old children. Professionally trained people administered the teaching program, and community groups participated by providing space and services. There were medical and dental services, social services, well-balanced meals, and parent education programs. Volunteers were welcome. The goal was and remains an effort to help the family.

Head Start has maintained its political popularity. It has been widely recognized as one of the most cost-effective and successful federal programs for children. "Hundreds of studies conducted on Head Start since 1970 indicate that, compared to other low-income children, Head Start children score better on standardized tests; achieve more in school and are less likely to fail a grade, drop out, or require special education classes. They are more likely to receive adequate medical care and to be of normal height and weight, with fewer absences from school due to illness and a better performance on physical test scores."[2] Head Start has received federal funding more continuously than any other program for children.

Today more than half of all women with a child under six years of age are working outside the home. Most of these women are in need of child care for their young children. The need for child care is especially critical in single parent families, because many of these families live below the poverty line. Another pressing need is the care of schoolage children before and after school because of the large number of working parents. The need for quality training of people to care for and teach these young children is equally important. Research suggests that there is a correlation between

[2]Children's Defense Fund. (1984). *A children's defense budget: An analysis of the president's FY1985 budget and children.*

teacher education and the quality of the child's preschool experience. "The primary predictor of the effectiveness or quality of child care programs has been found to be the caregiver's child development/child focused training."[3] The need for quality child care in all types of centers continues to be great in the 1980s.

Every era has seen the need for quality care of young children to meet some social or wartime crisis. The 1980s are no different, even though social and economic conditions may have improved.

The National Association for the Education of Young Children

In 1929 a group of nursery school teachers and college teachers of child development formed an association. They decided that this association would be open to anyone working in a field related to young children, including educators, social workers, nurses, doctors, psychologists, therapists, and parents. The group called themselves The Association for Nursery Education and was renamed in 1964 to become The National Association for the Education of Young Children (NAEYC). In 1985 it had a membership of approximately fifty thousand with state associations affiliated with the national association. NAEYC holds an annual meeting. It publishes a journal, *Young Children*, six times a year. It is concerned with children from infants through the age of eight.

Projects

Select an individual, an organization, or agency and report on the contribution this individual or group has made to the field of early childhood education.

For Your Further Reading

Berrueta-Clement, J. R., Schweinhart, L. J., Barnett, W. S., Epstein, A. S., & Weikart, D. P. (1984). *Changed lives: The effects of the Perry Preschool Program on youths through age 19.* Ypsilanti, MI: High/Scope Press. Every early childhood educator needs to be familiar with the findings of the Perry Preschool Program research, showing clearly that high quality preschool experience is cost effective to society.

Chattin-McNichols, J. P. (1981). The effects of Montessori school experience. *Young Children, 36*(5), 49–66. Reviews many comparative studies and shows in which areas of development Montessori programs exceed or are inferior to other programs.

---

[3]Public Policy Report, National Association for the Education of Young Children. (1981). Staff qualifications related to quality child care. *Annual Editions: Early Childhood Education 83/84.* Guilford, CT: Dushkin.

Cook, J. T. (1985). *Child daycare*. Davis, CA: International Dialogue Press. Comprehensive coverage of day-care history and economic dilemmas, particularly urging advocacy in the day-care crisis.

Rousseau, J. J. (1974). *Emile*. (B. Foxley, Trans.). London: J. M. Dent and Sons. (Reprinted from 1933). Also W. Boyd, (Trans. & Ed.). New York: Teachers College. An influential novel on child rearing and education first published in 1762. Rousseau believed that society was inherently corrupt; education should be from the child's immediate contact with the world of nature so that his innate goodness could flower.

Slaughter, D. T. (1982). What is the future of Head Start? *Young Children, 37*(3), 3–9. Reviews the history of Head Start, "which has accomplished everything but what it was originally supposed to accomplish: equal education opportunity"; discusses future prospects, now that we have newer models for helping families.

Spodek, B. (1985). Early childhood education's past as prologue: Roots of contemporary concerns. *Young Children, 40*(5), 3–7. Explores roots and recurring themes in early childhood education, including school entrance age, kindergarten and early reading, preschool as a social change agent, and concepts of knowledge.

Man and Airplane (boy, 3 years 3 months)

16 ◆ The Process of Learning in Early Childhood

Now we will look more closely at the learning process itself and how young children are helped to develop sound strategies for thinking and reasoning.

The development of knowledge in the early stages of growth is personal. It depends on personal relationships between learner and teacher. Learning is done by individuals, not by groups. Children who have shared experiences together may enjoy listening to stories in a small group or to music or poetry; but they do most of their learning as individuals, in different ways, at different rates, about things of immediate and personal interest. Just as they play first as individuals, then in parallel play, and only slowly in groups, so they grow through these same cycles in cognitive activities.

Without stimulation from the environment and encouragement from attentive adults, the child's more complex intellectual skills and competencies may fail to develop or may develop only in restricted ways. Too much inappropriate stimulation may be as damaging as lack of stimulation. The process of learning is exceedingly complex.

THE CHILD AS LEARNER OR "KNOWER"

We must remember that the child has learned a great deal before he enters school. He has had many experiences, and he understands his world on the basis of these experiences. He already "knows" a great deal, and our teaching must be based on a knowledge of and a feeling for his understandings. It is important for him not to skip any stages, psychological or intellectual, in his development.

Each child has his own pace and style of learning. Some children seem to learn best by watching. Some children learn best by manipulating and through trial and error. Some children stay with things much longer than others. The attention span is different for each child.

The young child, the "knower" we are concerned with, is still engaged in building a balance of trust in himself and others that will free him from too great mistrust and enable him to use his capacities. He is also still

Talking to a friend about her painting.

First Step Nursery School

engaged in moving beyond his infantile dependency and in achieving a greater measure of independence that will enable him to assert himself more actively in the learning process. Above all, he is engaged in using his initiative, in exploring, discovering, imagining, and going on to the new and untried. These three personality tasks, building a sense of trust, a sense of autonomy, and a sense of initiative, continue to be essential in learning.

As a learner the young child continues to use all his senses as he did in the sensorimotor stage, gathering impressions of the world around him and acting on these impressions. But he has also moved into the preoperational stage described by Piaget. He is doing more organizing and classifying of these impressions. He sees similarities and differences, develops systems in his thinking, and tests his conclusions. He is developing concepts. In water play, for example, he is no longer content just to splash, enjoying the feel and sight of water, but he fills containers, pours the water, and watches what happens. He may put various objects in the water; he finds an object that sinks and then tries to make others sink. He imagines and uses symbols in his play. After he has seen a boat on the lake, he pretends a box is a boat as he rocks it or "fishes" from it. He rehearses and clarifies concepts in dramatic play. He accommodates to what he has assimilated in more complex ways. His play reveals his progress. He makes things happen. If one block is not long enough for bridging a distance, he finds the one that fits the space.

The young child is increasing his competence in language expressions as well, and this ability makes possible greater complexity in thought. Words help him recall experience and organize and classify perceptions. He can communicate better than when he was younger. Verbal expressions help him clarify his own ideas.

In a center the child also learns from being with other children and with the adults there. He finds out more about how other children respond to his approaches and what he can and cannot do with them. He identifies with the teacher and learns from her. He "accommodates" to a greater range of social experiences.

The Properties of Water: An Example of Implicit Knowledge and Explicit Learning

Implicit knowledge and possibly explicit learnings come from experiences with water. It takes many years to reach an understanding of such a complex subject as the laws of floating bodies, but children begin to gain some of the necessary implicit knowledge through the daily experiences they have with water beginning in infancy. Children love to play in water. They are well motivated for learning here. What are some possible experiences with water? What explicit teaching may be done in this, or in any other area of experience?

Some Possible Experiences with Water

Bathing in water.

Washing one's face and hands, using soap, using water of different temperatures.

Turning the faucet on and off.

Pulling the plug in the basin, letting the water out, filling the basin.

Washing other things: doll clothes, a variety of fabrics or objects that feel different when wet, fabrics that are colorfast and those that are not.

Drying wet objects in sun, in shade, over heater.

Painting with water on different surfaces, seeing it dry in sun and shade.

Scrubbing table or floor, using wet cloth, mop, sponge.

Wringing out cloth, sponge, or mop.

Watching water being absorbed by blotter or sponge.

Flushing the toilet.

Pouring water, filling containers.

Using a hose to water plants, squirting streams of water.

Using a watering can with a nozzle or spray.

Feeling the spray of water, feeling the force of a stream of water.

Playing in water in a pool, swirling with stick, using a strainer.

Dropping objects in water, watching patterns made.

Floating different objects: light ones and heavy ones that sink or float.

Wading, swimming.

Bathing the doll baby or helping in bathing a real baby.

Blowing soap bubbles, indoors and outdoors in sunshine and in wind.

Implicit knowledge: this girl begins to understand the meaning of words like thin, thick, slippery, and smooth.

Santa Monica College, Child Development Center

Mixing substances with water: paint powder, powdered clay, flour, dry bread crumbs, salt, sugar, oil.

Dissolving substances like jello, and watching them set.

Watching kettle boil and steam condense.

Observing dew on grass, on cobwebs, on branches.

Observing frost patterns on windows.

Experiences with rain: watching it fall, feeling it on face, seeing it flow down slopes and in gutters, stepping in puddles.

Experiences with snow and hail: playing in snow, watching snow or hail melt, tasting snow, compressing it into balls, piling it, observing drifts and icicles hanging or melting.

Making ice cubes in refrigerator, and using them.

Making ice cream.

Caring for animals that live in water: fish, pollywogs, frogs, turtles.

Playing in water with sand and mud, digging channels for the water, putting all kinds of objects in the water, observing properties of water.

Out of these experiences, and many more, the child builds an implicit knowledge of some of the properties of water. He can begin to predict what will happen when he does certain things. He knows that water doesn't run uphill, for example. He can dig channels to lead the water where he wants it to go. He can begin to estimate what will float and what will sink. He has acquired a "bank" of knowledge about water.

How the Teacher Uses Experiences for Explicit Teaching

In addition to providing these experiences for the child, the teacher may call the child's attention to how water behaves. She may ask questions. She may make suggestions to extend the child's experimentation. She may describe what is happening and encourage him to describe it. She may give explanations in answer to his questions and help him explore.

The teacher may call a child's attention to the way his water paint evaporates in the sun in contrast to what happens in the shade. She may point out the way the water acts on the dry sand in contrast to the wet sand. She may point out the steam on the windows in the kitchen.

The teacher may ask questions as the child plays with water in a tub. "I wonder what would happen if you put that big piece of wood in the water?" and when he tries it she may ask, "What happened?" In other situations she may ask, "What happened when you added water to the clay powder?" or "Where do you think the steam comes from?" or "What makes the frost on our window?" or "I wonder what would happen if we put the ice in the sun?"

Through these experiences the child acquires some implicit knowledge about buoyancy, resistance, gravity, wave motion, and other principles. The teacher guides children in these steps towards "organizing facts

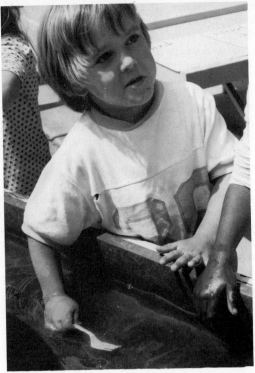

The child experiments with sinking and floating objects.

Jean Berlfein

He makes his choice.

Jean Berlfein

"What did you discover?"

Jean Berlfein

already internalized about the real world,"[1] so that these will be useful to them in the concepts they are building.

Clearing Up Misconceptions

The child begins early to reason, but his conclusions often reveal the limitations on which his reasoning is based. Four-year-old Melissa, for example, was full of excitement about the birth of a baby to an older sister. When she arrived at school, she told her teacher all about it. The teacher smiled as she remarked, "Now your mother is a grandmother." Melissa stopped, her eyes wide with surprise. Then she shook her head very positively. "Oh, no," she said, "My mother still lives with us." One gets an insight into what her concept of grandmother is based on as well as the different viewpoints of child and adult. The incident also shows us the difficulty a child has in thinking about relationships among people.

In helping the child gradually clear up misconceptions, we may ask questions such as, "Why do you think that?" or "How can you tell?" In doing this we are helping him examine his premises. There are probably few subjects about which the child has more curiosity and more misconception than the subject of where he came from, how he was conceived, how he was born, and how he grew. We can answer his questions by asking, "What do you think?" following the suggestions given by Selma

[1]M. Brearley and E. Hitchfield. (1970). *A guide to reading Piaget.* New York: Schocken Books.

Fraiberg in her excellent discussion, "Education for Love," in *The Magic Years*. We can use books such as Sara Bonnet Stein's *Making Babies*. We can give him information in simple words, giving only as much as he can understand or wants to know about at the moment. We should give only accurate, true information. The subject will need repeated clarification, but, bit by bit, his concepts will come closer to the facts.

In spite of explanations, children's misconceptions will persist until they are ready to understand. Francis said to his mother, "You're going to have to blow up your tummy, so we can have a baby." Francis was eager for a baby to arrive. The child keeps assimilating information in his personal ways, weaving it into the fabric of his experience. We do not always know what the meaning of it is to him.

Other questions likely to arise are in connection with toileting, as boys and girls use the toilets together. Here we have opportunities to make clearer the physical differences in the sexes and discuss the male and female roles. Changes in the roles of men and women in society are taking place, and children can begin to understand these changing roles.

The Teacher Helps the Child Distinguish between the Real World and the World of Fantasy

The thinking of children at this stage is largely personally oriented. Charles, described in an earlier chapter, could exclaim, "It doesn't wait for me," when he saw the water flowing away from him. This kind of perception of the world is revealed in the drawings of young children where the head or face is usually very large, because it is the part that is important for the child.

Fantasy and reality are often confused in children's thinking at this stage. What they think seems true to them whether it corresponds to reality or not. Children need help and time to make this distinction between reality and fantasy without having to reject their fantasies. They have a right to imagine and to create fantasies as well as a need to learn to identify reality.

It is sometimes a struggle for children to get the real world and the world of magic into their proper places. A child is fortunate when he has help from a parent or a teacher in learning to do so. His imaginative tales can be valued for what they are, delightful figments of the imagination and a method of escape that we can all use at times. It is fun to make up stories, but one should be clear about the differences between the pretend and the factual.

Francis, a four-year-old, tended to turn away from difficulties and deny unpleasant realities. He often tried to make his world be what he wanted it to be. He teased and successfully manipulated the succession of baby sitters who cared for him when he was not in the center while his mother worked. His teacher watched for opportunities to help him enjoy reality without distorting it. It was not difficult, for he was a friendly child, eager to please and to find a place for himself in the group.

> Francis is playing with dough at the table, patting, squeezing and folding it. He suddenly looks down and exclaims, "Hey! Hey, I made a turtle. I made a turtle!" He smiles a big smile and is obviously pleased with this discovery. With his hands he carefully forms the legs and head so they are more prominent. The other children start making turtles too. Francis exclaims to an approaching teacher, "Hey, look at my turtle!" He jumps off his chair. Jamie joins in excitedly, "Turtle, turtle, see my turtle!" The teacher admires the turtles.
>
> Francis says, "I didn't know I could make a turtle, but I did. I made a turtle." He then puts his hand behind the turtle and gives it a shove. The turtle sticks to the table and changes form slightly. Francis frowns and carefully unsticks it and shoves it again. This time it slides on the table but changes shape. He looks up at the teacher with a distraught expression and says, "My turtle can't walk."
>
> TEACHER: "Do you know why your turtle can't walk?"
> FRANCIS: "No—oh ya, because he is play-dough instead of real."
> TEACHER: "Yes, you know why."

Here we see Francis pleased with himself for making a turtle and then finding that the turtle does not fit in with his dream of a turtle. The teacher helps him return to a satisfying reality.

The Teacher Encourages the Use of Imagination

The teacher does not discourage the use of imagination by children. She encourages it. Imagination is valuable. We know that "hunches" and "brain storming" often produce worthwhile ideas with adults. Children are naturally good at using their imaginations, or "taking them out for a run," as someone has called it. As they become clearer about reality and fantasy, they have fun making up stories as well as describing real experiences. They play games of pretending as, "Wouldn't it be funny if . . ." or "This looks like a. . . ."

Thinking of alternatives or possibilities is an exercise for the intellect and the imagination. The teacher may ask, "How many ways are there to go to the store?" or "What do you think we will see when we get to the top of the hill?" or "What would you do if you found you were lost on the street?" or "What do you think we could make out of this?" Guessing and risking a guess are often valuable aids in problem solving if one can check on the results. Imaginative solutions are worth cultivating.

HOW ARE YOUNG CHILDREN MOTIVATED TO LEARN?

As we observe children, we see that they are most absorbed when they are most interested. They concentrate and they persist when they are really interested, just as we ourselves do. If we are to teach effectively, we need to understand the *interests* children are likely to have and the particular interests of the individual child. Only as we make available materials and experiences in which the child is truly interested can we facilitate his learning.

Purposeful activity grows out of interests, and it is this kind of activity which generates the energy that learning demands. Brearley puts it this way: "Teaching is a cultural task and our business is to gear these natural curiosities and interests to the traditional skills which the culture has built up and valued . . . ," adding that in teaching we need "the energy of his [the child's] willingness on our side."[2]

Young children are interested in *activity*, all kinds of physical movement, large and small muscle activities, indoor and outdoor play which

[2] M. Brearley (Ed.). (1970). *The teaching of young children: Some applications of Piaget's learning theory.* New York: Shocken Books.

Jumping provides for feelings of confidence and satisfaction.

San Diego State University. Courtesy Sam Hollander

gives a chance to explore the possibilities of what can be done with movement. Children find great satisfaction in climbing the jungle gym, digging in the dirt, and rolling in the snow.

There are many opportunities for cognitive learning in most of these activities. There are problems to be dealt with, things to be observed and compared.

Curiosity is a motivating force in children in the sensorimotor and preoperational stages of development. We need to provide a rich variety of firsthand experiences to be explored and acted upon. The curious child can use his experiences in "structured thinking" as he is ready. The teacher can supply words, ask questions, call attention to aspects of the experience and extend it. She can "deepen the interest into knowledge."

The *desire for love and appreciation* is also a strong motivating force in young children. It is a need that can easily be exploited unless we keep clearly in mind the child's purposes and his level of development. Too often we may be more concerned with our own purposes than with his. If we give the child approval for being "good" by our standards or for doing what *we* think is best, we may be limiting his development as an individual in his own right. We need to make sure that we acknowledge with approval the effort that went into constructing an airplane that satisfied *him*, or the control he exercised in not acting on the impulse to hit an offending companion, or the spontaneous sharing done among friends, or the imaginative observation, rather than giving approval only for achievements that satisfy us.

The supportive role of the adult is an important one. He or she gives support to the child by showing an interest in what the child does, by treating the child's questions with respect, by giving more attention to the positive than to the negative aspects of his performance, by generous giving of approval for real accomplishments.

The Urge Toward Mastery

Motivation depends on many factors. One of the strongest of these is the urge toward mastery of a problem and the satisfaction that all of us feel from performing with skill. We see this in a young child as he persists in working on a fastening until he succeeds in opening it and then turns to fresh fields of endeavor.

This urge toward competency, as Robert W. White has called it, is a strong motivating force as long as we feel that there is a hope of success. The strength of the urge diminishes if our efforts are continually blocked. The child who has lost hope of any success is not motivated to try. He has lost this powerful urge. When a child has lived in an environment that is largely unfavorable for successful learning, the teacher must work to reawaken his curiosity and zest for exploring and discovering. Above all she must help him rediscover his faith in his own competence. He must believe that he *can* succeed, if he tries. He must see himself as someone who is able to achieve. If the teacher is to help him, she must herself believe that the child can learn. She must believe in him and his capacities.

Under favorable conditions, the child's natural curiosity and his urge toward competency motivate him. He wants to learn and to gain skills. The teacher does not need to depend on extrinsic forms of motivation. The child wants to grow to be like the important adults around him. When these adults present themselves as "models" who work and achieve, they give direction to the child's efforts. He can work and become competent.

Bruner comments: "The will to learn is an intrinsic motive, one that finds its source and its reward in its own exercise."[3] He points out that the most lasting satisfactions lie in learning itself, not in extrinsic rewards. These do not give reliable nourishment "over the long course of learning." The urge toward competence is strong in a healthy child. He needs little else except encouragement to sustain his learning.

The teacher has a responsibility to guard this precious "will to learn" that motivates the child, or to reawaken it in children who may have lost it. She needs to help these children find "the confidence to try and to make mistakes, and the confidence to know that it is worth doing for its own sake. *And the daring to like yourself and trust your product.*"[4]

READINESS FOR LEARNING

Nurturing readiness for formal learning does not imply early teaching of school subjects. Most educators of young children are, and have always been, opposed to such pressures. As long ago as 1962, members of a colloquy held in Washington, DC, and called *Basic Human Values for Childhood Education* declared themselves "unreservedly opposed to pressures on children for early formal learning." They felt that "formal learning tasks may displace the informal play-type learning which involves imagination, fantasy, creative activities and the other higher mental processes, and in that way deprive the child of the very activities so necessary for his development."[5]

More recently, in 1984, the National Association for the Education of Young Children pointed out that teachers help children achieve sound intellectual learning through a curriculum that "encourages children to be

---

[3] J. S. Bruner. (1966). *Toward a theory of instruction.* Cambridge, MA.: Harvard University Press, p. 127.

[4] Vinnette Carroll, as quoted in *Christian Science Monitor*, November 29, 1969.

[5] Association for Childhood Education International. (1962). *Report of colloquy on basic human values for childhood education.* Washington DC: Author.

Mastery of trike rid-
ing: making this trike
go forward.

Valley College, Cam-
pus Child Develop-
ment Center

actively involved in the learning process, to experience a variety of
developmentally appropriate activities and materials, and to pursue their
own interests in the context of life in the community and the world."[6]

Children learn easily those things that they are developmentally ready to
learn. They construct their own knowledge from experiences and mistakes.
But their readiness needs to be nurtured. Jerome Bruner pointed out some
time ago that readiness may be a half-truth if one depends on readiness
alone. A good teacher is continually nurturing a child's readiness to move
forward into more advanced activities. For example, when a child has
mastered the skill of pounding large tacks into a board to his satisfaction,
he is ready for other experiences. The teacher provides nails and then a saw
so that the child can proceed to constructing an object, depending on his
interests, with all the learning involved in the construction. He also is
gaining confidence in his own ability to learn. The teacher will give
children choices, too, whenever possible to help them develop their
capacities in making decisions. Children can assume increasing responsibility as they are ready.

Each child grows and learns in his own manner and rate, nurtured by
opportunities, but without pressures. He becomes a more confident person
in the process of learning.

[6] National Association for the Education of Young Children. (1984). *Accreditation
criteria and procedures: Position statement of the National Academy of Early
Childhood Programs.* Washington, D.C.: Author.

Reading

Many experiences at the preschool level prepare a child for learning to read. One of the most important of these is a "reading atmosphere" fostered by people who are themselves interested in and enjoy books and who enjoy reading to the child from suitably selected books. Books become an important part of his world, too. As he sits with the adult, he observes her eye movements and becomes aware of the way she follows the line of print. She may use her finger to indicate where the words she is reading are appearing on the page and when she is ready for the page to be turned.

There are many opportunities to call the child's attention to words and their meaning. A "stop" sign on the street or a "stop" sign on the playground to indicate where the wagons and tricycles must stop, or a sign "store" on a block construction, or the sentence "This is a store" makes the child more aware of the written word (as the group was after a trip to the store). The child's name can be printed over his locker or cubby, on his paintings, or at the table where he sits for lunch. Later he may copy the teacher's lettering and write his own name. There may be discussion of the letters and comparisons with other people's names with the recognition of letters that are the same or different. Lotto games give the child practice in discriminating lines and forms, a skill needed in reading.

Handling tools, using scissors, drawing, and painting are some activities that promote the neuromuscular development which is required for reading and writing. Equally necessary is a wide variety of experiences with objects and people and situations that enable the child to understand what he will be reading later. All this is part of nurturing readiness to develop appropriate skills necessary for formal reading.

Adult Anxiety About a Child's Learning to Read

Adult anxiety often centers around children's reading. We see this in educational television programs and workbook activities for young children. Learning to recognize and write the letters of the alphabet is not an appropriate activity for most three-year-olds, but it is often included in these programs. Far more important as a basis for reading are the experiences we have mentioned.

When children have lacked this background, we give them help by providing what they have lacked rather than by working with them to master skills for which they lack the preparation. Skipping a stage does not promote optimum development in the end. Beginning without enough background may mean that the child struggles for months to achieve a level of skill he could reach with very little effort later. Some parents and teachers of young children grow anxious and attempt to push the child toward reading, not trusting him to learn, and thus not building his trust in himself. There is little point in learning to read before one has the background for understanding what one may read. Partial comprehension may become a habit. One only reads words. There will be individual differences in the age at which children are ready to begin reading, of course, and these differences can be respected.

In one center a three-and-a-half-year-old child was able to read quite well. His parents loved books and were pleased with his precocious development. The child was ready to demonstrate his skill on every occasion, but the other children were not interested. He lacked skill in riding a tricycle. He did not know how to use blocks or climb in the jungle gym. He did not know how to play. It was some weeks before he could make contact on his own with the children. He was full of fears and had wild fantasies. He was a child who needed a group experience.

When he left the group more than a year later, he was much more relaxed and was eating and sleeping better at home. While his motor skills were still below average for his age, he had made a great deal of progress in developing them as well as in developing his social skills. He was taking part in active group play in a more childlike way. His parents had revised their goals for him. They were pleased with his development, for they could see that he was a happier child. He will do well in school, but he also has a good chance of becoming a well-developed human being. He is sure to be less handicapped socially, emotionally, and even intellectually.

THE CHARACTERISTICS OF A GOOD THINKER

An important characteristic of a good thinker is a *feeling of confidence in himself*. Experiences in being successful encourage the child to persist and to believe in his own success. His teacher's belief in him and her expectations for him also give him confidence. This confidence enables him to face frustrations and failures and to use them, as the scientist does, for learning what does not work.

An ability to pay attention or concentrate is a characteristic of a good thinker. Providing what is of real interest to the child and allowing him time to complete an activity that interests him is one part of the teacher's contribution. She will note the materials that call forth the longest attention spans in children and supply more of them. She avoids interrupting purposeful activities when possible, keeping the schedule flexible to allow for concentration. A teacher reported that one four-year-old in her group worked for a full hour at the workbench making an airplane, using the tools and materials on hand there.

A good thinker makes a practice of *estimating* and *planning*. A child may say, "I need three pieces of wood to finish this." Afterward the teacher may say, if this is the case, "You thought you needed three pieces. Now you know you only needed two." Learning to estimate approximately what will be needed, how far it is around the playground, or how long it will take, and then finding out if the estimations were correct are characteristics of a thinker. The teacher can encourage these traits. She can also help the child check on results and *reflect*. As he sees similarities and differences, she can ask him, "Why?" or "How do you know?"

A good thinker uses his *imagination*. He is creative. Children often pretend in their play. "Pretend I'm the mother or the father or the baby" and proceed to imagine and act the role. Or they say, "Pretend I'm a lion and I'm going to eat you." They exercise their imaginations more actively than most adults do and, in fantasy, deal with all kinds of realities. Using imagination about personal relationships increases children's awareness of aspects of relationships. Here, too, the teacher can give direction to the thinking. "What would you have done if you had been this child?" she can say as they read a story together. Or she can ask, "What would you do if you found you were lost and didn't know your way home?" Thinking can take place in these discussions, and a pattern for solving difficulties can evolve as thinking begins to find its place along with action. Dramatic play of all kinds stimulates cognitive growth. Symbolic thinking depends on being able to imagine.

The good thinker needs to be able to *communicate* his thoughts. Language plays an important role in the development of the intellect. It is a means of clarifying thought as well as a means of communication. It nourishes the growth of the capacity to reason. We will discuss this further in the section on language.

Overcoming Blocks in Learning

A child may be blocked in learning because of fears that he may bring to the learning situation. Fear of making a mistake is one of the common fears. These fears may prevent him from daring to take necessary risks.

Blocks in learning may result from the child's attitude toward authority and authority figures. If the child is continually resisting authority, he is blocked in learning because there is inevitably a measure of authority and discipline necessary in a learning situation. He must in the end be able to discipline himself. The child needs to come to terms with his feelings about authority before he is free to learn as he might otherwise do. Discriminations of many kinds may inhibit learning. Meeting attitudes of discrimination or holding these attitudes is a block to learning in the areas involved.

Cognitive learning is best carried on under relatively conflict-free conditions. There should be an element of surprise or uncertainty or some disequilibrium, as an unanswered question, but not an element of conflict.

As part of her teaching role the teacher will try to help the child with any blocks that may hinder his learning.

In summary the conditions that favor intellectual growth are those in which the child feels secure and relatively free from conflicts and has confidence in himself and in his ability to cope with the problems presented. He does not learn readily when he is discouraged and sees little hope of success or when he feels alienated from others.

The next five chapters are about areas of learning in a curriculum for young children. We will suggest some activities and their values in each of these areas. Every teacher will want to explore and discover other opportunities to provide children with learning experiences in the areas, depending on the interests of the children in the group.

Project

Select an area and list all the possible ways in which children may be able to have experiences here. Indicate also what some of the explicit learnings might be. In what way might these be valuable for later learning? For example, what are possible experiences with colors, or with sounds?

For Your Further Reading

Brearley, M. (Ed.). (1970). *The teaching of young children: Some applications of Piaget's learning theory.* New York: Schocken Books. Describes implicit and explicit learning, as well as a simple and sound approach to classroom use of Piaget's theory.

Brown, J. F. (Ed.). (1982). *Curriculum planning for young children.* Washington, DC: National Association for the Education of Young Children. Articles from *Young Children* on learning, activities, teaching about the basic curriculum for young children.

Donaldson, M. (1978). *Children's minds.* New York: W. W. Norton. Challenges some of Piaget's findings and offers fresh insights into how children think.

Forman, G. E., & Hill, F. (Eds.). (1984). *Constructive play: Applying Piaget in the preschool* (rev. ed.). Reading, MA: Addison-Wesley. Open-ended activities and games for children to learn about the physical and social world as well as themselves.

Hendrick, J. (1986). *Total learning for the whole child: Holistic curriculum for children ages 2 to 5* (2nd ed.). Columbus, OH: Charles E. Merrill. Companion volume to Hendrick, J. (1984). *The whole child,* but much more than a curriculum guide. Strong emphasis on principles of learning.

Hohmann M., Banet B., & Weikart, D. P. (1979). *Young children in action: A manual for preschool educators.* Ypsilanti, MI: High/Scope Press. Curriculum guide to accompany Weikart, D. P., et al. (1971). *The cognitively oriented preschool curriculum.*

Baseball Players
(boy, 3 years)

17 ♦ Areas of Learning in the Program: Motor and Sensory Development

The curriculum encourages children to be actively involved in the learning process, to experience a variety of developmentally appropriate activities and materials, and to pursue their own interests in the context of life in the community and the world.[1]

In all the areas of learning in programs for young children, teaching begins at the point where the individual child is in his competencies and his understanding. We must remember that the child has already had many

[1]National Association for the Education of Young Children. (1984). *Accreditation criteria and procedures: Position statement of the National Academy of Early Childhood Programs.* Washington, DC: Author.

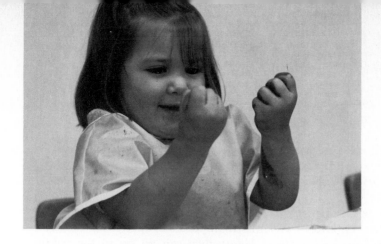

The child learns through the senses.

Santa Monica College, Child Development Center

295

experiences and has learned a great deal before he enters a center. He "knows" implicitly a great deal. Our teaching must be based on this knowledge.

Our task is to find out where the child is in his abilities and past experiences. We need to observe the child, consult with the parents who have guided his earlier learning, and build a relationship of trust with the child.

It is important not to skip any of the stages in intellectual or emotional development. When children have missed important experiences earlier, they need to have these experiences before they can go on to the next stages. Four-year-old Maria, for example, who had had little opportunity for play, at first explored the housekeeping corner more like a two-year-old child, before she went on to make use of the corner as four-year-olds usually do.

We will discuss curriculum areas in turn, beginning with sensorimotor aspects of learning.

PERCEIVING: SENSORIMOTOR LEARNING

Skills in Sensory Perception: Foundation for Concepts

The child learns about the world around him through his senses—seeing, hearing, feeling, tasting, and smelling—and through his kinesthetic sense. The greater the input of sensory impressions, the more material he has out of which to build concepts of what the world is like. He improves his tools for understanding the world as he improves the keenness of his sensory perception. The teacher provides for a wide variety of sensory experiences and encourages their use. Her role is an important one here.

A child with a sensory defect, such as a partially sighted child or a hearing-impaired child, is handicapped because he takes in less complete or less accurate impressions. He must make more effort to learn because of his sensory limitation.

Developing Motor Skills: Patterns of Response

Kinesthetic Sense and Motor Skills

The infant begins to perceive his world as he moves his hands, then his arms and legs, roots for the breast, and sucks. Much later he crawls, stands, begins to walk and broadens his horizons as he gains more control over his muscles. The child's kinesthetic impressions increase as he uses his body.

Acquiring skill in using body muscles is important for the young child. He gains confidence when he is able to control his muscles and can feel "in tune" with his own body, able to use it freely, following his own rhythms. His posture and the way he uses his body reveal attitudes he holds about himself. The child with good motor skills can do more about what he perceives. He has more confidence as he plays with other children and copes with situations.

A healthy child enjoys practicing until he masters a skill. The toddler goes up and down stairs or climbs over objects until he can do it easily. The nursery school age child will try out many methods of riding a tricycle after he has mastered the art of riding. He goes fast on it, cuts corners, rides close to objects.

He begins to know what it feels like to lift a weight, to roll down a slope, to throw. As he jumps from a box, he experiences distance and depth. Reaching out, falling, climbing, swinging, pushing a wagon, riding a tricycle—all play a part in refining kinesthetic perceptions. He enjoys his competency. It gives him confidence.

These children have implicit knowledge of space and of their bodies.

John Adams Children's Center

Skills in using large muscles develop through vigorous, active play. This kind of play usually takes place outdoors. Some of the activities that develop *large muscle* skills are:

Lifting and piling large hollow blocks, boxes, or short boards.
Pulling a loaded wagon or using a wheelbarrow for carrying objects.
Digging with shovel or spade.
Climbing on a jungle gym, rope ladder, or in a tree or over a box.
Swinging in a swing or on the rungs of a bar or a horizontal ladder.
Riding wheel toys.
Pounding nails, sawing, and using other carpentry tools.
Balancing by walking on low boards or on bouncing boards or on the trampoline.
Running, sometimes barefoot, on sand or grass.
Throwing balls through a hoop or throwing beanbags at a target, or just throwing.
Rhythmic activities to music.

Some of the activities that develop coordination in the use of *small muscles* are:

Activities in connection with dressing, buttoning, lacing shoes, pulling on boots, hanging up coat or towel.
Activities in connection with eating, such as using a spoon and fork, pouring juice or milk from a small pitcher into a cup or glass.
Play with all kinds of manipulative toys like trucks, cars, interlocking blocks, puzzles.
Using a paintbrush or large crayons or felt pen, or cutting with scissors.
Finger plays.

Good posture is important, too. It is encouraged by active play. It is also encouraged by making sure that chairs are of the proper height so that a child's feet are on the floor when he is seated and by making sure that a child sits only for short periods of time. Good posture may also be developed by dancing and games such as balancing a beanbag or a basket with a pad on one's head when marching.

Motor activities form an important part of the curriculum for young children. As the teacher observes the play, she may extend the range of experience by introducing a game of throwing beanbags at a target or of balancing on a walking board. She may rearrange the boards and boxes in new patterns to encourage more climbing. Part of her teaching will consist in making sure that children have a range of activities to develop coordination of large and small muscles.

With opportunity children can develop surprising skill. One four-year-old boy had extraordinary skill with tools. He could hammer a nail with accuracy, saw through boards, and use a screwdriver. His father had a workshop in their basement, and he had provided a small one for his son with proper tools. They often worked there together. This boy took the lead in the construction of a playhouse at nursery school. The project lasted several weeks, and he continued his interest in the project throughout the time, helping sustain the interest of other children in it.

There are many implicit cognitive learnings in motor activities. The child who has balanced on a walking board, built a high tower of blocks, bounced on a springing surface, swung on a set of rings or the horizontal ladder, rolled down an incline, or ridden his tricycle fast around corners knows implicitly some of the principles of physics which will later be the basis for explicit learning. His understanding of the abstract principles will be based on his own body experience with them in his play.

Seeing

Visual impressions are one of the most constant and valuable sources of learning for young children. An infant responds in an excited way to the sight of the breast or bottle being brought near him. He has learned a sequence of sights and sounds that allows him to anticipate the breast or bottle and predict this event. The older infant experiences an object as completely as possible by touching it, rolling it, pulling and twisting it, chewing on it, looking at it from all angles, and finally dropping it when he "understands" it. Donald Winnicott, in his chapter "Further Thoughts on Babies as Persons," has given us a delightful description of a ten-month-old baby "coming to know an object," a spoon, by playing with it.[2] Preschool children continue to learn by looking at, feeling, and doing something with the objects around them.

In favorable environments young children have many opportunities to see and come to know many objects. In unfavorable environments they may have fewer of these experiences. The effect of fewer experiences is that there are fewer impressions, which discourages children's curiosity and their urge to explore.

The teacher should be alert to the possibility of visual impairment in individual children. It is easy to misjudge the cause of behavior. The child with poor vision may be easily distracted or clumsy and may hold objects very close to his face. It is important to correct visual defects at an early age because defective vision impedes learning, especially in the very young child whose learning takes place largely through sensorimotor experiences. The teacher can make a simple vision test and can consult with the parents if there seems any likelihood of a problem.

Beauty in line, form, and color are important for children. They are helped to become more aware of beauty by having some lovely things to

[2] D. W. Winnicott. (1957). *The child and the outside world.* New York: Basic Books.

look at in the center, such as hanging plants, a beautiful picture in the entrance hall, and some of their own paintings attractively mounted and hung at a child's eye level.

Shapes and forms interest children. The teacher can help make these differences more explicit. Blocks can be arranged on shelves according to shapes and sizes. Big and small, long and short, wide and narrow are terms to learn in relation to objects seen as well as felt. There are different textures and patterns to be looked at as well as felt: the bark on trees, the tracks in sand or mud, or ripples made by waves. Experimenting with shadows, children can change shapes and sizes. Every teacher will build on what is available around her to give children more material for developing concepts through looking and examining what they see.

Hearing

Sounds are important to children. Interest in sounds and the capacity to listen and to discriminate sounds contributes to the development of speech. Children discover many sounds on their own as they explore materials. The teacher can extend these experiences by her comments: "You made a different sound when you hit the spoon against the can," or "Is it higher or lower this time?" Children often play with words and make up nonsense lines. They like the sounds of some phrases. The teacher can select stories and poems in which the words make music, or she can call attention to sounds.

Children today may live in such a confusion of noises that they fail to learn to identify individual sounds or to learn to listen. The teacher helps children listen to sounds—bird songs, the sound of an airplane, the eggbeater in the kitchen, the clock, a whisper, the rumble of a truck, the swish of feet in the leaves. She helps them make different sounds, hitting two things together, ringing a bell, making musical sounds by using a variety of instruments. A keen ear is a help to children as they go on learning and enjoying experiences.

At this stage of learning normal hearing is important for good development. The teacher is in a position to detect hearing impairment early. A child may seem inattentive because of a hearing loss. The teacher can make a simple test such as speaking to the child in a normal tone when his back is turned, or moving a ticking clock toward him and noting when he pays attention. If she suspects any hearing loss, she can consult with his parents. He may need hearing tests by a professional. Many children have been handicapped in school because of an undetected hearing loss.

Touching

Children are responsive to the feel of things. They learn from touching and need a wide variety of experiences with touching in order to develop adequate concepts about the world around them. They need help in making discriminations and in using the correct descriptive words. A teacher can exercise ingenuity in providing children with touch experiences and encouraging their personal descriptions of the feel of things.

Objects feel hard or soft, rough or smooth, firm or spongy, for example. A "feel box" with different objects hidden in it gives a child the chance to try to identify objects by their feel. Sorting games based on the feel of materials of different textures, or on shapes or sizes or forms may interest children. Children enjoy collecting different things that have special "feels," like stones and shells made smooth by the water, smooth beechnuts, or other objects that are smooth and hard. They enjoy the sensory delights of feeling things.

The teacher can provide a variety of materials of different textures in the "dress-up" area, such as squares of filmy gauze or chiffon, velvet, silk or soft wool or cotton, along with synthetic fibers. In each case the teacher uses the correct designation as she talks about the different materials.

The same object feels different at different temperatures, as the handlebars of a tricycle in the sun or the shade. Water feels different when it has turned to ice. The feel of a leaf when it is green and when it is dry is different, as is the feel of bark on different trees or the feel of different animals—a worm, a baby chick, a kitten. There is the feel of food as well as its taste to identify it. Some foods are soft and some are crunchy. The feel of clay when it is dry is different from its feel when wet and "gooshy." The child experiences these things, but the teacher reinforces and extends the experience by her comments or descriptive words. She may share the experience with him, describing it without asking any response from him. Children learn by touching and feeling.

Tasting

Children often comment on taste saying, "It tastes bad," or "good." There are more accurate terms, however, to describe the discrimination of tastes, and the teacher can introduce children to the terms *sweet, sour, bitter,* and *salty* with samples. Things that look the same do not always taste the same, such as pineapple and grapefruit juice, or a pinch of sugar and a pinch of salt. The most likely place for children to be interested in taste discrimination is at the table when they are eating.

Most of us know the taste of paste, playdough, and a wide variety of other things we use in school. Many young children also will bring objects and materials to their mouths to explore their taste and feel. Experiencing and describing tastes not only increase the child's awareness but also challenge his ability to express his perceptions. Enjoying tastes and flavors increases enjoyment in eating.

Smelling

There are many kinds of smells in the child's environment: the smell of food or flowers; the smell of clay, paint, or soap; the smell of freshly washed towels; the smell of wool when it is wet; and the smell of new shoes. Some smells are pleasant; some are unpleasant. The smell of food is good when one is hungry. Some flowers have a strong fragrance; some have a delicate fragrance. Almost everything has an odor that helps us to identify places, things, people, and animals.

Describing smells increases children's ability to express their perceptions and to describe their experiences. The teacher will comment on different odors or respond with appreciation when a child comments. She may help the child develop more awareness of odors by asking, "What does it smell like?" "Can you find where the odor comes from?" The teacher supplies a variety of experiences and can reinforce the child's learning by her interest and attention.

Mixing concrete for the signpost.

California State University, Chico. Child Development Laboratory

Finding out how to get the sign to stand up.

California State University, Chico. Child Development Laboratory

ORGANIZING SENSORY IMPRESSIONS: FORMING CONCEPTS

As children use their senses, they are storing up a multitude of impressions. In the course of doing this they begin to classify these impressions and to make distinctions. All furry animals are not kittens. An animal can be a kitty or a dog. Other children have mothers and fathers. Some children are bigger than others. When does tomorrow really come? It is often a confusing matter and there is an endless amount to learn. We can help children to organize, classify, and discriminate.

Identifying, associating, organizing, classifying, and perceiving relationships are important aspects of learning in the early years. Children do much of this in their play, but some of this is done through games and experiences devised to focus on developing these skills. They are learning to perceive basic relationships involving objects, space and time relationships, and cause and effect relationships.

To organize impressions, a child must be able to identify and label objects. All objects have *names*. The teacher will use the names of things in speaking to a child. She will call the child's attention to names, his own name on his locker or on his painting. She may point out signs when they are walking, the name of a street or a "stop" sign. She will give the child the name of any new object he meets.

Objects have *characteristics* by which they can also be identified. They may differ in color. They may be heavy or light or large or small. As she talks with children, the teacher will use descriptive words. The cup he is using is green. The box is large, but it is also light. Another box may be large and heavy. The teacher makes sure that the child has a chance to have experiences with many objects with different characteristics. She may introduce games that depend on identifying characteristics, such as "What can you find that is heavy?" or "What can you find that is light?" or "What can you find that is blue?"

It is important for the child to know about the *uses* and *functions* of objects as a way of learning about them. For example, the child paints with a brush, and he cuts with scissors. The teacher may ask, "What do you need when you want to cut the paper?" Some things have more than one use. We use water for several purposes. The teacher may ask, "What do we use water for?" In conversations the teacher and the children can talk about what things are used for, or what they might be used for.

Objects are *related* in many different ways. They may be the same, or they may be different. They may be similar, like plates and saucers. They may belong together in sets, like cups and saucers. There are size relationships. Some objects are large and some are small. There may be an order in size, from smallest to biggest. There are relationships in quantity, too, from a few to a lot. There are relationships in qualities. Some objects may be the same because they are soft or hard, or they may be different in these ways. They may be rough or smooth.

Making explicit the way in which things are alike or different is important. Things may be alike because of their function or their color or their size, for example. They may both be used for drinking but be different in color. Through many experiences with objects the teacher tries to help the child sharpen his ability to perceive, to make distinctions, and to classify. Matching and sorting games are useful here.

There are labels that refer to *position* in space, too, such as under, over, inside, outside, beside, on top of, below. The teacher can use these words as she gives directions: "Put the block on top of the box beside the truck." She can encourage the children to use specific words in describing where a thing belongs. She may introduce games in which children follow directions about placing or hiding objects.

The teacher will also help the child become more aware of *time* and the place of events in time. There is a time for lunch and a time for rest. One event comes before another event, or after it. There are days for school and days at home. There is a long time and a short time, and even a beginning and an end to an experience.

Things *change,* and some of the changes relate to time. A child is three, and then he is four. After the daytime comes the nighttime. Other changes are not related to time. Water freezes when it is put into the freezer or when it is very cold outdoors. A child is cold, and he gets warm when he runs. The teacher calls attention to these things, making them more explicit for the child, helping him to build concepts and to clear up misconceptions as he organizes his impressions.

Recalling and *remembering* involve making associations. Children enjoy recalling what they did once or what they saw when they were on a walk or trip. "Remember the fire engine. . . ." or, "Remember the baby colt and how he looked. . . ." It is good to be able to think about what one has experienced. It helps one learn and it solves problems. "Remember when you . . ." may help the child find a solution to the problem of how to make an airplane. Deciding what he needs to finish his airplane or boat may necessitate recalling what materials he used before and where he found them. He begins to plan this way.

Recalling will depend on *giving attention* in the first place. The teacher may introduce games that depend on paying attention and remembering, such as a game in which the child first looks carefully at some objects placed in front of him, then closes his eyes while one of these is removed, and, when he looks again, tries to remember the name of the missing object.

Many times children will surprise us by the new patterns they see or the associations they make. Children often have a fresh approach that can be nurtured by our appreciation.

Projects

1. Observe and record five examples of questions asked by a child. Indicate the circumstances briefly. How was each question answered? How would you evaluate each as a learning experience for the child concerned?
2. Observe and record incidents in which a child added to his store of sensory impressions in some area (for example, touch, sight, sound, smell, taste).
3. Observe and record incidents that give evidence of a child's learning:
   a. perceiving characteristics of an object
   b. perceiving functions of an object
   c. perceiving relationships
   d. ability to recall or associate perceptions

For Your Further Reading

Baker, K. R. (1966). *Let's play outdoors.* Washington, DC: National Association for the Education of Young Children. How teachers can make outdoor play worthwhile, with practical tips on sound play areas and equipment.

Engstrom, G. (Ed.). (1971). *The significance of the young child's motor development.* Washington, DC: National Association for the Education of Young Children. How physical activity relates to all areas of a child's development.

Hill, D. M. (1977). *Mud, sand and water.* Washington, DC: National Association for the Education of Young Children. How children's learning is advanced through natural, messy materials.

Kamii, C., & DeVries, R. (1980). *Group games in early education: Implications of Piaget's theory.* Washington, DC: National Association for the Education of Young Children. The role of competitive games in children's development, including game directions.

Skeen, P., Garner, A. P., & Cartwright, S. (1984). *Woodworking for young children.* Washington, DC: National Association for the Education of Young Children. Practical helps, even for adult beginners, to teach children woodworking.

Sullivan, M. (1982). *Feeling strong, feeling free: Movement exploration for young children.* Washington, DC: National Association for the Education of Young Children. Teaching ideas for a movement program for ages three to eight.

Once Upon a Time Story (girl,
4 years 8 months)

18 ◆ Areas of Learning in the Program: Language and Literature

LANGUAGE

Increasing the child's competence in the use of language is an important part of any program for young children. Social relations of all kinds are extended and improved as speech develops. Language is necessary for higher forms of thought processes.

Early Stages in Language Learning

Learning to talk is a complex learning process, and parents rightfully feel that the baby's first words mark a milestone in his development. A great deal of cognitive growth has taken place to make it possible. Yet it is worth noting that the ordinary, healthy child learns to talk without any formal teaching if he is in an environment where he hears plenty of speech.

The infant communicates by crying and by body movements, including mouth movements. He wriggles all over with delight when he is pleased. He stretches out his arms for what he wants and later he will point. He vocalizes and blows bubbles. His mouth movements and his other body movements tend to resemble those of his mother as she talks with him. He pays attention to sounds and uses visual cues in understanding meanings. He begins to understand that a word stands for an object long before he himself uses the word. His mother has used the word *bottle* as she brings it to him, and he understands.

As he moves into the stage in which he is becoming aware of the permanence of objects, that something exists even when he cannot see it, he recalls the bottle when he hears the word. The word calls up the image, an important function of language. Without the experience the word is of no use to him. When he comes to the stage of using words, he can communicate the idea of "bottle" by using the word himself or some reasonable attempt at the word, another significant achievement. It is interesting to note that for a long time the gesture is still the preferred method of communication if the object is in sight.

In the early stages a word often stands for a whole object or an experience. The word *hot*, for example, may mean the stove as well as the heat it gives off and the warning given to control action. With more experience the child will discover that the word refers to only one attribute of a stove and can be applied to other objects.

In this sensorimotor stage of development nothing takes the place of a wide variety of appropriate firsthand experiences with an object if the child is to develop concepts about it. The child needs to see, to touch, to taste, and to do something with the object if he is to understand its nature and the meaning of the label attached to it. If, for example, he can roll a ball, sit on it, bounce it, watch it float in the water or sink, and bite it, and if he can use several different types of balls, he stores up impressions that make up a more complete concept of "ball." He *knows* about balls. As adults we still learn in this firsthand way although we have added other ways of knowing.

Individual Differences in Use of Speech

In any group of children we observe great individual differences in the children's competence with language and their verbal "styles." Some children are always talking as they play. They sing or talk to themselves. When they are with other children, they chatter with them, describing what they are doing, giving directions, agreeing and disagreeing. Other children use very few words in the same situations, going quietly about the

This child has a first-hand experience with water, sand, and mud.

San Diego State University. Courtesy Sam Hollander

business of play although they show that they understand and are listening to what is being said. They give themselves less practice with speech. They may have other interests at the moment.

We can appreciate how much children are influenced by the speech they hear when we listen to the telephone conversations carried on during play in the housekeeping corner. Some children carry on long conversations about going to work, caring for babies, arranging parties. Other children, probably from homes where language use is restricted, tend to be monosyllabic in their telephone conversations. They are the children who may need some help if they are to develop competence with language.

We know that the child needs (1) variety and richness in experience, adapted to his level of understanding and (2) many experiences with speech, hearing speech and trying out the forms of speech, if he is to develop competence in the use of speech. Parents and teachers encourage children's speech by talking with them, by paying attention when the child speaks, and by responding appropriately, so that the communication is rewarding for them both.

The Young Child Develops Competence Without Being Corrected

An interesting finding in one recent study on language is that at home mothers do very little correcting of a young child's speech. They may correct errors of fact, but they tend to ignore errors in speech. Courtney Cazden, who has done extensive research on how children learn to speak, considers the commonsense view that holds that children learn a language by imitation and by having errors corrected is a myth. Learning by

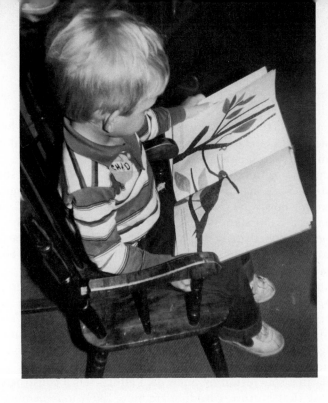

Chad "reads" about grasshoppers and trees.

Valley College, Campus Child Development Center

imitation and by correction is true only in a general sense, according to Cazden. Children appear to imitate some people and not others, depending on the affectional ties. They pick their own speech models. The teacher who accepts and respects the child is more likely to be imitated.

The Logic of Children's Speech

In learning to talk each child goes through stages that are strikingly similar from child to child and quite different from the adult speech that they hear. Children themselves are actively discovering language and trying to make some sense out of its structure. In this effort they apply their own logic to the structure. At one stage, for example, almost all children will say "foots," or "mouses." These are not words they are likely to have heard, but it shows that they have observed that an "s" is used to form plurals. They try applying this rule, a logical operation, only later to discover that there are exceptions. The same thing happens when they reach the conclusion that past tense is indicated by *-ed* and they begin saying "comed," "goed," "teached."

Here is an example. We see how some children correct their own mistakes. Pam, seeing the mice, called excitedly to the others, "Look, mices." Jason ran over to see and called to his companions, "Come and see the mouses." Later Pam, sitting with her elbows on the table while she watched the mice closely, suddenly asked, "When will the mice grow up?"

309

In phrasing her question Pam shows us that she had become aware of the correct singular and plural forms and had corrected her own usage. She had taken this step on her own, adding to her confidence in herself as an independent learner. Jason remained at the "mouses" stage, not yet ready for this discovery in language structure.

The child sometimes shows us the logic of experience as she views it. Two-year-old Susie shared in the excitement of welcoming her grandmother and her aunt who always came to visit together. Susie cried, "Grandmother, grandmother!" The family discovered that Susie thought the word grandmother applied to both. When the family insisted that the aunt's name was Aunt Helen, Susie would whisper in Aunt Helen's ear, "Grandmother."

The attempt to construct a logical grammar is evidence of an advance in thinking, although the errors introduced may seem more like a regression. The errors diminish as the child adds to his observations. All this goes on, not in any conscious way, of course, but as a formulation out of implicit knowledge from experiences. This process continues throughout life in the attempt to make sense out of conflicting evidence.

Coming to a conclusion by one's own efforts sets a constructive pattern for learning in the future. Children are more likely to remember what they themselves have discovered. Correcting children and calling attention to their errors tend to put them on the defensive unless they are very confident, like Susie. It may take away from the excitement of learning. The healthy child is an eager learner unless corrected too often and discouraged in making the effort.

Cognitive Skills Developed by the Need to Master Language

There is some evidence, as a result of recent studies in early language development, that "certain cognitive skills are exercised and thereby developed solely because of the need to master language."[1] While it is enough for the child to use his senses to discover the meaning of many words, he begins to meet words that he cannot understand by this method. He must deal with words like *how* and *why* by some other means. He uses the word in order to get enough responses to build a concept of its meaning. As Blank has put it, the child must "engage in a concentrated course of hypothesis testing." To do this he keeps asking a lot of "why" and "how" types of questions. From the answers he gets, he begins to attach some meaning to abstract terms about relationships or purposes.

---

[1] M. Blank. (1974). Cognitive functions of language in the preschool years. *Developmental Psychology, 10*(2).

The Importance of Questions

It is worth noting that mastering the question form is an evidence of intellectual growth. The question itself gives us clues as to the child's level of thinking. All this makes answering questions an important matter that deserves thought and attention. Pam's interesting question in the situation with the mice, "When will they grow up?" reveals that she is working on the aspect of time. The teacher's answer in this case was, "In about two weeks. Mice grow very fast." The answer was correct but probably very inadequate for Pam's concerns. How long is two weeks? Evidently it is connected with "fast." She will go on searching. Pam is nearly five and will be going to kindergarten soon. The teacher might have asked, "Are you thinking about growing up and going to a new school?" This might have led to a discussion on a subject important to Pam. Young children are often confused about time intervals, days of the week, years and phrases like "a little while ago." Until children have asked questions, tested out the answers, and corrected and refined their understanding, they cannot appreciate the meaning of these concepts.

When the Language at Home Is Different

A special situation exists in any group where some of the children speak a language other than English as their first language or speak a dialect other than standard English. These children must become competent in understanding a second language or another dialect.

Gone are the days, we hope, when children were not allowed to use their home language in school. All children should be encouraged to use all the speech they have. When a child does not speak English, it is important that the child or children have someone in the school who speaks their language. If the language of the minority group happens to be Spanish, for example, there should be a Spanish-speaking teacher or aide to talk with them, help with explanations, and encourage them in learning to become able to use English. If there is no Spanish-speaking teacher there may be a volunteer, a parent, or another child who speaks the language and can spend some time in the group.

Whatever the language, the center will help the English-speaking children learn about language differences and begin learning some other language themselves. Songs, games, and stories in other languages along with ones in English open the door for more language learning. American children whose experience with other languages is usually limited need such opportunities. Children learn readily at this age if all languages are respected and valued. A school with a mixture of nationalities has a chance to broaden the experience of all its children.

When the whole group consists of children with a first language other than English they adjust more readily if the language of the classroom is their own at first and English is introduced as a second language. There is considerable information about teaching English as a second language that may be helpful to the teacher in this situation. The teacher or some other person must be bilingual.

Other questions arise when children in the group speak a dialect other than standard English. Here again, it is important to respect the child's home dialect. Our attitudes are changing today because of recent studies about language. These studies indicate that all dialects are "systematic, highly structured language codes," different from but not inferior to one another. "The language variety one learns simply reflects where and with whom one lives, not the intelligence with which one is endowed."[2] Black dialect itself arose out of the culture of black people when this culture came in contact with white, Western culture. Dialects have developed in some native American groups in the same way.

Since it may be important for children to be able to speak standard English if they are to compete in an English-speaking country, the center should help them toward competency in that language while remaining comfortable with their home language or dialect.

An Environment That Stimulates Language Learning

We feel sure of some points: (1) Children learn the words they put to use, so we encourage speech and give children a great deal to talk about. For example, the teacher extends the child's vocabulary. The child exclaimed, "It went to the bottom," when he dropped a pebble into a pail of water. The teacher responded, "Yes, the pebble sank." At lunch the teacher may encourage children to recall their experiences, saying, "Do you remember when . . . ," and encourage each one to recount his version or to make plans for the future. (2) Talking with other children in play tends to stimulate more extensive and more sustained speech than talk with adults, in most cases. Opportunity for play, especially for sociodramatic play among children, should be provided. (3) One-to-one conversation between a child and an adult on a subject of interest to the child advances development in more complex forms of speech; so the teacher takes time for conversation with individual children.

WAYS IN WHICH THE TEACHER PROMOTES LANGUAGE COMPETENCE

The teacher serves as a model for the children in speech. They identify with her, and her warmth and responsiveness encourage their verbal

[2] C. Cazden, J. Baratz, W. Labov, and F. Palmer. (1981). Language development in day-care programs. In C. Cazden (Ed.). *Language in early childhood education* (rev. ed.). Washington, DC: National Association for the Education of Young Children.

expressions. In serving as a model she avoids using any direct way of changing children's language. She does not correct errors, although she may repeat correctly a word that has been mispronounced in the case of a very young child. She accepts the fact that children use the speech they are accustomed to hearing.

There will be nonverbal communication at times. A child brings his painting, and the teacher smiles and nods approval. There may be unspoken meanings behind some questions or statements a child makes. The teacher needs to be alert to the possibility of the fear or doubt that may be hidden in a question. She can put the fear or doubt into words that may help the child express his feelings more directly the next time.

The teacher stimulates children's growth in language competence in the following ways:

1. The teacher models grammatically *correct* speech. She uses *complete sentences* and *explicit words,* as in "Please bring me the red truck on the top shelf," rather than "Please bring that truck." The child has a pattern of exact speech in the first sentence but not in the second.
2. The teacher uses *variety* in her speech to help increase the child's vocabulary. She makes comments introducing new words as in the example, "The pebble sank."
3. The teacher asks *open-ended* questions rather than questions that can be answered by "yes" or "no." "What do you think will happen?"

Dramatic play settings provide opportunities for talking.

Hill an' Dale Family Learning Center.

"What would you do if . . . ?" "What is the problem?" in the case of a dispute, "I wonder if . . ." and "Where did the water go?"

4. The teacher *listens* carefully to what the child says and responds relevantly. She wants the child to feel that she values his words. Meeting with indifference when one speaks is discouraging to anyone.

5. The teacher *encourages talking.* Children gain speech competence by having many opportunities to use speech and by having a chance to talk about matters of interest to them to an interested listener. They gain language competence, too, as they talk among themselves as they play.

6. The teacher *monitors* her conversations with children occasionally to make sure she is not doing too much talking and to make sure she is encouraging speech in all of the children.

7. The teacher allows plenty of *time for conversations* with individual children. They may carry on a conversation as they wash the paint brushes together or prepare the snack. Conversations at the table may be between two children or between teacher and a child. On the way back to the center after a trip, conversations recalling the experience often take place.

8. Above all, the teacher plans *activities* which promote language. These will include such things as providing plenty of time, space, and props for *dramatic play.* Sociodramatic play is an excellent stimulus for speech production, as are *small-group projects* like cooking or a construction project. The teacher uses *games* to promote language such as describing objects, finishing a story, or guessing games where each child in turn guesses what a picture will be about when he has a peek at one small bit of the page. This guessing game appeals to four-year-olds. *Puppet play* encourages language just as simple *role playing* does for older children. *Excursions* to places of interest stimulate conversation, as do *reading* stories and poems and *telling stories* to children. The teacher can ask questions, "What do you suppose this book is about?" Interruptions while reading the story are welcomed for their language values. The teacher will need to develop skill in knowing the point at which she should continue the reading.

SPECIAL PROBLEMS WITH SPEECH

Some children may withdraw from trying to communicate because they are afraid, resentful, or disturbed in different ways. The teacher's task here is that of building a relationship of trust with the child before doing anything direct about his speech.

Young children often stutter, repeating words or syllables. They are in the process of learning to talk. They are eager to communicate, but they have not developed enough control to get the words out rapidly. Stuttering that is frequent and prolonged is a sign the child feels more pressure than he can manage comfortably. The teacher needs to make sure that any strains or pressures on the child are reduced. She will also help the child by giving him her undivided attention when he speaks to her. She will not say, "Speak more slowly." Calling the child's attention to the stuttering by asking him to speak more slowly may make him conscious of his speech. He becomes afraid of stuttering and is more likely to continue stuttering. The child who is free of undue pressure will probably stop stuttering as he becomes better able to control his speech muscles. It is interesting to note that types of speech defects vary in different cultures. Among certain Inuits and Native Americans, for example, no case of stuttering has ever been recorded. In our culture, it is more common among boys than girls, but there are cultures where the reverse is true.

There are children, too, who have defects of articulation in speech. They may have difficulty in saying the sounds of *r* or *th*. The adult helps these children by pronouncing the sound very clearly herself, repeating the word the child has said rather than asking him to repeat it. She wants him to hear the correct pronunciation and, in time, to imitate it without interfering with his spontaneity in verbal communication.

The whole curriculum plays a part in increasing the child's competence with language by offering him experiences to talk about and people to talk with. Speech is an important tool.

LANGUAGE AS SELF-EXPRESSION

RUTH EXPRESSES HER FEELING THROUGH LANGUAGE. Ruth is a delightfully verbal four-year-old whose spontaneity seems a gift from two accepting parents. Ruth welcomes approaches by others as gestures of friendliness. She disarms the most aggressive children by her own friendliness. She expresses her feelings freely in language that is fun to listen to.

"Wouldn't it be funny if I were an egg, or if I were a tomato and someone picked me in the garden?" she laughs as the group is returning from a trip to the farm.

She feels a part of whatever she sees and identifies closely with the world around her. "I'd like to have a comb like that," she says as she looks at the rooster. Patting the setting hen she exclaims, "I'd like to be a chicken and have someone pat me like this!"

Her imagination seizes on many things and weaves them into fascinating patterns. In the spring the nursery school had two ducks and a white rabbit. Ruth gave this version of the legend of the Easter Bunny when she came to school one morning: "When this bunny and the ducks grow up, we can teach them to paint eggs, can't we? The ducks will have the eggs, and the bunny will paint them, and when we come to nursery school there will be painted eggs all over, won't there?"

Ruth's feelings tumble out in words, and she finds these feelings easy to handle as she creates pictures of her world through language.

Language Is More Than an Avenue of Communication

Not all children use language as freely as Ruth, but for most children language is an important avenue of self-expression, not just an avenue of communication. They use it to express the delight they feel as well as the anger and resentment. They use it without regard to any listener. A young child will chatter to himself as he plays, or he will accompany his more rhythmic activities with singing.

Cindy is swinging and she talks to herself. "I'm going to ride a horsey, a horsey, a horsey. It's going to be a real big one. I'll be big, too, 'cause I ate my breakfast this morning."

When a group of children are happy and satisfied, they talk and sing as they play, even though they are not communicating with each other. Sometimes their singing is in the form of a chant, repeating sounds or words together in a rhythmic pattern. Sometimes their chanting is an expression of their delight in companionship as well as in sounds. Often these chants have an element of humor, as when Terry sang to the group, "Would you like to eat a hammer?" and the three other children replied together, "No." He continued the song with "Would you like to eat a tongue?" and they chorused, "No," and so on through a long list of nonsensical questions with the group replying "No" in great delight. This is not only language expression but it is also a form of group game which is beginning to make its appearance with four-year-olds, as we have noted earlier.

Teachers or parents should jot down these language expressions for the light they throw on the feelings or ideas and concepts of the child, as well as for their literary interest.

Children are helped by putting experiences into words when the experiences have an element of fear or of discomfort. Lynn, aged four years, nine months, reminisces pleasantly as he is swinging, about an experience which was not entirely pleasant.

> Last night my Daddy got a needle,
> A needle, needle, needle, needle,
> He took the sliver out of my hand,
> And it didn't hurt one bit,
> And it didn't hurt one bit,
> And I didn't cry at all.
> It didn't hurt at all.
> Last night my Daddy got a needle,
> And he stuck it in my hand
> Took the sliver out,
> And it didn't hurt one bit.
> And I didn't cry one bit,
> No, I didn't, 'cause it didn't hurt,
> Because he did it with a needle.
> Needle, needle, needle, needle.

Linda climbs high on the jungle gym and says, "I can climb right up here. Now look what I can do. I'm higher than Mommy now. She can't catch me. Now she can, now she can't." She expresses her delight in being up high, out of her mother's reach but not really out of touch. She reveals the ambivalence of her feelings.

Children enjoy hearing favorite songs and poems repeated over and over again until they know them by heart. They may sing them as they play. We can also encourage the use of language as a means of self-expression. This might be one way we keep open for the child an important avenue through which he can drain feelings, or share them with others, or find creative delight for himself. We also have for ourselves a valuable means of gaining insight into what experiences mean to the child as we listen to what he expresses through his words.

LITERATURE

Experiences with books are part of the daily program in a good center. A variety of well-chosen books should always be available under conditions that will encourage their proper use.

In selecting books a variety of sources are helpful in becoming acquainted with new books being published for children, and with children's literature in general. The children's librarian in the local public library is an important source of help to use in selecting books. Most centers depend on the library for many of their books. The books can be selected with the interests of individual children in mind, and the books can be changed frequently.

Bookshelves or a rack for books with plenty of soft cushions or comfortable chairs nearby makes it possible for a child to look at books while being relaxed. A heap of picture books piled on a small table can only lead to misuse of the books. Children cannot be expected to handle books carefully if the space is crowded; nor can they be expected to be interested in books for long if they are not comfortable.

A few colorful books laid out on a table near the bookshelf may serve to attract the children's attention to the books. Adding a new book or changing the selection available stimulates interest. Reading groups should be small, for the child likes to be close to the teacher and the book. He is easily distracted in a large group where he does not have this closeness. Reading need not be confined to one story period. Some children will want many opportunities to listen to stories, while others may not. Small informal groups formed when there is an interest meet these needs. In pleasant weather, reading can be done outdoors in a shady spot, and the new location creates new interest.

Looking at a child-made book.

Valley College, Campus Child Development Center

Books Should Fit the Interests of the Children

Variety in the books selected for the center library is important, for children differ in their interests, just as adults do. One boy showed no interest in books. He had evidently had few experiences with books at home, or else his experiences had been with books that were not suited to his level of development. But he did like cars, and one day he found a small book about cars. He looked at it carefully for a long time and then asked the teacher to read it to him while he listened attentively. For days he carried this book around. Sometimes he would stop and find someone to read it to him again. Then he began enjoying other books and joining the group when they listened to stories. Through the one book which was related to his interest he had begun to discover the world of books.

This case illustrates the importance of having books that are related to the children's individual interests. Each group will enjoy a somewhat different selection of books, depending on their particular environment and the experiences they have had. Books about trains will be popular in one place, and books about boats in another. Everywhere, children will enjoy books about boys and girls and animal pets, for they are all familiar with these subjects.

Books Should Present the Familiar World

In selecting books we must remember that the function of books for the young child is not to present new information, but to re-create for him the world he knows. By re-creation we strengthen his understanding of it. New knowledge should come from firsthand experiences and not from the printed page. We will find many city children thinking of milk as coming from a bottle no matter how many stories they have heard about the cow and her contribution to the bottle. Stories about cows have more meaning after a trip to the barn. Books like Harriet Huntington's *Let's Go Outdoors* present information that can be used in connection with experiences in the garden. It is fun for the children to find the pictures of earthworms and read about them after having discovered worms in their digging, or to find the picture of tadpoles when there are some tadpoles swimming in the bowl at school. Whatever the children's experiences, they can be broadened and enriched through books related to those experiences.

In the past many books presented an unrealistic or biased picture of the world. All the children in the stories were white, all mothers were homemakers, and all the strong characters were boys or men. Today we have books for children which present the world the child is experiencing:

Listening to a story.

First Step Nursery School

men and boys in caregiving roles, mothers in careers including nontraditional jobs, competent female heroines as well as male heroes, single parent families, and people of many racial and cultural groups.

Poetry Has an Important Place

Books of poetry are important in the center library. Children can appreciate the beauty and imagery of good poetry. They need to be introduced to it early and hear it read with expression. They love the rhythmic quality of words, the alliteration and repetition that are all part of poetry, beginning with Mother Goose rhymes and going on to the delightful verse of A. A. Milne or John Ciardi. Don Holdaway states, "Chant, song, dance, and linguistic rituals are among the most powerful forms of human learnings, primitively satisfying, deeply memorable, and globally meaningful. Much of its power comes from the sense of security, generated by repetitions, familiarity, and universality."[3] Children who are familiar with good poetry will often go on to create beauty with words themselves. Poetry may become a lifelong source of enjoyment for them.

Books Should Be Attractive and Interestingly Presented

Books which are desirable for a center are not only about familiar, everyday subjects, but also are short and written in simple, correct English with many clear illustrations in color. Pictures should be on the same page as the material they illustrate. There are many books that are reputedly for young children but fail to hold children's interest because they are not attractive in appearance and their vocabulary is above the child's level. The child who has these books will be less likely to develop an interest in them. He will be handicapped, for there are advantages in liking books. Much of what we learn later in life will be through books.

When we present stories to children, we must read slowly so that children have no difficulty in understanding. Anyone who has tried to follow a conversation in a foreign language with which he is not too familiar will understand how difficult even the ordinary rate of speech may be for the child who is listening to reading. As we read, we need to remember that children are still in the process of learning the language. We must read slowly with inflections that will clarify the meaning as well as add interest and variety. Teachers should be thoroughly familiar with the story and should be interested themselves.

In *telling* stories one has the advantage of being able to keep closer to the audience. Bringing in something related to the story such as caps, shells, or even a carrot adds to the interest. Telling as well as reading stories is an ability that every teacher should work to develop.

[3] D. Holdaway. (1979). *The foundations of literacy.* New York: Ashton Scholastic.

Effect of the Story on the Child

We have mentioned realistic stories as suitable for young children. The suitability of "fairy tales" and imaginative tales in general may well be raised here. At one time folk and fairy tales constituted almost the entire literary fare available to children, along with the moralistic tale. If one has a chance to look at samples of early literature for children, one will realize how much change there has been in books for children in the last hundred years. John Newbery is referred to as the "father of children's literature." He first took advantage of the market in children's books and published the pocket books of the eighteenth century. He was obliged to throw in sonnets from Shakespeare along with his Mother Goose to make it acceptable to the buying public of those days.

In selecting books today we are helped by knowing more about children's development. We know that arousing fear in them may be damaging, that there is a readiness factor in learning, and that children need help in understanding the world around them before they meet a terrifying unreal world. It is better to omit terrifying elements from stories until the child has had time to develop secure feelings and has confidence in his ability to meet the real world. This doesn't mean that stories for the child should lack action and suspense but that frightening elements should be left out. *Hansel and Gretel* is an example of a story not suitable for younger children. Some children will, of course, be readier at an earlier age than others for folktales, depending on their level of emotional development. Three- and four-year-olds are struggling with fears about possible body assaults and also struggling to sort out the real from the unreal. The price of introducing terrifying stories too early may be disturbed sleep and a child more timid than he need be in facing the new and unknown.

Imagination is fun when it is a play between the real and the unreal. Listen to the children's "jokes" to gain some concept of what is real and unreal to them. "How would you like to eat a horse?" draws a big laugh because they can perceive how impossible such a thing could be. They laugh at things like this because they know that they are not true, but what do they know about monsters and what they might or might not do? There are many stories of animals dressing and talking like people that may not be among the best in books for children. They may distort reality for children. As one child remarked, "I wonder why they make them talk like that."

Imagination is fun, too, when children use it with word sounds. As Connie uses the crayons, she talks. Holding up a red crayon she says to Judy, "Red, red, wet your bed." They both repeat this several times, giggling together. Then Connie adds, "Rain, rain, what's your name?" They repeat this several times with obvious pleasure. Judy leaves, and Connie continues, "Know what this is? A baby bat on his back!" She goes on, "Know what this is? Camel with a hammer in his hand. I saw a camel at the zoo. Camel, pamel." Like many four-year-olds, Connie likes words and the way they sound.

Selecting Books

In selecting books the teacher will find sources for help in the *Horn Book* magazine; resource books such as those by Norton (1983), Meek (1978), Glazer and Williams (1979); and the local library as she becomes acquainted with new books being published for children and with children's literature in general. Useful criteria for selecting children's books can be found in *Literature: Basic in the Language Arts Curriculum* (Stewig, 1983). A growing number of books are available for children on topics like death, the new baby, divorce, stepfamilies, hospitalization, handicaps, and other stressful situations. The book *Helping Children Cope* (Fassler, 1978), in which children's books are organized according to topic, will be particularly useful to teachers who are helping children cope with problems and conflicts. There are a number of excellent sources for multiethnic books. NAEYC has published a resource bibliography called *Cultural Awareness* (Schmidt & McNeill, 1978). We recommend that all centers purchase a few story, poetry, and informational or resource books each year. It helps a child's learning if the teacher can locate and use an informational or resource book with him when his interest in a particular subject is at a peak.

Projects

1. Select a child and record his speech as completely as possible for three ten-minute periods during one hour. Summarize your record and characterize his speech, covering such points as these: Is his speech used for self-expression or communication? Are there defects of articulation or defects in rhythm? How would you characterize his voice quality? For what purposes does he usually use speech? How many questions did he ask? What ideas and attitudes did he express in speech? Is his speech adequate for his purposes? How does his speech aid him in learning?
2. Select five books for this child on the basis of his interests and his stage of development, giving the name of the book, the author, and the reason for your selection.
3. Observe and record a situation in which the teacher made effective use of an experience to increase the child's language competence.

For Your Further Reading

Bos, B. J. (1983). *Before the basics: Creating conversations with children*. Roseville, CA: Turn the Page Press. A wonderfully enthusiastic approach to language experiences; many concrete ideas for activities.

Cazden, C. B. (Ed.). (1981). *Language in early childhood education* (rev. ed.). Washington, DC: National Association for the Education of Young Children. A widely referred-to collection of articles on language development at home or school, commercial language programs, dialect or ESL, and how language and reading are related.

de Villiers, P. A., & de Villiers, J. G. (1979). *Early language.* The developing child series. Cambridge, MA: Harvard University Press. Very readable overview of how early language develops.

Fassler, J. (1978). *Helping children cope.* New York: The Free Press. Bibliotherapy for dealing with problem areas; suggested book titles and helpful text on how to use the suggested books.

Garvey, C. (1984). *Children's talk.* The developing child series. Cambridge, MA: Harvard University Press. How talk is important in children's social development, and how children learn intangible rules of conversation.

Gottwald, S. R., Goldback, P., & Isack, A. H. (1985). Stuttering: Prevention and detection. *Young Children. 41*(1), 9-14. Identifies danger signs of stuttering; offers ways for teachers to enhance fluency; and offers help for stuttering referral.

Larrick, N. (1982). *A parent's guide to children's reading.* New York: Bantam Books. Good lists of books for children, periodically updated.

McAfee, O. D. (1985). Research report: Circle time: Getting past "Two little pumpkins." *Young Children. 40*(6), 24-29. A study of what takes place during circle times, plus practical suggestions for improving group times.

Schickedanz, J. (1985). *More than the ABC's: The early stages of reading and writing.* Washington, DC: National Association for the Education of Young Children. Written from a child development approach, this book offers parents and teachers sound ways to introduce "literacy learning."

The Dancing Turkey (boy, 4 years)

19 ◆ Areas of Learning in the Program: The Arts

Art media offer both child and adult an avenue for the discovery of self and for the expression of feeling. Creative expression through the arts, whether in language, music or dance, or the graphic or plastic arts, has an important place in the curriculum. The goal should be to "encourage creative expression and appreciation for the arts."[1]

We are interested in creative expression through art because of the satisfactions that this kind of expression brings. There is fulfillment and

[1] National Association for the Education of Young Children. (1984). *Accreditation criteria and procedures: Position statement of the National Academy of Early Childhood Programs.* Washington, DC: Author.

increased awareness in expression of feeling. We are happier when we are creative. All of us have within us warm, loving feelings, a responsiveness to beauty, to laughter, and to the richness of life itself. These are feelings that are good to express. With expression, we grow as people. Art is an important avenue for this kind of growth. When expression through art is blocked, the blocking limits personality growth.

We are also interested in opportunities for creative expression because such expression can serve as a safety valve, draining destructive feelings that might otherwise pile up to disturb us in unrecognized ways. As strains and tensions mount, it becomes important to have avenues for releasing these feelings.

We appreciate the art products of the child, too, not because of the talent shown, but because we can truly appreciate the effort that lies behind any achievement in controlling and expressing feeling in an art form.

Because of these values, it is essential that children have opportunities for creative expression through art media and that we recognize and protect the spontaneity of their expressions. By keeping many avenues of expression open in language, movement, and in the arts, we leave the child freer to grow as a person. We protect him against the effects of blocking and inhibitions that result when few avenues of expression are open. We help him to find the satisfactions that come from expressing himself freely, without fear and with confidence.

As we watch children in the center, we may become more aware of the avenues of expression through art that are open to us as adults. In the center we see children expressing a feeling through an art medium, but the need for expression and the values of expression may be as great for us as adults.

Here we will only suggest some of the ways in which children express themselves in language, music or dance, and in the graphic and plastic arts.

DRAWING AND PAINTING: AVENUES FOR EXPRESSION AND COMMUNICATION

Drawing and painting are important avenues through which young children may express their thoughts and feelings. They also use drawing and painting as a means to communicate when they have little language. Children may be telling something in the drawing or painting. They assume that we can receive the message.

Individual Differences

In art as in other areas there are wide individual differences in pace and rate of working. One child may paint a single picture carefully and slowly.

The artist at work.

First Step Nursery School

One picture is enough for him. His pace is slow and methodical. Another child may paint a series of pictures in rapid succession. Some children move early to representation. Other children scribble for a long time seeming to enjoy changing the paper. Still other children become absorbed in using color or texture and may explore these variables thoroughly. No one way is necessarily best; each child has his own pace of working.

No one art activity is equally satisfying to all children. One child may prefer to use a pencil to draw intricate lines, seeming to plan each stroke. He may prefer a small piece of paper. Another child may prefer paint and a wide brush. He may use a large piece of paper, cover it quickly, and allow his colors to drip. Another child may find that clay allows him to express his ideas and feelings best. He may enjoy the feel of clay or its potential for creating.

The Adult Role

Our role is to make sure that the child is well supplied with the materials he needs for drawing and painting, plenty of pencils or suitable pens, plenty of paper, paints of several different colors, space for undisturbed working. We may approve what he does when he shows us a product, but we do not give the child directions or set any kind of pattern. The product is the child's, his own creation, an expression in an art form of his feeling. We will encourage his effort. The time will come when the child will ask

This child enjoys the experience of painting.

Valley College, Campus Child Development Center

for something more from us as he matures. It is important that the child is free to express his thoughts and feelings without interference from adults.

The Process Rather Than the Product Is Important

Experiences in the graphic and plastic arts offer an important avenue through which individuals release their feelings and find satisfaction and an avenue for communication. Too many of us have had this avenue blocked by the teaching we have received at home or at school. We are convinced that we can't draw a straight line, and we probably are right. Nothing that we are likely to do will ever rate as a "work of art." But we probably could have drawn much better than we think and, more important, we could have found pleasure and emotional release in the process if we had had sound teaching, or at least had been left alone. The anxious attention on the product rather than the process, the many coloring books, and other "patterns" that were imposed on us have all served pretty effectively to prevent us from expressing ourselves through art. Yet art is an important means of expression and of releasing feelings as well as a source of satisfaction.

As we ourselves work with children, we must try to safeguard their use of art media as a means of self-expression by eliminating the use of coloring books or workbooks with young children. For every child, art can serve as an outlet for feeling if the process rather than the product is emphasized. It does not matter that there are differences in artistic ability, just as there are in music. Given an easel, paper and paint, and no directions, every child will paint. For some children painting will remain an important avenue through which they can express feeling all through their lives.

Drawing

Very young children seem to prefer drawing with a pencil on any kind of paper, usually placing the paper on the floor. Pencils lend themselves to simple as well as intricate drawings. Felt markers, flow pens, color ink pens, even chalk, and soft lead pencils may be used as well. Children will try these and may discover a preference for one or the other.

For reasons of convenience, many preschool children are limited to crayons in their art experiences at home. Crayons are a much "tighter" medium than paints and are used with more cramped movements. They are more suited to the level of representation that comes later. The child who continues to use crayons in preference to pencils or a brush is often a tense, tight child. Richard, for example, had a very difficult time adjusting to nursery school, and during this period he used crayons frequently. After he had relaxed and become more comfortable, he turned to the easel where he painted freely, seldom touching crayons again.

We will not waste many words on coloring books or workbooks. They are examples of pattern setting of the worst kind, preventing the child from expressing his own thoughts and feelings. Children who have often used coloring books and workbooks are unlikely to discover or to appreciate what art offers in the way of creative experiences. Heilman writes, "Children can become dependent upon these workbooks and the youngsters' own creative work can be seriously and negatively influenced."[2]

A Research Study of the Art Products of Young Children

Lark-Horovitz[3] has made one of the few intensive studies of the art of very young children from earliest childhood. With cooperation of a group of parents she collected all the art products the children had done in their homes or in centers. The parents were instructed to make paper and pencils

---

[2]H. Heilman. (1954). An experimental study of the effects of workbooks on the creative drawing of second grade children. Unpublished doctoral dissertation, The Pennsylvania State University.

[3]B. Lark-Horovitz. (1976). *The art of the very young—an indicator of individuality.* Columbus, OH: Charles E. Merrill.

or pens available without commenting on the artwork produced by their child. The children were selected because the mother was willing to cooperate, they were under a year old, and lived within traveling distance from Lark-Horovitz. They were not selected because of any indication of possible talent beyond the mother's willingness to participate. Lark-Horovitz continued to collect samples of the art done by many of these young children after they entered school. She found individual differences in very young children in the amount of artwork produced at home, the creativity displayed, and in the length of time art was a major interest. Some young children ceased showing interest in drawing after entering school. Only one or two went on to later careers in some form of the arts.

Her study showed some evidence of a relationship between art expression at an early age and language expression. The children in whose home art had been abundant and creative were later rated by their schools as superior in language development. It was as if the children's spontaneous expression in art had contributed to later expression in language.

The drawings used in this book at the beginning of each chapter have been selected from Lark-Horovitz' collection with the child's age, sex, and the title the child gave to his or her picture.

Painting

Providing opportunities for painting is important. A supply of large sheets of paper, several large brushes, and rich-colored paints should always be available. Two or more easels are needed. Sometimes children prefer to paint on a large sheet of paper on the floor or outdoors. Children are social. They may enjoy painting and talking together.

Painting needs a location relatively free from distraction. Aprons and a floor covering may be desirable. The primary colors should be supplied. Sometimes the teacher adds black or white if the children are interested in exploring other effects. Children will mix paints and discover other colors.

The opportunity to paint and the availability of appropriate supplies are all the child needs, but we can show our interest and our appreciation when the child wants these. We refrain from asking questions, and we do not give directions.

Using the Materials

Even the drip from a full brush can make fascinating patterns on paper. Some methodical children will wipe their brushes carefully because they want to make their pictures with no drips. Others may slop on the paint, expressing their own overflowing and as yet less well-controlled feeling, while others may drip the paint deliberately on the paper as they explore the possibilities of the medium. They do not all use the paint in the same way.

Greg picks up the brush from the jar with red paint and draws a circle. He puts red lines and dots inside the circle and then smears red paint in a few places outside the circle. "All done with this one," he says. On a fresh piece of paper he begins with paint from the orange jar and dabs the bright color on the paper in one spot, then uses broad, brisk strokes to paint with orange across the paper. He picks up the red brush and makes a few more strokes across the paper, covering very little of his previous work. He dabs a small amount of yellow in one spot near the corner of the paper and says again, "All done with this one."

Kay is a child for whom painting became a favorite medium for expression. When she first entered the group, she explored all the possible experiences with paint. The teacher watched her as she approached the easel with evident satisfaction on that first day. She painted on the paper with full brush strokes, using all the colors. Then she touched the tip of the brush to her tongue and stood relishing its taste. Next, she brushed it under her nose, getting its smell. Afterward she carefully painted the palm of her hand. She found out what paint felt like. She had enjoyed all the sensory experiences that paint offered, and she used it often during the time she attended.

Ginny is a child who delighted in the feel of paint on her skin. She usually ended a session at the easel by carefully painting her hands, arms, and face and then, just as carefully, washing off the paint, enjoying the sight of herself in the mirror all the while.

The youngest children usually do not intend to represent anything when they use paints. They are using art as a means of expressing themselves,

Painting out-of-doors, free of distraction.

Santa Monica College, Child Development Center

and paint as a medium whose possibilities they are beginning to explore. By the time they are three or four, they may name and describe what they are doing as they work; but we should be careful to avoid pushing them into naming their picture by asking questions. Again it is Kay who gives us a clue as she laughingly said when she put her painting away, "What is it? What is it?" The teacher asked her, "Is that what you think your mother will say when she sees your painting?" "Yes," replied Kay with a smile.

Left alone, children put down many of their experiences on paper, even though they may not add titles for our benefit. A large barn burned near one center in a spectacular night fire witnessed by some of the children and described vividly to the others. Following that, there were many paintings of "barns burning." Most of them were splotches of dark paint covered by red color. These pictures appeared again and again, and many of the children were probably helped to drain the fear which the fire had roused by expressing it in an art form, thus turning it into a more pleasant and manageable experience.

David was painting with a hard, circular movement. He talked as he painted. "I'm making a jungle. Look at my jungle. There's a lion. That's a trail and a river that the lion can't cross." With this painting David may have been expressing feelings about dangerous things that need to be controlled. They can be represented by lions in jungles with a river that sets a boundary. Through his painting he reduces his anxieties to more manageable proportions.

When we leave children free to use art media as avenues of self-expression, we gain a great deal of insight into what they are feeling as we observe what they paint and how they paint.

Fingerpaints Are Valuable

Fingerpainting allows a great deal of valuable, spontaneous expression. The pressure to keep clean may be less damaging to a child if he has this acceptable outlet for sensory experience and for messiness. Being messy with fingerpaints should reduce the need he feels to be messy in other places and times and lessen the damage he may suffer from having to limit himself at these places and times.

We learn something about the kinds of control that a child has built up as we watch him approach the new experience of using fingerpaints. Is his response wholehearted and immediate? Does he hesitate and withhold himself, finding participation difficult? In what ways does he enjoy the experience—by patting or squeezing or just poking the paint? Does he use a small bit of paint or a whole lot? Does he touch it with only one finger as though afraid of the sensation, or does he use his whole hand or even his arm?

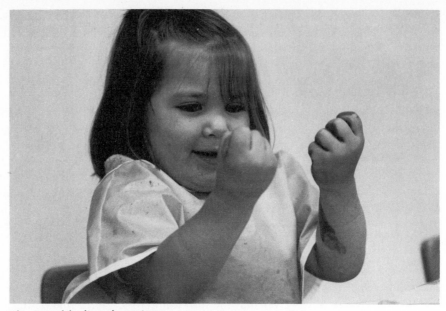

The joy of feeling the paint.
_____
Santa Monica College, Child Development Center

Changes in the child's behavior at the fingerpainting table will give us clues to changes taking place in behavior in other areas, too. Fingerpainting may help to free children for more creative activities in other areas. It offers a valuable avenue of release to children who have had too little chance for play with mud pies or for messy play at other times.

MODELING

Clay Is Another Desirable Medium

Clay may have many of the same values for children as fingerpainting. It offers a direct, sensory experience.

Children who have felt conflict over toilet training are especially likely to use it for release of feeling. The squeezing, patting, and pounding they do with clay serves to drain some of their resentment at interferences which they may have been unable to express in other ways. We often see a child make something out of clay and then destroy it by flattening it on the table. It is all right to smash clay, and one can get rid of hostile feelings in this way. It is a way of "acting out" that does no harm and may have much value.

Every center should have a crock or a tightly covered pail for storing clay. Because the sensory experiences offered by clay are important, it is wise to encourage handling it with the fingers rather than to introduce tools of any kind. We are less interested in products than in the process, and fingers are the best tools to achieve what we want. By making the clay wetter and thus messier, we may increase its value for some children. Some inhibited children, on the other hand, may be unable to touch clay at first if it is too wet and sticky. These children need to have clay that is only soft and moist until the barriers they have built up against messiness in any form are relaxed. The older preschool child who produces something that he values may find satisfaction in letting it dry, and later painting it. It may even be possible to fire the product to give it added value for the older child.

There is no art medium which seems more likely than clay to tempt the inexperienced adult into model making. The idea that one can play with clay, rolling it, patting it, feeling it without making anything, seems hard for even a well-intentioned adult to act on. Shades of past experiences in which it was necessary to "make" something operate against one's being content to play with the medium. We all need to be on our guard, or we will find ourselves making models that the children are only too prone to follow. Then we may have deprived them of the creative values in using clay.

Modeling with clay.

Valley College, Campus Child Development Center

Playdough is often used in centers and it provides a different experience than clay. It is easily made, less messy to use, and offers children the opportunity to see raw materials change. Playdough and clay both belong in centers and enhance modeling opportunities.

CUTTING AND PASTING

Before children can use scissors as a tool, they can tear paper for their use. As children are learning to cut, this activity is important in and of itself and need not serve any other purpose. The child makes snips to change the appearance of the paper. Changing the paper into small or large pieces *is* the activity. Most children will learn to cut if the teacher sits with them and snips paper herself at *their* level of cutting. Over time, as children become skilled in using scissors, they can use them as a tool to make shapes for collage, assemblage, or other activities.

Well-constructed blunt scissors with sharp blades should be provided for preschool children. Scissors should cut paper easily, but they must also be safe for children to use. Excellent plastic scissors that cut only paper are now available.

Pasting, like cutting, starts out as an activity that young children enjoy for its own sake. Children often place one piece of material over another with paste sandwiched in between; in this way they learn about the quality of paste. By using paste over time to attach paper and fabric to a variety of background surfaces, children learn how to accomplish their particular purpose. They make two-dimensional compositions called *collages*. Children can start pasting with paper or cardboard as a background surface and attach materials of various colors, textures, and shapes prepared by the teacher. Library paste is easy to handle and provides a beginning step. As other materials and adhesives are used children can become more selective in choosing materials and adhesives. Our goal is for the child to feel free and confident in his own expressions through collage. When he pleases himself, he pleases us, too.

There are many kinds of adhesives, such as library paste, white glue, liquid starch, vinyl plastic, and rubber cement. Each has its own unique qualities, and each is designed to accomplish a particular purpose. For example, a tissue paper collage can be made with liquid starch or library paste. Liquid starch will dry transparently and give a stained glass window effect to the tissue paper. As children use adhesives with various materials they learn which ones produce the effect they desire.

Many kinds of materials can be used for collage, such as candy wrappers, wire screen, cotton balls, confetti, and velvet. Teachers will search for all sorts of interesting materials with a wide variety of textures, shapes, and colors for children to use and become sensitive to the quality of the materials.

OTHER ART EXPERIENCES

Many other activities are related to art. Simple printmaking and weaving have value, and woodworking should be included in the art activities planned for young children.

The object of these activities is not the product. It is the experience of exploring and experimenting with color and texture, spaces, shapes, relations. Craft work, which may appeal to older children and adults, has no place in the young child's art experiences.

Children Need "Messy" Play Experiences

Children need the experiences of "messy" play that clay and fingerpainting offer. These experiences help to lessen the burden imposed on children by the effort to be clean. Because they are sensory experiences, they are deeply satisfying to children. As teachers we must look at our own attitude toward the sensory satisfaction of "messy" play. We may have suffered from training experiences in our childhood, so that it is hard for us to see children delighting in using sticky clay or gobs of fingerpaint. Unless we

These girls share their collage materials.

Valley College, Campus Child Development Center

can accept our own feelings, we may find ourselves avoiding the use of clay or fingerpaint. We may find ourselves depriving the child of a satisfying experience or, on the other hand, being unable to set limits when limitation is necessary because we are afraid of being too restrictive. We may need to take steps to handle our own feelings if we are to offer help to the children here.

It is probably important to mention that mud, sand, and water offer many of the same values to the child as clay. We might even consider clay and fingerpaints as sophisticated substitutes for the mud hole or mud puddles that have brought joy to the hearts—and fingers—of many healthy children. Children who have been denied access to mud and water have more need of experiences with clay and fingerpaints if they are to satisfy the desire for sensory experience that is strong in all young children. But children who use clay and fingerpaints will have a richer experience if they also know the feel of sand, both dry and wet, through their fingers and have dabbled in mud, and explored the possibilities of water play. A good center will supply these "down-to-earth" experiences, for they, too, are avenues of self-expression and among the most direct and satisfying open to a child.

MUSIC AND MOVEMENT

Music offers children an avenue of expression that is closely related to that of language. It is an avenue which is used by children everywhere. There is significance in the act of a mother as she rocks and sings to her child. The sound of a mother's voice, the feeling tones expressed in it, the rhythm of rocking are important to a child very early in his life.

The Tones of the Human Voice Tell Us a Great Deal

The child in a center will respond to the tone of the teacher's voice as much as to the words she uses. He will be reassured if her tone is confident and friendly, without regard to what she says. The "music" of the voice is an important medium for communicating feeling. As teachers and parents we need to be aware of the effect that the tones of our voices have on children. We need to use with effectiveness the important tool of voice quality as we work with children.

Just as the child senses meanings through the tone quality of adult voices, so we can be alert to what the child is communicating through the tones of his voice. The high-pitched tight, rapid speech of one child, the low, only half-articulated speech of another, the strong full tones of a third, all tell us a great deal about each of these children and what they are feeling. We can learn to identify more and more accurately what the voices of children reveal as we listen and observe.

Satisfying Activities Stimulate Singing and Dancing

When children are happy and content, when they are engaged in satisfying activities, especially rhythmic activities, they will sing. We can encourage musical expression when we help them find satisfactions and see that they have plenty of opportunity for rhythmic activities such as swinging, bouncing, pounding, running, or pedaling a tricycle. Two swings side by side make companionship possible under simple circumstances, so that the joy of having a friend may find expression along with the joy of movement through space. Swinging and singing go together. One school used a large truck inner tube for many rhythmic activities. Two or three children would sit on it and bounce, or the group would use it for a drum, pounding on it with their hands as they listened to music, or set their own rhythmic patterns. When a long board is placed between two low sawhorses, bouncing may take a rhythmic pattern, too. In fact there are endless ways in which rhythm can be introduced into the experience of children, bringing singing with it.

The teacher who can sing "on the spot" and move freely to music will encourage spontaneous responses in the children. Parents may be glad to bring to the center musical instruments they can play, so the children will

Music provides opportunities for expression.

First Step Nursery School

have a chance to see and hear wind, string, and percussion instruments. Activity and music go together. Singing around the piano may be fun, but it does not take the place of singing in connection with activities. There should be plenty of singing by the children and the teachers on the playground and through all the areas of play activity. There should be the opportunity for dancing wherever there are space and music.

The Ability to Keep Time Improves with Maturity Rather Than Practice

There is evidence that ability to keep time is not improved by practice but that it depends on maturity and innate ability. At four, a child keeps more accurate time than he did at three—whether or not he has had training. One four-year-old will keep better time than another, regardless of experience, because of innate differences in ability. But if a child has been subjected to pressure to "keep time with the music," he may find less enjoyment in music than he might, and he may feel less adequate in this area. There are individual differences in the rate at which a child develops a sense of time, but all children enjoy rhythmic experiences—if this enjoyment has not been interfered with. The more opportunity they have to move freely, either with music or without it, the more pleasure they will find and the more release for their feelings in this form of expression.

The Ability to Sing Improves with Practice

Ability to "carry a tune" responds to training, according to what we know at present. Singing with the teacher gives a child practice, but the teacher must value singing as a means of self-expression rather than as a skill, especially with the young child. She can help him enjoy this avenue of self-expression by bringing songs within the measure of his ability to sing them rather than setting him difficult patterns. Children's singing voices as a rule are not high-pitched. Children usually pitch their own songs below rather than above middle A, for example. Many of their own songs are sung in a minor key, quite different from the songs that we often give them to sing. Simple childlike songs, used in connection with activities, build skill and enjoyment of singing in the children.

The teacher with a musical background can encourage creative expression in singing by jotting down the songs that the children themselves sing in their play and then playing and singing these songs back to them later, in the same way that she encourages their stories and poems. Her interest will heighten their awareness of the creative possibilities of music.

In one center the violinist who was to bring her violin began playing the instrument as she walked down the hall. Many of the children heard the music and were eager to listen when she came into the room. She had introduced herself and her violin.

Listening Is Important

Another important experience that the program can offer is that of listening to good music through records or music played on the piano, the violin, the flute, or any other instrument. If the teacher herself is not a musician, she can often find someone who likes children and who will enjoy sharing music with them. This adds to the variety of the children's experience with music and increases their interest. Not all children may wish to listen each time such a music experience is offered. There should be no compulsion about listening, for this does not build desirable attitudes toward music. The child who does not wish to listen can respect the needs of the listening group for quiet by playing at the other end of the room himself or playing outside. Many times curiosity about a new instrument will bring even a nonlistener into the group for a time.

When a record player or a cassette recorder is used, it should be of good quality, and it should be played where a child can listen undisturbed. Some children will want to listen far more often than others. They should be free to listen without interfering with the play of other children or being interfered with themselves as they listen. With the proper physical setup, listening to music may form a large part of the music curriculum for some children at some periods.

Teachers can encourage a variety of experiences in listening, such as listening to bird songs, the peeping of baby chicks (if the center has raised some), and the many sounds to be heard on a city street. Watching and listening to a band practicing is an absorbing experience for children. They often reenact it later in their dramatic play.

Sometimes we find a child who spends a great deal of time listening to music or listening to stories. He may be doing this as a form of escape from facing difficulties, such as attempting to adjust to other children in play situations. The teacher needs to recognize this situation and to take steps to encourage the child to extend his interests. She can give him more support in his group relations and build up his confidence. It is important that the total pattern of the child's adjustment be understood. Music meets many emotional needs and should not serve only as an escape.

Children Enjoy Using Different Instruments

Every center needs a variety of sound instruments for the children to use freely, sometimes on their own and sometimes in a group under the teacher's direction. Drums and bells of all kinds are fun and can be easily available. But there are many other instruments: triangles, tamborines, cymbals, maracas, xylophones as well as simple shakers or sand blocks. An autoharp is a useful addition, easily used outdoors as well as indoors. Most children love to play the piano, and many of them will go to the piano to play and sing, turning the pages of a favorite songbook, perhaps with a friend beside them. With very little supervision children can use and enjoy the piano by themselves.

Body Movement Is a Natural Outlet for the Expression of Feeling

Dancing as well as singing will occur in many areas when children are free to act spontaneously. Running in the wind through falling leaves, crunching dry leaves underfoot in a marching rhythm, rolling down a grassy slope on the first warm spring day when space and sunshine seem to make everything burst into song and movement, all may be experiences in body movement for children.

One of the most natural and spontaneous forms of expression for a young child is expression through body movements. The teacher may be able to encourage the child to use his body saying, "Can you make your body into a round ball?" or "Can you make your body small or big?" When body movements become rhythmic and are used for the expression of feeling that the child wishes to communicate, they form a creative outlet.

When there is plenty of space, all children take delight in large, free body movements. A gymnasium or a large room equipped with full-length mirrors for modern dance practice, for example, inspires joyful and graceful experimentation with movements, especially if there is music to accompany the movement. It seems likely that opportunities to dance and play in front of full-length mirrors may add a dimension to the child's concept of himself as a person, especially for a child who has had little or no opportunity to see himself in a mirror.

Marching to music with a strong beat brings a response from children as well as adults. The strong beat sets the pattern, and the teacher enjoys the experience with the children. Drums and bells will extend the experience for the group. With opportunity and encouragement and increasing skill in using their bodies, they can translate many feelings into body movements.

The value of gymnastics for very young children is open to question. The regimentation required in training, the competitive aspects, the many failures, all these may interfere with healthy personality development. Young children at this stage in life are struggling to gain confidence in themselves and in their ability to use their initiative and make decisions. The rigid training required in gymnastics may distort this growth.

Values of Music and Movement

Music and movement have their greatest value for young children as avenues of self-expression. Children will use them in this way unless adults block them by offering patterns. The values that we seek are those that come with creativity.

To be in tune with one's body helps free a child from doubt about himself. It gives him confidence. For young children, simple actions like rolling over and over, getting up very slowly or very quickly, or pretending to lift something heavy help them to learn to control their movements and to have fun in doing this. Teachers, too, can discover the pleasure in free movement as they dance with the children in unpatterned ways.

Elaborate settings are not necessary for rhythm and music. In one of the wartime child-care centers a group of two-year-olds was playing in the limited area available to them. They had little in the way of play materials and less in the way of stable, continued contacts with reassuring adults. Their long day at school was followed by a home experience that offered little security to most of them. In the tiny court where they played, the wind was blowing one day. It picked up some stray pieces of toilet tissue (used to wipe drippy noses) and swirled them round and round in the corner of the cement courtyard. Observing this, one of the two-year-olds suddenly began turning and whirling with the bits of paper. Several children joined her, and in that bleak corner they did a graceful dance with the bits of tissue in the wind for a few brief minutes, and then ran off, laughing.

Children who are in groups in which there is plenty of expression through music have less need to drain off feeling in undesirable ways. They are likely to have fewer difficulties in working out relationships as they play together. When teachers are aware of the values that music and rhythm offer and the dangers of patterning these expressions, they can offer children many experiences in these areas, limited only by their own talent and resourcefulness and the limits imposed by the physical environment. The children will welcome these opportunities and profit from them. They will use them in creative ways.

Setting patterns for musical expression will serve to block the use of music or movement as a means of self-expression. If the teacher tries to show the child how to keep time, to fit his response into the pattern of the music she is playing, she is blocking him in the expression of his own feeling in response to the time. The skillful teacher will, instead, adapt the music to the child's own rhythm. She will give the children many opportunities to respond to music, but she will not attempt to dictate what their responses will be.

Projects

1. Look at a series of paintings done by one child over a period of weeks. What seems to remain the same? What changes in his paintings over the period: How would you characterize this child from looking at his paintings? What meaning does painting seem to have for him?
2. Watch two children using paint or clay. Note the differences in the way they use the material. Record their behavior and conversation. Indicate what values the experiences seemed to have for each child.

3. Over a period of observation note (a) the kinds and amounts of experience which the children have with rhythm and music, (b) the sounds that they appear to notice, and (c) their participation in musical or rhythmic group experiences. What differences do you observe in individual interest here and in ability?
4. Draw a floorplan of the room where you are observing and note how materials are arranged for art and music. Is there evidence of self-initiated activities? Where is the water supply? What colors are available for painting? Is the clay in a covered crock? Are the musical instruments available at the child's level? What musical instruments are there? Is there a record player? an autoharp? a piano? Assess the areas from the standpoint of developmentally appropriate activities for children under five.

For Your Further Reading

Bayless, K. M., & Ramsey, M. E. (1978). *Music: A way of life for the young child.* St. Louis, MO: C. V. Mosby. How to present musical experiences to children from birth through kindergarten. Musical developmental characteristics are listed. Discusses connection between music and language development.

Bos, B. J. (1978). *Don't move the muffin tins: A hands-off guide to art for the young child.* Carmichael, CA: The Burton Gallery. An exuberant book of ideas for arts and crafts activities. Includes the facilitating environment, role of adults, and presentation of materials in truly creative ways.

Goodnow, J. (1977). *Children drawing.* The developing child series. Cambridge, MA: Harvard University Press. Discusses how children's drawings are often indicative of their development, thinking, and problem solving.

Haines, J. E., & Gerber, L. L. (1984). *Leading young children to music: A resource book for teachers* (2nd ed.). Columbus, OH: Charles E. Merrill. Musical experiences for educational settings, including music-related activities for toddlers through eight-year-olds.

Lasky, L., & Mukerji, R. (1980). *Art: Basic for young children.* Washington, DC: National Association for the Education of Young Children. How art is important in children's learning, with many ideas for activities for two- to ten-year-olds. Why worksheets and patterns are never art.

Taylor, B. J. (1985). *A child goes forth: A curriculum guide for preschool children* (6th ed.). Minneapolis, MN: Burgess. An excellent activities guide, with each section including main principles, developmental characteristics, and application of principles as well as specific activities. Music and art chapters are excellent.

Car, Policeman, Stop Light (boy, 4 years 4 months)

20 ◆ Areas of Learning in the Program: The Sciences

The goal of learning in the field of science is to "encourage children to think, reason, question, and experiment."[1]

THE SCIENCES

Young children are explorers. They are curious and they investigate. Our role as adults is not to teach but to foster and protect children's urge to discover. We can provide an environment that invites exploring and

[1]National Association for the Education of Young Children. (1984). *Accreditation criteria and procedures.: Position statement of the National Academy of Early Childhood Programs.* Washington, DC: Author.

343

The sand box experience is extended with the addition of water.

First Step Nursery School

discovering, and we can avoid depriving children of the excitement of discovery and learning. It has been said that one only truly knows what one has discovered oneself. The healthy young child begins early discovering the world around him.

"My boat went to the bottom," says Drew. "It didn't do that yesterday." Drew is learning the properties of water. When his metal boat fills up with water it sinks. Yesterday it didn't do this because he had put it in the water in such a way that it didn't take on water. Drew's teacher says, "I wonder how you can get your boat to stay on top of the water." Drew discovers a way to get the boat to float. "I did it, I did it!" Indeed, Drew "did it," and he played with other objects, figuring out properties of water, properties of objects, and learning a great deal. Drew has confidence that he can figure things out. He is encouraged to think, reason, question, and experiment.

Children in favorable environments come in contact with many scientific experiences. The young child runs downhill and falls. He tries to pull a loaded wagon up the hill. He watches snow melt in the sun. He discovers a worm as he digs. He feeds a leaf of lettuce to the turtle. He watches a bulb sprout and finally blossom. He becomes aware of number, too. He has three candles on his birthday cake when he is three-years-old. He needs two blocks to finish his building.

Out of all these experiences the child develops ideas about the nature of the world. The teacher in the center helps him extend these ideas. She provides the opportunities for added experiences, and also by her comments and questions she gives more meaning to what the child is experiencing. We will look at each area in turn in this chapter.

MATHEMATICS

As children play, they handle objects and become aware of quantity. "I need more blocks to close up my wall," says Mark, as he figures out what he needs for his structure. They store up impressions of amounts and relationships that are essential for later stages in understanding mathematical concepts. "These are too big. I need smaller blocks," he tells Sue who is putting the play animals inside the enclosure. Learning that some objects are big, some small, and some are in between provides an important piece of information for the child in laying a foundation for understanding mathematical principles. The teacher may make the learning more explicit, saying, "You found just enough blocks to close your wall," or "It took just two blocks to close your wall." The teacher uses language that will help the child make sense out of the experience. Words like *the same as, different, high, low, balance, top shelf, bottom shelf, heavy,* and *light* enable the child to begin not only to understand what is happening but also to describe what is happening.

Kamii and DeVries state that, "Young children seem to have an interest in numbers when its use is at the appropriate level for them."[2] Mika says, "There are four cookies left." Her teacher responds, "Do we have enough for everybody to have one?" Piaget has made it very clear through his observations that learning to count does not mean that the child has an understanding of the numbers. The child gains this from his experiences. He "knows" two from having had many different experiences with two. He has two hands and two feet. At the table there is a chair for him and one for his friend. The teacher says, "Here are two chairs for two boys, just enough." Later she may say, "Do we have enough chairs for everyone at this table?" or "Do we have too many cups? Bring just enough cups for everybody at your table." Here the child is having direct experience with the very basis of number concept, one to one correspondence. "In beginning to construct number concepts it is best to avoid telling children to count. . . . The ability to count is one thing, and quantification is quite something else."[3]

[2]C. Kamii, & R. DeVries. (1976). *Piaget, children, and number.* Washington, DC: National Association for the Education of Young Children.
[3]Ibid.

The child playing in the doll corner selects the biggest doll. Then he sorts the doll clothes and finds the ones that fit this doll, discarding the smaller sizes. Children playing at the clay table want a lot of clay. They try to divide it, and one says, "You have more," or "Yours is biggest." They are having experiences which are part of understanding in mathematics.

In the sand area a child arranges containers in a row on the ledge, filling them with sand. As he fills them, he sees that they need different amounts. It takes much more sand to fill the big container than it does to fill the little one. The teacher may comment on these differences and on the relation of size and amount. The child may line the containers up in order from the biggest to the smallest.

In the housekeeping corner a child may line up the doll dishes and survey them with satisfaction. There are a lot! In contrast there are only a few cooking dishes. Things sometimes come in sets. The teacher may comment, "Are there enough lids for the pans?"

With a balance scale available, the child has a chance to weigh things and to compare weights. The teacher helps him put into words what he is discovering. She asks questions like, "I wonder what would happen if you put this rock on the scale."

The teacher provides measuring cups, one-cup, two-cup, or four-cup sizes, and measuring spoons. There are measurements to be made in

Examining a long bone with a magnifying lens.

California State University, Chico. Child Development Laboratory

Stacking blocks.

Valley College, Campus Child Development Center

cooking. It takes a cup of water to soften "this much" jello. A teaspoonful of salt is needed here, and two tablespoonfuls of sugar. The child at the workbench uses a ruler to measure the length of the piece he needs to complete his airplane. He measures it and saws the piece to measure.

There are many other situations in which the child makes estimates of quantity, the number of pens the box will hold as he puts away the pens, the number of blocks needed to go from the wall to the door, the amount of juice to pour into the cup, or the size of the serving on his plate. With the guidance of an alert teacher the center offers many experiences that give children a basis for understanding mathematical concepts.

Teachers may help children grasp sequencing of events by using language to expand what has happened. "We made playdough," says Jaimie. The teacher asks, "What did you do first . . . next . . . last," helping Jaimie put into words the sequence of events that occurred.

The concept of time is difficult for young children to grasp. As a child is bathed, dressed, played with, fed, and put to bed at somewhat regular times from birth, he is having opportunities for experiences that begin to form the basis for time perception.

By the time a child is two, he has learned to anticipate an immediate event, and he refers to time in the present "now." Later he will learn to place events in the past, present, and future. He lacks precision about these ideas. "A long time ago" may mean yesterday or last week, and "soon" may mean in the immediate future or in the next week.

Juan asked his teacher, "What time is it?" He was really asking, "When is my father coming?" A three-year-old understands time in terms of events that relate to him—"time to get dressed," "time to go outside and play," "time for a snack." A teacher who responds with a simple sequence of events is most helpful in teaching the child about time. For example, when a child says, "Help me, teacher!" it is more useful to say, "I'm helping Maria; I'll help you next," than to say, "In a minute" or "Soon."

PHYSICAL SCIENCE

Every child is interested in how things happen and where things come from. There are many opportunities in the simple, daily experiences of children to build up a fund of knowledge about the nature of the physical world around them. Megan was filling the small wading pool. She walked slowly and awkwardly with the heavy pail of water carefully pouring it into the pool. She proceeded to run back to the faucet with her empty pail for more. She begins to know intuitively what heavy and light mean by experiencing these terms with her own body. Paul tries to pull a heavy load in his wagon, and the teacher says, "It is too heavy. How can you make it lighter?" The language experience together with the real experience help the child to gain more understanding.

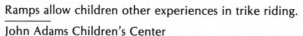

Ramps allow children other experiences in trike riding.

John Adams Children's Center

Rebecca gets off the tricycle and climbs into the wagon which Michael is pulling. She spies the pedal car and jumps off the wagon and climbs into the car. She rides the wheel toys and discovers differences in the ease of riding wheel toys of different sizes. She pulls and pushes toys on wheels. She steers with the wheel. Later, she turns the wagon upside down and tries the wheel, watching it rotate freely. She slows it down. She uses a pulley, pulling objects up and lowering them. She is laying a foundation for understanding some concepts in physics later on.

She wonders about many aspects of nature, the snow falling, hail bouncing on the roof or sidewalk, the rain evaporating in the sun and staying on the damp grass under the shade of the tree, the force of the wind that blew off the top of her shelter. She may blow soap bubbles outdoors and watch their colors and the direction they take as they float and burst. The teacher will give her simple explanations and suggest ways to find out more about the things that interest her. She will raise other questions. Rebecca's interests seem to be in physical science. All healthy young children are interested in the sciences as part of the world around them.

NATURAL SCIENCE

Children are interested in all living things. They enjoy watching growth and the changes it brings. In an earlier chapter we saw how teachers helped children in a city center extend their knowledge of seasonal changes.

A garden offers rich opportunities for learning and extending concepts about plant life. Children enjoy digging and planting seeds. There are many kinds of seeds, from the tiny carrot seed to the big, wrinkled nasturtium seed. They find seeds in pods as they gather nuts, peas, or beans. Picking fruit from a low tree and gathering the products of a garden are satisfying experiences when they are possible for children. But beans can be sprouted in a jar, and children can watch the unfolding of seeds kept moist in a dish. Bulbs will grow and flower in a window. The teacher and the children can talk about what they have planted and what will happen. Some children will participate eagerly, with a sustained interest. Others will show only a casual interest, but all will gain something.

There are seasonal changes to be noted in the garden. The leaves fall and can be gathered or heaped into piles for play. The children discover roots as they dig in the ground. They pick flowers or sprays of berries in the fall.

Watching pets and caring for them give children a chance to learn more about animals, how they eat, sleep, eliminate, and reproduce. The child is curious about many things. He can observe and discuss these things with other children and with the teacher. Fish need to be fed only occasionally, while the rabbit and the chickens are hungry many times a day. The bird splashes in his bath, but the baby ducks go right into the water. The turtle

Getting acquainted with a guinea pig.

San Diego State University. Courtesy Sam Hollander

moves very slowly, and the bird has to be kept in his cage because he flies away so fast and so far. Tadpoles slowly change into frogs. The baby chick is fluffy at first, but it finally grows feathers like the hen. There are many similarities and many differences among the animals children observe. These experiences make up a background for understanding.

In one center it was usually possible each spring to have a lamb for a few weeks. The children loved to give the lamb his bottle of milk in the morning. He would play with them. Often to the delight of the children, he managed to slip in an unguarded door and make straight for the kitchen, the direction from which his bottle appeared. A young kid one spring proved as adept as the children on the walking boards and in jumping over boxes. The children enjoyed his companionship.

When there are pets in a center, it is important to have adequate provisions for caring for them, a proper shelter, pens that can be cleaned easily and thoroughly. This, too, is part of what children need to learn about animals.

Trips to a farm to see other animals are sometimes possible, a cow with a calf, or sheep and pigs. It is sometimes possible to visit a hatchery at a time when chicks are hatching in the incubators. All these things extend the children's experiences.

Children in the city may extend their experiences with animals through visits to the zoo. Many zoos today have an area, planned for children, in which there are barnyard animals and other animals that can be petted and played with. City gardens may be limited to window boxes, but the feel and the smell of earth and the growing plants can still be there; only the space is restricted.

The young child constructs his knowledge from his own experience. He learns through his own direct involvement with the objects and through changes in the objects that are meaningful to him. Telling him answers that we have discovered ourselves will not help him in this process. The child has to structure his knowledge for himself. A teacher can be helpful in providing the opportunities for a child to learn ways of thinking, to learn ways to ask and answer questions, but she cannot shortcut the process for him.

Where Children Are Having Experiences with Animals, They Come in Contact with Death

If the children are having many experiences with animals, they are sure on some occasion to come into contact with death. The baby rats sometimes die, or a dog may get in and kill a chicken. The children may see a dead lamb when they visit the barn during lambing season, or they may discover a dead bird in the yard.

In their response to these experiences the children will reflect the attitudes of the adults with them. There is no need to hide death from children or to try to escape from facing it with them. It is a mystery, like life, and sometimes far less of a tragedy. The children will want to understand why the animal died, and they may be helped in their acceptance of the reality of death by touching and feeling to see how the dead animal differs from the living ones they have known. They will not be greatly disturbed by the event if the adult with them does not feel the need to dramatize or distort or escape from death herself. If the children can be helped to have sound, reassuring experiences in this area, they will be helped to face life as well as death with less fear. There is an end to everything: plants die, animals die, people die.

Questions about Babies

All children are interested in knowing where babies come from and how they grow. They are really interested in how they themselves were born. They are trying to develop concepts about where they came from and how they got here. They need simple, factual information on the subject. Occasions for giving this may arise when the pets in the school reproduce, and the children follow the sequence of events.

Children need to feel that it is all right to be interested and to ask questions about birth. The teacher needs to answer questions freely and with appreciation for the great significance of the subject for children. She will not burden them with more information than they want at any point, but she will make sure that they are given information when they want it. The information is needed in small doses, with time to digest it, and with

All children are interested in babies. Seeing a baby nursing is a new experience for this child.

Jean Berlfein

The mother understands. She explains to the group and they listen. The mother is a trustworthy source of information.

Jean Berlfein

They have accurate information. All watch baby nursing.

Jean Berlfein

many repetitions. The teacher will listen to conversations among the children on the subject and will be ready to clear up misconceptions. She will give simple information: "Babies start growing from an egg inside the mother. The father starts the egg growing."

Discussions about where they came from and how they were born will follow—how each one of them grew from an egg inside their mother, were fertilized or started growing by the father and protected inside the mother until they were big enough to be on their own outside. Later the children will need more information about the father's part.

Before offering information in answer to questions here, the wise teacher will herself ask the child, "What do you think happens?"[4] When the teacher understands what the child is imagining or how he is interpreting matters, she is in a better position to clear up his misconceptions and to give him the information he is seeking. The teacher may comment to clear up points, but she will understand that it takes time to build correct concepts, and she will not discourage thinking. We need only remember the richness of myth and legend that has come from attempts in the past to account for the wonder of creation.

Watching a mother nurse a baby is a fascinating experience for children who have not had baby brothers or sisters, as we can see in the pictures. The group of children watching the mother nursing her baby are absorbed in what they see. It seems apparent that the child in the first picture has never seen an infant nursing before. Her response is one of astonishment. The mother explains, and all the children look at her intently. The mother is a trustworthy source of information. This mother seems "in tune" with the children and is enjoying their interest. After the explanation all quietly watch the baby nursing, completely wrapped up in the wonder of the experience. Attitudes are being formed. The children are getting accurate information.

A few children who are interested may enjoy looking at pictures of prenatal growth in a book. There are other books with stories about babies that all children will enjoy hearing, like *Making Babies*, by Sara Bonnett Stein.[5] Conversations about babies are important for young children. There may be negative feelings expressed. The teacher should listen with respect, without discouraging such expressions, but she can suggest other interpretations or aspects.

Gaining some understanding about reproduction is an important part of learning in the early years.

[4]Refer to Selma Fraiberg's chapter "Education for Love" in her book, *The magic years.* (1959). New York: Scribner's.
[5]S. B. Stein. (1974). *Making babies: An open family book for parents and children together.* New York: Walker.

SOCIAL STUDIES

Children live in a community, and they want to understand it. Watch young children as they play out the roles of people they have met or experiences they have had in their daily lives. Becoming the truck driver, the doctor, the store clerk, the service station attendant, or the garage mechanic in dramatic play enables the young child to begin to understand the roles of different people. The teacher helps children by talking over questions of interest such as where people work or what firefighters or police officers do. Real experiences with these people as well as books, stories, and pictures depicting them help the child to understand better the roles of people in a society.

As children learn social roles, they also learn about the places where people work, both the physical structures and the surrounding environment. Michael and Jaime built an elaborate ramp for parking cars and included a block to represent where the attendant collected the money. Michael said, "My brother collects the money here." Michael was representing with blocks a situation that he knew about.

Children's experiences may be enriched by having visitors come to the school or by going on trips. The person who washes and polishes the floors in one school was invited to come and show the children the electric scrubber. Walking to the local library, to the shoe repair shop, or to the post office enables children to gain an understanding of how the community functions. They can talk about what they see and reenact these roles in their play later. A parent may bring to the center tools or a product that is part of his or her work, so that children will have clearer ideas of what parents do at work. It may be possible to arrange a trip to places where parents work. One center in a large office complex visited the snack bar owned by one of the parents. Children saw the big coffee maker, the rows of sandwiches being prepared, and the trays of fruit and cookies stored on shelves waiting for the noontime rush. They came back to their classroom and played snack bar for several days. A group on a college campus was invited to visit a classroom one day. The dramatic play afterwards reflected what they had seen.

Understanding Cultural Differences

Cultural diversity is the American norm. Recognition of and respect for a child's unique cultural heritage is essential. Culture provides a source of identity, a framework for interpreting the world, the basis for a feeling of belonging, and the basis for esthetic values.[6]

[6]National Association for the Education of Young Children. (1984). *Accreditation criteria and procedures: Position statement of the National Academy of Early Childhood Programs.* Washington, DC: Author.

At a very early age children are aware of people's physical and cultural differences.[7] There are racial differences. They can be seen, and children see them. A healthy racial/cultural identity plus skills in recognizing and combating racism are essential to all children's self-esteem and ability to function productively in a society. Racial identity is based upon a concept of "groupness," which young children have trouble understanding. A teacher or parent may help by using the family concept that is easier for the child to grasp. The child's physical and cultural characteristics are acquired from belonging to their family. A consultant in a school tells the story of entering a school at closing time, and as she walked up the stairs she heard a young child crying and screaming and the sound of small feet stamping. Around the corner came a little girl about four-years-old. The mother holding her hand saw the consultant and looked mortified at the precise moment that the child, seeing the consultant, looked at her mother and said loudly, "I told you I want to be Black." The child continued to yell, "I want to be Black! Can I be Black?" The consultant stopped in front of the girl, looked at her, put her hand out to touch her and said quietly, "You can't be Black." "But I want to be," she said. "Look at your mother." She did. The consultant said, "You look like your mother and daddy and your grandparents. I look like my mother, daddy, and grandparents. You can't ever be Black. Do you have Black friends in your class?" She smiled and said, "Yes." The consultant said, "You can have Black friends and you can ask your mother to buy you a Black doll and some books about Black children, but remember you can't be Black." The important point is that a child accepts his own identity.[8] Children whose parents come from different racial backgrounds have a further problem in identity because they are not likely to look like either parent.

Respect for cultural diversity of staff and children is one of the curriculum goals of the NAEYC Center Accreditation Project. Centers that have children of different racial origins within the group are fortunate. Children in these centers know that all people do not have the same color of skin or hair and do not all dress, eat, or even respond in the same way. They also know that all children go to the same center and make friends with people there. If every child feels that his differences are accepted, he can readily accept differences in others. They can all enjoy what these differences may offer.

Creating a Multicultural Classroom

The teacher can create a multicultural classroom that will help all children develop self- and group esteem. She can carefully select and hang pictures

[7]Council on Interracial Books for Children, Inc. (1983). Counteracting bias in early childhood education, *Interracial Books for Children Bulletin. 14*(7 & 8).
[8]Ibid.

of people of all races and cultures. Pictures should show both sexes and a variety of skin tones, eye shapes, and hair textures. Children should see pictures of people who look like them and people from their own culture in respected or leadership roles. This is important in classrooms of homogeneous grouping as well as in classrooms with cultural diversity. Pictures can be helpful in talking about differences. A teacher and a child were looking at a picture of a Japanese mother and her own child in the grocery store. The teacher asked, "Do you know someone like this?" This may help the young child talk about cultural diversity and perhaps clear up misconceptions or concerns the child might have about racial identity.

Using poems, songs, stories, music, and foods from different cultural traditions; hanging signs in a variety of languages; displaying art from other cultures; and providing toys, dolls, and puzzles that represent all races—all help to make a classroom multicultural. Making or collecting books about people who are different and avoiding any book with stereotypes are other important ways of creating an atmosphere of acknowledging and accepting cultural diversity. *Ten Quick Ways to Analyze Children's Books* is a helpful resource.[9] It is important to give children the opportunity to know from their own experience that people are different. The children themselves are different, but they are all growing up in the same country in one world.

Festivals and Holidays

In helping the children understand the meaning of festivals and holidays, the teacher must first be familiar with the cultural patterns represented by the children in her group as well as the area in which the center is located. In a neighborhood with a mixture of cultural customs there may be a variety of celebrations.

Children enjoy participating in celebrations, provided the celebrating is suited to the child's pace rather than the adult's and does not intrude on what the child himself is concerned with doing. The teacher should let the child choose to enter into the activity or ignore it.

The celebration of religious holidays is a very personal experience for family members. Living in a pluralistic society where respect for observances is important, teachers must plan very carefully if religious observances are to be recognized. Parents should be a part of the planning. Celebrations differ, but many of them involve the giving of gifts. Children enjoy making gifts for their parents and friends. These should be gifts that the child has planned and made rather than an assembly line gift suggested

[9]Council on Interracial Books for Children, Inc. (1980). *Guidelines for selecting bias-free textbooks and storybooks.* New York: Author.

by the teacher. Children can be helped with gift making projects by providing appropriate materials preceded by a planning session where ideas are generated.

There are other celebrations that children are likely to become aware of such as Halloween. Making a pumpkin face on the pumpkin, cutting the face out with the help of the teacher, and putting the candle inside are all part of the tradition of Halloween. Familiarity with a Halloween pumpkin at school may help children avoid being frightened, as they sometimes are, when trick or treating. Costumes and dressing up are a part of the Halloween festivities. One teacher thoughtfully collected a variety of costumes, clothing, and accessories to be saved for this special time. She allowed children the opportunity to assemble their own costumes and made sure a full-length mirror was available for them to see how they looked. Some centers emphasize cooking activities with pumpkins and autumn activities to enrich the Halloween theme and to play down its frightening aspects.

Holiday celebrations are important events in children's lives. In later years, these celebrations may be remembered as among the most significant events of the child's school experience. From the breaking of the piñata to the making of valentines children begin to know their social world. Every school will need to have some discussion with the parents in the community about what may be appropriate or inappropriate to include in these celebrations.

Birthdays are an important celebration for children. They can be shared with friends in the center and can add to the child's feeling of being an important and valued person. The celebration is best when it is simple, such as a birthday greeting by the teacher as the child comes in the morning. The children may make special cookies that day with one specially decorated for the birthday child. These may be served at snack time or lunch as children sing "Happy Birthday." It is wise to establish a policy of no presents or favors brought in by parents for the celebrations. The center birthday need not be like the one at home.

Trips Outside the School

We have referred to trips as a way of learning more about the world in which children live. In making a trip, the children may themselves use some of the community services. They may go by bus to a park or a zoo. Travel time should not be too long.

Trips may be made to some of the places that offer community services, such as a fire station. There they will have a chance to examine the fire engine, observe the long hoses and the ladders, perhaps try on a hat, or even sit on the seat of the truck. They will meet the people whose business it is to give fire protection to their community. There are many such opportunities for children to extend the range of their experiences about the role of workers. The teacher can make use of the experiences that her community offers, visiting industries that are within the range of the children's comprehension.

In planning trips the teacher should always visit the place herself before she takes the children there. In this way she can make sure that it is a suitable place for learning. She will know what hazards there may be and how to guard against them. Above all she will know how to prepare the children for the experience. Preparation for a trip is important. The children need to know what they are going to see, what to look for, and what to expect. They can be prepared for any unusual or unexpected events such as loud noises or sudden changes like a crane overhead. They are less likely to be startled. They can enjoy and profit more from the experience. In her visit beforehand, the teacher can also prepare the people there by making sure they know what to expect from young children. They are more likely to be able to do their part in making the experience a good one for the children.

Any instructions or prohibitions should be clearly stated before the children start. They should know what is expected of them, what they can do, and what is not permitted in the situation. They can enjoy being

A trip to the local farm.

California State University, Chico. Child Development Laboratory

responsible people if they understand what fits this role. The adults who are accompanying the children should also understand clearly what the rules are. There should be enough adults to enable each child to feel secure and free to explore at his own pace.

In planning trips the teacher will keep in mind that children learn most when there are familiar elements in the experience and when they can relate the unfamiliar to something they know. A child is likely to enjoy watching a cement mixer and men at work putting in a new driveway more than he will enjoy a trip to a factory with a lot of big machinery, the function of which he can hardly grasp. A hatchery with incubators full of eggs and tiny chicks is of great interest because he already knows something about eggs and chicks. He gets the most satisfaction out of simple experiences in which he can see clearly and, if possible, touch the things he sees.

On most trips there will be some children who will want to spend more time than others to satisfy their special curiosity about some aspect of the experience. Susan, for example, was most interested when the group visited the sheep barns one day, arriving just after a ewe had given birth to a lamb by cesarean section. Susan had recently been in the hospital for emergency surgery and had many questions. When the group moved on, she stayed behind with an assistant teacher who helped answer some of her questions and talked with her about how one feels about operations. It was important for Susan to have time to explore the subject thoroughly. It probably helped to reduce some of the anxieties that remained from her recent hospital experience. The rest of the children did not need this much time there.

Children profit from trips outside the school. If the group is small, it is easier for the teacher to be sure of the experience each child is having and to interpret for him what may need interpreting. There should always be two adults on every trip when there are more than three or four children. Emergencies arise, such as having to find a toilet for one child or maintaining a limit and taking a child back to the school when necessary. Many times parents are able and eager to help with trips and with transportation on trips. It is of real value for a parent and a teacher to share such an experience.

Projects

1. Outline a plan for introducing an experience in the school that will extend or enrich concepts or understandings in mathematics or in physical or natural science for some of the children in the group in which you are observing or participating.
2. Make a list of field trips that are desirable and possible for the children in your group and that might help to expand their concepts about work done in the community or about community services.

3. Outline a plan for a field trip for these children, indicating what the purposes of the trip would be, what preparations would be made beforehand by the staff, how the children would be prepared, and what follow-up activities there might be.

4. Talk with other people whose cultural or ethnic background differs from your own. Find out how their culture acknowledges celebrating a religious observance. Ask them to share a recipe for preparing an ethnic food or to tell a folktale that can be used with young children. Put these in a notebook called cultural awareness materials. Other items you may want to include may be pictures of children in their native dress and games children play.

For Your Further Reading

Baratta-Lorton, M. (1976). *Mathematics their way*. Reading, MA: Addison-Wesley. An exciting approach to hands-on experiential math, with photographs, materials, and math categories.

Blackwelder, S. R. (1980). *Science for all seasons: Science experiences for young children*. Englewood Cliffs, NJ: Prentice-Hall. Safe, easy-to-do experiments which help to satisfy young children's curiosity about the world around them.

Council on Interracial Books for Children. (1980). *Guidelines for selecting bias-free textbooks and storybooks*. New York: Author. Suggestions for choosing books free of stereotypes for children.

Endres, J. B., & Rockwell, R. E. (1980). *Food, nutrition, and the young child*. St. Louis: Times Mirror/Mosby. Information about nutrition and food for young children in educational settings.

Kamii, C. (1985). *Young children reinvent arithmetic*. New York: Teachers College. According to Piaget's theory, children construct number concepts on their own. Kamii is an eloquent spokesperson for how teachers can provide a constructivist mathematics curriculum.

Koblinsky, S., Atkinson, J., & Davis, S. (1980). Sex education with young children. *Young Children, 36*(1), 21–31. Also in J. F. Brown (Ed.). (1982). *Curriculum: Planning for young children*. Guidelines for teaching and bibliography of sex education books for children.

Nickelsburg, J. (1976). *Nature activities for early childhood*. Reading, MA: Addison-Wesley. Forty-four projects with small animals, plants, and activities indoors and in the ground; concepts and the author's wonderment are conveyed.

Ramsey, P. G. (1979). Beyond "Ten Little Indians" and turkeys: Alternative approaches to Thanksgiving. *Young Children, 34*(6), 28–32, 49–52. Five alternative curriculum themes which avoid stereotypes in observing Thanksgiving with young children.

Redleaf, R. (1983). *Open the door and let's explore: Neighborhood field trips for young children*. St. Paul, MN: Toys 'n Things Press. Easy field trips; includes learning goals, vocabulary, activities before and after the walk, songs, fingerplays, and books.

Schmidt, V. E., & McNeill, E. (1978). *Cultural awareness: A resource bibliography.* Washington, DC: National Association for the Education of Young Children. Detailed resources on Asian, Black, Native, and Spanish-speaking Americans, with multicultural books, posters, records, films, slides, and even dolls and museums listed.

Wanamaker, N., Hearn, K., & Richarz, S. (1979). *More than graham crackers: Nutrition education and food preparation with young children.* Washington, DC: National Association for the Education of Young Children. Teaching ideas about food and nutrition, including recipes and fingerplays.

Space Man (boy, 3 years 3 months)

21 ◆ Computers and Television

The era of technology has arrived and with it have come many changes in the environment. Computers, robots, electronic games, television, videocassettes, audiocassettes, and electronic piano keyboards are part of the rapid movement into technology. Television has brought many social changes, and computers may bring even more. Using this technology so that it enhances rather than diminishes our humanness should be a matter of concern to everyone.

COMPUTERS

We begin by looking at the use of microcomputers in the classroom with children under five years of age. Harriet Cuffaro of Bank Street College says, "In explaining, describing, hypothesizing, and questioning what computers can or will do in education, statements are also made, implicitly or explicitly, about the purpose of education, teaching, the content of curriculum, and the nature of the learner."[1]

Computers and the Early Childhood Classroom

Why use computers with young children? At present the materials usually found in early childhood settings include blocks, dress-up clothes, paints, paper, mud, sand, water, and books. They have been selected because they invite the active involvement and problem solving at a level developmentally appropriate for children under five. Do computers belong with these materials? Computers are new in the field of education, and much more research is needed before their values for young children can be established.

Let us look into an actual classroom experience with three- and four-year-old children in a center in which a computer was placed in an area of the room easily accessible to all of the children. The teacher began by introducing small groups of two or three children to the computer using the program LOGO.[2] LOGO is a computer language designed to intro-

[1] H. K. Cuffaro. (1984). Microcomputers in education: Why is earlier better? *Teachers College Record, 85*(4).
[2] LOGO was developed by Seymour Papert at the Massachusetts Institute of Technology.

Kevin selects the key to change the screen color.

Hill an' Dale Family Learning Center

duce children to the world of computer programming. Its aim is to make available to children a computer language using graphics. Children can create designs using a series of LOGO commands. A small triangle, referred to as a turtle, can be made to move forward, back, right, or left. Simple line designs are created by moving the turtle around the screen. The graphics created provide immediate results. The children see the results of the movements on the monitor. Background colors on the screen can be changed by typing in a series of commands. To clear the screen the child types *C* and *S*. The designs can be saved, used with other designs, and printed. The child is in control of what is happening and literally tells the computer what to do.

What kind of control does the child have at the computer? The young child building with blocks is aware of how he controls the blocks. The child playing with different objects in water is able to observe what happens and see the difference between the objects that float and those that sink. No one has to give him directions. He constructs his own knowledge. When using a computer, a child must follow specific instructions given by the teacher, and the teacher must supervise closely what the child does until he has memorized the steps to take. When problems occur, the teacher must provide the answers. It is difficult to be sure what knowledge the child is gaining while at the computer.

What must the child understand before he is able to control the computer without the teacher's directions? LOGO requires not only number and letter recognition on the keyboard but also recognition of the fact that some numbers are larger or smaller than others. Number concepts develop gradually out of firsthand experiences. Most children of three or four years have usually acquired understanding of number concepts only up to the numbers three or four. Rote memorization of numbers occurs with children of this age but not concepts of larger than or smaller than. Many young children have number recognition and can count up to ten or more but do not have a true concept of what these numbers mean.

LOGO is a graphic procedure in which children can make squares, circles, and other shapes. To make shapes involves not only understanding numbers but knowing that squares, rectangles, and triangles have specific geometrical features. The teacher in this center used games, paper, crayons, paints, stories, and songs to teach the children the concepts they needed to know in order to use LOGO. After much "teaching" this teacher decided that LOGO was a totally inappropriate experience for these children. In the next two or three years children will be having many more experiences with objects of different sizes and shapes, and they should be more ready for LOGO. Trying to hurry the process may interfere with sound learning.

After several months of using LOGO the teacher introduced another type of program, Computer Assisted Instruction (CAI). Computer Assisted Instruction is an educational approach to computing in which the computer program takes on the role of the teacher and drills or questions the child. The computer program, often in a game format, tells the child what to do. The child responds, and then is rewarded for giving the correct answer by a "happy face" appearing on the screen or by some other computer recognition. If a wrong answer is given, the child is informed by some sign. Sometimes the acknowledgment of an answer is so abstract that the child does not seem aware that the program is responding to something that he has done.

Computer Assisted Instruction has been largely designed along the lines of workbooks and ditto sheets. Research has shown that children need active experiences in doing and making as a foundation for later learning. Concept development does not result from using workbook and ditto sheets. These may delay or block intellectual development.

What is the value of originality and creativity? How much can Computer Assisted Instruction stimulate a child's creative capacity? The answers to these questions depend on what the teacher believes about the learning process. At present Computer Assisted Instruction appears to offer little to stimulate the child's creative capacities. These qualities are developed by self-initiated activities.

The teaching of number recognition and the alphabet serves as the basis for most of the computer games. Some of the programs attempt to teach spatial relationships such as *on top of*, *next to*, *beside*, *bottom*, *top* or visual discrimination of, for example, the same or different shapes. These concepts are probably better taught and learned in routine daily activities, such as when children are handling objects, moving a play car next to another car, or putting a block on top of another one to build a tower. The young child is a doer rather than a watcher. Early childhood educators should avoid educational schemes that are not in keeping with developmentally appropriate experiences for children.

Social Experiences and Impulsive Behavior

Children approach the computer with different temperamental styles, different cognitive styles, and different social needs. Matt had trouble settling down to activities and was often disciplined because of his behavior. He often sat down at the computer to play one of the games. At the computer he seemed able to control his impulsive behavior, carefully pressing the keys so the computer would do what he wanted. Matt appeared to feel motivated to gain control over his body. When he first sat down at the computer his little chubby fingers were dancing with action. After a few unsuccessful attempts to type in the instructions necessary to play the game he finally got his hands under control and very deliberately pressed the keys with success. Patricia Vardin-Barker[3] has reported that

---

[3]P. Vardin-Barker. (Summer, 1984). Microcomputers, robots, and electronic toys. *Proceedings of the Early Childhood Education Conference of Teachers College, Columbia University.*

Developing independence at the computer. Mika handles the floppy disk.

Hill an' Dale Family Learning Center

She inserts the disk into the disk drive.

Hill an' Dale Family Learning Center

She closes the disk drive.

Hill an' Dale Family Learning Center

She presses the restart key.

Hill an' Dale Family Learning Center

impulsive children are often able to develop the controls needed to program and focus at the computer. Again, we may wonder if this is the best way to develop body control and impulse control.

Children can play games at the computer that require responding to patterns on the screen that are either the same or different. This is a visual discrimination task for young children found in many workbooks. A correct choice brings a melodic tune, and an incorrect choice brings an unpleasant sound. Children can be actively involved in the game, talking to each other, taking turns, and watching what is happening on the screen. The computer can contribute to social development and rouse interest, but so can playing together with blocks or in the housekeeping center. There are many other experiences that probably enhance social development more effectively than the computer does.

Emotional Responses of Young Children to the Computer

Some children seem to benefit emotionally from using a computer as a way to make the transition from home to center. One child who was new to the center in September used the computer in this way. The first thing Danny did when he entered the classroom was to go to the computer which was near the entrance and the teacher. Danny recognized numbers and letters, so he found the computer games a satisfying experience. As time went by Danny played less with the computer and more with the other children, and he enjoyed the many activities that were available. By December he was not using the computer at all. He had become comfortable with this new experience of being in school. Children will find different sources of security in their transition from home to center.

Some children at the computer showed symptoms of stress such as sucking a finger and facial expressions suggesting anxiety when they did not know what to do and needed help.

The Attention Span of Young Children at the Computer

The attention spans of young children at the computer differed. Few children used the computer as long as Danny did, although several children returned to the computer frequently. The novelty of the computer, along with a screen like that in a television and the presence of an adult, all seemed to contribute to the popularity of the computer in this center.

Differences Between the Interest of Boys and Girls

Observational records were kept at the center which showed how often and how long children used the computer. Girls and boys in this center showed equal interest in the computer. There were individual differences in interest and ability, but there was no evidence to suggest boys took to the computer more than girls. Dr. Douglas H. Clements of Kent State University has stated that "Most studies reveal lack of sex differences in the computer use of younger children, but a consistent bias in favor of boys in older students. Several authorities have suggested, therefore, that the early years are the ideal time to introduce the computer in school."[4] Research in sex equity suggests that boys take to the computer more than girls do beginning at about the third grade.

Playing Games at the Computer

One of the popular games children played at the computer was a memory game in which thirty-six cards appear on the screen, all neatly lined up in the correct order. All the child has to do is press a key to get the game started. To end the game all the child has to do is turn off the power. The computer makes such games very tidy and solves many of the problems such as conflicts in social relationships, the problem of keeping track of the parts, of arranging the parts, and figuring out what to do when there is a missing part. The computer games are already designed, and there is no opportunity for children to use their own imagination in creating their

---

[4]J. Parker. (1984). *Some disturbing data: Sex differences in computer use.* Paper presented at the annual National Educational Computing Conferences, Dayton, OH.

play. Young children at play often make up their own games, changing the rules as they play. Games with set rules will appeal to these children when they are older.

Summary

The time may soon come when children will need to be able to use a computer. Computers will be common equipment in schools, and teachers will be trained in using them and in teaching children in the primary grades and high schools how to use them. More homes will have home computers. Computers are revolutionizing the business world and are a help to students, teachers, homes, and people in many professions.

More research is needed about the age at which a child will profit most in learning to use computers. At present, computers for children under school age seem questionable. Computers are an expensive addition to an educational program for young children, and few teachers are trained in their use. Computers require a great deal of teacher time with one individual. More important, they are far less effective in promoting development in learning with young children than the educational programs in quality early childhood programs that already exist. They may even interfere with sound learning. Development proceeds by stages, and each stage contributes to sound growth. No stage can be skipped. It takes time for a child to grow. Pushing children's development may create problems in healthy growing. We can conclude that the computer has some values in a classroom, but these values can be obtained in less expensive and more effective ways when teaching young children under the age of five.

TELEVISION

Television viewing and computer use by young children have some similarities. However, television sets are found in most homes and many schools while computers, as yet, are not. Most children do a lot of television viewing, and this is having an effect on their lives. Television viewing limits the child's time for play, which is his natural avenue for learning. Play is an active process in which the child is doing and imagining. Television is a passive process. It may reduce the child's capacity for self-initiated activities. Watching television may take the place of reading for older children.

Television is a mass medium. It cannot be adapted to the individual needs of children and their individual readiness for an experience. The personal element so necessary for the young child is lacking. Misconceptions cannot be discovered and cleared up. Amassing facts, partially understood, does not promote sound learning. For older children television can and does offer material that broadens their horizons, just as reading does, with television adding the vividness of pictures and movement. For young children, however, the excitement, speed, noise, and constantly changing stimuli are probably bewildering and overwhelming. Children lack the background for interpreting the rapidly changing sequence of events. Children need actual, concrete experiences and the world presented in small enough doses. This is not what television offers them. Young children believe what they see on television. They are still trying to sort out what is real from what is fantasy or fiction, and television does not make this easier for them.

Television Viewing Is Likely to Impoverish and Distort Play

Television is having an effect on the dramatic play of young children. Patterns appear in the child's play that are a reflection of what he has seen on the screen. In some of the portrayals of aggressive behavior on television programs, children seem to find patterns for playing out their own aggressive feelings. While we are not sure what the effect of television may be on young children, we can be certain that it is desirable for the child to re-enact what he sees on television programs. In this way he is doing something about what he sees, trying to understand it better and make it less frightening. At the same time it is important to remember that if these roles are too frightening, disorganizing, or cause a child to lose control, playing them out will not enable him to cope. Rather, it will do the very opposite. Teachers must redirect, limit, or stop this play as well as accept the child's feelings and let him know she is protecting him.

Here is an example of the play of two four-year-old boys. It seems influenced by television in the beginning but turns into a familiar picnic situation in the end.

Kevin and Michael were playing together in the housekeeping corner. After rearranging the furniture, they picked up the suitcases. Michael opened his. It was full of clothes and other articles. Kevin opened his and seemed disappointed because it was empty. Michael poured some of the contents of his suitcase into Kevin's. He then proceeded to put on some dark glasses and picked up the suitcase and left. Kevin called good-bye to him.

Michael came back into the housekeeping corner, saying to Kevin, who was playing with a string of beads, "We're robbers. Come on, robber."

"They'll be here in seven minutes. Call the police," Kevin answered him.

Michael picked up the phone and pretended he was calling the police.

"They're coming right away," said Michael.

"Call the cowboys," said Kevin. "Come on, let's hurry; go on outside and I'll be there in a minute before the cowboys come. Go on outside, don't walk on the lawn. I'll be with you in a moment." Michael went outside the housekeeping corner.

"Come on back in; we'll eat a light supper first," Kevin said. "Hurry up, now, hurry up. If you don't want to set the table, I will," he added. (All this time Kevin was separating the plastic beads as he talked.)

Kevin told Michael to get some more silverware and put it in the suitcase.

Michael made a sound like a siren.

Kevin said, "Put more silverware in the suitcase."

"Let's take the plates, too," Michael replied. He got the cups, more plates, and silverware. They worked together to shut the suitcase.

"Now let's go," said Kevin, and they ran out of the housekeeping corner into the adjoining room and unpacked the suitcase.

"We're having a picnic," said Kevin. Kevin filled the sugar bowl and creamer with water. They set out the dishes. Michael had previously put a phone in the suitcase, so he took it out. They pretended to eat. Michael picked up the phone and made a call. "Let's drink some more tea," said Kevin, and they did.

"Would you help me snap these beads together, Michael?" asked Kevin. "You'd better."

So Michael started putting the beads together. "You make you a string, and I'll add onto mine," Kevin said.

Michael replied, "Leave a lot for me. Here, I'll put some more in a cup for you and some for me." They put the beads together, working very hard.

Kim came in and Michael popped up and said, "We're playing house, and you can't come in."

Kevin repeated this.

Kim stood on one side watching. Kevin and Michael then packed everything in the suitcase and returned to the other room.

Kevin and Michael are friends. Each makes suggestions that the other accepts. They improvise as they play. Themes and roles change. Robbers, cowboys, police, and family roles mix. Michael defers to Kevin who seems to be the leader, but who does not dominate the play. Michael makes his own suggestions, too. They start by playing together in the housekeeping area and sharing materials there. Then Michael leaves, putting on dark glasses and carrying a suitcase, perhaps taking the role of a father leaving for work, but he soon returns with the suggestion, "We're robbers." The play becomes more animated. They hurry. They call the police, then the cowboys, while Kevin warns, "Don't walk on the lawn," a prohibition which may have puzzled him at some time. They both seem to feel that in being robbers they are playing a dangerous role, and calling the police helps them. After each move made as robbers, they seem to find reassurance in deciding to pretend to eat, a familiar homemaking activity. Having called the police, they decide to "have a light supper first." After having taken the silverware and dishes, they decide to have a picnic and they pretend to eat and later begin playing with beads in a very ordinary play situation.

They have played out a series of situations which have an element of fear and anxiety and which they do not understand. They have found some resolution. They are ready for less exciting play. One feels they are reassured and ready to end the episodes. They have made a point of sharing with each other, but they exclude Kim when she tries to join them. They show us how much confusion exists for them in regard to roles different people play.

Programs Planned for Children

There are television programs planned especially for young children. When these are planned by people who are well informed about children's developmental needs and have had experience with children, the programs may be of benefit. "Mr. Rogers" is an example of such a program. However, there are some programs designed to give the parents the role of being stupid, unable to solve everyday problems. These programs do not portray a healthy family situation and threaten the trust on which the child depends. Caricaturing this role is confusing and possibly damaging to the child's confidence in adults. The adult needs to check on what the child is viewing, sometimes watching with the child and talking about what they have seen. The wise adult will set a limit on television viewing.

Many of the programs for children are planned with a view to satisfying parents who feel it is important to push young children into learning to read, write, and count. A confusion exists for these parents between learning the *ABC*'s or how to count to ten and true education that is the result of understanding what young children gain through concrete experiences in doing and making. A child who has had plenty of experiences in playing with blocks, for example, understands the meaning of *many* or *few* or one, two, three. He has laid a foundation for later understanding of mathematics. The child who has had many experiences of looking at books, having books read to him, finding out what books have to offer, is usually a child who learns to read easily. This child's teacher may have introduced the sounds of the letters of the alphabet rather than the names as a first step in reading. Each child has his or her own rate in learning. Pushing a child before he has a basis for understanding is likely to disrupt and undermine later learning.

Concern Over Violence in Television Programs

One of the gravest concerns about television viewing for young children is the amount of violence they see as they watch television. Violence on television may give older children and adults some release and a chance to drain off some hostile, aggressive feelings, but young children are still in an acting out stage. They have not developed much inner control as yet. They tend to hit, bite, or kick, and their impulses are strong. They are not sure of the difference between acceptable and unacceptable behavior.

Television seldom makes the difference clear. It does not offer young children much help in controlling impulsive behavior or of limiting the acting out of feelings. Conflicts are usually resolved violently on television with no apparent consequences. The evidence from studies so far suggests that adults are wise to protect young children from terrifying, incomprehensible material that too often makes up television viewing. One must conclude that television viewing certainly does not belong in quality programs for young children and that home viewing must be thoughtfully supervised by adults.

The Use of Video Cassettes in Centers

Video tapes, video monitors, and video cassette recorders are popular items in many homes. Video tapes of cartoons, stories, and children's programs are readily available for very low rental fees. A word of caution concerning young children and the use of video cassettes in centers is suggested. Children thrive on active experiences appropriate to their stage of growth and development. Television is a passive experience and as stated earlier does not belong in centers.

Projects

1. Visit a local computer shop and examine the various types of computer programs available for children under the age of five years. Write a critique of this experience noting the responses for correct or incorrect answers, clarity of information, format, and your opinion of the value of the program for young children.

2. Visit a local early childhood center that uses computers. Observe how they are used, which programs are used, sex differences, teacher involvement, children's attention span, location of the computer in the classroom, and value of the experience for children.

3. Plan a visit to a local computer shop for a small group of children. Arrange to have computer programs for children under five available to use. Observe which programs hold the children's attention, any sex differences, how long the children stay with the program, and social interaction of the children.

4. Watch television with a small group of children and observe their behavior. Report on their attention span, involvement with the characters on the screen, and general interest.

5. Watch several television programs designed for young children. Evaluate the quality of the programs based upon your knowledge of early childhood principles.

For Your Further Reading

Brady, E. H., & Hill, S. (1984). Research in review: Young children and microcomputers: Research issues and directions. *Young Children*, *39*(3), 49–61. Comprehensive overview of best current opinions on this topic, pointing out issues on which research is needed. Considers issues of age, gender, special education, economic equity, teacher education, and administrative uses.

Burg, K. (1984). The microcomputer in the kindergarten. *Young Children*, *39*(3), 28–33. Begins with anecdotal accounts of how kindergarteners derive different social, language, and motor learnings from the classroom computer; concludes with caution that computers must be supplemental rather than basic in the kindergarten curriculum.

Greenfield, P. M. (1984). *Mind and media: The effects of television, video games, and computers.* The developing child series. Cambridge, MA: Harvard University Press. Urges the use of research to see how these media can promote social development and thinking skills. Is encouraging on positive aspects of the three media.

Honig, A. S. (1983). Television and young children: Research in review. *Young Children*, *38*(4), 63–76. Considers child's functioning in relation to TV: passive versus active learning, achievement, violence and aggression, sex role learning, prosocial programs, and effects on family life; concludes with how adults can take charge.

Nieboer, R. A. (1983). *A study of the effect of computers on the preschool environment.* Urbana, IL: ERIC Clearinghouse on Elementary and Early Childhood Education (ED 234 898). Establishing a computer activity center in the preschool did not dominate classroom activity or create unique management problems.

Sloan, D. (1984). *The computer in education: A critical perspective* (Special Issue). *Teachers College Record*, *85*(4). Entire issue devoted to articles on uses of and cautions for educational computing.

PART SIX

◆

CONCERNS
OF PARENTS
AND TEACHERS

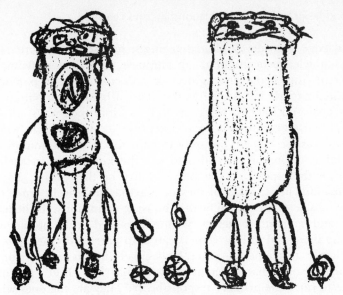

Mummy and Daddy on Skis (boy, 4 years 7 months)

22 ◆ Teachers and Parents Work Together

To bring up children in personal and tolerant ways, based on information and education rather than tradition, is a very new way; it exposes parents to many additional insecurities. . . .[1]

The twentieth century has brought so much that is new that we may find it difficult to appreciate how many "additional insecurities" parents face, as Erikson puts it. Through the centuries in different parts of the world there have been traditional ways of bringing up children. Parents for the most part have followed these traditions. Only recently has a body of

[1]E. Erikson. (1959). *Identity and the life cycle* (Vol. 1, No. 1). New York: International Press.

knowledge been developing that might be useful for parents in the way that knowledge is useful to an engineer or a doctor. Being a parent is different from being an engineer or a doctor. Being a parent is a deeply personal experience as well as one that calls for information. It demands "personal and tolerant ways" as well as "informed ways" of functioning. We are just beginning to give attention to the possible ways in which parents can be helped, not only to gain the "information and education" available at present, but also to use the knowledge in their individual ways, with respect for the individuality of their child. Parents have a tremendous job to do, and they do it remarkably well. Some of them face many obstacles because of health, housing conditions, the demands of their jobs, and many other factors. We are interested in the problems of parents. We are interested in how centers can help parents do their job.

When a child enters a center, he begins living in two environments, each requiring somewhat different adjustments. The child's parents will continue to carry the primary responsibility. They are the ones who know the child more intimately. The teacher brings her knowledge of child growth and development and her understanding of a number of children. Many teachers are themselves parents. All teachers gain in understanding the children in their group when parents share with the teacher their knowledge of their individual child. The insights of both parent and teacher may grow in the sharing. Such sharing will depend on communication and also on the basic respect parents and teachers have for one another. If there is a sense of mutual respect, the parent and teacher will be better able to give optimum support to the child as he moves from home to center and back to the home.

PARENTS ARE IMPORTANT PEOPLE TO A CHILD

Of most importance to the child are their parents and what they think, feel, and do. Ricky, for example, spent most of the morning in school making a table. After he had made it, he painted it, working intently with long strokes of the brush. He asked the teacher if it could be painted different colors. When she agreed that would be a good idea, he used blue, yellow, and orange, and then he painted a part with one color over another to make another color. He announced that he had made the table for his daddy. He asked the teacher almost pleadingly, "Do you think my Daddy will love it?" "Yes, I think he will love it," she answered.

As he intently brushed the table with paint he said, "I am doing a good job. A painter should do a good job. I can paint better than other children." He seemed satisfied as he looked at the table, and he said hopefully, "We'll wrap it up with a string around so it won't come open. It is a surprise. Will he know what it is?"

The teacher answered, "If he doesn't, you can tell him." Ricky excitedly answered, "I *can* tell him it is a table for him." Here we see a child eager to please a parent, putting his best effort into a product, planning and anticipating, hoping it will be a good thing.

A less confident child can be seen in this example. Tommy, a three-year-old who has never attended a center before, and his mother arrive on the first morning with anxiety showing plainly on their faces. They had met the teacher and visited the day before, but they still do not seem to feel at all sure of what the experience will be like. Tommy's mother sits down on the chair the teacher indicates is for her. When Tommy finally leaves her to explore some trucks and calls for help, she only goes to him after she asks the teacher, "Is it all right for me to help him?"

She watches him closely and only occasionally appears to notice what other children are doing. She quickly turns away when she observes a dispute. Once another child grabs the small truck Tommy is using. He burst into tears and rushes to his mother who holds him tightly and does not conceal her concern. One feels her uncertainty and her disapproval of many of the situations that occur. She volunteers few comments. When she relates an incident about Tommy to the teacher, she says, "I know what I did was wrong." She seems to pass judgment on herself and others and expects the same from them. Perhaps being in a school situation makes her feel like this because of her own childhood experiences.

The anxiety Tommy's mother feels makes it more difficult for Tommy to feel secure in the center. The teacher needs to help this mother gain confidence in the center and what it offers. She will try to reassure this mother of the staff's interest in Tommy. The teacher will help Tommy find activities he enjoys, and she may manage to interest a friendly, sociable child in including Tommy in the play. Whenever possible, the teacher will join the mother in observing and commenting on what is happening. It may take time before Tommy and his mother really trust the center and its program. The wise teacher needs to understand that parents may have mixed feelings about leaving their child.

In entering a young child in a center a parent is taking a step that will mean important changes in their relationship. The child may quickly become more independent than he has been. He will have experiences in which the parent does not share. If the child is developing well, he will find satisfying relationships with other children and with his teachers. Parents may find it hard to share responsibility for the child with the teacher.

The parent who has enjoyed her child's babyhood may find it difficult to accept the child's liking the center and his readiness to leave her. The parent who may have found the care of a young child unusually difficult may also be reluctant to let him go. Parents may be afraid of shirking their

An adult helps this child roll up his sleeves.

First Step Nursery School

responsibility. They may find it hard to accept their realistic need to have some time free for outside work or time free from the demands that every young child makes. Centers help meet the needs of parents as well as the needs of children.

The mother who is enrolling a child in an early childhood program because she expects to be working outside the home will be influenced in her feelings about the center by the way she feels about her job. She may be looking forward to working and may be satisfied about arrangements at home. She is likely to be glad, in this case, to have the child enter the center even though she has some regrets about the necessary separation. If she wishes she did not have to work, she may find it very difficult to help the child enter into the group, and she may need reassurance from the staff. Most parents are able to help the child with separation if they themselves feel confident in the center.

Children who have had brothers or sisters in the center previously usually adapt more easily than those who have not, less because they themselves are familiar with the program than because their parents feel at home there. If the parent has accepted group experience for the child, the child is likely to find it easy to do the same.

Most parents enjoy watching the spurt in growth that usually occurs in the child during the first few months in a center. Changes appear in the child's language, his social skills, ideas about himself, and in what he can do. As one mother remarked, she found herself enjoying her child much more after he started attending the center. He seemed more like a person to her.

Teachers Need to Be Aware of the Feelings of Parents

Most parents feel strongly about matters pertaining to health. Frequently teachers are less alert than parents to adjusting a child's clothing to changes in temperature or activities. They may be less concerned about wet feet or wet sleeves. Teachers are not the ones who are up at night with the sick child, nor do they have the same heavy emotional investment in the child as the parent. Good parent-teacher relations are based on mutual understanding. The inexperienced teacher must train herself to be very careful in matters involving health. With experience, she will come to appreciate the parent's viewpoint. If she is careful, she relieves the parent of a source of anxiety and makes a better relationship possible.

Teachers should provide aprons and smocks for "messy" play and have changes of clothing available when needed in the center. Parents often have errands and shopping to do on their way home from their workday. Parents appreciate teachers who are aware of their feelings about the child's appearance. This is another way to build good relationships between the school and the home.

Some parents are likely to feel anxious about the behavior of their children. Such parents may be older than the average parent of a preschool child, or they may have backgrounds of professional experience unrelated to young children. They may have had little background to help them understand the growth impulses of young children. They are likely to see failure for themselves in the childlike behavior of their offspring. They need reassurance from a teacher who accepts them and their children as they are.

Parents from minority groups may differ in their cultural traditions and their attitudes about the child's center. They may have difficulty in understanding what the center is attempting to do for their child. They themselves are likely to have met discrimination and may find it difficult to trust the teacher and the center. The teacher needs to give special consideration to the needs of these parents. She must try to learn all she can from them about their expectations and make any suitable adjustment in her program. She should inform herself about the cultural patterns the parents represent. She can strengthen her own program for the children if she incorporates elements from the different cultures with the help of the parents. All parents will have something to contribute. Doing so helps confirm for the children the validity of the mixed culture in which they live.

PARENTS PRESENT DIFFERENT PROBLEMS

Parents Want to Know about Their Child in the Center

Parents are interested in what happens to their child while he is at the center. They may see rapid changes taking place in their child. Not all the changes taking place will seem desirable to them. Growth seldom proceeds smoothly. They may find a quiet, docile child becoming more aggressive and defiant after he has been in the center for a while. He may not share his toys as willingly as he did earlier. His vocabulary may be increasing rapidly, but it may contain words that the parents find quite unacceptable. These parents may be critical of aspects of the program.

These criticisms should be considered carefully by the teacher to see whether situations should be handled differently as well as to identify and understand what may lie behind the complaint. It is a step in the growth of understanding when a criticism is expressed by the parent, accepted by the teacher, and a mutual understanding reached. Questions and criticisms can often be cleared up by frank discussion so that they do not block the growth of more positive relationships.

Some parents may not ask questions. These parents may work and have little or no time to observe. It may be easier for them to leave matters to the teacher, and they may find it difficult to question a teacher about what she is doing. It is important in these cases to find occasions when the teacher can mention to the parent something about what the child did that day, such as painting a colorful picture, or her observations of his interest in a special activity or his skill with puzzles. She may raise a question herself about the child's behavior. In doing this she shows her interest in the child. She is also helping the parent ask questions or express her concerns. If the caregiver is not the parent, the teacher needs to help the caregiver in the same way.

Sometimes a parent may be late in coming for the child at the end of the day's session. A late parent means a longer day for a teacher. It requires patience and understanding on the part of the teacher, but there are often good reasons for a parent's being late. The teacher needs to accept the parent's reason and handle the situation matter of factly. If a parent is repeatedly late, the teacher must discuss the situation with the parent. She should state clearly what it means to the staff in the center and discuss with the parent what can be done about the problem. It may be better to hold the discussion in the morning or by appointment rather than at the time the parent arrives late. The teacher must take into account her own feelings as well as those of the parent, but she needs to make a firm statement for the sake of the staff. If the problem lies in the parents' hours of employment, for example, the parent will need to talk the situation over with the employer so that the hours can be adjusted. If this cannot be done, the parent may need to find another center.

Parents Are Concerned about Their Child's Safety

Teachers have always been alert to protect the physical safety of children, but they define safety more in terms of a well arranged environment and good supervision. Parents are reassured to see climbing equipment that is sturdy and used on resilient surfaces, dangerous appliances and substances not accessible to children, safety rules followed on walks, visible fire extinguishers and fire drills, and other procedures showing care for physical well-being.

Parents today have deep concerns about protecting their children from abduction, sexual molestation, and physical abuse. They seek help in knowing how to protect their children from such terrifying experiences. They worry about molestation and abuse in centers for young children because of widespread publicity about a few cases. Some divorced or separated parents have to alert the center to the threat of the child's abduction by the non-custodial parent. Parents ask more frequently if it is permissible for them to visit the center unannounced at any time. Teachers must respond with understanding and reassurance to these parental concerns.

Teachers can help in several ways. An upset parent needs to be listened to even more than she needs explanations of the center's policies. However, the center does need to have clearly defined policies and procedures, and parents need to be informed about them when the child is first enrolled. Reminders of the center's policies can be made on a parent bulletin board or in a newsletter. It may be uncomfortable to challenge a person who arrives to pick up a child who is not the authorized person, but parents are grateful in the long run to know that teachers exercise such caution. Some centers now include discussions of safety as part of their curriculum. Some excellent books for young children have been published recently. These books and curriculum ideas on safety for young children are designed to help them feel reassured and competent; they are not intended to frighten them.

If parental concerns about child abduction, molestation, and abuse are persistent, teachers may wish to plan a group discussion (see pp. 389–390). Workshops have been given in many communities to help parents and teachers gain confidence in dealing with these issues of child safety. Teachers can also make available to parents recent books and articles through a newsletter, bulletin board, or lending library. Parents appreciate knowing about community resources that are available, such as where to get help when abuse or molestation is suspected. Teachers need to have this information for their own use as well as to give to parents. Teachers play an important role in providing information and reassurance to parents in this sensitive area.

GOALS IN WORKING WITH PARENTS

In working with parents there are two main goals. The first goal is to help parents gain confidence. The parent who feels confident is better able to enjoy her child and better able to learn about the needs of children and to use this knowledge more effectively.

The second goal is that of helping parents gain the insights and the knowledge that may improve their contribution to a child's development. The teacher who helps parents feel more confident and who is skillful in providing sound information has achieved important goals in her work.

How Do We Help Parents Gain More Confidence in Themselves?

The center and the teacher may help parents feel that they are important in many small but significant ways.

Does the center provide a comfortable place for parents to sit when they are waiting, a bulletin board with attractive, interesting material on it, and some magazines and books for browsing or lending? Does the teacher try to make parents feel welcome at the center? Does she take time to point out something of interest that may be happening in the center? Has she been clear about the acceptable times to bring and call for the child and about decisions that are hers to make and those that the parent should make?

The parent will gain confidence if the teacher takes the time to listen to what the parent wants to tell her. The teacher will try to "listen with the third ear" to understand any meaning that lies behind the words. It is important for the parent to feel that she is being understood. In her relationship with the parent, the teacher will show interest, give encouragement, and avoid blame and criticism.

In all our relationships as teachers with parents we must respect the deep feelings involved in any parent-child relationship. We must remember that life with young children brings many frustrations and makes many demands, although it also brings much satisfaction and joy. We must respect parents if we are to help them feel confident. Good relationships are built on awareness and sympathy.

What Knowledge Will Be Useful to Parents?

Our second goal in working with parents is to help them gain more understanding about children and their needs. Along with the intuitive understanding most parents have about their own child, they can benefit from more information or added knowledge. Much of what we have learned as teachers of young children will also be useful to parents. We have a responsibility for sharing our knowledge of child development with

Climbers enhance physical development.

First Step Nursery School

them and for doing this in a way that does not interfere with the parents' own unique knowledge of their child.

What knowledge may be especially useful to parents? What might be included in a parent education program? We will suggest some information that might be included in a discussion program:

1. The values of play and of activity for the young child, with emphasis on letting the child touch things and explore as much as possible.
2. The kinds of play materials and play opportunities that are appropriate at different ages and stages, with emphasis on simple, raw materials, dramatic and creative materials, and homemade equipment.
3. Ways in which a child is helped to develop competence in speech, including the importance of talking with a child and listening to his speech, the importance of opportunities with books and stories, and the importance of expanding the child's own language.
4. Information about the way in which a child learns, and the value of answering a child's questions, of helping him ask questions, and of helping him to discover for himself.
5. Understanding about the kind of help that promotes development, such as giving directions or making suggestions in a positive rather than in a negative way; giving a child enough, but not too much or too confusing kinds of experience; letting him take his time; preparing the child for new or difficult situations; playing a supporting role rather than a critical one.

6. The value of helping a child learn to distinguish between fantasy and reality while still enjoying and using his imagination.
7. The importance of putting feelings into words as a way of understanding and controlling action and how this verbalization may be done.
8. The value of play with other children and ways in which a child is helped in getting along with others.
9. Information about development and growth needs, especially about the extent of individual differences in children.
10. Understanding of the stages in cognitive growth, concept formation, the value of imagination in the thought process, and the contribution made to intellectual growth by a rich variety of experiences.

With more knowledge, parents' expectations for the child become more reasonable. Parents can take more interest in the child's development, watching growth patterns evolve that are reassuringly similar to those of all children, yet unique in wonderful ways. They are better able to treasure the individuality of their child as a result of their increased understanding of growth and development.

HOW DO PARENTS LEARN?

Parents, or any of us, learn in a variety of ways. We learn by *observing* a skillful person as he performs a job. We learn by *discussion*, raising questions and expressing feelings and attitudes. We learn by *doing*, putting into practice what we have seen and discussed. When observation, discussion, and active participation take place under favorable conditions, they result in sound learning. A good parent education program will include opportunities for all three kinds of activities.

Observation

Parents should feel free to observe at any time. Observation in centers is an important opportunity for parents to see their child with other children and find that in some respects he is like others and in some respects he is unique. Through observation parents may find ideas for play materials, activities, and ways of handling situations. Sometimes the child's behavior with other children and adults will need to be interpreted by the teacher. She can explain why a situation was handled in one way and not another or what she believes a bit of behavior may mean. Observations may make clear the significance and value of behavior that parents may not have noticed before.

Parents should be encouraged to observe and have an opportunity to talk with the teacher about what they see. Such discussions can be arranged after center hours. If the center has adequate observation space, parents

Friendships are important.

First Step Nursery School

will find it easier to observe without distracting their child and other children.

The teacher may wish to observe a child at home in order to gain insight into his behavior at the center or to help build a relationship with the child. She will arrange with the parent and child for a visit. The teacher can gain understanding about the child's interests, skills, abilities, and relationships with others from a home visit.

For a child, and for the parents too, the visit of the teacher may have a great deal of significance. The visit demonstrates to the child that he is an important person to her. And parents, even though they may feel somewhat anxious and strained, may still appreciate the visit. Parent-teacher relationships can be more comfortable as a result of this opportunity to visit outside the center. Afterward, it may be easier for a parent to ask questions important to her and for the teacher to understand what these questions mean.

Individual Conferences

Individual conferences represent one of the most valuable ways in which teachers and parents can share their observations of the child. The teacher and the parent may hold many informal conferences at arrival or dismissal times or by telephone. Planned conferences may be held at regular intervals. Through conferences both parent and teacher can become more aware of how each may be of help to the other. As parents and teachers look at what is happening and pool their thoughts about the child, they may gain new appreciation for what he is like.

The initial contact between teacher and parent is important even if it takes place by telephone. The parent's first impressions will influence her attitude toward the center and will somehow be conveyed to the child. The first conference (described in Chapter 9) will probably occur as the child is about to enter the center. At this time parents are encouraged to talk about their child and they have the opportunity to raise questions about the center. The teacher listens, and together she and the parents try to understand what the experience of entering the program may mean to the child. They decide the roles each will play in helping the child to adjust. There may be several short conferences for parents and teacher to share information during the adjustment process. The communication between parents and teacher at this time establishes conferences as matter-of-course events. Teachers accept the responsibility for creating an atmosphere in which communication is easy, honest, and direct.

Individual conferences can be held at regular intervals during the year, perhaps near the midpoint, and at the end of the year. At these times, the teacher's observation of the child's progress on a variety of dimensions can

A parent and teacher get together.

California State University, Chico. Child Development Laboratory

be discussed. The teacher's observations of the child can be compared with the parent's observations of the child at home. The teacher knows the child at the center, and the parent knows the child at home.

In the conferences the teacher has with parents, she helps them approach problems, not by giving answers, but by listening to what solutions the parent has tried. She helps the parent select a course of action from those discussed. Only the parents know the child, the situation in the home, and what they themselves can do. The responsibility for solving most problems belongs to the parent, and the teacher should not attempt to take over this responsibility any more than she should solve a child's problem for him. She tries only to help the parent to solve a problem by listening, asking questions to clarify a point, or suggesting factors that may be related. She may point out the possible meanings of a course of action to a child and help parents think about a variety of alternative solutions. The experienced teacher does not offer advice or pass judgment, but she needs to show confidence that there is a solution.

Every teacher needs education and experience in conferencing. She also needs the opportunity, especially as a beginning teacher, to plan and later discuss the parent conferences she has with a professional person, such as her director, a supervisor, or a consultant. A beginning teacher may benefit from participating in some conferences with an experienced teacher. She learns from analyzing her own experience and identifying the meanings in both her responses and those of the parents. In-service education is important for developing skills in conferencing.

Group Discussions

Group discussions provide parents with the opportunity to have contacts with other parents. These contacts are not the same as those in the ordinary social event. Here they meet as parents. They can share their concerns and talk about common problems. As a group they are all concerned with their children. It is often a relief for them to know that they are not alone in facing some problems. They may get help from each other in solving a specific problem.

Some mothers with young children are likely to feel rather isolated and without many outside contacts. Some employed mothers have few opportunities to talk with other parents of young children. They need contact with other adults who are interested in children. With the support of other parents, a parent may find it easier to let the child be more independent. Many adults live far from their own families and cannot turn to their parents for support. They may be relatively alone in facing uncertainties which they hesitate to share with friends. They are in need of the extended family experience, which the center offers through group meetings.

There are many kinds of group experiences. Some centers have general group meetings, held in the evening, for mothers and fathers. The more the chance for parent participation, the more the individual parent will gain. Techniques can be used to bring about participation even when groups are large. If the parents share responsibility with the staff for making plans, or take on the responsibility themselves, the experiences are likely to come closer to what parents really want and thus be more valuable to them. A parent committee may plan the programs.

Sometimes parents bring up particular situations for discussion. It is only natural that parents will wish to discuss the particular problem of their own child, but the discussion leader will need to keep relating the specific example to general principles or group interests. "Is this a problem which occurs frequently?" "Have some of you met this problem in other types of situations?" "Shall we look at reasons why this behavior appears in children just at this point in their growth?" Parents can be encouraged to bring in *typical* situations for discussion at a meeting. Problems that are not typical are better discussed by parent and teacher in a conference.

It is helpful to have some agreement before discussion starts on the length of time of a meeting. It is seldom wise to have a discussion of more than an hour and a half. Frequently small groups will stay to talk more informally about points which have been raised, and this is a valuable part of the experience for them.

When meetings are being planned, teachers must consider the busy lives and diverse work hours of the parents who will attend. Some centers have arranged to have informal coffee hours during hours when children are at the center. A discussion is led by someone on the staff. Other centers have had success with Saturday morning open houses for parents and children, in which the parents can experience some of the children's activities and can chat informally with teachers over puzzles and playdough. There are also work meetings in which parents and teachers repair and paint equipment and talk as they work. Whether parents and teachers meet in the evening in a discussion group or in some other manner, it is important to meet the convenience of parents.

A lending library with books and pamphlets is useful to parents, as is a bulletin board where teachers and parents can share things that have stimulated their thinking.

Parents can also learn from *participating* in the center. Most centers welcome parents who come in as volunteers, helping in the program, such as on an excursion or field trip, bringing in a musical instrument to play, providing objects of interest, helping with a cooking project, storytelling, or dancing. Discussion and evaluation by parents and staff afterward make parents' participation a valuable experience for all.

Centers such as Head Start programs and cooperative nursery schools use parents as assistant teachers. Parents have a great deal to contribute to the center. They need an adequate orientation in the procedures of the program for the particular center in which they will be sharing responsibilities with a trained teacher. They need to attend regular meetings in which there is discussion of current problems, review and planning of learning opportunities for the children, and an opportunity to raise questions, especially those about their own uncertainties or resistances.

In addition to the problems faced by teachers routinely, parents who are assistant teachers in the group in which their child is enrolled face the added problem of having two roles, that of teacher and that of parent for her child. Playing these two roles at the same time is often a very difficult task. Parents in cooperative nursery schools know this problem. Patience is required on the part of everyone involved. Some children do better on the days when their mothers are not present.

THE CENTER SUPPORTS PARENTS

The center has a responsibility for parent education. More is being done today, and much more needs to be done in the future, as we learn more about ways of helping parents. We can ask ourselves, "What would we like to find in a center to help us with the task of being a parent?"

Many centers have waiting lists with names of parents who hope to enroll their children. These parents are interested, and the center can offer them opportunities for learning through discussion groups, through conferences and consultation services, and, in some cases, through home visits and home teaching. Classes for expectant parents have proved to be of value, as have parent-infant and parent-toddler classes. Centers need to be doing much more to help both fathers and mothers find success and satisfaction in carrying on their roles in "informed" ways.

Parents who have lacked educational opportunities themselves can learn ways of supporting their children's learning. In some experimental and federally sponsored programs teachers are going into homes and helping mothers of infants and very young children find ways to enrich the experiences there. In other programs, teachers are going into homes to work with the child to augment what the school is doing and to demonstrate to the individual parent how she may help her child. This kind of home visiting program appears to be very effective in supplementing a child's school experiences. It results in improved performance in learning, according to research done by Weikart and others.[2]

[2]D. P. Weikart, D. J. Deloria, & S. Lawsor. (1974). A report on longitudinal evaluations of preschool programs. In S. Ryan (Ed.). *Results of a preschool intervention project* (Vol. 1). Washington, DC: U.S. Department of Health, Education, and Welfare (No. OHD 74-24).

With more general awareness of the role of education, more parents are becoming aware of the role they themselves can play in the process of helping children learn. Children will benefit from this greater awareness by parents if *all* aspects of learning are emphasized. They will also benefit if parents do not work too hard at trying to be teachers.

The teacher remains in a key position to help parents value what the child is and does. She can help the parent see a relationship between a single bit of behavior and the total growth pattern. In this way she may help the parent gain a perspective and yet keep a sense of closeness to the child. She will not stress techniques. Techniques are not enough, however good they may be. They may even interfere with spontaneous relationships. It is not so much what people do as how they feel about what they do that is important. "What parents need all along is enlightenment about underlying causes, not advice and not instruction as to procedure."[3]

As the teacher works with different parents, she will strive to understand the differences in their feelings. In working with them she will gain much that will help her in her own understanding of children. She, in turn, may help the parents in their understanding of children. Working together, teachers and parents will find the satisfactions that come with confidence, skill, and understanding.

Projects

1. Observe a group of children at the end of the school day. Note what individual parents do and say as they call for their children.
2. A parent has many roles. What conflicts may arise in playing these roles?

For Your Further Reading

Adams, C., & Fay, J. (1981). *No more secrets: Protecting your child from sexual assault*. San Luis Obispo, CA: Impact Publishers. An excellent short book for parents of children up to twelve who want help in talking to their children about sexual assault. Written in helpful question and answer form.

Berger, E. H. (1981). *Parents as partners in education: The school and home working together*. St. Louis, MO: C. V. Mosby. Aims at producing a partnership between parent and the professional teacher, paraprofessional caregivers, community workers, and parent educators. Includes chapters on parents of exceptional children, abused children, and home-based programs.

Brazelton, T. B. (1985). *Working and caring*. Reading, MA: Addison-Wesley. For working parents about how to hold a job and raise a family. Another fine book by pediatrician Brazelton.

Cataldo, C. Z. (1986). *Parent education for early childhood*. New York: Teachers College. Deals with child-rearing topics from infancy through early primary grades, and offers methods for parent education as well as content.

[3]D. W. Winnicott. (1957). *The child and the outside world*. New York: Basic Books.

Evans, J., & Ilfeld, E. (1982). *Good beginnings: Parenting in the early years*. Ypsilanti, MI: High/Scope. Organized around seven stages in infant/toddler development, the book uses Piaget's theoretical framework in defining parental roles.

Fassler, J. (1978). *Helping children cope: Mastering stress through books and stories*. New York: The Free Press. Sections on death, separation experiences, hospitalization and illness, lifestyle changes, and other crises like natural disasters and a parent going to prison. Lists of suggested books with excellent suggestions on how to use them.

Galinsky, E. (1982). *Between generations: The stages of parenthood*. New York: Berkley Books. Discusses the development of parents as their children progress through their stages of development.

Honig, A. S. (1979). *Parent involvement in early childhood education* (rev. ed.). Washington, DC: National Association for the Education of Young Children. Parents need child development knowledge and a variety of ways to be involved in their child's early education. The revised edition adds up-to-date issues in parenting like role of fathers and single parenthood.

Hymes, J. L., Jr. (1974). *Effective home-school relations* (rev. ed.). Carmel, CA: Hacienda Press. A book full of good ideas for the "how-to" of parent-teacher relationships, but more: the qualitative aspects of home-school relations.

Spilke, F. S. (1979). *What about the children? A divorced parent's handbook*. New York: Crown Publishers.

Spilke, F. S. (1979). *The family that changed: A child's book about divorce*. New York: Crown Publishers. This pair of books offers warm and helpful ideas for children from three to six and their parents. The parents' book includes issues not often discussed, like grandparents' roles and a parent living with someone without marriage.

Self-Portrait (girl, 5 years)

23 ◆ Becoming a Professional Person

"I am persuaded that good teachers, first of all, must hold strong commitments and convictions from which their practices flow."[1] Hymes's statement is about becoming a professional person and developing a philosophy.

   As we begin to work with young children and their families in the early
childhood field, how do we develop a philosophy based on commitments
and convictions? How does one become a professional person? Here is an
example in which a beginning teacher was faced with violations of
professional standards.

[1]J. L. Hymes, Jr. (1981). *Teaching the child under six* (3rd ed.). Columbus, OH:
Charles E. Merrill.

Selma, a student aide in a licensed day-care center, comes in at the busy noon hour to help with lunch and to get children ready for naps. She notices that there are often too many children for the licensed number. She brings the matter up with the director, who replies, "Yes, I have to be over-enrolled so that I'll have my licensed number every day, to make up for illnesses and vacations." Selma goes along with this but with growing concern. The director asks her to come in as an extra one morning because the licensing inspector is expected. Another day the fire inspector arrives, and the director sends Selma out the back door to take several children for a walk.

Professional standards certainly are being violated in this center. What should Selma do as a professional person in the difficult situation she faces? In the process of becoming a professional, Selma should find answers for some of these kinds of problems. She must explore her commitments and convictions as she develops a philosophy.

Teachers need time to become truly professional persons, just as children need time to develop. With time and experience each individual will discover guidelines and will construct a philosophy. These will serve as a basis for decision making as she teaches. Each one will develop ethical standards to guide her in work with children and parents. In this way teachers will grow professionally.

Every profession has or should have agreed-upon guidelines for conduct. The medical and legal professions are examples. As more knowledge becomes available and society changes, standards need to change. Standards in early childhood education covered only matters of health care at first. Today they include many more areas because more is known about the developmental needs of young children. Social changes, too, require improved standards. The need for care for infants, toddlers, preschoolers, and school-age children is urgent as increasing numbers of mothers are employed. There is now a pressing need to consider better standards for group care to meet the new problems.

Early childhood education has few agreed-upon standards or codes of conduct at present. The NAEYC has recently proposed standards for the profession; but, in practice, quality programs and good teachers are responsible for maintaining professional standards. Beginning teachers will find many sources of support as they continue to learn about professional conduct.

PROFESSIONAL GROWTH IN ETHICS AND ETHICAL STANDARDS

One of the most important areas for teachers' professional growth is that of ethical standards. Many questions raised today are ethical issues such as confidentiality of records or obtaining research data from children as subjects. The need to develop a code of ethics for the early childhood profession has become clear.[2]

Selma faced dilemmas for which ethical guidelines are urgent. Teachers can act with more confidence when they have some guidelines for correct or "right" behavior, especially when there are temptations to behave otherwise. With guidelines teachers find it easier to act in the best interests of the child, the parent, and the program, rather than to act expediently. They may find it easier to be clear about what they will not do or will not allow to be done under any circumstances.

Confidentiality

Ethical standards or codes of conduct include confidentiality. Teachers must consider all information about families confidential.

Teachers serve many needs, not only for the child but also for the parents. Decisions made by teachers about what is in the child's and family's best interests should be in accord with ethical guidelines. Teachers may have glimpses into intimate family situations. Teachers often need to contact public health clinics, child protective services, legal authorities, and other community agencies. They may need to contact the family physician. When making these contacts they need to be clear about what information can be shared without breaching confidentiality.

Confidentiality means sharing information only with those staff members who are directly involved. It means keeping all notes on children and families carefully filed and not left out for others to read. It means making sensitive telephone calls in private. It means never talking to one parent about another parent. It also includes asking permission from a family before talking with any outside agencies. Beginning teachers should respect the policies of the center concerning its ethical standards. They need to consult with their supervisor when difficult situations arise, as they clarify their own feelings and beliefs.

A code of ethics covers more than confidentiality. Ethical guidelines become important when teachers are confronted with difficult choices which may carry a risk to themselves, the child, the parent, or the center. There may be several ways of looking at a problem depending on the circumstances. Standards of ethics should be discussed with more experienced teachers before coming to conclusions. There are no easy answers

---

[2]L. G. Katz. (1977). *Ethical issues in working with children*. Urbana, IL: ERIC Clearinghouse on Elementary and Early Childhood Education (ED 144 681).
S. Feeney & K. Kipnis. (1985). Professional ethics in early childhood education. *Young Children, 40*(3) 54–57.
E. Ward. (1977). A code of ethics: The hallmark of a profession. In B. Spodek (Ed.). *Teaching practices: Reexamining assumptions*. Washington, DC: National Association for the Education of Young Children.

Teachers' observations must be kept confidential.

California State University, Chico. Child Development Laboratory

to some of these questions, but there are resources available and support from others in solving ethical problems.

PROFESSIONAL GROWTH IN RELATIONS WITH OTHERS

With Children

In working with children teachers make use of all the knowledge they have gained in their training about child growth and development and about children's needs at different stages of development. All through this book we have presented material about understanding children and ways to meet their needs in a quality program. We have pointed out the dangers of labeling children and the need for objective observations.

Nonprofessional or unprofessional responses of teachers are likely to come from personal preference or folk wisdom.[3] Teachers responding professionally look for the meaning of the child's behavior. They look at the curriculum and the physical environment to see if better planning

[3]L. G. Katz. (1984). The professional early childhood teacher. *Young Children,* *39*(5).

could benefit children's learning and prevent difficulties from occurring. They look at age-expected behaviors for the children and above all at what they know about the individual child from careful observation.

With Parents

What professional standards are involved when teachers work with parents? We have discussed one of the ways in which teachers act professionally with parents by treating information from them with the utmost confidentiality.

The relationship between teacher and parent differs from the personal relationship between friends. It is a professional relationship, concerned with an educational experience, the individual child's well-being, and with the part the parents share in this. Some teachers may seek personal friendships with the parents. In these cases, the teacher's own need for friendship may stand in the way of developing a professional relationship.

Teachers who can offer a professional relationship to parents must have a real understanding of themselves. They must be able to recognize their own needs and feelings in relationships with others. They must be able to respond to parents' needs, not to satisfy their own personal needs. Teachers accept parents, but they do not depend on feeling accepted by them.

Teachers need to listen carefully when parents discuss problems with them. They can be ready to share their knowledge and their experiences with parents. If teachers feel that the problem needs specialized help, they should be familiar with the referral resources in the community so that they can refer the parent appropriately. For example, teachers are frequently the first to observe that a child may have a hearing impairment or a vision problem. Teachers can suggest a referral, but the parent must be the one to make the decision.

Here are some examples of situations teachers may face with parents. Decisions are not easy to make in these cases.

> A father angrily insists that the teacher spank his child when the child "misbehaves."
> A mother requests that her unusual dietary preferences for the child be followed, even though there is no health reason involved.
> A child who has been kidnapped in the past by the noncustodial parent sees that parent watching outside the fence of the center.
> A child tells the teacher information indicating that the parent may be breaking the law.

If teachers suspect that a child may be abused, physically, emotionally, or sexually, they are faced with the necessity of reporting immediately to the appropriate authorities. Professional teachers put the welfare of the child above any conflicting concerns; they should report promptly all cases of suspected abuse. In many states there are penalties for failure to report. Reporting suspected abuse is not a dilemma or choice: it is a necessity.

With Colleagues

Teachers of young children are likely to be part of a teaching team, as there are always two adults with the group. Close working relationships, frequently in sensitive situations, make it important to maintain professional relationships with all colleagues, teachers, aides, the custodian, the secretary, and others.

Some aspects of the working conditions of teachers in early childhood centers leave much to be desired. Morale may be poor because of unpaid overtime, lack of adequate breaks, unequal division of labor among staff, and inadequate opportunities for decision making.[4] While improved pay and working conditions are the real issues, there are ways teachers can support each other to make the center a more satisfying workplace. Other centers may be more fortunate with good morale among the staff in spite of poor pay.

The center may bring in consultants, preferably on a regular basis, to provide staff development or to focus on problems of individual children. It is helpful when the center's director observes individual classrooms and gets acquainted with children in order to consult with teachers. Individual conferences between the director and the teachers are important.

Professional growth for teachers means learning to listen to colleagues' points of view. Flexibility and compromises are often necessary in working with others if these do not damage the standards of the center. Regular discussions about teaching methods and different situations at the center help to prevent conflict.

Teachers should be careful to share the workload as equally as possible and to be fair about breaks, substituting, or carrying an extra load when necessary. They need to take their share of chores such as shopping for curriculum materials, cleaning up in the kitchen, mending books or broken equipment, and doing the laundry as necessary. When teachers support one another, they create a center in which morale is good.

THE PROFESSIONAL TEACHER CONTINUES LEARNING

The process of learning to teach seems to occur in developmental levels, just as children go through stages of development. Teachers have their

---

[4]M. Whitebrook, C. Howes, R. Darrah, & J. Friedman. (1982). Caring for the caregivers: Staff burnout in child care. In L. G. Katz (Ed.). *Current topics in early childhood education* (Vol. 4). Norwood, NJ: ABLEX.

own patterns as they learn to teach, but awareness of stages may be helpful to some teachers as they think about their own development.[5]

Lilian Katz suggests that there may be developmental stages that some teachers experience in teaching young children. The first stage may be one of *survival*, during which teachers may be surprised at the gap between their high hopes and the realities of day-to-day work with children. The next stage is one of *consolidation*, when they may pull together what they have learned and look forward to gaining more skill in working with individual children. Then may come a stage of *renewal*, when teachers begin looking for ideas about new materials and procedures. New approaches in the field are of interest. Teachers finally reach a stage of greater *maturity* after several years. They feel freer to develop their own ideas and to become more creative in teaching. They become more concerned about the underlying philosophy of early childhood education.

As we have said in Chapter 3, people in any profession need to continue to learn. Learning becomes more interesting as professionals discover new aspects of their work, new questions, and new solutions to problems. Teachers continue their learning through educational activities, support, and opportunities which are appropriate to their professional experience, like some of the following:

Professional Affiliation

1. Joining a professional organization, such as the National Association for the Education of Young Children and the Organisation Mondiale pour L'Education Prescolaire (OMEP).
2. Attending professional conferences and workshops.
3. Subscribing to professional journals and newsletters.

Continuing Education

4. Working toward a certificate of competence from a community college, a four-year-college or university; toward state licensing; or toward the Child Development Associate certificate.
5. Planning ahead for future study, possibly a further degree.

Job Market

6. Investigating career opportunities in the field.
7. Preparing and updating a professional resumé. Preparing well for job interviews.

---

[5]L. G. Katz. (1972). Developmental stages of preschool teachers. *Elementary School Journal*, *23*(1).
E. Frede. (1985). How teachers grow: Four stages. *High Scope ReSource*, *4*(1).

Activities for Professional Renewal

8. Visiting other early childhood programs.
9. Participating actively in staff meetings and in-service training sessions.
10. Participating in the center accreditation process recently developed (1984) by the National Association for the Education of Young Children.[6]
11. Keeping an up-to-date curriculum activities file.
12. Maintaining comprehensive files of books, articles, pamphlets, clippings, and ideas for oneself, for colleagues, and for parents.
13. Participating in research projects.

Teachers attending their first conference of the National Association for the Education of Young Children, surrounded by perhaps 15,000 people from all kinds of programs across the nation, are likely to experience pride and renewed commitment to their chosen career. They will feel a part of a powerful movement on behalf of young children and their families.

Teachers also become more professional by speaking out effectively for children. Hymes calls on "all teachers of young children to take on the role of child advocate. . . . The continuing shortage of programs plus the increasing threats to quality create a pressing need for teachers to be good friends to *all* young children, and to know how to act on their allegiance."[7]

[6]National Association for the Education of Young Children. (1984). *Accreditation criteria and procedures: Position statement of the National Academy of Early Childhood Programs*. Washington, DC: Author.
[7]Hymes, op. cit.

A panel at a professional conference.

California State University, Chico. Child Development Laboratory

Participating in research in the classroom.

California State University, Chico. Child Development Laboratory

TAKING CARE OF ONESELF AS A PROFESSIONAL PERSON

In becoming professional, teachers need to maintain good health, learn to handle stress, and use social support systems and the evaluations of self and others for continued learning.

Self-Care and Maintaining Good Health

Teachers of young children need to be in good health to have the energy and vitality to maintain enthusiasm for their work. It takes stamina to work for long hours with a group of lively children. Habits of good nutrition, vigorous exercise, sufficient sleep and deep relaxation, with regular breaks for recreation, are needed to maintain health and energy.

Teachers need to cultivate interests of their own and to participate in leisure activities outside teaching hours. Achieving a healthy balance between work and leisure is essential.

Stress Management

Closely related to self-care is stress management. Stress and "burn-out" in the child care profession have recently been the subject of research.[8] Staff

[8]M. Whitebrook, C. Howes, R. Darrah, & J. Friedman (1982). Caring for the caregivers: Staff burnout in child care. In L. G. Katz (Ed.). *Current topics in early childhood education* (Vol. 4). Pp. 211–235. Norwood, NJ: ABLEX.

turnover because of stress results in "talent drain" and is expensive for centers and for the individual.

What are the causes of stress in early childhood teaching? The nature of the work itself makes heavy demands on the teacher's energy. Close personal relations with young children who have many needs and require constant attention are often a drain on a teacher's strength by the end of the day.

Frequently working conditions are not good, as we have mentioned. Early childhood education does not usually receive high priority in educational budgets. When these factors are combined with low pay, lack of benefits, and low status, it is easy to see that teachers of young children may face stress.

In spite of these factors, working with children gives real enjoyment. Supportive staff relationships also bring satisfaction along with personal growth opportunities.

Teachers can join together to work toward higher pay, better job benefits, and improved working conditions such as smaller child-staff ratios, availability of substitutes, and more control over policy and decision making. To be successful they need more community support.[9]

Social Support Systems

The presence of a network of supportive people helps teachers in their professional growth. Regular staff meetings are very important in providing such support. Staff meetings have been found to be directly related to good staff morale if teachers have felt helped by them in dealing with difficult situations.[10] In full-day centers it can be very difficult to find hours when the staff can be together to conduct business, make decisions, and fulfill a supportive function for one another. In staff discussions everyone should feel free to express ideas and feelings and to bring up problems. Staff meetings may also be used for in-service training. When everyone is encouraged to contribute, staff meetings will be seen as a productive use of time.

Making and Using Evaluations

All centers do some evaluating of the work of staff members in formal or informal ways.

The National Association for the Education of Young Children has included evaluation in its system for voluntary review of centers leading to nationally recognized accreditation. "The director (or other appropriate

[9]Ibid.
[10]C. Maslach & A. Pines (1977). The burnout syndrome in the day care setting. *Child Care Quarterly, 6*(2), 100–113.

person) evaluates all staff at least annually. . . . The evaluation includes classroom observation. Staff are informed of evaluation criteria in advance. . . . Staff have an opportunity to evaluate their own performance."[11]

Supervisors are usually the people who formally evaluate teachers. A good head teacher or director is a source of help. She is usually encouraging and supportive and able to point out to the teacher what has been done well and where improvement is needed. The supervisor may refer to an incident that the teacher has handled well or to some planning by which the teacher avoided conflicts. A teacher gains confidence under such a supervisor, becoming better able to discover strengths. Evaluation should be a positive experience, helping the teacher become more effective.

Teachers evaluate each other in informal ways, and they need to be sensitive in recognizing and benefiting from these evaluations.

Parents, too, do some evaluating of teachers. Parent-teacher conferences may give teachers an opportunity to discover how parents feel. Some centers formally include parents' evaluation of teachers in yearly reviews.

Children do some evaluating as shown in their behavior when they feel free to express their feelings.

Self-evaluation is very important, possibly the most important form of evaluation. Some centers use videotaping to assist teachers in self-evaluation. Self-evaluation enables teachers to pull together all the different kinds of evaluation and gain from them.

The NAEYC accreditation criteria state, "At least annually, parents, staff, and other professionals are involved in evaluating the program's effectiveness in meeting the needs of children and parents."[12]

BECOMING A PROFESSIONAL IN THE FIELD OF EARLY CHILDHOOD EDUCATION

It takes time and experience to become a professional in the field of early childhood education, and the process continues through one's working life. Much depends on circumstances and on opportunities. One person may begin teaching in a very favorable situation with plenty of support and inspiration from working with good teachers as models. It may be hard work with many discouraging moments, but teaching becomes more and more interesting each year. Another person may find it harder to become confident and competent but should find the effort worth it in the end.

[11]National Association for the Education of Young Children. (1984). *Accreditation criteria and procedures: Position Statement of the National Academy of Early Childhood Programs*. Washington, DC: Author.
[12]Ibid.

We do not always see clearly the progress we have made. A successful episode in handling two aggressive boys; the development of an exciting new curriculum unit; a gratifying conference with a troubled parent; an exciting regional workshop with new ideas—any or all of these experiences add to our growth as a professional.

A student teacher once predicted that she would feel professional "when I have it all together." Her master teacher replied, "Then that might be *never*. Just as with children's development, our professional development is a process, not a product."

Projects

1. Arrange to attend a staff meeting in a center. Observe how ideas are introduced, the process of decision making, and how involved the staff members appear to be.
2. Make an appointment to "shadow" a center's director for at least one hour. Make notes on the several kinds of activities and responsibilities you see being carried out, in terms of planning, leading, evaluating, and any other.
3. In a center where you participate, note some ways in which teachers get help in staying "alive" professionally. How does the center encourage staff development activities?
4. Interview someone who has worked in early childhood education for more than ten years to find out why the person chose the profession, what kinds of work she has done in the field, what she sees as problems and new trends in the field, or something else that interests you.

For Your Further Reading

Katz, L. G. (1972). Developmental stages of preschool teachers. *Elementary School Journal*, *23*(1) 50–54. Describes stages teacher may go through as they progress in their career, along with kinds of support and training needed in each stage.

Katz, L. G. (1984). The professional early childhood teacher. *Young Children*, *39*(5), 3–10. Describes behaviors of professional, nonprofessional, and unprofessional teachers in relation to what is being learned by children.

National Association for the Education of Young Children. (1984). *Accreditation criteria and procedures: Position statement of the National Academy of Early Childhood Programs*. Washington, DC: Author. Guidelines for quality programs, the basis for the center accreditation process started by NAEYC in 1984. Every early childhood teacher should be acquainted with this publication.

Seaver, J. W., Cartwright, C. A., Ward, C. B., & Heasley, C. A. (1984).*Careers with young children: Making your decision* (rev. ed.). Washington, DC: National Association for the Education of Young Children. Helpful workbook to assist in choosing an early childhood career; gives examples of careers in five different strands and a large number of job titles.

Ward, E. (1977). A code of ethics: The hallmark of a profession. In B. Spodek (Ed.). *Teaching practices: Reexamining assumptions.* Pp. 65–69. Washington, DC: National Association for the Education of Young Children. One of the first— and best—written codes of ethics for early childhood education.

Whitebrook, M., Howes, C., Darrah, R., & Friedman, J. (1982). Caring for the care-givers: Staff burnout in child care. In L. G. Katz (Ed.). *Current topics in early childhood education* (Vol. 4). Pp. 211–235. Norwood, NJ: ABLEX. Examines factors that lead to staff burnout; based on their survey of child-care teachers.

House, Sun, and Sky (girl, 3 years 9 months)

24 ◆ Accepting Our Common Responsibilities

We live in a democratic nation with a Constitution and a Bill of Rights. With rights go responsibilities for all of us as citizens. Among our common responsibilities are those relating to families and children. There have been many changes in this century. Many of these have benefited families. Others have created new problems.

Research has greatly increased our knowledge in many areas. How much of this research has advanced our knowledge about the development of children? How much more do we know about their needs for healthy growth and the development of their capacities? How much of this knowledge is made easily available to those caring for young children?

How much is society doing to implement what we know so that all children may grow up in favorable environments? What standards exist, and how are they enforced? These are some of the questions that need to be raised, and we share this responsibility. Parents, teachers, employees, the business world, the general public, and the government need to be concerned.

In a period with rapid changes such as we have experienced, education plays an important role in helping people meet changes, adapt, and learn. Throughout this book we have been looking for ways to increase our understanding of children and the ways in which they grow and learn. We have found that observing them will teach us a great deal about human behavior, and that, if we are to handle children wisely, we must understand something about ourselves. The kind of people we are influences what we do for children.

The longer we study, the more we appreciate the complexities of human behavior, and the more we hesitate to propose ready-made formulas for solving problems or setting standards as to what an individual child ought or ought not do.

We have taken a big step forward when we have learned to *observe* children, to recognize the *uniqueness* of each individual, to search for the *meaning behind an act, to accept the child and have confidence in his potential growth*. We have taken a big step when we have learned to make our contribution to the child through reducing the difficulty of the problems he must face, through enriching his experiences, through providing him with optimum opportunities for learning, and through helping him to find avenues for creative satisfactions, rather than by depending on admonition and interference. We can assume responsibility for defining and maintaining limits for the child's behavior with confidence because we understand better his developmental needs.

Research findings have called attention to the importance of infancy and toddlerhood in giving direction to development, not only in physical growth but in intellectual and personality growth as well. Healthy parental bonds established in this sensitive period influence all aspects of development. Yet very few employers are willing to give women leave, paid or unpaid, for up to six months or a year to take care of a baby. Many mothers feel that they cannot afford to take such leave, either because of the needed earnings or because their job status would be in jeopardy.

We also have evidence that opportunities to play with other children are essential for sound personality development. Play alone as well as play with adults and children helps the child resolve emotional problems arising out of the developmental process itself. In the early years play is a most effective mode of learning. Play, to be of most use to the child, needs the guidance of an adult who is aware of its possibilities and a group small enough for the adult to build a relationship of trust with each child. The early years are the important ones for learning and for personality development.

While interest in early childhood education grows steadily along with a demand for it, there is a serious shortage of well-trained teachers for young children.[1] Teacher education programs are at risk because of reduced budgets. This problem exists primarily because of the low pay and low status in this field. Licensing standards deteriorate when teacher shortages exist. The gravity of this situation demands state and local help.

The nutritional status of children who live in families below the poverty line has been declining through the 1980s as federal food programs have been reduced.[2] Many of these families have unemployed adults, and all the members of these families suffer.

Some changes have been beneficial such as the improved status of women and greater educational opportunities, along with conveniences that can lighten housework. Other changes have not been beneficial, such as crowding in the cities with problems of pollution, lack of adequate decent housing, lack of parks, playgrounds, and public transportation. Through the centuries parents have been concerned about the welfare of their children, but today individual parents may be less able than those in the past to provide their children with a healthy environment. Families are in need of more support if they are to fulfill their functions well.

Schools are an important part of a community. To the extent that a community plans its facilities and services well, it benefits its schools, for the school does not exist as an agency apart from the community. It suffers as a result of divisions and conflicts among citizens. Schools are nurtured by their community, and they in turn nurture community life.

Today's citizens are interested in dealing with problems as they become aware of them. Some businesses have begun to provide child care for the young children of their employees or provide an allowance to help with the fees employees pay for child care. A few centers near retirement homes have encouraged contacts between senior citizens there who enjoy children and welcome the opportunity to become "grandparents" for interested children. More citizens are taking an active part in the effort to find solutions to problems such as air pollution or dangers in the disposal of nuclear waste, for example, or the burden the rapidly growing budget deficit poses for us and for future generations.

The National Association for the Education of Young Children has taken an important step in its efforts to raise standards in the field of early childhood education. In 1984 it published a position statement dealing

[1]*Child Care Employee News*, Summer/Fall 1985.
[2]Children's Defense Fund. (1984). *A children's defense budget: An analysis of the president's FY 1985 budget and children*. Washington, DC: Author.

with standards of early childhood programs.[3] It is not enough just to provide care for young children, but we must also aim for quality care in all programs. This publication outlines the criteria for high quality early childhood education programs, based on the best knowledge we have at present.

Only as we continue to study children and learn from them and as we try to understand ourselves better, can we expect to judge what will benefit each individual child. Our concern should include all children.

As students, teachers, and parents we must accept the challenge put to us by Chisholm[4] almost half a century ago: "Dare any of us say that he or she can do nothing about the desperate need of the world for better human relationships?"

For Your Further Reading

Friedman, D. (1983). *Encouraging employer support to working parents: Community strategies for change*. New York: Center for Public Advocacy Research. Trends, strategies, and resources for building good programs for young children with employer support.

Hymes, J. L., Jr. (1985). *Early childhood education: The year in review, a look at 1984*. Carmel, CA: Hacienda Press. Each of the fourteen annual editions provides valuable reading for information on key trends in early education in the past year.

National Association for the Education of Young Children. (1984). *Accreditation criteria and procedures: Position statement of the National Academy of Early Childhood Programs*. Washington, DC: Author. In accepting our common responsibilities, we can rely on these criteria to provide a vision of excellence in early childhood programs.

Washington, V., & Oyemade, U. J. (1985). Changing family trends: Head Start must respond. *Young Children, 40*(6), 12–19. Head Start must make changes to adapt to family changes, like the feminization of poverty, teenage parenting, employed mothers, and continued long-term poverty.

Werner, E. E. (1984). *Child care: Kith, kin, and hired hands*. Baltimore, MD: University Park Press. Implications of alternate caregiving for parents, social policy, and social action. The child care debate will be stimulated by the predictions in this book.

---

[3]National Association for the Education of Young Children. (1984). *Accreditation criteria and procedures: Position Statement of the National Academy of Early Childhood Programs*. Washington, DC: Author.

[4]B. Chisholm (January, 1949). Social responsibility. *Science*.

Bibliography

Abt Associates. (1978). *National day care study: Preliminary findings and their implications.* Cambridge, MA: Author.

Ad Hoc Day Care Coalition. (1985). *The crisis in infant and toddler care.* Washington, DC: National Association for the Education of Young Children.

Adams, C., & Fay, J. (1981). *No more secrets: Protecting your child from sexual assault.* San Luis Obispo, CA: Impact Publishers.

Adams, L., & Garlick, B. (Eds.). (1979). *Ideas that work with young children* (Vol. 2). Washington, DC: National Association for the Education of Young Children.

Ade, W. (1982). Professionalization and its implications for the field of early childhood education, *Young Children, 37*(3), 25-32.

Adolf, B., & Rose, K. (1982). *Child care and the working parent: First steps toward employer involvement in child care.* New York: Children at Work.

Alexander, D. (1983). *Children's computer drawings.* Urbana, IL: ERIC Clearinghouse on Elementary and Early Childhood Education (ED 238 562).

Alger, H. A. (1984). Transitions: Alternatives to manipulative management techniques. *Young Children, 39*(6), 16-25. Also in J. F. Brown (Ed.). (1984). *Administering programs for young children.* Pp. 89-97. Washington, DC: National Association for the Education of Young Children.

Allen, K. E. (1980). Research in review: Mainstreaming: what have we learned? *Young Children, (35)*5, 54-63.

Almy, M. (Ed.). (1968). *Early childhood play: Selected readings related to cognition and motivation.* New York: Simon and Schuster.

Almy, M. (1975). *The early childhood educator at work.* New York: McGraw Hill.

Almy, M. (1984). A child's right to play. *Young Children, 39*(4), 80. Also in J. F. Brown (Ed.). (1984). *Administering programs for young children,* p. 68. Washington, DC: National Association for the Education of Young Children.

Almy, M., & Genishi, C. (1979). *Ways of studying children: An observation manual for early childhood teachers* (rev. ed.). New York: Teachers College.

Alston, F. K. (1984). *Caring for other people's children: A complete guide to family day care.* Baltimore, MD: University Park Press.

American Montessori Society. (n.d.). *Accredited teacher preparation programs.* New York: Author.

Andress, B. (1980). *Music experiences in early childhood.* New York: Holt, Rinehart and Winston.

Anglin, L. W., Goldman, R., & Anglin, J. S. (1982). *Teaching: What it's all about.* New York: Harper & Row.

Arnstein, H. (1978). *What to tell your child: About birth, illness, death, divorce and other family crises.* New York: Condor.

Aronoff, F. W. (1969). *Music and young children.* New York: Holt, Rinehart and Winston.

Ashton-Warner, S. (1963). *Teacher.* New York: Simon and Schuster.

Association for Childhood Education International. (1962). *Report of colloquy on basic human values for childhood education.* Washington, DC: Author.

Auerbach, S. (1982). *Choosing child care: A guide for parents.* San Francisco: Institute for Childhood Resources.

Axline, V. (1964). *Dibs: In search of self.* Boston: Houghton Mifflin.

Baden, R. K., Genser, A., Levine, J. A., & Seligson, M. (1983). *School-age child care: An action manual.* Boston: Auburn House.

Baker, K. R. (1966). *Let's play outdoors.* Washington, DC: National Association for the Education of Young Children.

Baker, K. R. (Ed.). (1972). *Ideas that work with young children*. Washington, DC: National Association for the Education of Young Children.

Balaban, N. (1985). *Starting school: From separation to independence (A guide for early childhood teachers)*. New York: Teachers College.

Baratta-Lorton, M. (1976). *Mathematics their way*. Reading, MA: Addison-Wesley.

Baskin, L., & Spencer, M. (1983). *Microcomputers in early childhood education*. Urbana, IL: ERIC Clearinghouse on Elementary and Early Childhood Education (ED 227 967).

Baumrind, D. (1972). Socialization and instrumental competence in young children. In W. W. Hartup (Ed.). *The young child: Reviews of research* (Vol. 2). Pp. 202–224. Washington, DC: National Association for the Education of Young Children.

Bayless, K. M., & Ramsey, M. E. (1978). *Music: A way of life for the young child*. St. Louis, MO: C. V. Mosby.

Bell, D. R., & Low, L. M. (1977). *Observing and recording children's behavior*. Richland, WA: Performance Associates.

Belsky, J., & Steinberg, L. D. (1978). The effects of day care: A critical review. *Child Development, 49*, 929–949.

Bentzen, W. R. (1985). *Seeing young children: A guide to observing and recording behavior*. Albany, NY: Delmar.

Berger, E. H. (1981). *Parents as partners in education: The school and home working together*. St. Louis, MO: C. V. Mosby.

Berne, P. H. & Savary, L. M. (1985). *Building self-esteem in children*. New York: Continuum Publishing.

Bernstein, J. E. (1977). Helping young children cope with death. In L. G. Katz (Ed.). *Current topics in early childhood education* (Vol. 1). Pp. 179–189. Norwood, NJ: ABLEX.

Berrueta-Clement, J. R., Schweinhart, L. J., Barnett, W. S., Epstein, A. S., & Weikart, D. P. (1984). *Changed lives: The effects of the Perry Preschool Program on youths through age 19*. Ypsilanti, MI: High/Scope.

Bettelheim, B. (1976). *The uses of enchantment*. New York: Alfred A. Knopf.

Biber, B. (1967). *Young deprived children and their educational needs*. Washington, DC: Association for Childhood Education International.

Biber, B. (1977). A view of preschool education. In B. D. Boegehold, H. K. Cuffaro, W. H. Hooks, & G. J. Klopf (Eds.). *Education before five*. New York: Teachers College.

Biber, B. (1985). *Early education and psychological development*. New Haven: Yale University Press.

Bibliography of Books for Children Committee. (1984). *Bibliography of books for children*. Washington, DC: Association for Childhood Education International.

Blackwelder, S. R. (1980). *Science for all seasons: Science experiences for young children*. Englewood Cliffs, NJ: Prentice-Hall.

Blank, M. (1974). Cognitive functions of language in the preschool years. *Developmental Psychology, 10*(2).

Blau, R., Brady, E. H., Bucher, I., Hiteshew, B., Zavitkovsky, A., & Zavitkovsky, D. (1977). *Activities for school-age child care*. Washington, DC: National Association for the Education of Young Children.

Blom, G. E., Cheney, B. D., & Snoddy, J. E. (1986). *Stress in childhood: An intervention model for teachers and other professionals*. New York: Teachers College.

Boegehold, B. D., Cuffaro, H. K., Hooks, W. H., & Klopf G. J. (Eds.). (1977). *Education before five*. New York: Teachers College.

Bos, B. J. (1978). *Don't move the muffin tins: A hands-off guide to art for the young child*. Carmichael, CA: The Burton Gallery.

Bos, B. J. (1983). *Before the basics: Creating conversations with children*. Roseville, CA: Turn the Page Press.

Bowlby, J. (1975). *Separation anxiety: A critical review of the literature*. New York: Child Welfare League of America.

Bowlby, J. (1982). Attachment and loss: Retrospects and prospect. *American Journal of Orthopsychiatry, 52*(4), 664–678.

Bradbard, M. R., & Endsley, R. C. (1978). Developing a parent guide to quality day care centers. *Child Care Quarterly, 7*(4), 279–288.

Bradbard, M. R., & Endsley, R. C. (1979). What do licensers say to parents who ask their help with selecting quality day care? *Child Care Quarterly, 8*(4), 307–312.

Brady, E. H., & Hill, S. (1984). Research in review: Young children and microcomputers: Research issues and directions. *Young Children, 39*(3), 49–61.

Braun, S. J., & Edwards, E. P. (1972). *History and theory of early childhood education.* Worthington, OH: Charles A. Jones.

Brazelton, T. B. (1974). *Toddlers and parents: A declaration of independence.* New York: Delacorte.

Brazelton, T. B. (1981). *On becoming a family.* New York: Delacorte.

Brazelton, T. B. (1983). *Infants and mothers: Differences in development.* New York: Delacorte.

Brazelton, T. B. (1984). *To listen to a child: Understanding the normal problems of growing up.* Reading, MA: Addison-Wesley.

Brazelton, T. B. (1985). *Working and caring.* Reading, MA: Addison-Wesley.

Brearley, M. (Ed.). (1970). *The teaching of young children: Some applications of Piaget's learning theory.* New York: Schocken Books.

Brearley, M., & Hitchfield, E. (1966). *A guide to reading Piaget.* New York: Schocken Books.

Briggs, D. C. (1970). *Your child's self-esteem: The key to his life.* Garden City, NY: Doubleday.

Brittain, W. L. (1979). *Creativity, art and the young child.* New York: Macmillan.

Bromwich, R. (1981). *Working with parents and infants: An interactional approach.* Baltimore, MD: University Park Press.

Brown, B. (1985). Head Start: How research changed public policy. *Young Children, 40*(5), 9–13.

Brown, J. F. (Ed.). (1982). *Curriculum planning for young children.* Washington, DC: National Association for the Education of Young Children.

Brown, J. F. (Ed.). (1984). *Administering programs for young children.* Washington, DC: National Association for the Education of Young Children.

Brown, N. S., Curry, N. E., & Tittnich, E. (1971). How groups of children handle common stress through play. In N. E. Curry, & S. Arnaud (Eds.). *Play: The child strives toward self-realization.* Pp. 26–38. Washington, DC: National Association for the Education of Young Children.

Bruner, J. S. (1966). *Toward a theory of instruction.* Cambridge, MA: Harvard University Press.

Burg, K. (1984). The microcomputer in the kindergarten. *Young Children, 39*(3), 28–33.

Burket, L. L. (1981). *Positive parental involvement in the area of reading during preschool years and primary grades.* Urbana, IL: ERIC Clearinghouse on Reading and Communication Skills (ED 216 324).

Burtt, K. G., & Kalkstein, K. (1981). *Smart toys for babies from birth to two.* New York: Harper & Row.

Burud, S., Aschbacher, P., & McCroskey, J. (1984). *Employer supported child care: Investing in human resources.* Boston: Auburn House.

Butler, D., & Clay, M. (1979). *Reading begins at home.* Exeter, NH: Heineman.

Bynum, B. J. (1982). *How parents can help their children in reading.* Urbana, IL: ERIC Clearinghouse on Reading and Communication Skills (ED 218 588).

Caldwell, B. (1977). Aggression and hostility in young children. *Young Children, 32*(2), 4–13.

Caldwell, B. (1984). One step forward, two steps back. *Young Children, 39*(5), 48–50.

Caldwell, B. M., & Freyer, M. (1983). How can we educate the American public about the child care profession? *Young Children, 38*(3), 11–17.

Caldwell, B. M., & Hilliard, A. G. III. (1985). *What is quality child care?* Washington, DC: National Association for the Education of Young Children.

Campbell, P. F., & Fein, G. G. (1986). *Young children and microcomputers.* Englewood Cliffs, NJ: Prentice-Hall.

Carlsson-Paige, N., & Levin, D. E. (1985). *Helping children understand peace, war and the nuclear threat.* Washington, DC: National Association for the Education of Young Children.

Carlsson-Paige, N., & Levin, D. E. (1986). The Butter Battle Book: Uses and abuses with young children. *Young Children, 41*(3), 37-42.

Cataldo, C. Z. (1986). *Parent education for early childhood.* New York: Teachers College.

Cataldo, C. Z. (1983). *Infant and toddler programs: A guide to very early childhood education.* Reading, MA: Addison-Wesley.

Catron, C. E., & Kendall, E. D. (1984). Staff evaluation that promotes growth and problem solving. *Young Children, 39*(6), 61-66. Also in J. F. Brown (Ed.). *Administering programs for young children.* Washington, D.C.: National Association for the Education of Young Children.

Cazden, C. B. (Ed.). (1981). *Language in early childhood education* (rev. ed.). Washington, DC: National Association for the Education of Young Children.

Cazden, C. B., Baratz, J. C., Labov, W., & Palmer, F. H. (1981). Language development in day care programs. In C. B. Cazden (Ed.). (1981). *Language in early childhood education.* (rev. ed.). Pp. 107-125. Washington, DC: National Association for the Education of Young Children.

Cazden, C., Bryant, B., & Tillman, M. (1981). Making it and going home: The attitudes of Black people toward language education. In C. B. Cazden (Ed.). (1981). *Language in early childhood education* (rev. ed.). Pp. 97-106. Washington, DC: National Association for the Education of Young Children.

CDA National Credentialing Program. (n.d.). *The child development credential.* Washington, DC: Author.

Chall, J. S. (1983). *Stages of reading development.* New York: McGraw-Hill.

Chattin-McNichols, J. P. (1981). The effects of Montessori school experience. *Young Children, 36*(5), 49-66.

Cherry, C. (1971). *Creative movement for the developing child: A nursery school handbook for non-musicians* (rev. ed.). Belmont, CA: Fearon.

Cherry, C. (1972). *Creative art for the developing child: A teacher's handbook for early childhood education.* Belmont, CA: Fearon.

Cherry, C. (1976). *Creative play for the developing child: Early lifehood education through play.* Belmont, CA: Fearon.

Cherry, C. (1981). *Think of something quiet: A guide for achieving serenity in early childhood classrooms.* Belmont, CA: Pitman Learning.

Cherry, C. (1983). *Please don't sit on the kids: Alternatives to punitive discipline.* Belmont, CA: Pitman Learning.

Children's Defense Fund. (1982). *Employed parents and their children.* Washington, DC: Author.

Children's Defense Fund. (1984). *A children's defense budget: An analysis of the president's FY1985 budget and children.* Washington, DC: Author.

Children's Defense Fund. (1985). *A children's defense budget: An analysis of the president's FY1986 budget and children.* Washington, DC: Author.

Children's Defense Fund. (1986). *A children's defense budget: An analysis of the president's FY1987 budget and children.* Washington, DC: Author.

Chisholm, B. (1949). Social responsibility. *Science, 109*, 27-30, 43.

Clarke-Stewart, A. (1982). *Daycare.* The developing child series. Cambridge, MA: Harvard University Press.

Clemens, S. G. (1983). *The sun's not broken, A cloud's just in the way.* Mt. Rainier, MD: Gryphon House.

Cleverley, J. F., & Phillips, D. C. (1986). *Visions of childhood: Influential models from Locke to Spock* (rev. ed.). New York: Teachers College.

Cohen, D., & Stern, V. (1983). *Observing and recording the behavior of young children* (4th ed.). New York: Teachers College.

Cook, J. T. (1985). *Child daycare.* Davis, CA: International Dialogue Press.

Cook, R. E., & Armbruster, V. B. (1983). *Adapting early childhood curricula: Suggestions for meeting special needs.* St. Louis, MO: C. V. Mosby.

Coopersmith, S. (1967). *The antecedents of self-esteem.* San Francisco: W. H. Freeman.

Council on Interracial Books for Children.

(1980). *Guidelines for selecting bias-free textbooks and storybooks*. New York: Author.

Council on Interracial Books for Children. (1983). Counteracting bias in early childhood education. *Interracial Books for Children Bulletin, 14*(7 & 8).

Croft, D. J. (1976). *Be honest with yourself: A self-evaluation handbook for early childhood education teachers*. Belmont, CA: Wadsworth.

Croft, D. J., & Hess, R. D. (1985). *An activities handbook for teachers of young children* (4th ed.). Boston: Houghton Mifflin.

Cuffaro, H. (1974). Dramatic play: The experience of block building. In E. Hirsch, (Ed.). (1974). *The block book*. Pp. 69–87. Washington, DC: National Association for the Education of Young Children.

Cuffaro, H. K. (1984). *Microcomputers in education: Why is earlier better?* Teachers College Record, *85*(4).

Curran, D. (1983). *Traits of a healthy family*. Minneapolis, MN: Winston Press.

Curran, D. (1985). *Stress and the healthy family*. Minneapolis, MN: Winston Press.

Curry, N. E., & Arnaud, S. (1971). *Play: The child strives toward self-realization*. Washington, DC: National Association for the Education of Young Children.

Curry, N. E., & Tittnich, E. M. (1975). *Ready or not, here we come: The dilemma of school readiness* (rev. ed.). Pittsburgh: University of Pittsburgh, Arsenal Family and Children's Center.

Davidson, J. (1980). Wasted time: The ignored dilemma. *Young Children, 35*(4), 13–21.

Day, D. E., & Sheehan, R. (1979). Elements of a better preschool. In L. Adams, & B. Garlick (Eds.). *Ideas that work with young children* (Vol. 2). Pp. 219–227. Washington, DC: National Association for the Education of Young Children.

Day, M. S., & Parker, R. K. (Eds.). (1977). *The preschool in action: Early childhood programs* (2nd ed.). Boston: Allyn and Bacon.

de Villiers, P. A., & de Villiers, J. G. (1979). *Early language*. The developing child series. Cambridge, MA: Harvard University Press.

Dittmann, L. L. (Ed.). (1977). *Curriculum is what happens* (rev. ed.). Washington, DC: National Association for the Education of Young Children.

Dittman, L. L. (Ed.). (1984). *The infants we care for*. Washington, DC: National Association for the Education of Young Children.

Dittmann, L. L. (1985). *Finding the best care for your infant or toddler*. Washington, DC: National Association for the Education of Young Children.

Dixon, G. T., & Fraser, S. (1986). Teaching preschoolers in a multilingual classroom. *Childhood Education, 62*(4), 272–275.

Donaldson, M. (1978). *Children's minds*. New York: W. W. Norton.

Dunn, J. (1977). *Distress and comfort*. The developing child series. Cambridge, MA: Harvard University Press.

Dunn, J. (1985). *Sisters and brothers*. The developing child series. Cambridge, MA: Harvard University Press.

Early Childhood and Literary Development Committee of the International Reading Association. (1986). Literacy development and pre-first grade. *Young Children, 41*(4), 10–13.

Edwards, C. P. (1986). *Promoting social and moral development in young children: Creative approaches for the classroom*. New York: Teachers College.

Elkind, D. (1981). *The hurried child: Growing up too fast too soon*. Reading, MA: Addison-Wesley.

Elkind, D. (1986). Formal education and early childhood education: An essential difference. *Phi Delta Kappan, 67*(9), 631–636.

Elkind, D. (1986). *The miseducation of children: Superkids at risk*. New York: Alfred A. Knopf.

Emlen, A. C. (1982). *When parents are at work: A three-company survey of how employed parents arrange child care*. Urbana, IL: ERIC Clearinghouse for Elementary and Early Childhood Education (ED 230 265).

Endres, J. B., & Rockwell, R. E. (1980). *Food, nutrition, and the young child*. St. Louis, MO: Times Mirror/Mosby.

Endsley, R. C., & Bradbard, M. R. (1981). *Quality day care: A handbook of choices for parents and caregivers*. Englewood Cliffs, NJ: Prentice-Hall.

Engstrom, G. (Ed.). (1971). *The significance of the young child's motor development*. Washington, DC: National Association for the Education of Young Children.

ERIC Clearinghouse on Reading and Communication Skills. (1983). *Children's books, 1982: A list of books for preschool through junior high school age*. Urbana, IL: ERIC Clearinghouse on Reading and Communication Skills (ED 229 780).

Erikson, E. H. (1963). *Childhood and society* (2nd ed.). New York: W. W. Norton.

Esbensen, S. B. (1986). *Hidden hazards on playgrounds for young children*. Ypsilanti, MI: High/Scope.

Evans, J., & Ilfeld, E. (1982). *Good beginnings: Parenting in the early years*. Ypsilanti, MI: High/Scope.

Faber, A., & Mazlish, E. (1980). *How to talk so kids will listen and listen so kids will talk*. New York: Avon.

Fassler, J. (1978). *Helping children cope: Mastering stress through books and stories*. New York: The Free Press.

Feeney, S., Christensen, D., & Moravcik, E. (1983). *Who am I in the lives of children?* Columbus, OH: Charles E. Merrill

Feeney, S., & Kipnis, K. (1985). Professional ethics in early childhood education. *Young Children, 40*(3), 54-57.

Feeney, S., & Margarick, M. (1984). Choosing good toys for young children. *Young Children, 40*(1), 21-25.

Flemming, B. M., Hamilton, D. S., & Hicks, J. D. (1977). *Resources for creative teaching in early childhood education*. New York: Harcourt Brace Jovanovich.

Forman, G. E., & Hill, F. (Eds.). (1984). *Constructive play: Applying Piaget in the preschool* (rev. ed.). Reading, MA: Addison-Wesley.

Forman, G. E., & Kuschner, D. S. (1983). *The child's construction of knowledge: Piaget for teaching children*. Washington, DC: National Association for the Education of Young Children.

Forsyth, I. (Ed.). (1983). *Language matters: Writing and the developing child*. London: The Ebury Teachers' Centre.

Fraiberg, S. (1959). *The magic years: Understanding and handling the problems of early childhood*. New York: Scribners.

Frede, E. (1984). *Getting involved: Workshops for parents*. Ypsilanti, MI: High/Scope.

Frede, E. (1985). How teachers grow: Four stages. *High Scope ReSource, 4*(1), 10-12.

Freedman, P. (1982). A comparison of multi-age and homogeneous age grouping in early childhood centers. In L. G. Katz (Ed.). *Current topics in early childhood education* (Vol. 4). Pp. 193-209. Norwood, NJ: ABLEX.

Freudenberger, H. J. (1977). Burnout: The occupational hazard of the child care worker. *Child Care Quarterly, 6*(2), 90-99.

Frick, R. (1986). Viewpoint 1: In support of academic redshirting. *Young Children, 41*(2), 9-10.

Friedman, D. (1983). *Encouraging employer support to working parents: Community strategies for change*. New York: Center for Public Advocacy Research.

Frost, J. L. (1986). Children in a changing society: Frontiers of challenge. *Childhood Education, 62*(4), 242-249.

Frost, J. L., & Henninger, M. L. (1979). Making playgrounds safe for children and children safe for playgrounds. *Young Children, 34*(4), 12-24. Also in D. W. Hewes (Ed.). (1979). *Administration: Making programs work for children and families*. Pp. 101-108. Washington, DC: National Association for the Education of Young Children.

Frost, J. L., & Klein, B. L. (1979). *Children's play and playgrounds*. Boston: Allyn and Bacon.

Furman, E. (1978). Helping children cope with death. *Young Children, 33*(4), 25-32. In J. F. Brown (Ed.). (1982). *Curriculum planning for young children*. Pp. 238-245. Washington, DC: National Association for the Education of Young Children.

Galinsky, E. (1982). *Between generations: The stages of parenthood*. New York: Berkley Books.

Garvey, C. (1977). *Play*. The developing child series. Cambridge, MA: Harvard University Press.

Garvey, C. (1984). *Children's talk*. The developing child series. Cambridge, MA: Harvard University Press.

Gerber, M. (Ed.). (1979). *Resources for infant education*. Los Angeles, CA: Resources for Infant Education.

Gilligan, C. (1982). *In a different voice: Psychological theory and women's development*. Cambridge, MA: Harvard University Press.

Gilstrap, R. (Ed.). (1981). *Toward self-discipline: A guide for parents and educators*. Washington, DC: Association for Childhood Education International.

Glazer, J., & Williams, G. (1979). *Introduction to children's literature*. New York: McGraw-Hill.

Goelmann, H., Oberg, A., & Smith, F. (Eds.) (1984). *Awakening to literacy*. Exeter, NH: Heinemann Educational Books.

Gonzalez-Mena, J. (1979). What is a good beginning? *Young Children, 34*(3), 47-53.

Gonzalez-Mena, J. (1981). English as a second language for preschool children. In C. B. Cazden (Ed.). (1981). *Language in early childhood education* (rev. ed.). Pp. 127-132. Washington, DC: National Association for the Education of Young Children.

Goodnow, J. (1977). *Children drawing*. The developing child series. Cambridge, MA: Harvard University Press.

Gottwald, S. R., Goldback, P., & Isack, A. H. (1985). Stuttering: Prevention and detection. *Young Children, 41*(1), 9-14.

Greenberg, M. (1979). *Your children need music: A guide for parents and teachers of young children*. Englewood Cliffs, NJ: Prentice-Hall.

Greenfield, P. M. (1984). *Mind and media: The effects of television, video games, and computers*. The developing child series. Cambridge, MA: Harvard University Press.

Greenman, J. T., & Fuqua, R. W. (Eds.). (1984). *Making day care better: Training, evaluation and the process of change*. New York: Teachers College.

Griego, M. C., Bucks, B. L., Gilbert, S., & Kimball, L. (1981). *Tortillitas para mama*. New York: Holt, Rinehart and Winston.

Grollman, E. A. (Ed.). (1967). *Explaining death to children*. Boston: Beacon Press.

Grollman, E. A. (1976). *Talking about death: A dialogue between parent and child*. Boston: Beacon Press.

Gutek, G. L. (1968). *Pestalozzi and education*. New York: Random House.

Haines, J. E., & Gerber, L. L. (1984). *Leading young children to music: A resource book for teachers* (2nd ed.). Columbus, OH: Charles E. Merrill.

Hall, E. T. (1966). *The hidden dimension*. Garden City, NY: Doubleday.

Hammond, C. H. (1986). "Not ready! Don't rush me!" *Childhood Education, 62*(4), 276-280.

Harms, T. (1979). Evaluating settings for learning. *Young Children, 25*(5), 304-306, 308. Also in D. W. Hewes (Ed.). *Administration: Making programs work for children and families*. Pp. 187-190. Washington, DC: National Association for the Education of Young Children.

Harms, T., & Clifford, R. (1980). *Early childhood environmental rating scale*. New York: Teachers College.

Hartup, W. W. (Ed.). (1972). *The young child: Reviews of research* (Vol. 2.). Washington, DC: National Association for the Education of Young Children.

Hartup, W. W., & Smothergill, L. (Eds.). (1967). *The young child: Reviews of research* (Vol. 1). Washington, DC: National Association for the Education of Young Children.

Haswell, K. L., Hock, E., & Wenar, C. (1982). Techniques for dealing with oppositional behavior in preschool children. *Young*

Children, 37(3), 12–18. Also in J. F. Brown (Ed.). (1982). *Curriculum planning for young children.* Pp. 221–227. Washington, DC: National Association for the Education of Young Children.

Hatch, N. (1977). A revised workweek for caregivers. *Day Care and Early Education, 4*(3), 15–16.

Hazen, N., Black, B., & Fleming-Johnson, F. (1984). Social acceptance: Strategies children use and how teachers can help children learn them. *Young Children, 39*(6), 26–36.

Heilman, H. (1954). *An experimental study of the effects of workbooks on the creative drawing of second grade children.* Unpublished doctoral dissertation, The Pennsylvania State University.

Hendrick, J. (1984). *The whole child: Early education for the eighties* (3rd ed.). St. Louis, MO: Times Mirror/Mosby.

Hendrick, J. (1984). What makes a good day for children? In J. Hendrick (Ed.). (1984). *The whole child: Early education for the eighties* (3rd ed.). St. Louis, MO: Times Mirror/Mosby.

Hendrick, J. (1986). *Total learning for the whole child: Holistic curriculum for children ages 2 to 5* (2nd ed.). Columbus, OH: Charles E. Merrill.

Herr, J., & Morse, W. (1982). Food for thought: Nutrition education for young children. *Young Children, 38*(1), 3–11.

Hess, R., & Croft, D. (1983). *Teachers of young children* (3rd ed.). Boston: Houghton Mifflin.

Hewes, D. W. (Ed.). (1979). *Administration: Making programs work for children and families.* Washington, DC: National Association for the Education of Young Children.

Hill, D. M. (1977). *Mud, sand, and water.* Washington, DC: National Association for the Education of Young Children.

Hirsch, E. S. (1971). *Transition periods, stumbling blocks of education.* New York: Early Childhood Education Council of New York City.

Hirsch, E. S. (1983). *Problems of early childhood:*

An annotated bibliography and guide. New York: Garland.

Hirsch, E. S. (Ed.). (1984). *The block book* (rev. ed.). Washington, DC: National Association for the Education of Young Children.

Hohmann, M. (1983). *Study guide to "Young children in action."* Ypsilanti, MI: High/Scope Press.

Hohmann, M., Banet, B., & Weikart, D. P. (1979). *Young children in action: A manual for preschool educators.* Ypsilanti, MI: High/Scope Press.

Holdaway, D. (1979). *The foundations of literacy.* New York: Ashton Scholastic.

Holt, B. G. (1977). *Science with young children.* Washington, DC: National Association for the Education of Young Children.

Honig, A. S. (1979). *Parent involvement in early childhood education* (rev. ed.). Washington, DC: National Association for the Education of Young Children.

Honig, A. S. (1983). Research in review: Television and young children. *Young Children, 38*(4), 63–76.

Honig, A. S. (1983). TV violence and child aggression: Research review. *Day Care and Early Education, 10*(4), 41–45.

Honig, A. S. (1985). *Love and learn: Discipline for young children.* Washington, DC: National Association for the Education of Young Children.

Honig, A. S. (1985). Research in review: Compliance, control and discipline. (Part I). *Young Children, 40*(2), 50–58.

Honig, A. S. (1985). Research in review: Compliance, control and discipline. (Part II). *Young Children, 40*(3), 47–52.

Honig, A. S. (1986). Research in review: Stress and coping in children. (Part I). *Young Children, 41*(4), 50–63.

Honig, A. S. (1986). Research in review: Stress and coping in children. (Part II). *Young Children, 41*(5), 47–59.

Honig, A. S., & Lally, J. R. (1981). *Infant caregiving: A design for training.* Syracuse, NY: Syracuse University Press.

Hoot, J. L. (Ed.). (1986). *Computers in early*

childhood education: Issues and practices. Englewood Cliffs, NJ: Prentice-Hall.

Hostetler, L. (1984). Public policy report: The nanny trap: Child care work today. *Young Children, 39*(2), 76-79.

Hostetler, L., & Klugman, E. (1982). Early childhood job titles: One step toward professional status. *Young Children, 37*(6), 13-22.

Howes, C. (1985). *Keeping current in child care research: An annotated bibliography.* Washington, DC: National Association for the Education of Young Children.

Hoyles, M. (Ed.). (1979). *Changing childhood.* An International Year of the Child publication. London: Writers and Readers Publishing Cooperative.

Huntington, H. E. (1939). *Let's go outdoors.* New York: Doubleday.

Hymes, J. L., Jr. (1958). *Behavior and misbehavior: A teacher's guide to action.* Englewood Cliffs, NJ: Prentice-Hall.

Hymes, J. L., Jr. (1974). *Effective home-school relations* (rev. ed.). Carmel, CA: Hacienda Press.

Hymes, J. L., Jr. (1975). *Early childhood education: An introduction to the profession.* Washington, DC: National Association for the Education of Young Children.

Hymes, J. L., Jr. (1978). *Living history interviews: Early childhood education.* Book 1: *Beginnings* (out of print). Book 2: *Care of the children of working mothers.* (1978). Book 3: *Reaching large numbers of children.* (1979). Carmel, CA: Hacienda Press.

Hymes, J. L., Jr. (1981). *Teaching the child under six* (3rd ed.). Columbus, OH: Charles E. Merrill.

Hymes, J. L., Jr. (1985). *Early childhood education: The year in review, A look at 1984.* Carmel, CA: Hacienda Press.

Hymes, J. L., Jr. (1986). *Early childhood education: The year in review: A look at 1985.* Carmel, CA: Hacienda Press.

Hyson, M. C. (1979). Lobster on the sidewalk: Understanding and helping children with fears. *Young Children, 34*(5), 54-60.

Hyson, M. C. (1982). Playing with kids all day: Job stress in early childhood education. *Young Children, 37*(2), 25-32.

Hyson, M. C., & Eyman, A. P. (1986). Approaches to computer literacy in early childhood teacher education. *Young Children, 41*(6), 54-59.

Isaacs, S. (1930. Reissued in 1966). *Intellectual growth in young children.* New York: Schocken Books.

Isaacs, S. (1929. Reissued in 1968). *The nursery years: The mind of the child from birth to six years.* New York: Schocken Books.

Isaacs, S. (1933. Reissued in 1972). *Social development in young children.* New York: Schocken Books.

Isenberg, J. P., & Jacobs, J. E. (1982). *Playthings as learning tools: A parents' guide.* New York: John Wiley.

Ives, S. B., Fassler, D., & Lash, M. (1985). *The divorce workbook: A guide for kids and families.* Burlington, VT: Waterfront Books.

Jervis, K. (Ed.) (1985). *A guide to attachment, separation and loss: Strategies for helping two to four year olds.* Los Angeles: Edna Reiss Memorial Trust.

Jewett, C. L. (1982). *Helping children cope with separation and loss.* Harvard, MA: The Harvard Common Press.

Johnson, H. M. (1972. Originally published 1928.). *Children in "The Nursery School."* New York: Agathon.

Jones, E. (1977). *Dimensions of teaching-learning environments: Handbook for teachers.* Pasadena, CA: Pacific Oaks College.

Jones, E. (Ed.). (1978). *Joys and risks in teaching young children.* Pasadena, CA: Pacific Oaks College.

Jones, E. (1978). Teacher education: Entertainment or interaction? *Young Children, 33*(3), 15-23.

Jones, E. (1986). *Teaching adults: An active learning approach.* Washington, DC: National Association for the Education of Young Children.

Jorde, P. (1982). *Avoiding burnout: Strategies for managing time, space, and people in early childhood education*. Washington, DC: Acropolis Books.

Kamii, C. (1982). *Number in preschool and kindergarten: Educational implications of Piaget's theory*. Washington, DC: National Association for the Education of Young Children.

Kamii, C. (1984). Obedience is not enough. *Young Children, 39*(4), 11-14.

Kamii, C. (1985). Leading primary education toward excellence: Beyond worksheets and drill. *Young Children, 40*(6), 3-9.

Kamii, C. (1985). *Young children reinvent arithmetic*. New York: Teachers College.

Kamii, C., & DeVries, R. (1976). *Piaget, children and number*. Washington, DC: National Association for the Education of Young Children.

Kamii, C., & DeVries, R. (1980). *Group games in early education: Implications of Piaget's theory*. Washington, DC: National Association for the Education of Young Children.

Katz, L. G. (1972). Developmental stages of preschool teachers. *Elementary School Journal, 23*(1), 50-54.

Katz, L. G. (1977). Challenges to early childhood educators. In L. G. Katz (Ed.). (1977). *Talks with teachers*. Pp. 57-66. Washington, DC: National Association for the Education of Young Children.

Katz, L. G. (Ed.). (1977). *Current topics in early childhood education* (Vol. 1). Norwood, NJ: ABLEX.

Katz, L. G. (1977). Education or excitement? In L. G. Katz (Ed.). (1977). *Talks with teachers*. Washington, DC: National Association for the Education of Young Children.

Katz, L. G. (1977). *Ethical issues in working with children*. Urbana IL: ERIC Clearinghouse on Elementary and Early Childhood Education (ED 144 681).

Katz, L. G. (1977). *Talks with teachers*. Washington, DC: National Association for the Education of Young Children.

Katz, L. G. (1977). Teachers in preschools: Problems and prospects. *International Journal of Early Childhood, 9*, 111-123. Also in

L. G. Katz (Ed.). (1977). *Talks with teachers*. Washington, DC: National Association for the Education of Young Children.

Katz, L. G. (Ed.). (1979). *Current topics in early childhood education* (Vol. 2). Norwood, NJ: ABLEX.

Katz, L. G. (1979). *Helping others learn to teach: Some principles and techniques for in-service educators*. Urbana, IL: ERIC Clearinghouse on Elementary and Early Childhood Education.

Katz, L. G. (Ed.). (1980). *Current topics in early childhood education* (Vol. 3). Norwood, NJ: ABLEX.

Katz, L. G. (1980). Mothering and teaching: Some significant distinctions. In L. G. Katz (Ed.). (1980). *Current topics in early childhood education* (Vol. 3). Pp. 47-63. Norwood, NJ: ABLEX.

Katz, L. G. (Ed.). (1982). *Current topics in early childhood education* (Vol. 4). Norwood NJ: ABLEX.

Katz, L. G. (Ed.). (1984). *Current topics in early childhood education* (Vol. 5). Norwood, NJ: ABLEX.

Katz, L. G. (1984). *More talks with teachers*. Urbana IL: ERIC Clearinghouse on Elementary and Early Childhood Education (ED 250 099).

Katz, L. G. (1984). The professional early childhood teacher. *Young Children, 39*(5), 3-10. Washington, DC: National Association for the Education of Young Children.

Katz, L. G. (Ed.). (1985). *Current topics in early childhood education* (Vol. 6). Norwood, NJ: ABLEX.

Katz, L. G., & Ward, E. (1978). *Ethical behavior in early childhood education*. Washington, DC: National Association for the Education of Young Children.

Kellogg, R. (1969). *Analyzing children's art*. Palo Alto, CA: National Press.

Kemmer, E. (1984). *Violence in the family: An annotated bibliography*. New York: Garland.

Kempe, R. S., and Kempe, C. H. (1978). *Child abuse*. The developing child series. Cambridge, MA: Harvard University Press.

Klaus, M., & Kennell, J. (1976). *Maternal-infant bonding*. St. Louis, MO: C. V. Mosby.

Klinman, D. G., & Kohl, R. (1984). *Fatherhood U.S.A.: The first national guide to programs, services, and resources for and about fathers*. New York: Garland.

Klinzing, D. G. (April, 1985). *A study of the behavior of children in a preschool equipped with computers*. Paper presented at the meeting of the American Educational Research Association, Chicago, IL.

Knowles, D. W., & Reeves, N. (1983). *But won't granny need her socks? Dealing effectively with children's concerns about death and dying*. Dubuque, IA: Kendall/Hunt.

Koblinsky, S. A. (1983). *Sexuality education for parents of young children: A facilitator training manual*. Fayetteville, NY: Ed-U Press.

Koblinsky, S., Atkinson, J., & Davis, S. (1980). Sex education with young children. *Young Children, 36*(1), 21-31. Also in J. F. Brown (Ed.). (1982). *Curriculum planning for young children*. Pp. 160-170. Washington, DC: National Association for the Education of Young Children.

Koblinsky, S., & Behana, N. (1984). Child sexual abuse: The educator's role in prevention, detection, and intervention. *Young Children, 39*(6), 3-15.

Kostelnik, M. J., Whiren, A. P., & Stein, L. C. (1986). Living with He-Man: Managing superhero fantasy play. *Young Children, 41*(4), 3-9.

Kotin, L., Crabtree, R. K., Aikman, W. F. (1981). *Legal handbook for day care centers*. Washington, DC: U.S. Department of Health and Human Services.

Kritchevsky, S., Prescott, E., with Walling, L. (1977). *Planning environments for young children: Physical space* (2nd ed.). Washington, DC: National Association for the Education of Young Children.

Krogh, S. L., & Lamme, L. L. (1985). "But what about sharing?" Children's literature and moral development. *Young Children, 40*(4), 48-51.

Kubie, L. S. (1948). The child's fifth freedom. *Child Study, 25*, 67-70, 88.

Kübler-Ross, E. (1983). *On children and death*. New York: Macmillan.

LaBarre, W. (1949). The age period of cultural fixation. *Mental Hygiene, 33*, 209-221.

Landreth, C. (1972). *Preschool learning and teaching*. New York: Harper & Row.

Languis, M., Sanders, T., & Tipps, S. (1980). *Brain and learning: Directions in early childhood education*. Washington, DC: National Association for the Education of Young Children.

Lark-Horovitz, B. (1976). *The art of the very young: An indicator of individuality*. Columbus, OH: Charles E. Merrill.

Lark-Horovitz, B., Lewis, H., & Luca, M. (1973). *Understanding children's art for better teaching*. Columbus, OH: Charles E. Merrill.

Larrick, N. (1982). *A parent's guide to children's reading*. New York: Bantam Books.

Lasky, L., & Mukerji, R. (1980). *Art: Basic for young children*. Washington, DC: National Association for the Education of Young Children.

Lazar, I., & Darlington, R. B. (1978). *Summary: Lasting effects after preschool: Final report to the Education Commission of the States*. Urbana, IL: ERIC Clearinghouse on Elementary and Early Childhood Education.

Lazar, I., & Darlington, R. B. (1982). Lasting effects of early education: A report from the Consortium for Longitudinal Studies. *Monographs of the Society for Research in Child Development. 47* (2-3, Serial No. 195).

Leach, P. (1981). *Your baby and child: From birth to age five*. New York: Alfred A. Knopf.

Lee, M. W. (1983). *Early childhood education and microcomputers*. Urbana, IL: ERIC Clearinghouse on Elementary and Early Childhood Education (ED 231 503).

Leeb-Lundberg, K. (1985). *Mathematics is more than counting*. Wheaton, MD: Association for Childhood Education International.

Leighton, D., & Kluckhorn, C. (1947). *Children of the people: The Navaho individual and his development*. Cambridge: Harvard University Press.

LeShan, E. (1978). *What's going to happen to me? When parents separate or divorce*. New York: Four Winds.

Lichtman, A. J., & Challinor, J. R. (Eds.).

(1979). *Kin and communities*. Washington, DC: Smithsonian Press.

Lickona, T. (1983). *Raising good children: Helping your child through the stages of moral development*. New York: Bantam Books.

Lipinski, J. M. (1983). *Competence, gender and preschoolers' free play choices when a microcomputer is present in the classroom*. Urbana, IL: ERIC Clearinghouse on Elementary and Early Childhood Education (ED 243 609).

Logue, M. E., Eheart, B. K., & Leavitt, R. L. (1986). Viewpoint: Staff training: What difference does it make? *Young Children, 41*(5), 8–9.

Lomax, E., Kagan, J., & Rosenkrantz, B. (1978). *Science and patterns of child care*. San Francisco: W. H. Freeman.

Long, S. M., & Batchelor, B. (Eds.). (1979). *When there is crisis: Helping children cope with change*. Terre Haute, IN: Indiana Association for the Education of Young Children.

Long, T. J. (1983). *Working parents, schools and children in self-care*. Urbana, IL: ERIC Clearinghouse on Elementary and Early Childhood Education (ED 238 552).

Long, T. J., and Long, L. (1983). *The handbook for latchkey children and their parents: A complete guide for latchkey kids and their working parents*. Urbana, IL: ERIC Clearinghouse on Elementary and Early Childhood Education (ED 245 569).

Lurie, R., & Neugebauer, R. (Eds.). (1982). *Caring for infants and toddlers: What works, what doesn't* (Vol. 2). Redmond, WA: Child Care Information Exchange.

Maccoby, E. E. (1980). *Social development: Psychological growth and the parent-child relationship*. New York: Harcourt Brace Jovanovich.

Magid, R. Y. (1983). *Child care initiatives for working parents: Why employers get involved*. New York: American Management Association.

Maier, H. (1969). *Three theories of child development*. New York: Harper & Row.

Marion, M. (1981). *Guidance of young children*. St. Louis, MO: C. V. Mosby

Maslach, C., & Pines, A. (1977). The burnout syndrome in the day care setting. *Child Care Quarterly, 6*(2), 100–113.

Mattingly, M. (1977). Introduction to symposium: Stress and burnout in child care. *Child Care Quarterly, 6*(2), 127–137.

McAfee, O. D. (1985). Research report: Circle time: Getting past "Two Little Pumpkins." *Young Children, 40*(6), 24–29,

McAfee, O. (1985). *Group time in early childhood centers: An exploratory study*. Urbana, IL: ERIC Clearinghouse on Elementary and Early Childhood Education (ED 251 243).

McCarthy, J., & May, C. R. (Eds.). (1974). *Providing the best for young children*. Washington, DC: National Association for the Education of Young Children.

McDonald, D. T. (1979). *Music in our lives: The early years*. Washington, DC: National Association for the Education of Young Children.

McMillan, M. (1919). *The nursery school*. New York: E. P. Dutton.

McNamee, A. S. (Ed.). (1982). *Children and stress: Helping children cope*. Washington, DC: Association for Childhood Education International.

McNeill, E., Allen, J., & Schmidt, V. (1975). *Cultural awareness for young children*. Dallas, TX: The Learning Tree.

McVickar, P. (1972). *Imagination: Key to human potential*. Washington, DC: National Association for the Education of Young Children.

Meddin, B. J., & Rosen, A. (1986). Child abuse and neglect: Prevention and reporting. *Young Children, 41*(4), 26–30.

Meek, M., et al. (1978). *The cool web: The pattern of children's reading*. New York: Atheneum.

Meisels, S. J. (1985). *Developmental screening in early childhood: A guide* (rev. ed.). Washington, DC: National Association for the Education of Young Children.

Miller, C. S. (1984). Building self-control: Discipline for young children. *Young Children, 40*(1), 15-19.

Mitchell, G. (1979). *The day care book: A guide for working parents to help them find the best possible day care for their children.* Briarcliff Manor, NY: Stein and Day.

Moore, S. (1977). Old and new approaches to preschool education. *Young Children, 33*(1), 69-72.

Moore, S. G., & Cooper, C. R. (1982). *The young child: Reviews of research* (Vol. 3). Washington, DC: National Association for the Education of Young Children.

Morado, C. (1986). Public policy report: Pre-kindergarten programs for 4-year-olds: Some key issues. *Young Children, 41*(5), 61-63.

Morado, C. (1986). Public policy report: Pre-kindergarten programs for 4-year-olds: State involvement in preschool education. *Young Children, 41*(6), 69-71.

Morgan, G., Curry, N., Endsley, R., Bradbard, M., Rashid, H., & Epstein, A. (1985). *Quality in early childhood programs: Four perspectives.* Ypsilanti, MI: High/Scope.

Moyer, J. (Ed.). (1985). *Selecting educational equipment and materials: For school and home.* Wheaton, MD: Association for Childhood Education International.

Mugge, D. (1976). Taking the routine out of routines. *Young Children, 31*(3), 209-217. Also in D. Hewes (Ed.). (1979). *Administration: Making programs work for children and families.* Pp. 89-95. Washington, DC: National Association for the Education of Young Children.

Murphy, L. B., & Leeper, E. M. (1970). *Away from bedlam.* DHEW Publication No. (OCD) 72-18. Washington, DC: U. S. Department of Health, Education, and Welfare, Office of Child Development.

Murphy, L. B., & Leeper, E. M. (1970). *Preparing for change.* DHEW Publication No. (OCD) 72-17. Washington, DC: U.S. Department of Health, Education and Welfare, Office of Child Development.

National Association for the Education of Young Children. (1981). Public policy report: Staff qualifications related to quality child care. In *Annual Editions: Early Childhood Education, 83/84.* (1983). Guilford, CT: Dushkin.

National Association for the Education of Young Children. (1982). *Business incentives for providing child care as a benefit to employees: Sources for further information.* Washington, DC: Author.

National Association for the Education of Young Children. (1982). *Early childhood teacher education guidelines for four- and five-year programs.* Washington, DC: Author.

National Association for the Education of Young Children. (1982). *What are the benefits of quality child care for preschool children?* Washington, DC: Author.

National Association for the Education of Young Children. (1983). *Careers in early childhood education.* Washington, DC: Author.

National Association for the Education of Young Children. (1983). *How to choose a good early childhood program.* Washington, DC: Author.

National Association for the Education of Young Children. (1984). *Accreditation criteria and procedures: Position statement of the National Academy of Early Childhood Programs.* Washington, DC: Author.

National Association for the Education of Young Children. (1984). *A beginner's bibliography.* Washington, DC: Author.

National Association for the Education of Young Children. (1984). *Como escoger on buen programa de educacion pre-escolar.* Washington, DC: Author.

National Association for the Education of Young Children. (1984). *How to plan and start a good early childhood program.* Washington, DC: Author.

National Association for the Education of Young Children. (1984). *NAEYC position statement on nomenclature, salaries, benefits, and the status of the early childhood profession.* Washington, DC: Author.

National Association for the Education of Young Children. (1984). *NAEYC position statements on child care licensing and family day care regulation.* Washington, DC: Author.

National Association for the Education of Young Children. (1985). *Caring for infants and toddlers: A discussion with Bettye Caldwell.* (Video tape number 801). Washington, DC: Author.

National Association for the Education of Young Children. (1985). *The child care boom: Licensed programs, 1977 to 1985.* Washington, DC: Author.

National Association for the Education of Young Children. (1985). *A classroom with blocks.* (filmstrip). Accompanies E. Hirsch (Ed.). *The block book* (rev. ed.). (1984). Washington, DC: Author.

National Association for the Education of Young Children. (1985). *Computers and young children: A discussion with Barbara Bowen.* (Video tape number 802). Washington, DC: Author.

National Association for the Education of Young Children. (1985). *Culture and education of young children: A discussion with Carol Phillips.* (Video tape number 803). Washington, DC: Author.

National Association for the Education of Young Children. (1985). *Curriculum for preschool and kindergarten: Discussion with Lilian Katz.* (Video tape number 804). Washington, DC: Author.

National Association for the Education of Young Children. (1985). *Discipline: A discussion with Jimmy Hymes.* (Video tape number 805). Washington, DC: Author.

National Association for the Education of Young Children. (1985). *Environments for young children: A discussion with Elizabeth Prescott and Elizabeth Jones.* (Video tape number 806). Washington, DC: Author.

National Association for the Education of Young Children. (1985). *Guidelines for early childhood education programs in associate degree granting institutions.* Washington, DC: Author.

National Association for the Education of Young Children (1985). *In whose hands? A demographic factsheet on childcare providers.* Washington, DC: Author.

National Association for the Education of Young Children. (1985). *Love and learn: Discipline for young children.* Washington, DC: Author.

National Association for the Education of Young Children. (1985). *Play and learning: A discussion with Barbara Biber.* (Video tape number 807). Washington, DC: Author.

National Association for the Education of Young Children. (1985). *Reading and young children: A discussion with Jan McCarthy.* (Video tape number 808). Washington, DC: Author.

National Association for the Education of Young Children. (1986). NAEYC position statement on developmentally appropriate practice in programs for 4- and 5-year-olds. *Young Children, 41*(6), 3–19.

National Association for the Education of Young Children. (1986). NAEYC position statement on developmentally appropriate practice in early childhood programs serving children from birth to age 8. *Young Children, 41*(6), 20–29.

Nebraska State Board of Education. (1984). What's best for 5-year-olds? *High Scope ReSource, 5*(2), 3–8.

Nickelsburg, J. (1976). *Nature activities for early childhood.* Reading, MA: Addison-Wesley.

Nieboer, R. A. (1983). *A study of the effect of computers on the preschool environment.* Urbana, IL: ERIC Clearinghouse on Elementary and Early Childhood Education (ED 234 898).

Norton, D. (1983). *Through the eyes of a child: An introduction to children's literature.* Columbus, OH: Charles E. Merrill.

O'Brien, M., Porterfield, E., Herbert-Jackson, E., & Risley, T. R. (1979). *The toddler center: A practical guide to day care for one- and two-year-olds.* Baltimore, MD: University Park Press.

Papert, S. (1980). *Mindstorms: Children, computers, and powerful ideas.* New York: Basic Books.

Parke, R. D. (1981). *Fathers.* The developing child series. Cambridge, MA: Harvard University Press.

Parker, J. (1984). *Some disturbing data: Sex differences in computer use.* Paper presented at the annual National Educational Computing Conference, Dayton, OH.

Pettygrove, W., Whitebook, M. & Weir, M. (1984). Research report: Beyond babysitting: Changing the treatment and image of child caregivers. *Young Children, 39*(5), 14-21.

Pflaum, S. (1978). *The development of language and reading in young children* (2nd ed.). Columbus, OH: Charles E. Merrill.

Phelan, G. (1979). *Family relationships.* Minneapolis: Burgess.

Phillips, D., & Whitebook, M. (1986). Who are child care workers? The search for answers. *Young Children, 41*(4), 14-20.

Phillips, J. L., Jr. (1981). *Piaget's theory: A primer.* San Francisco: W. H. Freeman.

Phinney, J. S. (1982). Observing children: Ideas for teachers. *Young Children, 37*(5), 16-24.

Phyfe-Perkins, E. (1981). *Effects of teacher behavior on preschool children: A review of research.* Urbana, IL: ERIC Clearinghouse on Elementary and Early Childhood Education (ED 211 176).

Piaget, J. (1952). *The origins of intelligence in children.* New York: W. W. Norton.

Piaget, J. (1970). Piaget's theory. In P. Mussen (Ed.). *Carmichael's manual of child psychology.* Pp. 703-732. New York: John Wiley.

Piaget, J. (1970). *Science of education and the psychology of the child.* New York: Orion Press.

Pincus, L., & Dare, C. (1978). *Secrets in the family.* New York: Harper Colophon Books.

Pitcher, E. G., Feinberg, S. G., & David, A. (1984). *Helping young children learn* (4th ed.). Columbus, OH: Charles E. Merrill.

Plato. (1969). (P. Shorey, Trans.). *The republic.* London: William Heinemann.

Pogrebin, L. C. (1981). *Growing up free: Raising your child in the 80's.* New York: Bantam Books.

Powell, D. R. (1986). Research in review: Effects of program models and teaching practices. *Young Children, 41*(6), 60-67.

Provence, S., Naylor, A., & Patterson, J. (1977). *The challenge of day care.* New Haven: Yale University Press.

Pugmire, W. (1977). *Experiences in music for young children.* Albany, NY: Delmar.

Radomski, M. A. (1986). Professionalization of early childhood educators: How far have we progressed? *Young Children, 41*(5), 20-23.

Ramsey, P. G. (1979). Beyond "Ten Little Indians" and turkeys: Alternative approaches to Thanksgiving. *Young Children, 34*(6), 28-32, 49-52.

Ramsey, P. G. (1982). Multicultural education in early childhood. *Young Children, 37*(2), 13-24. Also in J. F. Brown (Ed.). (1982). *Curriculum planning for young children.* Pp. 131-142. Washington, DC: National Association for the Education of Young Children.

Ramsey, P. G. (1986). *Children's understanding of diversity: Multicultural perspectives in early childhood education.* New York: Teachers College.

Raskin, L. M., Taylor, W. J., & Kerckhoff, F. G. (1975). The teacher as observer for assessment: A guideline. *Young Children, 30*(5), 339-344. Also in L. Adams, & B. Garlick (Eds.). (1979). *Ideas that work with young children* (Vol. 2). Pp. 228-233. Washington, DC: National Association for the Education of Young Children.

Redl, F., & Wineman, D. (1952). *Controls from within.* Glencoe, IL: Free Press.

Redleaf, R. (1983). *Open the door and let's explore: Neighborhood field trips for young children.* St. Paul, MN: Toys 'n Things Press.

Richarz, A. S. (1980). *Understanding children through observation.* St. Paul, MN: West Publishing.

Riley, S. S. (1984). *How to generate values in young children: Integrity, honesty, individuality, self-confidence, and wisdom.* Washington, DC: National Association for the Education of Young Children.

Rogers, D. L., & Ross, D. D. (1986). Encouraging positive social interaction among young children. *Young Children, 41*(3), 12-17.

Rossi, A. S. (Ed.). (1978). *The family.* New York: W. W. Norton.

Rousseau, J. J. (1974. Reprinted from 1933). (B. Foxley, Trans.). *Emile.* London: J. M. Dent and Sons. (Also published by New York: Teachers College, Columbia University, W. Boyd, Trans. & Ed., 1962.)

Rubin, Z. (1980). *Children's friendships.* The

developing child series. Cambridge, MA: Harvard University Press.

Rutter, M. (1981). Social-emotional consequences of day care for preschool children. *American Journal of Orthopsychiatry, 51*(1), 4-28.

Rutter, M. (1981). *Maternal deprivation reassessed* (2nd ed.). New York: Penguin Books.

Ryan, S. (Ed.). *A report on longitudinal evaluations of preschool programs* (Vol. 1). *Results of a preschool intervention project*. D. P. Weikart, D. J. Deloria, & S. Lawsor. (1974). Washington, DC: U. S. Department of Health, Education, and Welfare. Publication No. (OHD) 74-24.

Saracho, O. N., & Spodek, B. (1983). *Understanding the multicultural experience in early childhood education*. Washington, DC: National Association for the Education of Young Children.

Sarnoff, C. (1976). *Latency*. New York: Jason Aronson.

Schafer, W. (1987). *Stress management for wellness*. New York: Holt, Rinehart and Winston.

Scheffler, H. N. (1983). *Resources for early childhood*. New York: Garland.

Schickedanz, J. (1983). *Helping children learn about reading*. Washington, DC: National Association for the Education of Young Children.

Schickedanz, J. (1986). *More than the ABC's: The early stages of reading and writing*. Washington, DC: National Association for the Education of Young Children.

Schickedanz, J. A., York, M. E., Stewart, I. S., & White, D. A. (1983). *Strategies for teaching young children*. Englewood Cliffs, NJ: Prentice-Hall.

Schirrmacher, R. (1986). Talking with young children about their art. *Young Children, 41*(5), 3-7.

Schmidt, V. E., & McNeill, E. (1978). *Cultural awareness: A resource bibliography*. Washington, DC: National Association for the Education of Young Children.

Schowalter, J. (1979). When dinosaurs return: Children's fascination with dinosaurs. *Children Today, 8*(3), 2-5.

Schwarz, J. C., & Wynn, R. (1971). The effects of mother's presence and previsits on children's emotional reaction to starting nursery school. *Child Development, 42*, 871-882.

Seaver, J., Cartwright, C., Ward, C., & Heasley, C. A. (1984). *Careers with young children: Making your decision* (rev. ed.). Washington, DC: National Association for the Education of Young Children.

Seefeldt, C., & Tinney, S. (1985). Dinosaurs: The past is present. *Young Children, 40*(4), 20-24.

Seefeldt, C. (Ed.). (1986). *The early childhood curriculum: A review of current research*. New York: Teachers College.

Segal, M., & Adcock, D. (1981). *Just pretending: Ways to help children grow through imaginative play*. Englewood Cliffs, NJ: Prentice-Hall.

Seiderman, S. (1978). Combating staff burnout. *Day Care and Early Education, 5*(4), 6-9.

Shade, D. D. (1983). *Microcomputers: A close look at what happens when preschool children interact with age-appropriate software*. Urbana, IL: ERIC Clearinghouse on Elementary and Early Childhood Education (ED 243 608).

Sheehy, E. (1977). *Children discover music and dance*. New York: Teachers College.

Skeen, P., Garner, A. P., & Cartwright, S. (1984). *Woodworking for young children*. Washington, DC: National Association for the Education of Young Children.

Slaughter, D. T. (1982). What is the future of Head Start? *Young Children, 37*(3), 3-9.

Sloan, D. (Ed.). (1984). *The computer in education: A critical perspective* (Special Issue). *Teachers College Record, 85*(4).

Smilansky, S. (1968). *The effects of sociodramatic play on disadvantaged preschool children*. New York: John Wiley & Sons.

Smilansky, S. (1971). Can adults facilitate play in children?: Theoretical and practical considerations. In N. E. Curry, & S. Arnaud. (1971). *Play: The child strives toward self-realization*. Pp. 39-50. Washington, DC: National Association for the Education of Young Children.

Smith, C. A. (1986). Nurturing kindness through

storytelling. *Young Children, 41*(6), 46–51.

Smith, N. R. (1983). *Experience and art: Teaching children to paint.* New York: Teachers College.

Soderman, A. K. (1984). Viewpoint: Formal education for four-year-olds? That depends. . . . *Young Children, 39*(5), 11–13.

Soderman, A. K. (1985). Dealing with difficult young children: Strategies for teachers and parents. *Young Children, 40*(5), 15–20.

Souweine, J., Crimmins, S., & Mazel, C. (1981). *Mainstreaming: Ideas for teaching young children.* Washington, DC: National Association for the Education of Young Children.

Spilke, F. S. (1979). *What about the children? A divorced parent's handbook.* New York: Crown.

Spilke, F. S. (1979). *The family that changed: A child's book about divorce.* New York: Crown.

Spock, B., & Rothenberg, M. B. (1985). *Dr. Spock's baby and child care.* New York: E. P. Dutton.

Spodek, B. (Ed.). (1977). *Teaching practices: Reexamining assumptions.* Washington, DC: National Association for the Education of Young Children.

Spodek, B. (1985). Early childhood education's past as prologue: Roots of contemporary concerns. *Young Children, 40*(5), 3–7.

Spodek, B. (1985). *Teaching in the early years* (3rd ed.) Englewood Cliffs, NJ: Prentice-Hall.

Spodek, B., & Walberg, H. J. (Eds.). (1977). *Early childhood education: Issues and insights.* Berkeley, CA: McCutchan.

Spodek, B. (Ed.). (1986). *Today's kindergarten: Exploring the knowledge base, expanding the curriculum.* New York: Teachers College.

Sprung, B. (Ed.). (1978). *Perspectives on non-sexist early childhood education.* New York: Teachers College.

Squibb, B. (1980). *Family day care: How to provide it in your home.* St. Paul, MN: Toys 'n Things Press.

Stein, S. B. (1974). *Making babies: An open family book for parents and children together.* New York: Walker.

Stevens, J. H., & Mathews, M. (1978). *Mother/child father/child relationships.*

Washington, DC: National Association for the Education of Young Children.

Stewig, J. W. (1983). *Literature: Basic in the language arts curriculum.* Urbana, IL: ERIC Clearinghouse on Reading and Communication Skills (ED 232 188).

Stone, J. G. (1978). *A guide to discipline* (rev. ed.). Washington, DC: National Association for the Education of Young Children.

Storm, S. (1985). *The human side of child care administration: A how-to manual.* Washington, DC: National Association for the Education of Young Children.

Strom, R. (1977). *Parent and child in fiction.* Belmont, CA: Brooks/Cole.

Sullivan, M. (1982). *Feeling strong, feeling free: Movement exploration for young children.* Washington, DC: National Association for the Education of Young Children.

Taylor, B. J. (1985). *A child goes forth: A curriculum guide for preschool children* (6th ed.). Minneapolis, MN: Burgess.

Taylor, B. W. (1982). *Case studies in child development.* Belmont, CA: Brooks Cole.

Taylor, H. (1983). *Microcomputers in the early childhood classroom.* Urbana, IL: ERIC Clearinghouse for Elementary and Early Childhood Education (ED 234 845).

Taylor, K. W. (1981). *Parents and children learn together* (3rd ed.). New York: Teachers College.

U.S. Department of Health and Human Services, Administration for Children, Youth and Families, Day Care Division. (1981). *A parent's guide to day care.* Mt. Rainier, MD: Gryphon House.

Uphoff, J. K., & Gilmore, J. (1986). Viewpoint 2: Pupil age at school entrance—How many are ready for success? *Young Children, 41*(2), 11–16.

Vardin-Barker, P. (1984). *Microcomputers, robots, and electronic toys.* Proceedings of the Early Childhood Education Conference. New York: Teachers College.

Verzaro-O'Brien, M., LeBlanc, D., & Hennon, C. (1982). Industry-related day care: Trends and options. *Young Children*, 37(2), 4–10. Also in J. F. Brown (Ed.). (1984). *Administering programs for young children*. Pp. 194–200. Washington, DC: National Association for the Education of Young Children.

Wadsworth, B. J. (1978). *Piaget for the classroom teacher*. New York: Longman.

Wagner, D. A., & Stevenson, H. W. (Eds.). (1982). *Cultural perspectives on child development*. San Francisco: W. H. Freeman.

Wakefield, A. P. (1979). Multi-age grouping in day care. *Children Today*, 8(3), 26–28.

Wanamaker, N., Hearn, K., & Richarz, S. (1979). *More than graham crackers: Nutrition education and food preparation with young children*. Washington, DC: National Association for the Education of Young Children.

Ward, E. (1977). A code of ethics: The hallmark of a profession. In B. Spodek (Ed.). *Teaching practices: Reexamining assumptions*. Pp. 65–69. Washington, DC: National Association for the Education of Young Children.

Warren, R. M. (1977). *Caring: Supporting children's growth*. Washington, DC: National Association for the Education of Young Children.

Washington, V., & Oyemade, U. J. (1985). Changing family trends: Head Start must respond. *Young Children*, 40(6), 12–19.

Waxman, S. (1979). *Growing up feeling good: A child's introduction to sexuality*. Los Angeles, CA: Panjandrum/Aris Books.

Weber, E. (1984). *Ideas influencing early childhood education: A theoretical analysis*. New York: Teachers College.

Weikart D. P. (1986). Basics for preschoolers: The High/Scope approach. *High Scope ReSource*. 5(2), 1, 22–23.

Weikart, D. P., Rogers, L., Adcock, C., & McClelland, D. (1971). *The cognitively oriented curriculum: A framework for preschool teachers*. Washington, DC: ERIC-National Association for the Education of Young Children Publication.

Weissbourd, B., & Musick, J. S. (Eds.). (1981). *Infants: Their social environments*. Washington, DC: National Association for the Education of Young Children.

Werner, E. E. (1984). *Child care: Kith, kin, and hired hands*. Baltimore, MD: University Park Press.

Werner, E. E. (1984). Resilient children. *Young Children*, 40(1), 68–72.

Werner, E. E., & Smith, R. S. (1982). *Vulnerable but invincible: A longitudinal study of resilient children*. New York: McGraw-Hill.

White, B. L. (1985). *The first three years of life* (rev. ed.). Englewood Cliffs, NJ: Prentice-Hall.

White, R. W. (1968). Motivation reconsidered: The concept of competence. In M. Almy, (Ed.). *Early childhood play: Selected readings related to cognition and motivation*. New York: Simon and Schuster.

Whitebook, M. (1986). Viewpoint: The teacher shortage: A professional precipice. *Young Teacher*, 41(3), 10–11.

Whitebook, M., Howes, C., Darrah, R., & Friedman, J. (1982). Caring for the caregivers: Staff burnout in child care. In L. G. Katz (Ed.). *Current topics in early childhood education* (Vol. 4). Pp. 211–235. Norwood, NJ: ABLEX.

Willert, M. K., & Kamii, C. (1985). Reading in kindergarten: Direct vs. indirect teaching. *Young Children*, 40(4), 3–9.

Williams, L. R., & Gaetano, Y. D. (1985). *ALERTA: A multi-cultural, bilingual approach to teaching young children*. Reading MA: Addison-Wesley.

Willis, A., & Ricciuti, H. (1975). *A good beginning for babies: Guidelines for group care*. Washington, DC: National Association for the Education of Young Children.

Winn, M. (1977). *The plug-in drug: Television, children, and the family*. New York: Viking.

Winn, M. (1983). *Children without childhood: Growing up too fast in the world of sex and drugs*. New York: Penguin Books.

Winnicott, D. W. (1957). *The child and the outside world*. New York: Basic Books.

Winnicott, D. W. (1971). *Playing and reality*. New York: Basic Books.

Winnicott, D. W. (1974). *The maturational process and the facilitating environment*. New York: International Universities Press.

Worden, P. E., Kee, D. W., & Ingle, M. J. (1985). *Preschoolers' alphabet learning activities with their parents: Picture-books vs. personal computer software.* Paper presented at the meeting of the Society for Research in Child Development, Toronto.

Work/Family Directions. (1985). *A guide to child care regulations in (your state).* Washington, DC: National Association for the Education of Young Children.

Yamamoto, K., (Ed.). (1972). *The child and his image: Self-concept in the early years.* Boston: Houghton Mifflin.

Zavitkovsky, D., Baker, K. R., Berlfein, J. R., Almy, M. (1986). *Listen to the children.* Washington, DC: National Association for the Education of Young Children.

Ziajka, A. (1983). Microcomputers in early childhood education? A first look. *Young Children, 38*(5), 61-67. Also in J. F. Brown (Ed.). (1984). *Administering programs for young children.* Washington, DC: National Association for the Education of Young Children.

Zigler, E. F., & Gordon, E. E. (Eds.). (1982). *Day care: Scientific and social policy issues.* Boston: Auburn House.

Zimmerman, K., & Herr, J. (1981). Time wasters: Solutions for teachers and directors. *Young Children, 36*(3), 45-48.

INDEX